The
Musical Mind

The cognitive psychology of music

JOHN A. SLOBODA

Department of Psychology, University of Keele

OXFORD PSYCHOLOGY SERIES NO. 5

OXFORD
UNIVERSITY PRESS

OXFORD
UNIVERSITY PRESS

Great Clarendon Street, Oxford OX2 6DP

Oxford University Press is a department of the University of Oxford.
It furthers the University's objective of excellence in research, scholarship,
and education by publishing worldwide in

Oxford New York

Athens Auckland Bangkok Bogotá Buenos Aires Calcutta
Cape Town Chennai Dar es Salaam Delhi Florence Hong Kong Istanbul
Karachi Kuala Lumpur Madrid Melbourne Mexico City Mumbai
Nairobi Paris São Paulo Singapore Taipei Tokyo Toronto Warsaw

with associated companies in Berlin Ibadan

Oxford is a registered trade mark of Oxford University Press
in the UK and in certain other countries

Published in the United States
by Oxford University Press Inc., New York

First published 1985

Reprinted in paperback 1986

Reprinted 1987 (with corrections) 1988, 1989,1990, 1991, 1993, 1994,
1996, 1997, 1999 (with corrections), 2000 (twice)

A catalogue record for this book is available from the British Library

Library of Congress Cataloging in Publication Data
(Data available)

ISBN 0 19 852128 6 (pbk)

Printed in Great Britain
on acid-free paper by
Bookcraft (Bath) Ltd., Midsomer Norton

Editors:

James L. McGaugh
Nicholas J. Mackintosh
Anne Treisman
Endel Tulving
Lawrence Weiskrantz

OXFORD PSYCHOLOGY SERIES

Preface

When it was first suggested that I should write a book on the cognitive psychology of music, I had no clear conception of what sort of book might be the outcome. As I began to take stock of the existing literature, it became clear that there was a gap that needed to be filled. On one side of this gap could be placed the vast majority of the psychological research on music. On the other side was the experience and insight of the musician, as expressed both through his practices and through the rigorous disciplines of musicology, music theory, and analysis. It seemed, to me at least, that the psychology of music related rather little to what musicians actually did, and so was failing to tackle questions of central musical importance.

There are several reasons why this state of affairs might have arisen. One is that many psychologists studying music have not had the good fortune to receive extended musical training, and so have had a limited range of musical insights and intuitions to guide their work. The difficulties caused by this are akin to the difficulties that might be experienced by someone attempting to carry out psycholinguistic research on a language that he did not know at all well, and without a thorough grounding in linguistics. Even psychologists *with* musical expertise have often seemed to detach their scientific work from their musical knowledge.

Another reason is that theoretical developments in the psychology of music have been slow. Experimentalists have tended to construct micro-theories to account for their own results so that research from different sources cannot easily be synthesized. Only in the last few years have people well-grounded in both psychology and music begun to construct psychologically interesting theories of musical functioning which might be capable of unifying and giving direction to a wide range of research endeavours.

A third reason is that psychological research has been dominated by the view that one must understand the most peripheral and simple aspects of intellectual functioning as a prelude to the study of more central and complex aspects. Although this view is now accepted to be largely misconceived, a vast amount of so-called 'music' research has concentrated on the processes involved in the perception of single tones. Topics such as the representation of large-scale musical structure, performance, and composition, have received comparatively little attention. Yet these are the topics which are of most direct relevance to musicians.

A fourth and related reason is that psychologists have, rightly, wished to conduct their research with rigorous control and measurement. It is much easier to construct brief auditory stimuli to exact specifications whilst constraining subjects to simple yes/no responses, than it is to to allow subjects the freedom to indulge in some complex but musically interesting behaviour in response to complex musically structured conditions. Yet the latter *can* be done with rigour, and is beginning to be done with increasing frequency.

Fifth, and finally, writers on the psychology of music have tended to address themselves exclusively either to the professional psychologist or to the music educator and educational researcher. There has been little fruitful dialogue between psychologists and practising or academic musicians. This may not be entirely the fault of psychologists, but few psychologists seem to have been really concerned to break the interdisciplinary barrier.

I have written with this barrier very much in mind, and have tried to offer something to both the psychologist and the musician. The psychologist will, I hope, find a coherent account of the important research carried out in this area. He will also be exposed to some of the questions and issues which have not yet stimulated a great deal of research. These questions arise as I critically examine the field through the eyes of a musician, but also through the eyes of a cognitive psychologist who finds psychologists of music slow to accept the wider perspectives which cognitive science has brought to other branches of psychology in the last decade. I have assumed a moderate degree of musical literacy in my readers. To have done otherwise would have made my task impossibly slow. Likewise, an acquaintance is assumed with the broad range of topics and methods embraced by scientific psychology, although I have attempted to write in such a way that detailed knowledge in specific areas is not required. I have made liberal reference to suitable introductory reading where the general reader might wish to seek further information.

Musicians will, I hope, find that cognitive psychology has something to offer in helping them understand the mental bases of their skills. I have not, however, set out to provide a 'recipe book' of psychological aids to specific musical problems. Rather, I have tried to highlight and elucidate some basic characteristics of musical skills and the cognitive mechanisms which serve them. An understanding of these underlying factors will, hopefully, allow musicians to formulate better solutions to some of their problems.

I am very much aware that the subject I present abounds with loose ends and unsolved problems. I have not tried to give the field more substantiality than it has. What I hope to have done is to describe the main achievements in this rapidly growing area up to the end of 1982 or thereabouts, and map out some important topics and questions which need more attention than they have received.

My own approach to the cognitive psychology of music has been most greatly influenced by the writings of Christopher Longuet-Higgins who, in the early 1970s, was asking and answering important questions about the psychological representation of extended tonal music at a time when many others were hooked on peripheral questions. I gratefully acknowledge his encouragement and support, which has been directly instrumental in getting this book finished. I am also grateful to several people for putting me on the track of material that I otherwise would have discovered much later or not at all. Alan Mosley first told me about the work of Heinrich Schenker; Michael Durand first showed me the fascinating story revealed by ink changes in Mozart's operatic autographs; and Ian Hunter introduced me to David Sudnow's unique account of his own improvisatory development, as well as opening my eyes to the profound contrasts between skills of literate and non-literate people.

Several people deserve special mention in connection with the immediate preparation of this book. I am grateful to Stephen Banfield, Ian Hunter, Pamela Liebeck, George Pratt, Henry Shaffer, Ursula Sharma, my wife Judith, and anonymous reviewers for the Oxford University Press, for reading portions of the first draft and offering useful comments. My late father also made detailed comments on the earlier portion of the book which much improved its intelligibility, and I dedicate this book to his memory. I am particularly grateful to the Senate of the University of Keele for the award of a Keele Research Fellowship in 1982 which allowed me the uninterrupted time required to complete the first draft. I gratefully acknowledge the secretarial help of Dorothy Masters and Margaret Woodward, and technical assistance from John Coleman and the Keele University Computer Centre.

The psychology of music is a rapidly growing subject, and it is exciting to be directly involved in that growth. I have enjoyed writing this book, but I am also aware that the field has leapt forward even in the two years I have taken out of the laboratory to complete it. I am now anxious to return to the laboratory. My principal hope is that psychologists who enjoy reading this book will also be stimulated to repair to the laboratory and render some of my critical comments obsolete.

J. A. S.

July 1983

Christopher
Long ver-Higgins

Preface to the 1999 reprinting

The text of *The Musical Mind* was completed in 1983. Fifteen years have now passed since then, and a new printing makes it timely for me to say something about the progress of music psychology since 1983. In effect, I need to justify why any reader should turn to this book, given the substantial progress in the field since that time. Fifteen years is a long time in science, and anyone wishing to enter the field of music research as an active participant cannot do so without concentrating their attention on materials published in the last five years or so. However, it seems that *The Musical Mind* has served a variety of constituencies outside the research laboratory. Musicians, students, and interested lay-people have been kind enough to say that they have found something of more lasting value in the book. This pleases me, for it was never my intention to provide a comprehensive textbook, of the kind that could be straightforwardly updated by the addition of new sections every few years. I wanted, as I hope I expressed in the Preface to the first printing, to address the field from a critical perspective (in which I saw psychologists as insufficiently interested in making their research relevant to the interests and concerns of musicians) and highlight areas of investigation which I felt to be important, regardless of the quantity of research that had been published in those areas.

This Preface is not in any sense, an exhaustive summary of where the cognitive psychology of music has got to since 1893. That would require another book. Rather, it is a brief evaluation of the development of some of the key themes that I identified. It therefore is probably best read *after* consulting the relevant chapters, rather than before, and I have therefore referenced all my comments to the numbered sections and page numbers of the chapters. I have tried to be selective in my citation of more recent research, favouring books and review articles over specific empirical studies unless these latter are of foundational significance. In this way, interested readers will gain the fastest access to recent surveys of specific areas of research.

Music, language, and meaning

My organizing principle for discussing links between language and music was the tripartite distinction between phonology, syntax, and semantics (2.3(h) ff. pp. 22–65). In so far as music could be mapped on to this distinction, it seemed appropriate to think of music and language as overlapping (both functionally and conceptually). In 1983 my broad conclusion was that evidence for equivalence at the phonological and syntactic level was rather impressive, but that musical and linguistic semantics operated in rather different ways, in so far as the scanty research literature in music allowed any definite conclusions at all.

About phonology (2.4, pp. 23–32) I wish to add rather little. The ability to make categorical distinctions between musical elements is a foundational aspect of music perception and performance. My treatment concentrated on pitch and duration. More recent research has widened the range of dimensions about which we have knowledge. Of these, timbre is undoubtedly the most significant (Hajda, Kendall, Carterette, and Harchberger 1997).

The study of psychological aspects of musical syntax (2.5, pp. 32–57) has seen phenomenal growth since 1983. To me, the most interesting feature of this growth is that it has been largely driven organically by developments within experimental psychology, rather than developments within musicology. Our understanding of pitch relations has deepened largely through the application of traditional psychophysical techniques to long-established cultural conceptualizations of tonality (e.g. Krumhansl 1990) rather than in response to new theory, even when that theory is explicitly psychologically oriented (e.g. Lerdahl and Jackendoff 1983: Narmour 1989, 1992). Earlier (Sloboda 1986) I predicted that Lerdahl and Jackendoff's *Generative Theory of Tonal Music* (1983) would give the kind of new impetus to music psychology research that Chomsky (1965) gave to psycholinguistics. With a few brave exceptions (e.g. Deliege 1987) I have been proved entirely wrong about that. More fruitful growth points have been at the junctions between psychology and neuroscience, partly as a result of the rise of connectionism and neural-net modelling (see Bharucha 1991), but also as a result of a range of new techniques which allow direct measurement of the overlap of brain activity between language and music processing (e.g. Besson 1997; Patel and Peretz 1997). One possible reason for the slowness for psychology to take on new musicological theorizing is that such work attempts to grapple with sytactical issues at the global as well as the local level (i.e. pertaining to entire movements and not just single phrases). Our methods for studying global cognition are still in their infancy, and psychology is still best suited to studying our interactions with materials lasting seconds rather than minutes.

Interest in musical semantics (2.6, pp. 57–65) has increased considerably since 1983. A particularly acute philosophical contribution has been made by Raffman (1993) who pointed out that the phrase 'music has meaning'. can mean both 'music has semantics', and 'music has personal significance' (as in 'music means a lot to me'). Much conceptual confusion has been created by previous unclarity on this point. The psychology of musical semantics is concerned with the mapping and explanation of relationships, between musical elements and their non-musical connotations, which are often emotional (e.g. Juslin 1997), but by no mans always need be so (e.g. Watt and Ash 1998). Over and above semantics, music can be used to achieve valued psychological states, including emotional states, and an explanation of these effects requires an understanding, not only of cognitive psychology, but also social psychology (Hargreaves and North 1997), therapy (Bunt 1994), and the psychology of motivation (Sloboda and Davidson 1995). Cognition remains central to this aspect, however, since there is now some evidence to support Meyer's (1973) contention (2.6, pp. 64–5) that violations of structural expectancy (describable in syntactic terms) contribute in a very direct way to the intensity of experienced emotion, if not its content (Krumhansl 1998; Sloboda 1991).

Music performance

My treatment of performance (3) was also based round three issues, sight-reading, rehearsal, and expert performance. A great deal of new work has been done in the latter two areas, almost nothing in the first.

The emphasis on sight-reading in 1983 (3.2, pp. 68–90) largely reflected my own research interests, in which reading was a dominant theme at that time. Despite the fact that notational competence remains central to much musical skill and development, there is little more known about it than in 1983. Waters and Underwood (1998) report a study on eye movements which summarizes the small recent literature.

The study of rehearsal (3.3, pp. 90–3) has seen a recent renaissance as a result of the rise of a branch of cognitive psychology known as 'expertise studies' (see Ericsson and Smith 1991). This area was foreshadowed by seminal work on problem-solving (1 p. 8) begun by Simon and colleagues, and has led to detailed investigations of the conditions under which skilled individuals improve their skills. Not only do we understand much more about the details of effective musical practice (e.g. Ericsson, Krampe, and Tesch-Romer 1993; Jorgensen and Lehmann 1997), but we have a much clearer idea of the social, motivational, and emotional factors which allow unusually high levels of musical achievement to develop (Manturszewska 1990; Davidson, Howe, and Sloboda 1997). This work is entirely in keeping with the 'demystification' of talent and genius, which characterized my approach in 1983 (see 1 pp, 3–6), and which has been a central theme in the cognitive psychology of creativity and achievement ever since (e.g. Howe, Davidson, and Sloboda 1998; Weisberg 1993)

The section on expert musical performance was, in 1983, largely conceptual (3.4, pp. 93–101), and driven by the hope that psychologists would begin to study it. This hope has been fulfilled beyond all expectations. Work begun in Europe by Shaffer (pp. 98–9) and Gabrielsson (p. 30), built on by their students (Clarke 1995; Juslin 1997; Todd 1985), and taken up enthusiastically in the US (e.g. Palmer 1996, 1997, Repp 1990, 1997) has confirmed my hypotheses that expert performance depends upon the flexible deployment of structural knowledge. One reason why this area of work progressed much faster than I expected was the development of MIDI (Musical Instrument Digital Interface) technology, which allowed for easy storage and manipulation of performances through commercially available industry-standard equipment. This now allows the achievement in days of what it took Shaffer years to develop. A notable feature of much of this research is its use of entire pieces of music performed in naturalistic contexts, thus meeting demands of ecological validity, and forming one of the really productive meeting points between psychologists and practising musicians, for whom 'performance studies' is now an established subdiscipline, sharing many of the technologies and methodologies developed in psychology (e.g. Rink 1995). These developments recently allowed the opportunity to revisit the question of fingering strategies (Sloboda, Clarke, Parncutt, and Raekallio 1998), and do the research suggested in 1983 (3.4, pp. 96–7), a source of some personal satisfaction.

Composition and improvization

Despite a considerable general interest in creativity and the products of creative individuals (e.g. Simonton 1996), the amount of new work on cognitive processes in composition and improvisation since 1983 has been small. A collection of preliminary studies in this area (Sloboda 1998) has not led to major subsequent developments. In general, what little work there is focuses on detailed analyses of improvisations (e.g. Jarvinen 1995). The only study of composition published in a major music psychology journal this decade is a small expert–novice comparison on a classroom composition exercise (Colley, Banton, Down, and Pither, 1992). It is hard to understand why so little attention has been paid to these areas. Admittedly, they pose methodological problems; but it is possible that their neglect also reflects the general neglect of musical creativity in the arena of the high art or 'classical' tradition which dominates schools, colleges, and universities. Whatever the reason, it means that my 1983 chapter remains as pertinent today as it did then.

Listening to music

The notion that music listening draws on general auditory mechanisms designed for a range of detection tasks in the natural world (5.2, pp. 154–66) has now motivated an active research area called 'Auditory Scene Analysis' of which Bregman's (1990) contribution is the defining work (see also McAdams and Bigand 1993). The most impressive application of this work to music is undoubtedly the series of studies by Huron (e.g. 1991, 1993) which show, through computer-based analyses of very large corpuses of classical compositions, that composers have intuitively conformed to many of the perceptual principles that allow, for instance, separate musical voices to be heard as separate perceptual objects. A natural consequence of this line of work is the demonstration that, at many levels, what experts and novices extract from their hearing of music is remarkably similar, despite the effects of training. Significant evidence of these commonalities has been provided by in a series of studies on cue-abstraction while listening to complete compositions (Deliege and Melen 1997). This work has also been supported by the strong theoretical claim (Lerdahl 1998) that certain structural features (intended by, for instance, some avant-garde composers) are simply incapable of being detected by natural hearing mechanisms, and this accounts for their difficulty and relative unpopularity among listeners.

Given that memorizing music is such a central and ecologically pertinent aspect of musical cognition, I tried to give significant coverage to memory for extended musical sequences in my treatment of listening (5.4, pp. 174–93). A number of books treating music perception and cognition have been published since (chronologically: Howell, Cross, and West 1995; Dowling and Bartlett 1996; Riess-Jones and Holleran 1990; Butler 1992; Aiello 1994; Deliege and Sloboda 1997). It is surprising how little explicit attention is given to memorization (although the role of memory is implied in studies of recognition and other forms of judgment). The most comprehensive coverage of memory is given by Dowling and Harwood (1986) although it reviews almost the same materials as I did. Only two other chapters focus primarily on memory and recall (Sloboda and Parker 1985; Krumhansl 1990). Curiously, the most extended examination of the memorization process since 1983 has been provided through the study of anomalous cognition displayed by autistic musical savants (Miller 1989). It would be fair to say that the predominant strand in recent research on music listening has been to further our understanding of the experience of pitch, within the context of western tonal music (e.g. Cuddy 1997; Cross 1997; Krumhansl 1991; Sloboda 1992). Since memorization requires integration of information across all relevant domains, pitch, rhythm, melody, and large-scale structure, it is perhaps unsurprising that our understanding of it has not progressed as fast as one would have liked. More integrative syntheses in other areas of the kind attempted by Parncutt (1994) for rhythm and metre are required.

Learning and development

Since 1983, substantial progress has been made in our understanding of the development of musical awareness from birth to school age (Deliege and Sloboda 1995; Trehub, Schellenberg, and Hill 1997). One of the most interesting new findings relating to the first year of life (6.2.1, pp. 198–202) is that infants have musical preferences which seem to be informed by an appreciation of such high-level musical features as phrase structure (e.g. Jusczyk and Krumhansl 1993). The scaffolding for early musical development provided by parent–child interaction is now much better understood (Papousek 1995).

In middle childhood two research strands have developed. On the one side is research into autonomous or naturalistic musical behaviour, such as song singing (Davidson 1994), or spontaneous notations (Bamberger 1991), following in the tradition of Moog and Gardner (6.2.2, pp. 202–5). On the other are experimental studies, using paridigms developed for the study of adult cognition and which allow direct comparison between different age groups on the same materials, (e.g. Drake 1993; Lamont 1998). However, it would be fair to say that adult cognition still accounts for the vast majority of work in music cognition, and there is still much to be understood about the development of musical cognition.

Perhaps as a result of the slowness of the developmental literature to progress, there have been a few successful applications of cognitive psychology to musical education and training. My enthusiasm for production systems as a theoretical tool (6.3, pp. 215–29) proved to be overstated. The rise of connectionism as an alternative theoretical framework both rendered production-system theorizing unfashionable, and at the same time seemed to disable or inhibit experimental work which might apply this theorizing to concrete musical learning situations (Morrongiello 1992). Instead, the predominant interest of the last few years has been in ways in which involvement with music might aid developmental progress in other areas of cognition (Sharp, Benefield, and Kendall 1998). This may reflect pressures on music within the school curriculum in many countries.

Work on the assessment of musical ability (6.4, pp. 233–8) has not been a major concern of recent research within the cognitive tradition. By and large there is too little clarity concerning what precise cognitive skills are being tapped by many ability tests, and predictive validity is generally low. Individual researchers seem to devise their own tests to suit their particular research question (e.g. Macpherson 1995), with the consequent loss of generality.

Culture and biology

Cross-cultural issues have continued to be a neglected aspect of the study of musical cognition. Comparisons of oral and literate cultures are almost non-existent, notable and pioneering exceptions being the work of Arom and colleagues on perception of scales and tuning in Central Africa and Indonesia (Arom, Leothaud, and Voisin 1997) and that of Kessler and colleagues on perception of tonality in Bali (Kessler, Hansen, and Shepard 1984). Indeed, even studies of western music show a worrying narrowness, concentrating on perception and performance of high-art classical music to the near exclusion of other forms.

In relation to biology, on the other hand, new techniques such as Magnetic Resonance Imaging (MRI) and Positron Emission Tomography (PET) have revolutionized the amount and quality of information available concerning brain activity during music engagement. Most of the work in music is in the somewhat better-established area of Event-Related Potentials (ERPs) (see Besson 1997). Much of this has focused on the measuring of musical expectancy as a function of manipulations of structure. There are also some excellent case studies on individuals with brain damage which add to our knowledge of functional dissociation (see Patel and Peretz 1997).

The scientific milieu

It is not possible to conclude this brief update without reference to the very changed intellectual climate for the study of music psychology. In 1983, researchers in this topic had only just begun to co-ordinate their activities intentionally. Fifteen years later the activities of the field are co-ordinated by major national and international scholarly bodies, including the Society for Music Perception and Cognition (SMPC), the European Society for the Cognitive Sciences of Music (ESCOM), as well as the Deutsche Gesellscahft fur Musikpsychologie (DGM), Japanese Society for Music Perception and Cognition (JSMPC), and the Society for Research in Psychology of Music and Music Education (SRPMME). A major international conference, the International Conference on Music Perception and Cognition (ICMPC) is held every two years in a different part of the world. When the conference was last held in Europe, in 1994, there were over 200 papers presented. The major journals in the field, *Music perception* and *Psychology of music* go from strength to strength.

Despite the great advances made, challenges remain. The relationship between music cognition and more traditional academic disciplines remains problematical. I see music cognition as primarily a science, with most of its roots in psychology, but with important inputs from linguistics, computer science, and philosophy. However, the subject matter, music, is traditionally studied from within faculties of fine arts. Attempts to locate music cognition teachers and researchers within arts contexts has never proved easy. The assumptions of scientists and artists about how to approach the subject matter are usually too different. This means that the dialogue between scientists and musicians has been and remains problematical.

Another challenge relates to the lack of cohesion within the discipline of music cognition itself. Understanding the phenomenon of music requires inputs from many disciplines, and even from many parts of the discipline of psychology. For instance, the areas covered in this book touch social psychology, developmental psychology, educational psychology, neuropsychology, as well as cognitive psychology. Each of these has its own theories, nethdologies, and preoccupations. To become truly expert in any one of them could take a lifetime. Music psychology is, thus, not a coherent discipline, but a loose confederation of disciplines converging around the same object of study. It is hard, therefore, to agree on what the important problems are, or how they should be addressed. International funded research collaborations, such as those found in medicine or physics, are absent from music psychology, with the result that the discipline grows by accretion, each researcher or group making their own idiosyncratic contribution. Governments and other funding agencies are, in general, not interested enough to impose discipline through national or international research policies.

Finally, both psychology and music are undergoing rapid changes as disciplines. Both are entering 'post-modern' phases where some of the earlier certainties are evaporating. In psychology, the hope for a unified theory of mind, possibly in the form of some computational model has faded. In music, activities such as historical musicology, which were once considered the unshakable foundations of the discipline, are being supplanted by a range of interdisciplinary approaches within what is sometimes characterized as 'the new musicology' that relativize, and to a certain extend, undermine the central focus of tranditional musicology, on the historical canon of 'masterworks' which universities study, and music academies prepare young musicians to perform.

These interesting problems form, in themselves, part of my justification for not attempting a thoroughgoing revision of this book. The *Musical mind* was written from within a point of some stability and self confidence in the historical development of cognitive psychology. To reflect the feel of today's intellectual climate, and to foresee some important questions for the next millenium, would require an altogether different approach from a refocused perspective. And two things are very clear to me about that approach: (1) it would need to take much more account of the messy world of emotion and motivation, to balance the precisions and tidinesses of cognition; (2) it would need to encompass a far greater range of the world's musics, cultures, and sub-cultures than the classical art tradition that has moulded the discipline up to this point.

References

Aiello, R. (Ed.) (1994). *Musical perceptions*. Oxford University Press, New York.
Arom, S., Leothaud, G. and Voisin, F. (1997). Experimental ethnomusicology: an interactive approach to the study of musical scales. In I. Deliege and J. A. Sloboda (Eds) *Perception and cognition of music*. Psychology Press, Hove.
Bamberger, J. (1991). *The mind behind the musical ear*. Harvard University Press, Cambridge, Mass.

Besson, M. (1997). Electrophysiological studies of music processing. In I. Deliege and J. A. Sloboda (Eds.) *Perception and cognition of music*. Psychology Press, Hove.

Bharucha, J. J. (1991). Pitch, harmony and neural nets: a psychological perspective. In P. Todd and D. G. Loy (Eds), *Music and connectionism*. MIT Press, Cambridge, Mass.

Brehman, A. S. (1990). *Auditory scene analysis: the perceptual organisation of sound*. MIT Press, Cambridge, Mass.

Bunt, L. (1994). *Music therapy: an art beyond words*. Routledge, London.

Butler, D. (1992). *The musicians' guide to perception and cognition*. Schirmer, New York, .

Chomsky, N. (1965). *Aspects of the theory of syntax*. MIT Press, Cambridge, Mass.

Clarke, E. F. (1995). Expression in performance: generativity, perception and semiosis. In J. Rink, (Ed.) *The practice of performance: studies in musical interpretation*. Cambridge University Press, Cambridge.

Colley, A., Banton, L., Down, J., and Pither, A. (1992). An expert–novice comparison in musical composition. *Psychology of Music*, **20.2**, 124–38.

Cross, I. (1997). Pitch schemata. In I. Deliege and J. A. Sloboda (Eds.) *Percetion and cognition of music*. Psychology Press, Hove.

Cuddy, L. (1997). Tonal relations. In I. Deliege and J. A. Sloboda (Eds.) *Perception and cognition of music*. Psychology Press, Hove.

Davidson, L. (1994). Songsinging by young and old: a developmental approach. In R. Aiello (Ed.) *Musical perceptions*. Oxford University Press, New York.

Davidson, J. W., Howe, M. J. A., and Sloboda, J. A. (1997). Environmental factors in the development of musical performance skill in the first twenty years of life. In D. Hargreaves and A. C. North (Eds.) *The social psychology of music*. Oxford University Press, Oxford.

Deliege, I. (1987). Grouping conditions in listening to music: an approach to Lerdahl and Jackendoff's grouping preference rules. *Music Perception*, **4.4**, 325–60.

Deliege, I. and Melen, M. (1997). Cue abstraction in the representation of musical form. In I. Deliege and J. A. Sloboda (Eds.) *Perception and Cognition of Music*. Psychology Press, Hove.

Deliege, I. and Sloboda, J. A. (Eds.) (1995). *Musical beginnings: the origins and development of musical competence* Oxford University Press, Oxford.

Deliege, I. and Sloboda, J. A. (Eds.) (1997). *Perception and cognition of music*. Psychology Press, Hove.

Dowling, W. J. and Harwood, D. L. (1996). *Music cognition*. Academic Press, New York.

Drake, C. (1993). Reproduction of musical rhythms by children, adult musicians, and non-musicians. *Perception and Psychophysics*, **53**, 25–33.

Ericsson, K. A., Krampe, R. T., and Tesch-Romer, C. (1993). The role of deliberate practice is the acquisition of expert performance. *Psychological review*, **100**, 363–406.

Ericsson, K. A. and Smith, J. (1991). *Towards a general theory of expertise: prospects and limits*. Cambridge University Press, Cambridge.

Hajda, J. M., Kendall, R. A., Careterette, E. C., and Harshberger, M. L. (1997). Methodological issues in timbre research. In I. Deliege and J. A. Sloboda (Eds.) *Perception and cognition of music*. Psychology Press, Hove.

Hargreaves, D. J. and North, A. C. (1997). *The social psychology of music*. Oxford University Press, Oxford.

Howe, M. J. A., Davidson, J. W., and Sloboda, J. A. (1998). Innate talent: reality or myth? *Behavioural and Brain Sciences*, **2**, 399–442.

Howell, P., Cross, I., and West, R. (Eds.) (1995). *Musical structure and cognition*. Academic Press, London.

Huron, D. (1991). The avoidance of part-crossing in polyphonic music: perceptual evidence and musical practice. *Music Perception*, **9.1**, 93–104.

Huron, D. (1993). Note onset asynchrony in J. S. Bach's Two-Part Inventions. *Music Perception*, **10.4**, 435–44.

Jarvinen, T. (1995). Tonal hierarchies in jazz improvisation. *Music Perception*, **12.4**, 415–37.

Jorgensen, H. and Lehmann, A. (Eds.) (1997). *Does practice make perfect? Current theory and research on instrumental music practice*. Norges Musikkhogskole, Oslo.

Jusczyk, P. and Krumhansl, C. L. (1993). Pitch and rhythmic patterns affecting infants' sensitivity to musical phrase structure. *Journal of Experimental Psychology: Human Perception and Performance*, **19**, 1–14.

Juslin, P. (1997). Emotional communication in music performance: a functionalist perspective and some data. *Music Perception*, **14**, 383–418.

Kessler, E. J., Hansen, C., and Shepard, R. N. (1984). Tonal schemata in the perception of music in Bali and in the West, *Music Perception*, **2**, 131–65.

Krumhansl, C. L. (1990). *The cognitive foundations of musical pitch*. Oxford University Press, Oxford.

Krumhansl, C. L. (1990). Internal representations for musical perception and performance. In M. Riess-Jones, and S. Holleran (1990) (Eds.). *Cognitive Bases of Musical communication*. American Psychological Association, Washington D.C.

Krumhansl, C. L. (1991). Music psychology: tonal structures in perception and memory. *Annual Review of Psychology*, **42**, 277–303.

Krumhansl, C. L. (1998). An exploratory study of musical emotions and psychophysiology. *Canadian Journal of Psychology*, **51**, 36–52.

Lamont, A. (1998). Music, education, and the development of pitch perception: the role of context, age, and musical experience. *Psychology of Music*, **26.1**, 7–25.

Lerdahl, F. (1988). Cognitive constraints on compositional systems. In J. Sloboda (Ed.) *Generative processes in music: the psychology of composition, performance, and improvisation*. Oxford University Press, London.

Lerdahl, F. and Jackendoff, R. (1983). *A Generative theory of tonal music*. MIT Press, Cambridge, Mass.

McAdams, S. and Bigand, E. (Eds.) (1993). *Thinking in sound: The cognitive psychology of human audition*. Oxford University Press, Oxford.

MacPherson, G. (1995). The assessment of musical performance: development and validation of five new measures. *Psychology of Music*, **23.2**, 142–61.

Miller, L. K. (1989). *Musical Savants: exceptional skill in the mentally retarded*. Erlbaum, Hillsdale, NJ.

Morrongiello, B. (1992). Effects of training on children's perception of music: a review. *Psychology of Music*, **20.1**, 1992.

Narmour, E. (1989). *The analysis and cognition of basic melodic structures.* University of Chicago Press, London.

Narmour, E. (1992). *The analysis and cognition of melodic complexity.* University of Chicago Press, London.

Palmer, C. (1996). On the assignment of structure in music performance. *Music Perception,* **14**, 21–54.

Palmer, C. (1997). Music performance. *Annual Review of Psychology,* **48**, 115–38.

Parncutt, R. (1994). A perceptual model of pulse salience and metrical accent in musical rhythms. *Music Perception,* **11.4**, 409–64.

Papousek, M. (1995). Intuitive parenting: a hidden source of musical stimulation in infancy. In I. Deliege, and J. A. Sloboda (1995) (Eds.) *Musical beginnings: the origins and development of musical competence.* Oxford University Press, Oxford.

Patel, A., and Peretz, I. (1997). Is music autonomous from language? A neuropsychological approach. In I. Deliege and J. A. Sloboda (Eds.) *Perception and cognition of music.* Psychology Press, Hove.

Raffman, D. (1993). *Language, music, and mind.* MIT Press, Cambridge, Mass.

Repp, B. (1990). Patterns of expressive timing in performances of a Beethoven Minuet by nineteen famous pianists. *Journal of the Acoustical Society of America,* **88**, 622–41.

Repp, B. (1997). The aesthetic quality of a quantitatively average music performance: two preliminary experiments. *Music Perception,* **14.4**, 419–44.

Riess-Jones, M. and Holleran, S. (Eds.) (1990). *Cognitive bases of musical communication.* American Psychological Association, Washington, D.C.

J. Rink, (Ed.) *The practice of performance: studies in musical interpretation.* Cambridge University Press, Cambridge.

Sharpe, C., Benenfield, P., and Kendall, L. (1998). *The effects of teaching and learning in the arts.* Qualifications and Curriculum Authority, London.

Simonton, D. K. (1996). Creative expertise: a life-span developmental perspective. In K. A. Ericsson (Ed.) *The road to excellence: the acquisition of expert performance in the arts and sciences, sports and games.* Erlbaum, Mahway, NJ.

Sloboda, J. A. (1986). Cognitive psychology and real music: the psychology of music comes of age. *Psychologica Belgica,* **26.2**, R.

Sloboda, J. A. (Ed.) (1988). *Generative processes in music: the psychology of composition, performance, and improvisation.* Oxford University Press, London.

Sloboda, J. A. (1991). Music structure and emotional response: some empirical findings. *Psychology of Music,* **19**, 110–20.

Sloboda, J. A. (1992). Psychological structures in music: core research 1980–1990. In. J. Paynter, T. Howell, R. Orton, and P. Seymour (Eds.). *Companion to contemporary musical thought.* Routledge and Kegan Paul, London.

Sloboda, J. A. and Davidson, J. W. (1995). The young performing musician. In I. Deliege and J. A. Sloboda (Eds.) *The origins and development of musical competence.* Oxford University Press, London.

Sloboda, J. A., Clarke, E. F., Parncutt, R., and Raekallio, M. (1998). Determinants of finger choice in piano sight reading. *Journal of Experimental Psychology: Human Perception and Performance,* **24.1**, 185–203.

Sloboda, J. A., and Parker, D. H. H. (1985). Immediate recall of melodies. In P.

Howell, I. Cross, and R. West (1995) (Eds.) *Musical structure and cognition.* Academic Press, London.

Todd, N. P. M. (1985). A model of expressive timing in music. *Music Perception*, **3**, 33–58.

Trehub, S., Schellenberg, G., and Hill, D. (1997). The origins of music perception and cognition: a developmental perspective. In I. Deliege and J. A. Sloboda (Eds.) *Perception and cognition of music.* Psychology Press, Hove.

Waters, A. J. and Underwood, G. (1998). Eye movements in a simple music-reading task: a study of expert and novice musicians. *Psychology of Music*, **26.1**, 46–60.

Watt, R. and Ash, R. (1997). A psychological investigation of meaning in music. *Musicae Scientiae*, **2.1**, 33–54.

Weisberg, R. W. (1993). *Creativity: Beyond the Myth of Genius.* Freeman, San Francisco.

Contents

1. Music as a cognitive skill

The reason that most of us take part in musical activity, be it composing, performing, or listening, is that music is capable of arousing in us deep and significant emotions. These emotions can range from the 'pure' aesthetic delight in a sound construction, through emotions like joy or sorrow which music sometimes evokes or enhances, to the simple relief from monotony, boredom or depression which everyday musical experiences can provide.

If someone from a civilization without music were to ask us why our civilisation supported so much musical activity, our answer would surely point to this capacity of music to heighten emotional life. Of course there are other reasons for individuals or societies to make use of music. Because much musical activity is also social activity it can come to have many social meanings, offering a variety of social rewards to those who participate in it. For instance, knowledge about certain types of music is a prerequisite for full membership of particular subcultures. The adoption of music for use in formally defined social situations allows people to earn a living through music. Aspects of musical training, such as the need for discipline and co-operation, may be held to be generally worth while. And so on. However, we may label these social motivations as secondary, if only because they are so closely tied to particular cultures. The emotional factor is, however, transcultural. It seems unlikely that music could have penetrated to the core of so many different cultures unless there were some fundamental human attraction to organized sound which transcended cultural boundaries.

If emotional factors are fundamental to the existence of music, then the fundamental question for a psychological investigation into music is *how* music is able to affect people. Seen with the cold eye of physics a musical event is just a collection of sounds with various pitches, durations, and other measurable qualities. Somehow the human mind endows these sounds with significance. They become symbols for something other than pure sound, something which enables us to laugh or cry, like or dislike, be moved or be indifferent.

There are two reasons why this issue leads us straight into the realms of cognitive psychology. The first is that most of our responses to music are learned. This is not to deny the possibility of some primitive responses to music shared by the whole species. For instance, loud fast music is arousing, whilst soft, slow music is soothing. Certain pitch ranges and timbres seem particularly attractive to infants, as do simple repetitive rhythms. But these primitive tendencies cannot account for the subtle and multidimensional nature of the adult response to music, nor can they account for the many significant cultural differences in response. I can still recall the surprise I felt when, after hearing a rather jolly sounding Greek folk song, my Greek companion indicated that this was a desperately sad piece of music. No doubt, an understanding of the words was partly responsible for her different view of the music; but I realized that my own response was determined by the major key, the simple and open harmonies, and the general rhythmic impetus. These qualities are, in fact, common to most Greek folk music. More subtle differences, undetected by me, are responsible for the communication of affect.

A second pointer to the cognitive component of our emotional responses is the fact that they are not to be explained simply in terms of 'conditioning'. Conditioning theory (amusingly called the 'Darling, They're Playing Our Tune' theory by Davies 1978) supposes that a piece of music acquires the emotional significance of the circumstances in which it happened to be heard. On this theory, the form and content of the music is irrelevant to its acquired emotional character. Only its context is important. Although this type of conditioning may occur in certain circumstances, and may help explain particular idiosyncrasies of musical taste, there are several observations which show that it is inadequate as a complete explanation for emotional responses:

1. Listeners within a musical culture generally agree on the emotional character of a given piece of music, even though they may have never heard it before (Hevner, 1936). Conditioning theory, in contrast, would predict wide individual differences according to circumstances of hearing.

2. The emotional character of a piece of music is not unitary and unchanging. On the contrary, experienced listeners to some types of music are able to identify a web of differing emotions which are evoked by the detailed sequence of events, and which become more finely differentiatied the better the music is known. Conditioning theory, in contrast, would lead one to expect that a piece of music would always be dominated by a single generalized emotional tone acquired from the conditioning context.

3. Our emotional response to the very same music can vary considerably from hearing to hearing. For instance, there have been occasions when the last movement of Tchaikovsky's Sixth Symphony has moved me to tears of grief, and others on which it has left me completely unmoved. What remained the same about my mental state on the different occasions was my *knowledge* that this was music *expressing* extreme grief, regardless of my emotional response to it.

An analogy which I find helpful is that between music and humour. When hearing a joke the listener must first understand it; he must perceive and identify the constituent words, recognise them as sentences, form a mental representation of the propositions that the sentences assert, and then determine the nature of the incongruity, double meaning, or whatever that makes the joke. Thus, to 'get the joke' involves a large set of cognitive processes, drawing upon knowledge of language and the world. After this the listener may, depending on his mood and taste, experience an emotional reaction involving laughter. So there is both a cognitive and an affective stage to his response. The cognitive stage is a necessary precursor of the affective stage; a listener cannot find a joke funny unless he understands it. However, the affective stage does not *necessarily* follow the cognitive stage. A person may understand a joke perfectly well without being moved to laughter by it. So it is with music. A person may understand the music he hears without being moved by it. If he *is* moved by it then he must have passed through the cognitive stage, which involves forming an abstract or symbolic *internal representation* of the music. The nature of this internal representation, and the things it allows a person to do with music, is the central subject matter of the cognitive psychology of music.

The way in which people represent music to themselves determines how well they can remember and perform it. Composition and improvisation require the generation of such representations, and perception involves the listener constructing them. These representations, and the processes which create them, are not directly observable. We have to infer their existence and nature from observations of the way in which people listen to, memorize, perform, create, and react to music.

Because such activities are learned, they may be viewed as skilled behaviours. Although composing and performing are universally acknowledged to be skills of some complexity, one must also remember that more commonplace activities, such as the ability to whistle a familiar melody, or to detect a 'wrong sounding' note in an unfamiliar melody, are also complex skills which are capable of shedding light on the nature of internal representations in music. What makes the composer or performer special is his rarity rather than anything *fundamentally* different about his mental equipment.

To illustrate this point, let us take two contrasting examples of musical skill and see what a cognitive psychologist might make of them. The first is the much quoted incident in the life of the young Mozart who, denied access to the score of Allegri's *Miserere*, listened to two church performances and then wrote it out from memory. The primary source for the authenticity of this incident is a letter from Mozart's father dated 14 April 1770 (Anderson, 1966). Such an accomplishment, although by no means unique, is well beyond the capacity of most people, and has become one of a handful of legends about the apparently superhuman powers of great musicians. In discussing this example the psychologist Farnsworth (1969) claims that Mozart's 'eidetic' memory was responsible for his ability. Eidetic memory is a peculiarly vivid, almost hallucinatory, recall which is alleged to be present in some children. On this view, the unusual accomplishment is the result of possessing unusual mental powers, since most people do not possess eidetic memory.

An alternative explanation is that Mozart was more adept, through experience, at doing something we all do when trying to memorize complex material; that is, to identify patterns in the material, thereby remembering groups as single units or 'chunks'. It is difficult to decide between these two alternatives with respect to Mozart's memory, since we cannot test him further. There is, however, contemporary evidence which tends to favour the latter explanation. For instance, there has been much recent interest in the abilities of game players with various levels of expertise to remember game positions. Chase and Simon (1973) asked chess players of varying standards to examine boards taken from actual games for five seconds and then attempt to reproduce the boards from memory. Players in the category of chess master were able to reproduce the boards almost perfectly, whereas novices did very poorly. This is, perhaps, unsurprising, and similar results have been obtained when musicians and non-musicians are asked to reproduce the positions of a few notes displayed briefly on a stave (Halpern and Bower 1982; Sloboda 1976a). The really important result is that when chess players were asked to reproduce random boards which could not have occured in any rational game, the masters and novices performed equally, and very poorly. This shows that masters do not have better visual (eidetic) memory than novices. They are superior *only* when the material to be remembered makes some sense, and can be grouped into strategic 'chunks' (e.g. a pawn chain, a fork, a concealed check). This is confirmed by detailed observation of the way masters carry out the reproduction task. They tend to recall all the members of a chunk together, with pauses between separate chunks.

For a chess master, the mental representation of a chess position is not a copy of the physical board. It is a more abstract *structural* description of the meaningful relationships between groups of pieces. Through many years of experience he has acquired automatic perceptual mechanisms which rapidly pick out frequently occuring strategic patterns from the input. It has been estimated that the master must be able to recognise several thousands of patterns in this way.

Most musical material has just as much patterning and structure as a chess position. Within particular idioms there are many regularly occuring patterns (e.g. chords, scales and arpeggios) and someone exposed to an idiom will rapidly become familiar with them. Patterning also occurs on a larger scale. Thematic repetition is a cornerstone of most music, certain harmonic progressions are ubiquitous, and so on. The master can make use of all this patterning when building up a representation of a piece of music.

My second example is commonplace. Nearly everybody is capable of identifying well known melodies, or of recalling them if given the title (e.g. 'Yankee Doodle', 'Frère Jacques', 'God Save the Queen'). What makes this observation particularly important in the current context is that a precise pitch, speed, or medium is not crucial for identification, nor will a person necessarily reproduce a melody at a pitch he has ever heard before. For instance, Attneave and Olson (1971) asked people to sing the NBC chimes from various given starting notes. The chimes are broadcast several times each day as a station identifier for the American National Broadcasting Corporation, but they are always played at the same pitch. The experimental subjects were able to transpose the chimes to any starting note within their range instantly and effortlessly. This is one of several demonstrations that people do not remember simple melodies in terms of precise pitches and durations but in terms of patterns and relationships. The NBC chimes remain identifiably the same so long as the pitch and duration *ratios* between the notes remain constant. This simple demonstration of musical memory already demonstrates how it is a *abstraction* from the physical stimulus. Sequential structure also influences untrained musicians. For instance, music which conforms to the rules of diatonic tonal harmony is much easier for Western listeners to remember than is music which breaks these rules. Some of the most important demonstrations of this are reviewed in Chapter 5, which examines the processes involved in listening to music. Here I wish to stress the closeness of the analogy to the chess experiments. Music which does not contain familiar patterns and structures cannot easily be represented in a listener's memory.

If expert and commonplace musical achievements are to be explained in the same sort of way, how are we to account for the *differences* between experts and novices? The most important factor is probably the *number* and *complexity* of the structural features in terms of which the listener is capable of representing music. The 'ordinary' listener is probably aware only of the musical 'foreground', noticing small patterns which are made up from a few adjacent notes. The Mozarts of the world probably share this level of representation, but have overlaid it with higher-order grouping processes which form single 'background' units from groups of 'foreground' units. The same process could be repeated on the new units to form even larger units, building up a hierarchical schema which could span a piece of music lasting several minutes.

A second difference between trained and untrained musical memories may lie in the degree of awareness that the memorizer has of the structures he is using. Commonly, musical training involves acquiring the vocabulary in terms of which to describe the structure of music. Elements of this vocabulary (e.g. cadential sequence, tonic chord, passing note) often function as means for extending memory capacity. A musician can be consciously looking out for instances of such structures. This does not imply that such structures are not available to untrained people. The evidence suggests, rather, that untrained musicians have implicit knowledge of that which musicians can talk about explicitly. In this respect, music is similar to language. Ordinary people speak their natural language according to the same grammatical rules as professional linguists even though they may have very limited conscious knowledge of those rules.

The 'representation of musical structure' is a unifying concept for the various topics treated in this book; and it may be helpful at this point to give a brief sketch of the topics to be covered, and the approach I shall be taking to them.

One of the key features of any cognitive skill is speed. A process such as reading or listening is useless if it cannot keep up with the inflow of new material. Mozart had not only to notice structural relationships in the piece he memorized, he also had to perform all the necessary mental operations quickly enough to keep abreast of the music. Skilled performance must also be rapid and fluent. This has led psychologists to think that performance is controlled by the same sort of hierarchical structures as seem to account for input skill. Here, highly automated procedures control detailed performance while the performer is free to attend to higher-order aspects. For instance, the experienced sight reader confronted with a familiar scale passage will not need to make conscious decisions about which fingers to use for which notes. His hand will automatically take up the right configuration, while his attention may be on expressive factors, or on mentally preparing the following phrase. When we hear the phenomenal speed of a virtuoso performance, we can render it explicable, although no less of an achievement, by recalling that what strikes the ear as 20 separate notes may well be, for the performer, a single integrated and automated unit. What makes the achievement impressive is the many hundreds of hours' practice which may be needed to develop the degree of automation required. In examining psychological investigations of music performance (Chapter 3) we shall find considerable evidence for abstract high-level structures governing all aspects of skilled performance.

When we turn to the creation of music through composition or improvisation (Chapter 4), we shall find that the same notions of structured representation and rapid deployment of structural units are helpful in understanding these skills. Succesful composition relies on the ability to be sensitive to very large-scale structures, so that detailed working out can be governed by a conception of the overall framework. This applies to any large creative endeavour, such as writing a book. Without some unifying conception the author will find it hard to co-ordinate and shape the many sub-sections. Success in improvisation relies on structural grasp too, but also on the ability to rapidly choose appropriate, yet novel, elements to fill the slots in a basic script. Improvisers achieve their best results when working within a highly constrained form (e.g. jazz blues, fugue), whereas composers are more likely to achieve successful innovation of forms.

Since a basic premise of this book is that we *learn* the structures that we use to represent music, an examination of the learning process itself is central to our concerns (Chapter 6). This process can be seen as having two phases. The first is developmental enculturation. This is the learning that takes place as a result of our exposure to the normal musical products of our culture in childhood, together with the acquisition of simple skills like the ability to reproduce short songs. The knowledge acquired at this stage is not, on the whole, the result of self-conscious learning or teaching effort. Rather, children simply acquire the knowledge through their everyday social experiences. In consequence such knowledge tends to be universal in a culture, and is the ground on which more specialized skills may be built. The second phase is, then, the acquisition of specialized skills through training. These skills are not universal within a culture, and are what turn ordinary citizens into 'musicians'. Our treatment of enculturation can be only descriptive. The treatment of specialized skills should arguably be prescriptive as well. Musicians have some right to expect that cognitive psychologists should be particularly well qualified to advise teachers and students on the self-conscious acquisition of skill.

Because musical skills are culturally transmitted, it follows that they may vary significantly between cultures. Many writers on the psychology of music talk about Western tonal music as if it were the only type of music. Whilst ignorance prevents me from dwelling on music from other cultures at any length, Chapter 7 contains an attempt to evaluate just how far some of the cognitive principles which underlie Western musical skill are relevant to other forms of music.

Most contemporary thought in cognitive psychology is functional, in that it attempts to discover the *principles* of structure and operation which would allow an information handling system to behave in the way we observe humans to behave. We have to keep in mind, however, that these principles are *in fact*, in our case, realized in the structures and functions of the *brain*, and that it is worthwhile finding out what we can about the brain in relation to the skills we examine. Studies reviewed in Chapter 7 reveal that, as with other cognitive skills, components of musical skill appear to have specific brain localization. The functional organization of the brain is modular, with specific portions doing specific jobs.

I began this chapter with reference to what is, humanly, the most important psychological fact about music; that it carries emotional significance or meaning for us. To say this prompts the thought that music is, in some respects, like a language. Although many writers on music have used this analogy in a loosely metaphorical way, there is now a growing body of theory and data which make a more rigorous assessment possible. Chapter 2 attempts such an assessment. It is possibly the most technical of the chapters, but is central to the book in that it provides a source of ideas about the nature of cognitive representations in music. These ideas are put to work elsewhere in attempting to understand specific musical skills. I hope, though, that the selective reader will be able to read the other chapters in isolation, and still obtain a broad idea of how music is represented in the mind, and why an understanding of these representations is so central to an understanding of all the skills discussed.

Before going further, I must say something about the term 'cognitive psychology' itself and its role in this book. Cognitive psychology is a fairly new branch of psychology. It is also a rapidly changing discipline, and a generally acceptable definition of its aims and boundaries would be hard to produce. The emergence of an identifiable discipline coincided approximately with the publication of Broadbent's seminal *Perception and Communication* (1958). It marked the advent of a cautious experimental mentalism, which showed that it was possible to subject processes such as attention and recognition to rigorous laboratory investigation. Subjects were not required to introspect on these processes but to perform tasks from whose accuracy or speed of execution could be inferred something about the internal structure of the system controlling these tasks. It was another nine years before Neisser's influential *Cognitive Psychology* (1967) gave the discipline its name, but during the years spanned by these two books the preoccupations of researchers in this field remained quite narrowly defined. The research concentrated on 'input' skills, including the recognition of letters, words, and other simple stimuli, in artificially simplified laboratory surroundings. Major theoretical disputes centred on questions of capacity: how many items could be held in memory at once? were cognitive operations on incoming stimuli performed in series or in parallel? The 1970s saw a broadening of the field in several directions. One development was a greater interest in higher cognitive processes and the control of complex behaviour, and an allied interest in the organization of knowledge and its deployment in cognitive skills. Several influences were important here. One was a renewal of interest in problem-solving behaviour, much neglected since the 1930s. Newell and Simon's *Human Problem Solving* (1972) is arguably the most important contribution to this branch of the subject, and is also a prime example of another very important influence on cognitive psychology—the growth of the science of artificial intelligence. The opportunity to embody theories in working computer programs has stimulated concern with theories of cognitive functioning which are specific enough to predict actual instances of behaviour, but which are broad enough to account for a wide range of cognitive achievements.

The second major development of recent years has been the attempt to study cognitive skills in situations more closely resembling those in which people would normally employ them outside the laboratory. Thus, concern has focused on how people deal with extended and meaningful material rather than on fragmented, meaningless stimuli. This movement has brought in its train an increased interest in developmental aspects of cognition, and cultural variance; and a greater commitment to finding practical applications for cognitive research. Neisser's second book, *Cognition and Reality* (1976) has been a rallying point for this approach, and some of the first fruits of research in this vein are exemplified by collections such as Gruneberg, Morris, and Sykes' *Practical Aspects of Memory* (1978).

Luckily for the beginning student there are now many excellent introductions to the subject available (e.g. Anderson 1980; Solso 1980), although they sometimes tend to exaggerate the stability and unity of the subject. Claxton (1980) provides some more candid and critical assessments, although some of the arguments will be difficult for beginners to follow. In this book I identify, although fairly loosely, with what I perceive as the mainstream of current cognitive research outlined above. The focus is on empirical study of what people *do* with music, rather than what they *say* they do, and, where possible, I address myself to the real-life behaviour of musicians, rather than to their behaviour in artificially constricted laboratory situations. I try to give as much prominence to output skill (e.g. performing) and higher cognitive functioning (e.g. composition) as I do to input skill (e.g. listening). Finally, my criterion for selecting empirical studies to describe is that they should have a particular theoretical or practical importance. I make no claim to provide a complete survey of the literature.

The cognitive psychology of music is still a very young discipline and there are several areas of enquiry which have not yet received detailed empirical attention. I have felt it important to identify some of these areas, and say something about the kinds of questions which need to be asked. In this respect the book looks forward to the future, and is not simply a statement of the current position. I have freely used my experiences and intuitions as a practising musician to augment and complement experimental findings; indeed the section on composition would hardly have been possible without them. Here, as elsewhere, my aim has been to stimulate scientific thinking and experiment. If some of the ideas in this book are proved wrong through new research no-one will be more pleased than I.

The last purpose of this chapter is to place this book in the context of other writing on the psychology of music, and to suggest some further general reading in the area. Some aspects of the psychology of music fall outside the concerns of this book. I make little mention of musical taste or preference, and the reader is referred to Farnsworth (1969) for an introduction to this area. I do not deal with social applications of music (e.g. to industry or therapy). Farnsworth is quite useful here, and Priestley (1975) and Alvin (1975) are two of several introductions to music therapy. There is also a *Journal of Music Therapy*. Purely educational research falls outside the scope of this book. Two main journals in this area are the *Journal of Research into Music Education* and *Psychology of Music*. Sensory psychology and psychoacoustics are not covered in any detail. The *Journal of the Acoustical Society of America* is a prime source of research in this area. Plomp (1977) offers a recent synthesis, and Moore (1982) provides a sensible introduction to the area. Research on music reported in the main perceptual journals tends to be of this sort. My last area of exclusion concerns psychometric approaches to musical ability. Shuter-Dyson and Gabriel (1981) provide a useful summary of research in this tradition.

General collections of papers by Critchley and Henson (1977), Clynes (1982) and Deutsch (1982a) are useful source books for the whole subject. A recent book by Davies (1978) approaches nearest to the orientation of this book, although his emphasis, and that of a new journal *Music Perception*, is on the processes involved in listening. Finally, the journal *Psychomusicology* has recently been founded with an editorial policy which closely fits the aims of this book. The name, although new and unwieldy, is perhaps the best single-word description for the subject which this book explores.

2. Music, language, and meaning

2.1. Introduction

This chapter begins by looking at two influential theorists, the linguist Chomsky and the musicologist Schenker. Their theories have some striking similarities. They both argue, for their own subject matter, that human behaviour _must_ be supported by the ability to form abstract underlying representations. Two of man's highest and most complex products seem to display something central about his intellect.

Chomsky and Schenker gained their principal insights from examining the _structure_ of language and music rather than from examining linguistic and musical _behaviour_. Recent empirical work has shown that music and language share behavioural as well as formal features; and so the chapter moves on to review this work. The major portion of the chapter is organized around the subdivision of language and music into three components: phonology, syntax, and semantics. Phonology concerns the way in which a potentially infinite variety of sounds are 'parcelled up' into a finite number of discrete sound categories which constitute the basic communicative units. Syntax concerns the way in which these units are combined into sequences. A major concern of those studying syntax has been the discovery of rules which reliably produce legal sequences and eliminate illegal ones. Semantics concerns the way in which meaning is carried by the sequences so constructed. Particular fixed combinations of phonological units can have fixed meanings, but it is a characteristic of both language and music that meaning is also carried by the ordering and combination of elements in longer sequences.

The concern of this chapter is not only to describe linguistic and musical rules or categories, but also to examine the degree to which psychological evidence confirms their reality. A linguist searches for the neatest and most economical way of describing a language's structure. A _psycholinguist_ seeks the description which most closely resembles the psychological processes by which language is produced and understood. And so it must be for the psychomusicologist.

2.2. Chomsky and Schenker

The cognitive psychology of language almost owes its very existence to the linguist Noam Chomsky. His radical approach to the problem of describing language structure (Chomsky 1957, 1965, 1968) was the main impetus to the formation of the discipline of psycholinguistics, and the impact of his work still reverberates around the psychological laboratories of the world. As is the case with all seminal thinkers his work has attracted as much cogent opposition as it has support, but it is doubtful if any current approach to language owes nothing to him.

One of Chomsky's main claims has been that, at a deep level, all natural languages have the same structure, and that this structure tells us something universal about the human intellect. Many writers on music have been attracted to the idea that there are musical universals; maybe that there is something particularly natural about tonality. Could it be that Chomsky's theses receive independent support from music? A few writers seem to think so. For instance, Leonard Bernstein has recently celebrated his discovery of the 'Chomsky connection' with characteristic exuberance (Bernstein 1976). Sundberg and Lindblom (1976) have written a 'Chomskyan' grammar for a set of Swedish folk-songs; and researchers in artificial intelligence have written programs for parsing music which share formal properties with language programs. For the most part, however, psychologists investigating music have not been eager to pursue this path, preferring to treat music as a totally independent phenomenon.

There are, of course, good scientific reasons for approaching the study of music without too many presuppositions, but my own attitude to this issue has been profoundly affected by the writings of the German musicologist Heinrich Schenker (1868–1935) which have been gaining influence in contemporary analytic thought (e.g. Schenker, 1935). There are some striking parallels between Schenker's views on music and Chomsky's on language. For instance, Schenker would wish to claim that, at a deep level, all good musical compositions have the same type of structure, and that this structure reveals to us something about the nature of musical intuition. There is no evidence to suggest that Chomsky knew of Schenker's work at the time of formulating his theories of language. It appears, therefore, that similar ways of viewing language and music arose quite independently in two creative intellects steeped in their own subject matter.

My view is that the linguistic analogy in music deserves serious attention; although I would make three qualifying remarks. Firstly, it would be foolish to claim that music is simply another natural language. There are many fundamental differences which cannot be overlooked, the most obvious being that we use language to make assertions or ask questions about the real world and the objects and relationships in it. If music has any subject matter at all, then it is certainly not the same as that of normal language. Secondly, this analogy can clearly be exploited in metaphorical, poetic ways, of which scientists are right to be wary (e.g. 'music is the language of the emotions'). However, this does not exclude the possibility of a more rigorous use of the analogy. Indeed, it is arguable that the most productive scientific analogies are those which fire the imagination as much as they fuel empirical and theoretical endeavours. Thirdly, it is an open question just how far the analogy can be pursued, and its application is subject to the weighing of empirical evidence and argument that characterizes any scientific endeavour. In other words, the analogy is something to be evaluated, not assumed.

What, then, are the main similarities between Chomsky and Schenker? Perhaps the most fundamental similarity concerns the differentiation between *surface* and *deep* structure. Surface structure is, roughly, the form taken by a linguistic (or musical) sequence as it is uttered (or written). The two sentences 'John phoned up Mary' and 'John phoned Mary up' have different surface structures; and so do the two musical sequences given in Example 2.1. Nevertheless, in both cases we would wish to say that there is a particular closeness between the two sequences, which is not simply a result of their containing the same elements in a different order (e.g. the closeness would not be shared by 'Phoned John up Mary'). In the language example we would wish to say, at the least, that the two sentences *mean* the same thing. Chomsky proposed that we could capture the closeness of such sentences within a grammar, if we assigned them to the same deep structure. This deep structure is an abstract entity, not itself a sentence, from which both surface structures can be derived by the application of *transformation* rules.

Example 2.1.

In order to represent the deep structure of a sentence it is useful to employ an 'immediate constituent tree' notation as shown in Figs. 2.1–2.3. Each tree has a single *node* at its head; S for sentence. This node can be decomposed into two or more nodes at the next lower level. The rules governing the decomposition of nodes are called the generative (or rewrite) rules of the grammar. One generative rule allows S to be rewritten as NP + VP (noun phrase + verb phrase). Other rules allow further rewriting (e.g. VP goes to V + NP). At the lowest level, individual words can be specified. For many simple sentences, immediate constituent analysis of this kind gives a satisfactory account of their structure because words connected to a single node are next to one another. Grammatical relation is signalled by sequential adjacency. In Fig. 2.1 'The' has a closer grammatical relation to 'girl' than any other word in the sentence. An informal way of testing the grammatical relation of two words is to see whether they could be replaced by a single word to form a new meaningful sentence. Thus, 'The girl' could be replaced by 'Mary', and 'hit the ball' by 'sang'; but 'girl hit the' cannot be so replaced.

There are, however, many sentences where an immediate constituent analysis does not capture our intuitions about the grammatical relation of words. In Fig. 2.2 we find that the constituent tree links 'up' to 'Mary', whereas one

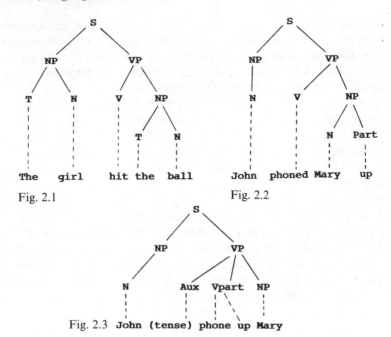

Fig. 2.1

Fig. 2.2

Fig. 2.3 John (tense) phone up Mary

Fig. 2.1–2.3. Examples of immediate constituent trees for English sentences. Key: S = sentence, NP = noun phrase, VP = verb phrase, T = article, N = noun, V = verb.

may feel that 'up' is, in fact, more related to 'phoned'. What is more, we can introduce longer sequences between 'phoned' and 'up' without destroying this relation. For instance, 'John phoned the brown eyed girl he met for the first time yesterday up' is an acceptable sentence. Chomsky's solution to this problem is to propose that the deep structure is a tree in which words having close grammatical relationship are governed by the same node. So 'John phoned up Mary' and 'John phoned Mary up' are given the *same* deep structure, shown in Fig. 2.3. Note that the symbols in the bottom row (the terminal string) do not constitute a sentence. There are some obligatory transformations that must be performed (in this case the inflection of the verb form to indicate tense). Other transformations are optional, such as the moving of 'up' to the end of the noun phrase governed by the verb phrase. These transformations generate the various different surface structures that a single deep structure may exhibit.

Turning now to the music sequences in Example 2.1, although Schenker analysis would rarely be applied to such trivial excerpts, we can note some interesting parallels to the language examples. Schenker would give both excerpts the same deep structure (*Ursatz*). This deep structure always has two components: a fundamental melodic line (*Urlinie*) which, in this case, is the progression 3–2–1 in the scale of A major, and a bass arpeggiation

(*Bassbrechung*) which, in this case, is the progression I–V–I in the same key. In each excerpt the melodic C receives no explicit representation in the deep structure. Rather, it is an interpolation between the notes of the *Urlinie* which results in expansion or *prolongation* of the material. However, no amount of appropriate prolongation destroys the integrity of the *Ursatz* or the fundamental interdependence of its elements. For instance, Example 2.2 possesses precisely the same deep structure as both sequences in Example 2.1. The asterisked notes show the *Ursatz*. The relation of the melodic B to the preceding C is not weakened by the intervening notes, just as the relationship of 'phoned' to 'up' is not weakened by intervening words.

Example 2.2.

The source of the *Ursatz* (the top node in a hypothetical constituent structure tree) is the chord of the tonic triad. It must, however, be admitted that neither Schenker nor any of his followers have produced anything approaching a formal generative grammar for deriving *Ursatze* from triads, or for transforming an *Ursatz* into an acceptable composition through prolongation. What they have shown is that *Ursatze* are discoverable in a very large body of tonal compositions. One aim of modern linguists is to produce a set of generative and transformational rules which generates all and *only* acceptable sentences of a language like English. While Schenkerians might claim that all good compositions are built upon *Ursatze*, they would not claim to be in possession of rules which would generate *only* good music. Schenker's method is, in essence, analytic, not generative.

There are three significant contrasts between Schenkerian and Chomskyan structures which we should note before proceeding. Firstly, the *Ursatz* is, in itself, a legal although trivial piece of music. It obeys rules of counterpoint and harmonic progression just as do the 'surface' elements. Schenker analysis proceeds by a recursive 'reduction' of a finished composition, eliminating subsidiary prolongations to reveal a harmonic and contrapuntal 'skeleton'. This skeleton is then further reduced by the very same methods over and again until the simplest and most fundamental structure is revealed. In contrast, as we have already noticed, Chomskyan deep structures are not, in themselves, acceptable sentences.

Secondly, the transformations applied to an *Ursatz* result in a lengthening and complexifying of the music. Very long movements containing hundreds of notes may be subsumed under a single *Ursatz*. To demonstrate this was one of Schenker's major achievments. In contrast, Chomskyan deep structures govern only single sentences, which are typically short, and a common effect of applying transformations is condensation rather than expansion. For instance the sentence 'John likes Mary and John likes Jane' mirrors rather closely the deep structure which would normally be transformed and shortened to 'John likes Mary and Jane.'

Thirdly, differentiation between pieces of music is achieved at the surface level rather than at the level of deep structure. According to Schenker there are very few different types of *Ursatz*. If the *Ursatz* determined the significance of music, then there would be very little for composers to say. Much of the 'meaning' of any piece of music is given to it through the actual surface details. In language it is different. The significance of a sentence, in practical discourse, lies almost entirely in its deep structure. There are an indefinite number of deep structures, corresponding to all the different propositions thata language can express. Transformations of these deep structures often *reduce* differentiation because, for instance, different deep structures can be transformed into identical surface structures—as in 'Bill shot the man with a gun'. This is ambiguous: one possible deep structure would have Bill doing the shooting with a gun; the other would have the man possessing a gun.

The demonstration that events quite far apart in both linguistic and musical sequences can have a close structural relationship has two major consequences. The first is that whatever grammars are eventually shown to be fully adequate for language and music, they must be more powerful than 'finite state' grammars. Chomsky (1957) provided the classic proof that this type of grammar is inadequate for a natural langauge. In such a grammar, words are generated one at a time, each word determining the set from which the next word may be chosen. The rules are thus 'context independent'. It does not matter in which context a word is found; exactly the same set of consecutive words is permissible in each case. In a finite state grammar, for instance, the word 'washes' must allow both 'himself' and 'herself' to follow, since 'the boy washes himself' and 'the girl washes herself' are both correct English sentences. Yet such a grammar would allow 'the boy washes herself', which is unacceptable. To improve on a finite-state grammar we must introduce 'context sensitive' rules which take into account more than the immediately preceding word. The same arguments apply by analogy to music.

The second consequence is more directly psychological. If music and language have properties which demand grammars of a certain complexity, then humans must have the psychological resources to represent such grammars. This claim is hardly controversial nowadays, but it is incompatible with the radical behaviourism of Skinner (1957) and others which dominated many branches of psychology at the time of Chomsky's early work. Their basic claim was that behavioural sequences were brought about by simple causal chains in which a given response was triggered by an immediately preceding stimulus (which could, in verbal behaviour, be internal feedback from the preceding word uttered). Today, Lashley's (1951) classic argument for hierarchical models of sequential behaviour, in which the whole sequence is, in crucial respects, mapped out in the mind before any behaviour is initiated, is the basis of standard theory (see, for instance, Martin 1972, and Shaffer 1976). A speaker is able to produce grammatical sentences precisely because he is able to represent each sentence as a unified structure in which the parts have the kinds of relationships between them which are exemplified in a deep-structure tree. Similarly, as Schenker would claim, a composer is able to produce a masterwork precisely because he has an intuition of the *Ursatz* underlying it, which guides and unifies the process of generating the individual notes.

As this chapter progresses I shall return to Chomsky and Schenker on several occasions. I will not, however, be able to provide a detailed analysis or critique of either transformational grammar or Schenker analysis. To do so would require lengthy excursions into linguistics and musicology. For a useful introduction to Chomsky's work the reader is referred to Lyons (1970). Greene (1972) and Fodor, Bever, and Garrett (1974) provide psychological assessments of transformational grammar. A criticism of Chomskyan linguistics may be found in Robinson (1975).

A difficulty with approaching the work of Schenker is that good English translations of all his major writings are not yet available. The major English-speaking musicologists to employ Schenkerian concepts are Salzer. (1952) and Forte (1962). Yeston (1977) has made a collection of articles on Schenker, and a recent critical approach is provided by Narmour (1977). It is worth emphasizing that Schenker's work does not occupy the central position in musicological thought that Chomsky's work does in linguistics. Schenker did not present his ideas with the formal precision of Chomsky, and their application to anything other than mainstream classical compositions is problematical.

2.3. Other comparisons between language and music

Although the Chomsky–Schenker parallel seems one of the most striking links between language and music, it is not, of course, the only one. Before reviewing selected research in detail I would like to list, and comment upon, some of the other major similarities between language and music.

(*a*) Both language and music are characteristics of the human species that seem to be *universal* to all humans and *specific* to humans. To say that language and music are universal is to say that humans have a general capacity to acquire linguistic and musical competence. There may, of course, be special reasons why particular individuals do not acquire competence (e.g. brain damage, lack of appropriate experience). The claim that language is *specific* to humans has been the subject of psychological controversy. Clearly, there seems to be no other species whose natural communication shares all the features of human language, but attempts to teach chimpanzees a modified human language (Gardner and Gardner 1969) have met with enough success to sustain lengthy argument in the psychological literature. On balance, most psychologists would conclude that such studies, whilst possibly forcing us to reassess our ideas about chimpanzees' mental capacities, do not seriously challenge the specificity hypothesis. Although chimpanzees have learned modest vocabularies of sign-language words, they use and combine them in ways which do not go significantly beyond the capacities of a normal two-year-old human child, and the human effort required to produce and sustain this behaviour is prodigious.

The specificity hypothesis for music has not been subject to the degree of psychological assessment that has been devoted to language. However, it is clear that the functions of music for man find no parallel in the animal world; many of the most highly patterned sound behaviours (e.g. bird song) are relatively rigid intra-specific signals of territory, aggression, warning, etc. I shall discuss more fully in Chapter 7 the question of whether non-human primates display capacities in virtue of which man's musical origins could be explained. Certainly, no serious scientific effort has been made to exploit such capacities. For now, a quote from Williams (1980) will suffice to typify the generally accepted conclusion about non-human music. 'In the vocalising of apes we do not find the elements, nor even the beginnings of the chant and dance ritual of primitive man.'

(*b*) Both language and music are capable of generating an unlimited number of novel sequences. People can produce sentences they have never heard before, and composers can write melodies which nobody has ever produced before. Animal 'languages' in contrast usually contain a finite (and small) set of utterances which exhaust the communicative repertoire.

(*c*) Children seem to have a natural ability to learn the rules of language and music through exposure to examples. Spontaneous speech and spontaneous singing are first exhibited at around the same age (between one and two years). Language development proceeds through intermediate forms to model adult grammar at about the age of five. The studies reviewed in Chapter 6 show an analogous progression for music.

(*d*) The natural medium for both language and music is auditory–vocal. That is, both language and music are primarily received as sequences of sounds and produced as sequences of vocal movements which create sounds. Thus, many of the neural mechanisms for analysing input and producing output must be shared. The most universal of all musical forms is the song, where words and music are intimately combined.

(*e*) Although the auditory–vocal mode is primary, many cultures have developed ways of writing down music. In such notational systems the writer expresses the sequence he wishes to communicate as a set of written symbols, and the receiver retrieves the message by decoding the visual symbols. Although most people acquire the ability to understand and use spoken language without specific tuition, reading and writing has usually to be taught *after* a person is a competent user of spoken language. Many cultures have no notational systems for their language or music, and many individuals in literate cultures have difficulty in acquiring literacy. Adult illiteracy is acknowledged to be a major social problem in nearly all literate cultures, and inability to sight read bedevils a great number of music performers (see Chapter 3). The inability to deal with notation is all the more striking when, as is the case with standard Western notations, the grammatical structure is actually made more explicit in the notated form than in the spoken form. For instance, English orthography marks each word with a gap, and each major segment with a punctuation mark; whereas in speech words and clauses run together with no explicit marker. In standard musical notation key, metre, phrasing, and other structural information is explicitly signalled by notational elements; whereas in the auditory mode the listener must frequently work this out from the note sequence itself (see this chapter, section 5, and Chapter 5).

Although literacy is hard to acquire, its acquisition can profoundly alter cognitive functioning. Activities such as the accurate memorisation of long passages, or extended composition, would be impossible without it. In Chapter 7, I shall be exploring some of the ways in which literate and non-literate musical activity differ.

(*f*) Receptive skills precede productive skills in development. Children can understand sentences using certain constructions before they can invent sentences using those same constructions. In music, children are able to respond to musical devices before they can use these devices to make their own music. Generally, most adults retain a severe production deficiency in music. Although they may be able to learn to reproduce specific musical sequences, and although they may develop complex analytic listening abilities, they can be totally incapable of producing novel musical sequences of a style and complexity similar to those they are competent to deal with receptively. So, for instance, a listener may have a deep knowledge of Mozart's symphonies, as evidenced by his ability to recall, describe and classify them, or to analyse their structure, yet he may be totally unable to generate a theme, let alone a whole work, which is original yet 'Mozartian'.

(*g*) The forms taken by natural language and natural music differ across cultures, but some universal features constrain these forms. The fact that there are different forms has the consequence that people familiar with a particular form are often unable to deal appropriately with other forms. Thus, a native English speaker is unable to understand Chinese. Similarly, someone whose musical culture has consisted of English nursery rhymes is unlikely to be able to understand Tibetan chant. In both language and music, there are varying degrees of formal difference. For instance, spoken Slovakian is quite similar to spoken Polish, and so a native Pole will have partial success in understanding a Slovak speaker. Similarly, Mozart has more in common with nursery rhymes than Tibetan chant, so someone familiar with nursery rhymes will have partial success in understanding

Mozart. Formal differences arise because there is a certain degree of arbitrariness about the precise sounds used to realize linguistic and musical forms. In language, any pronounceable set of sounds will do as a word, provided that all users know its function. Similarly, there are many ways of signalling grammatical dependency, from word ordering to inflection.

Given the diversity in linguistic and musical forms, it seems initially puzzling that one should wish to claim that there are universal features nonetheless. One form of the argument for linguistic universals runs something as follows. The role of language is to express thought. The form of human thought is innate and common to all humans. The deep structure of an utterance is closely related to the thought it represents (whether or not is is identical *to* the thought need not concern us here). In order to represent a thought faithfully, the deep structure is constrained in certain ways. In other words, because all human prelinguistic thoughts have the same type of form, then all linguistic deep structures which represent them must have the same kind of form. In order to turn the deep structure into a sentence, the speaker must transform it into a linear sound sequence which supplies the necessary information to a listener. These transformations are thus doubly constrained; by the nature of the vocal apparatus shared by all humans (which determines the general surface appearance of an utterance); and by the deep structure which they must carry through to the surface. This argument draws in many complex issues in philosophy, linguistics, and cognitive psychology. For instance, if language expresses propositions, does this imply that human thought is propositional? If so, what role does imagery play in thought (Pylyshyn 1973, Kosslyn and Pomerantz 1977)? Rather than pursue these issues, our purpose here is to see what a similar argument might look like for music.

The first question we must ask is whether there is any entity which bears the same relationship to a musical sequence as a thought bears to a linguistic sequence. A thought is not, in itself, a linguistic sequence on the argument we have outlined. It exists independently of language and could be entertained by a non-linguistic or pre-linguistic human. Is there any form of mental activity which could take place in a mind without musical knowledge that could be somehow *expressed* by a musical sequence? Such activity would be, precisely, one which could find musical expression in such natural but diverse forms as a Tibetan chant or a nursery rhyme. One suggestion is that the mental substrate of music is something like that which underlies certain types of story. In these stories a starting position of equilibrium or rest is specified. Then some disturbance is introduced into the situation, producing various problems and tensions which must be resolved. The story ends with a return to equilibrium. The underlying representation for music could be seen as a highly abstracted blueprint for such stories, retaining only the features they all have in common. The learning of a musical language could then be seen as the acquisition of a way of representing these features in sound. Maybe, *but, tonic triad is a western thing?*

therefore, we should look more closely at Schenker's *Ursatz* for insight into the possible nature of universals; for, as a deep structure, it is likely to have a close resemblance to the underlying thought representation of music.

The *Ursatz* is derived from a tonic triad. The tonic triad is a fundamental musical structure built on the natural harmonic series. Leaving aside octaves, which we may hold to be harmonically equivalent, the triad is the chord which results from combining the three lowest distinct harmonics of a note (the second, third, and fifth harmonics). If the fundamental note is C then these harmonics are C, G, and E, respectively (the fourth harmonic is a further C). For Schenker, this tonic triad represents the ultimate resting place in music, the place from which it starts and to which it returns. It has this function precisely because it is present in many natural periodic sounds (*Klang in die Natur*). When an elastic medium of any sort is set in periodic motion, it will produce sound waves corresponding to twice, three times, four times, the lowest (fundamental) frequency of vibration, and so on (see Jeans 1937, for an introduction to the physics of sound in relation to music). These sounds constitute the harmonic series, although higher harmonics are usually very faint compared to the fundamental and lower harmonics. The tonic triad is 'natural' in a very real sense because it is audibly present in most natural sounds.

Example 2.3. An *Ursatz*, the fundamental Schenkerian structure.

If we examine an *Ursatz* such as that given in Example 2.3, we find that all its notes are contained in the tonic triad (of G major in this case) except the middle note of the upper line (the *Urlinie*). At the midpoint of the *Urlinie* we thus find a departure from the resting position which is established at either end of the *Ursatz*. Tension and discord have been introduced; but it is *motivated* tension. One may argue that in good stories neither the tensions nor their resolutions are arbitrary. We find it unsatisfactory when the author introduces some *deus ex machina* to extricate the hero from a seemingly impossible situation. We prefer it when the kernel of the solution is somehow implicit in what has gone before. For instance, the villain's evil designs have within them them the seeds of their own destruction; the internal dynamics of a relationship lead the partners to the brink of breakdown and also provide the final resources to save it; and so on. Similarly, the *Ursatz* satisfies because it is not just *any* note (say F) which introduces tension. It is, in this case, an A which has two highly important pivotal functions. Firstly, it creates a linear progression in the *Urlinie*, B–A–G. The line has its own logic or pattern (two consecutive linear descents of one scale step) so that, in one sense, the A becomes an inevitable consequence of travelling from the B to the G.

Secondly, it creates, together with its accompanying bass note, the elements of a new triad based on D (A is the third harmonic of D). The tension-inducing element thus operates by attempting to set up a 'rival' triad. In the final chord of the *Ursatz* we witness the 'defeat' of this rival system. Let us, then, hypothesize that one appropriate 'deep' universal for musical thought is to be summarized in the phrases 'creation and resolution of motivated tension'. This notion has a family resemblance to the 'implicative' theory of L. B. Meyer (see this chapter, section 2.5).

What, if anything, can we say about the universal features of music brought about by 'surface' constraints, i.e. the constraints dictated by the fact that music is primarily vocal, and thus melodic? Firstly, since the deep structure has discrete phases, then the surface constituents must display discreteness or discontinuity, whether at the level of 'episode' or 'note'. At the very least, music must contain two discrete aspects of a sound event which begin 'in unity' with one another, move to a state of 'disunity' and then return to unity.

Second, there must be sound dimensions along which distance can be measured. The tension-inducing elements must be more distant from the initial elements along one of these dimension than the final elements. So, clearly, linear time cannot be this dimension, because the middle tension-inducing elements will always be closer in time to the beginning of the music than will the resolving terminal elements.

Third, sounds must be capable of being classified along a *second* independent dimension of sound representing distance. This is so that *motivated* tension can be introduced. As we have seen, motivated tension is achieved when an element is discrepant on one dimension (e.g. harmony) but unified on another (e.g. scale), thus displaying ambiguity. The system of tonality may be seen as one particularly satisfactory solution to the problem of representation that is consistent with these constraints. Within the tonal system there are two ways of representing the closeness of two notes with definite pitch. One is scalar: notes are close if their pitches are as near to one another as the scale allows. The other is harmonic: notes are close when their pitch *ratios* are those between low harmonics in the harmonic series. Thus, a given note can be close to another on the scalar dimension whilst being distant on the harmonic dimension, and *vice versa*. It is possible that one reason for tonality's success is that its dimensions of closeness are ones which it is easy for people to work with. We return to this issue in greater detail in Chapter 7.

(*h*) It is common to consider a human language as comprising three components: phonology—a way of characterising the basic sound units of a language; syntax—the rules governing the way in which sound units are combined; and semantics—the way in which meaning is assigned to sound sequences. Music seems to break down quite naturally into the same three components, and the following sections take a more detailed look at research on these three aspects of language and music.

2.4. Musical phonology

All utterances of a natural human language like English can be analysed into a small set of basic speech–sound classes called 'phonemes'. The characterization of a phoneme is somewhat technical, but many phonemes correspond directly to letters. Thus, the word 'cat' has three phonemes, one for each letter. Each phoneme can be thought of as a certain sound pattern, having certain frequency and duration parameters, typically produced by a characteristic combination of lip, tongue, and vocal chord motion. The continuing debate about the extent to which phoneme characteristics are invariant in different sound environments need not concern us here (Cole and Scott 1974; Liberman, Cooper, Shankweiler, and Studdert-Kennedy 1967). Two points about phonemes are of special significance. One is that most phonemes are characterized by a *range* of sounds along particular dimensions rather than totally specific values. The other is that different languages divide up the sound continuum in different ways. Thus, two sounds which are distinct phonemes in one language may be heard as the same phoneme in a different language. Hence the well documented difficulty encountered by people trying to learn a language having substantially different phonology to their own. They simply fail to hear important distinctions. The human tendency to perceive speech *categorically* provides much of the explanation for these phenomena.

Categorical perception is best described by means of a specific example. It appears that the principal determiner of whether one hears a consonant as voiced (e.g., /d/) or unvoiced (e.g., /t/) is the time relationship between the onset of two components of the sound known as the first and second formants (f_1 and f_2). Formants are bursts of sound occupying discrete frequency bands. A typical speech sound will have four such bands. The first formant is the name for the lowest frequency band present, the second for the next highest, and so on. Such sounds can be synthesized by machine, and it appears that the optimal /d/ is heard when the onsets of f_1 and f_2 are simultaneous. In contrast, the optimal /t/ is heard when f_1 commences about 60 ms after f_2. With a machine it is possible to synthesize sounds with onset delays intermediate between 0 and 60 ms, and then discover how listeners classify them. If we generalize from other perceptual studies where one dimension is varied between two extreme values, our expectation would be that as onset delay increased from 0 to 30 ms, listeners would hear a sound less and less like /d/. When the midpoint was reached we would expect to hear an ambiguous sound, and then, as the delay approached 60 ms, the sound would become more and more like /t/.

The actual result of such an experiment is very different (Liberman, Harris, Kinney, and Lane 1961). Up to about 20 ms delay there is almost no change in the perceived sound. Subjects identified nearly all the sounds as absolutely clear /d/s, indiscriminable from the case where the delay was zero. Then over a very small range of delay (about 10 ms) perception 'flipped over' to /t/. Further increases in delay produced no perceptible change, all sounds beyond this boundary being indiscriminable from the case where the delay was a full 60 ms.

It has been found that this type of effect is demonstrable for nearly all phonemic distinctions, and this shows that the level of analysis of which we are habitually aware has discarded much of the specific information present in the sound. From sounds which vary continuously on a number of dimensions we extract a few categories into which all normal speech sounds are assigned. These are the categories which feed onto higher level syntactic and semantic analyses.

It appears that we acquire the categories of our native language very early in life. A set of studies by Eimas and his colleagues (Eimas 1975; Eimas, Siqueland, Jusczyck, and Vigorito 1971) has demonstrated that three-day-old infants already categorize sounds in the same way as adults. This precocious ability strongly suggests the existence of special learning mechanisms for speech patterns, since—of course—infants categorize differently according to the language they are exposed to in the first few days of life.

These features of language seem to have some rather close musical parallels. The basic 'phoneme' of music is a 'note'. Like a phoneme a note is characterized by frequency and duration parameters. Within a particular musical culture, all music is composed from a small set of these notes, chosen from an indefinitely large set of possibilities. Different cultures, however, choose different subsets of possible notes for their music. The selection takes place along two dimensions of sound: frequency and duration; these merit separate discussion.

2.4.1. *Categorical perception of frequency*

The perceived pitch of a musical sound is, in most naturally occurring instances, determined by its fundamental frequency of vibration. The exceptions to this will not concern us here. Furthermore, we will assume that octaves are musically equivalent in the context of this discussion. The 'phonology' of pitch thus concerns the way in which the octave is subdivided. The subset(s) of pitches chosen by a musical culture constitutes the musical scale(s) of that culture.

There is some evidence that people brought up within one musical culture have difficulty in perceiving and reproducing scales of another culture. It is hard to find convincing contemporary evidence for this since the Western diatonic scale has infiltrated most cultures through the broadcasting media. There is, however, some ethnomusicological data which shows how tunes which have migrated from one culture to another have been adapted to the new scale (Cohen and Cohen 1973). Hodeir (1956) has put forward the interesting hypothesis that the 'blue notes' in the jazz scale came about through the efforts of African musicians (from a culture using a pentatonic scale) to assimilate the diatonic scale of the North American culture. If we represent the diatonic scale as a sequence of note names (e.g. C, D, E, F, G, A, B) then the proposed pentatonic scale would use only C, D, F, G, and A. Users of the pentatonic scale would have no normal representation for the diatonic E and B of this example. When attempting to reproduce a Western melody using these notes, Africans would have heard them as 'mistuned' notes falling somewhere between D and F or A and C. Accordingly they would 'fish' for these notes when playing or singing, producing something which would sound unstable and mistuned to Western ears. Gradually this accidental feature would become formalized as part of the jazz style—the flattened third and seventh. One must emphasize that this is an unproven hypothesis and does not receive universal acceptance (Virden and Wishart 1977).

The psychological principle underlying such examples appears to be the categorical nature of pitch perception. It has been demonstrated in laboratory conditions by Locke and Kellar (1973). They presented listeners with triads in which the tuning of the middle note (the third of the chord) was systematically varied from major to minor, passing through several intermediate pitches. The outside pitches were always 440 Hz (A) and 659 Hz (E). The middle note varied between 554 Hz (C sharp) and 523 Hz (C natural). There were two experimental tests. In one, subjects heard a single chord (the standard) and then, after a short delay, were required to say whether each of a sequence of chords was the same as, or different from, the standard. In the other test, subjects heard pairs of chords in which the middle notes differed by a few Hz at most. They were required to say whether the chords were the same or different. In both tests, musician subjects showed clear evidence of categorical perception. Fig. 2.4 shows the mean responses for 15 musicians. The hatched line shows the result of the first test when the standard was 554 Hz (A major chord). Almost all chords with middle notes above 546 Hz were heard as A major. Almost all chords with middle notes below 540 Hz were heard as A minor. The evidence suggests a category boundary at about 542 Hz.

The data from the second test (full lines) corroborates this picture. The four lines are for different degrees of separation of the test pitches. In each case there is a clear peak in discrimination at the category boundary. That is, when members of the pair of chords straddle the boundary, discrimination is good. When they are both on the same side of the boundary, discrimination is poor.

Interestingly, non-musicians did not show such clear evidence of categorical perception. The discrimination functions have peaks at around

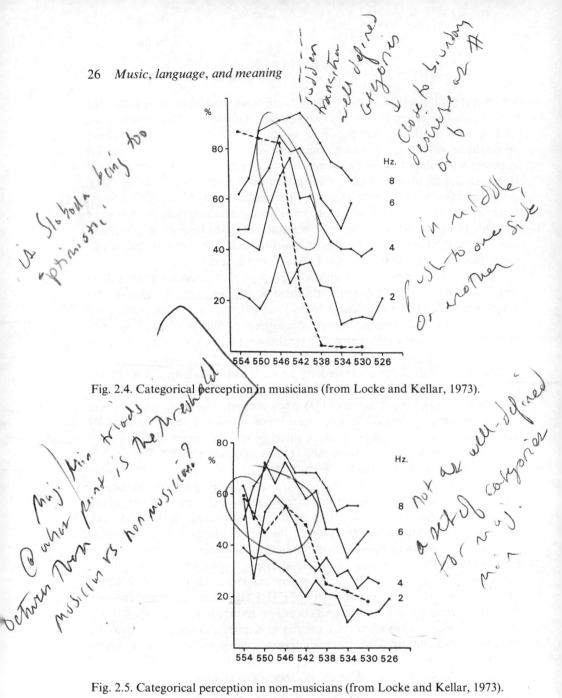

Fig. 2.4. Categorical perception in musicians (from Locke and Kellar, 1973).

Fig. 2.5. Categorical perception in non-musicians (from Locke and Kellar, 1973).

Figs. 2.4. and 2.5. Key: the dashed line gives the data from the categorization test; the full lines give the data from the discrimination test at various pitch separations; the abscissa represents the frequency of the middle note of the chord; the ordinate represents percent correct judgement.

546 Hz, but the comparisons to a standard show a more smoothly declining function: the greater the pitch difference, the less likely a 'same' judgement (see Fig. 2.5).

This study raises several issues. Firstly, there is the question of the accessibility to listeners of the *uncategorized* frequency information. In the speech studies it would appear that this information is not normally available to conscious perception. In music, however, this information certainly *can* be made available to consciousness. If it were not so, then no chord could ever sound badly tuned—the assimilation to categories would 'complete' the perceptual experience. The music listener, we must conclude, has some ability to operate both within and outside the categorical mode.

A second question is, therefore, what perceptual contexts encourage categorical perception? For most listeners the likely answer is that the context must be one which provides a framework for the construction of a musical scale. This framework will supply, at the very least, two simultaneous (or closely consequent) notes, such that one can act as a 'tonic' for the other. The notes of a musical scale are defined not absolutely but relatively, so that a scale can be constructed on any pitch using a characteristic set of frequency ratios to generate the notes. Thus, what music listeners carry in their memories are not the absolute pitches of any particular scale, but procedures for generating a scale from any given tonic. In Locke and Kellar's study this framework was supplied by the invariant outer notes of the chord which maintained a 3:2 frequency ratio throughout. This identified them, within diatonic tonality, as the tonic (first step) and dominant (fifth step) of a diatonic scale. This framework imposed a categorization on the middle note as the submediant (third step) of either a major or a minor diatonic scale. Had the experiment been carried out using only a single variable note without chordal context, then it is unlikely that any categorization would have taken place. Data from normal psychophysical studies support this assertion. There is no evidence of discontinuity in the discrimination functions for single frequencies.

A third question concerns the genesis of categorization within the individual. The music data suggest that, unlike language, mere exposure to tonal music is insufficient to bring about categorical perception. Some aspect of musical training heightens the tendency to categorize. For instance, most musical training involves learning note names and scale terminology. It is possible that possessing verbal labels increases the likelihood of categorical information being extracted and stored. Another possibility is that, for some musicians, each category becomes associated with a prototypical 'absolute' frequency band. This is possible, at least in Western cultures, because there are generally agreed conventions about the precise frequencies to which instruments should be tuned. Concert A is defined as 440 Hz. Such frequencies could come to represent the 'central' positions of scale categories for listeners, with deviant pitches being assigned to the nearest prototype.

There is considerable evidence for an ability that could support such behaviour. It is called 'absolute pitch' or 'perfect pitch' and is possessed by a significant minority of trained musicians. This is an accurate long-term memory for prototypical pitches and their associated scale names; and I shall discuss it more fully in Chapter 5. We do not know, unfortunately, how many of Locke and Kellar's 'musician' subjects possessed absolute pitch.

A different type of evidence for assimilation of music to scale categories is provided by Dowling (1978). In this study subjects were required to judge pairs of brief melodies as the same or different. In some cases the second melody (which was always at a different pitch from the first) was an exact transposition of the first melody. In other cases, the second melody was a 'tonal answer' to the first; that is, the melodic contour was transposed up or down *within the same key*. This has the consequence that the exact intervals of the original melody are not preserved. Example 2.4 is an illustration of the type of melodic stimulus used by Dowling. Example 2.5 is an exact transposition of it. Example 2.6 is a tonal answer starting on the same note as 2.5. Dowling found that his subjects could not consistently discriminate exact transpositions from tonal answers. One plausible explanation for this finding is that, at least for unfamiliar melodies, subjects code melodies as contours in which the *number* of scale steps between adjacent notes is represented, but not the precise pitch distance.

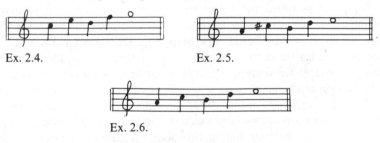

Ex. 2.4.   Ex. 2.5.

Ex. 2.6.

Examples 2.4–2.6. Examples of stimuli used by Dowling (1978).

2.4.2. *Categorical perception of duration*

One of the most well researched areas in this field concerns the perception of plucked and bowed string notes (Blechner, Day, and Cutting 1976; Cutting and Rosner 1974; Cutting, Rosner, and Foard 1976). In a carefully designed series of experiments, Cutting and his colleagues have demonstrated that variations in rise time (the time from sound onset until the time when waveform amplitude reaches its peak) are responsible for the perception of this quality, rise times of 30 ms or less giving rise to 'plucked' sounds, and those of 60 ms or more producing 'bowed' sounds. The discrimination function shows a peak at the category boundary (around 40 ms) and troughs within each category. The interest of this phenomenon is threefold. First, it exactly matches the functions for the categorical perception of a phonetic distinction in speech; the one displayed between the words 'chop' and 'shop'. This also depends on rise times and shows a category boundary at about 40 msec (Cutting and Rosner 1974). Secondly, adaptation to a sound well within one category shifts the category boundary towards the unadapted category. This exactly matches speech perception data (Eimas and Corbit 1973). Thirdly, infants as young as two months demonstrate categorical perception for these sounds (Jusczyck, Rosner, Cutting, Foard, and Smith 1977), just as they do for many speech sounds (Eimas 1974; Eimas *et al.* 1971).

These findings have been used to dispute the view that speech perception involves unique psychological processes and mechanisms. Cutting *et al.* (1976) state that 'it is evident that the arsenal of empirical findings which once distinguished speech perception as a unique type of auditory perception is being steadily depleted.' It seems, in fact, that we possess some perceptual mechanisms which are present from an early age and are deployed in both speech and music perception to produce categorical perception. The reason why the same physical attribute (rise time) gives rise to different perceptual experience in speech and music is probably that the acoustic contexts are different. There is evidence that the nature of the immediately following vowel/note affects the way in which the rise portion is heard. For instance, the sound patterns for stop consonants (like /t/ and /p/) are heard as chirps when presented in isolation (Mattingley, Liberman, Syrdal, and Halwes 1971). They require a subsequent vowel in order to be heard as speech sounds. Similarly, Cutting *et al.* (1976) show that synthetic musical sounds must persist for at least 250 ms after the initial rise in order to be heard as plucked or bowed.

The issue of context also assumes central importance in the second major aspect of musical duration that I wish to discuss. This is the perception of the duration of a note. The results of standard psychophysical tests tell us that when two successive isolated tones are presented for discrimination of duration (i.e. subjects must say which is longer), then the longer the sounds are, the greater must be the difference between them if it is to be reliably detected (Woodrow 1951). In music, however, absolute durations are less important than the rhythmic implications which notes acquire through their immediate context. Fundamental to most Western music is the concept of a *beat*, a musical pulse which underlies any melody. In general, notes will either begin on the beat or at some simple subdivision of the beat (half, third, and quarter being common). This fact is reflected in musical terminology and notation, where there exists a limited set of categories for describing durations of notes. These categories are, for the most part, divisions of a longer category into two equal halves. Thus, there are two crotchets (quarter notes) to every minim (half note); two quavers (eighth notes) to every crotchet, and so on. In a particular performing situation, one of these symbols may be defined as having a particular duration (for instance, 'crotchet = 120' is a standard way of indicating that there should be 120 crotchet beats per minute). Thus, all the other symbols acquire a defined duration which is exactly double, or half that of the standard. None the less, in any human performance it is certain that there will be significant deviations from these defined durations.

In all empirical studies which have measured times between the beginnings of successive notes, such deviations have been found in abundance (Michon 1974; Seashore 1938; Shaffer 1981b; Sloboda 1983), even when the performer has been asked to produce absolutely strict rhythms (Gabrielsson 1974). None the less, identification of intended rhythm is a commonplace accomplishment for listeners, who are continually faced with the potentially confusing phenomena of *rubato* and gradual changes in speed. In contrast, accurate perception of deviations from metricality is difficult, and requires much specific training. It is almost impossible for one performer to imitate another *exactly*. All this strongly suggests that listeners achieve a categorization of the durations of the notes they hear into crotchets, quavers, etc.

In the light of these considerations it becomes a little easier to understand some puzzling data provided by Sternberg, Knoll, and Zukofsky (1982) who showed that three highly trained professional musicians, including Pierre Boulez, were unable to reproduce non-standard subdivisions of a beat accurately. In the experiments subjects heard a series of regular beats at one second intervals, one of which was followed by a click at a delay ranging from one eighth to seven eighths of a beat. They were then required to place an equivalent click after a subsequent beat. The reproduction of the shorter subdivisions (less than one third of a beat) were systematically in error, all being overestimates. In contrast, reproduction was very accurate when the subdivision was half, three quarters, five sixths, or seven eighths of a beat. A similar pattern of results was obtained when the subjects were asked to *estimate* the delay of a click by giving a verbal categorization (e.g. 'between one eighth and one seventh of a beat'), except that in this situation the errors were *under*estimates. Why were these subjects so poor? Maybe accurately reproduced and estimated delays correspond to frequently occuring rhythmic patterns in music, which are readily categorized. In Fig. 2.6 I have written out the experimental stimuli in musical notation. The first, second, and fourth notes in each example correspond to the regular beats, and the third note corresponds to the click. The lower half dozen notational forms will be familiar to most performing musicians. It is hard to think of well-known examples of the upper four. These are precisely the ones that caused difficulty for the subjects used by Sternberg *et al*. Perhaps they are particularly hard to perceive as examples of distinct rhythmic categories.

Just as in the discussion of categorical perception of pitch, one would not wish to claim that categorical perception of duration makes finer temporal discriminations impossible. We *can* hear rhythmic imprecision and *rubato* with appropriate training, but fine differences in timing are more often experienced not as such, but as differences in the quality (the 'life' or 'swing')

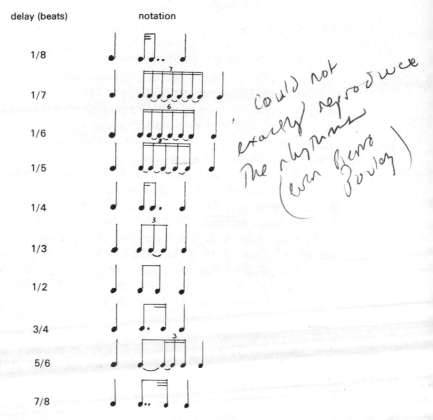

delay (beats)   notation

Could not exactly reproduce the rhythms (even Benn Powley)

Fig. 2.6. Stimuli used by Sternberg, Knoll, and Zukofsky (1982), expressed in conventional rhythmic notation.

of a performance. This accounts in part for the intangibility of performance style (see Chapter 3). Differences in style are due to real differences in performance, but many of them cannot be consciously categorized by most listeners. Most of us have only global and imprecise means of capturing our experience of style difference.

My discussion of musical phonology has been designed to illustrate one fundamental feature of music behaviour. That is, we tend to categorize our musical experience along the available dimensions of sound, giving importance to differences between categories at the expense of differences within categories. The notions of scale and metre are the fundamental concepts underlying musical phonology (although timbre and intensity are arguably additional dimensions). The similarities between language and music in this respect are striking, although categorical perception in music is neither as complete nor as universal as it appears to be in language. To understand the musical significance of categorization we must now turn to the way notes are combined with one another. This is the subject matter of musical syntax.

2.5. Musical syntax

2.5.1. *The psychological reality of grammar*

The attempt to construct formal descriptions of musical structures is a central concern of musicology (see, for example, Bent 1980). Schenker is only one of many people who have attempted to characterize the sequential regularities of music in terms of rule systems. Since music, like language, is a human product, we can legitimately suppose that the observed structure of music tells us something about the nature of the human mind that produces it. But what? An extreme view would be that the rules of a musical (or linguistic) grammar are the very psychological procedures that someone uses to generate music (or language). This view has been strongly criticized on a number of grounds, both for music (Laske 1975) and for language (Olson and Clark 1976). One of the strongest arguments is that there is no such thing as a unique grammar for any body of data. Different rules, applied in different orders, can produce exactly the same set of sentences or musical sequences. The mere discovery of a single workable grammar is, therefore, no guarantee that *this* grammar is the one that best describes psychological processes of generation. Another argument derives from the observation that humans can (and deliberately do) violate the rules which seem to account for some of their behaviour. Thus, people *do* speak ungrammatically, and composers *do* violate the formal conventions within which they work. A formal syntax or grammar is a closed system whose sole purpose is to generate the set of sequences stipulated as 'grammatical'. The psychological generation of language is, in contrast, a process whose purposes are wider. The intention to communicate a particular meaningful proposition is the psychological motivation behind most utterances, and if a speaker has good reasons to suppose that he will be understood even without correct grammar, then he may disregard grammatical conventions. In music, the intention to violate a listener's expectancies may lead to a comparable freedom with the grammar.

The modest view supported by more psychologists is that some features of grammars have implications for the general way in which we think about psychological processes. One implication of the generative approach exemplified by Chomsky's work is that we decide what to say by the application of a finite set of rules (or procedures) to some unspoken proposition we wish to utter, rather than by having to recall, by association, the correct utterance for each separate proposition. On an associationist view, it is impossible to know how to express the proposition that, say, John loves Mary until one has learned the verbal formula 'John loves Mary' and is able to recall it when required. On the generative view, a speaker may never have heard or uttered the sentence 'John loves Mary' yet still be capable of producing it to express the appropriate proposition. This is done in the following way. A person's knowledge that John loves Mary is to be characterized, roughly, as knowledge that a certain person, John, is the agent of some activity, loving, this activity being directed towards a recipient, Mary. The person then *constructs* the appropriate sentence by reference to rules which stipulate how general relationships between agents and objects are expressed. One form of expression is given by the formula, agent + active verb + recipient. In simple three element propositions the conditions for this formula to be applied are satisfied, so, with appropriate knowledge of the vocabulary items 'loves', 'Mary', and 'John', the speaker can utter them in the correct order. Because the number of acceptable sentences in a language like English is indefinitely large, and because we are all capable of generating acceptable sentences that we may not have heard before, it seems inevitable to conclude that we store rules for constructing sentences rather than (or at least in addition to) storing sentences themselves.

A second, and related, implication is that listeners will be able to sort utterances they hear into acceptable and unacceptable categories. Thus, most people can tell that a novel utterance is ungrammatical, even though they judge another equally novel utterance to be acceptable. Since neither utterance has prior associative meaning, it seems incontrovertible that the utterances are being assessed in virtue of their conformation to a set of rules of construction. Hard questions arise, however, when we try to specify exactly what rules are invoked. Is a generative grammar, as such, the principal mental tool? If so, then a listener would have to judge a quasi-sentence like 'John the apple ate' ungrammatical by somehow running the grammar 'in reverse' and failing to condense the sentence to a single node. Alternatively, he might try generating sentences according to the grammar and fail to come up with a match. The trouble is that either of these processes may involve an indefinite number of steps. If one used the second process one could not, strictly speaking, be certain that a sentence was ungrammatical until one had generated all possible sentences, and noted the absence of the sentence in question. Since we may argue that the number of English sentences is indefinitely large, this is clearly a very implausible psychological mechanism. More plausibly, people have 'metaknowledge' about the grammatical systems they work with. For instance, someone may know that, in English, a sentence never starts with a verb in the indicative mood. This is not itself a rule of the generative grammar (although statements of this sort are sometimes confusingly referred to as grammatical rules). It is a generalization about the *products* of the grammar. Or again, it seems likely that people use non-syntactic considerations in judging sentences. Given 'John the apple ate', a listener might attempt to work out a plausible proposition including all the elements mentioned (which would presumably entail the apple being eaten by John) and then discovering how he or she would naturally express the proposition, rejecting the given utterance if it did not match his or her own.

A third implication, and one that I wish to examine in some detail, since it relates to comparable experimental data in language and music, is that, regardless of our conclusions about the equivalence of generative grammars to psychological processes, the *structures* embodied in such grammars have psychological reality. Briefly, this claim is that elements of an utterance which are closely linked to one another in the grammar are closely linked psychologically, in whatever form of cognitive representation a speaker or listener may make of a sentence or melody. If the structure of a sequence is best represented in a grammar as a tree of the sort shown in Figs. 2.1–2.3, then the claim would be that adjacent items governed by the same node are closer in 'psychological space' than are adjacent items governed by different nodes. Figure 2.7 shows an idealized constituent tree which might equally well be a proposed structural tree for a linguistic or a musical sequence containing eight elements. The nodes are indicated by letters, the terminal elements that constitute the actual sequence are indicated with numbers. Taking, as an example, elements 3 and 4, we see that they are very closely linked in the structure. They are both subsumed under node E, and more remotely by node B. In constrast, elements 4 and 5, whilst also being adjacent members of the sequence, are not closely linked in the structure. Element 4 is 'governed' by node B, whilst element 5 is 'governed' by node C.

An experimental technique developed to investigate this claim involves subjects listening to short well-formed sequences of language or music over which an audible click has been superimposed, at a particular point. Subjects are asked to indicate exactly when they hear the click to occur by reporting the syllable or note which seemed to be simultaneous with it. The initial results of applying this technique have been reported for language by Fodor and Bever (1965) and Ladefoged and Broadbent (1960); and for music by Gregory (1978) and Sloboda and Gregory (1980). The basic findings in both domains are easily summarized. Firstly, click location is quite inaccurate. Secondly, clicks appear to migrate perceptually to boundaries between structural groupings. For instance, in the sentence 'That he was happy was evident from the way he smiled', a click occurring during the fourth word tended to

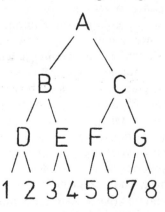

Fig. 2.7. An idealized constituent tree structure.

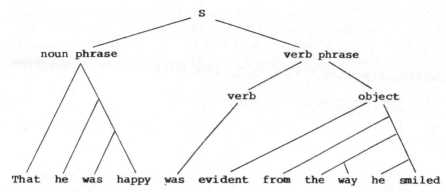

Fig. 2.8. Constituent tree analysis of a sentence used in Fodor and Bever's (1965) study.

be heard as coming later than its actual time of occurrence. If the click occurred during the fifth word, it was heard early. A constituent analysis of the sentence (Fig. 2.8) assigns the first four words to the major node NP (noun phrase) while the rest of the sentence makes up VP (the verb phrase). In structural terms, therefore, words 3 and 4 are close, as are words 5 and 6. Words 4 and 5, though, are not structurally close. The experimental results show that these structural relations are represented psychologically. It seems that there is a tendency to represent closely related elements as 'un-interrupted', so that an extraneous event (the click) gets pushed towards a point where the structural links are weak.

A pictorial analogy of the process may be obtained if one imagines the words (or notes) of a sequence to be laid out in a line on a surface. Each major structural grouping is covered by a smooth hemispheric dome. The click can then be envisaged as a small pellet dropped on to the surface from a position vertically above its real location in the sentence. When it hits the surface of the dome its final position will be determined by the slope of the dome at that point. Pellets falling near the apex of the dome are likely to be displaced rather little; pellets falling near the edge are likely to roll off into the space between.

The music results are to be explained in a similar way to the language results. Here, the main structural unit is the musical phrase. In Sloboda and Gregory's (1980) experiment, each melody contained two metrically equal phrases, and, in one condition, equal durations for all the notes. Example 2.8 shows one such melody. Musicians generally agree that the first phrase ends on the fourth note of the second bar. In this experiment the notes were computer-generated and exactly equal in all respects other than pitch. In physical terms, therefore, notes 4 and 5 of the second bar are as close to one another as notes 5 and 6 (arguably even closer since they are at the same pitch). Structurally, however, notes 4 and 5 are distant. A click placed on note 5 had a higher tendency to 'migrate' backwards than any other placement of the click, confirming that listeners were representing the phrase boundary in a special way. The migration tendency was enhanced by melodies which marked the phrase boundary with a long note (see Example 2.7) but reduced by melodies which did not have a 'normal' harmonic structure (Examples 2.9 and 2.10).

Ex. 2.7.

Ex. 2.8.

Ex. 2.9.

Ex. 2.10.

Examples 2.7–2.10. Examples of stimuli used by Sloboda and Gregory (1980).

The precise interpretation of such 'click' experiments has been the subject of some controversy in the literature (Olson and Clark 1976). For instance, Reber and Anderson (1970) presented subjects with sentences over which *no* click had been superimposed, but told their subjects that very faint clicks were present. Subjects were asked to detect the location of the 'clicks'. They tended to locate clicks at phrase boundaries. Thus, argue Reber and Anderson, the earlier results are explicable by a bias subjects display to place their responses at phrase boundaries rather than by a perceptual migration. However, it may be argued that a tendency to organise *any* aspect of cognitive behaviour, be it perceptual or response-orientated, on the basis of phrase structure is good evidence for the psychological reality of grammatical structures. More worrying, perhaps, are studies like those of Bond (1971) and Lehiste (1972) who found that non-grammatical cues, like pauses and stresses, were more important than syntax in determining the nature of the migration. In Sloboda and Gregory's study pauses (long notes) were also found to elicit click migration. However, in both these cases, no harm is done to the general thrust of our argument if it is acknowledge that pausal and stress patterns in speech and music can be generated by a grammar along with the word ordering (see Chomsky and Halle 1968, for langauge; and Martin 1972, and Sundberg and Lindblom 1976, for music). In other words, it may be *because* they occur in a systematic syntax-related fashion that stresses and pauses become psychological 'magnets' for clicks in individuals with long experience of a particular grammar.

'Clickology' is not the only way that the psychological reality of grammatical structures can be demonstrated. For instance, if phrases are psychological units, then one might expect processing within a single phrase to proceed more rapidly or effectively than processing which requires integration of information from two phrases. This prediction has been confirmed by Green and Mitchell (1978) who showed that language readers' pauses are longest after fixations which complete major grammatical units. Also, Levin and Kaplan (1970) have shown that the eye–voice span in language reading tends to extend to a phrase boundary, and Sloboda (1974, 1977a) has shown the same for music reading. Span, here, is defined as the number of words (or notes) that a reader can produce after the text has suddenly and unexpectedly been removed. It is a measure of how much has been taken in ahead of what is actually being said (or played). The findings suggest that readers take in material up to the boundary of the current phrase quite soon after starting to read it, but then 'mark time' until the execution of that phrase is almost complete before sweeping rapidly on to the next boundary.

In the discussion so far I have been deliberately vague about musical syntax and its nature. I wished, for purposes of exposition, to let it be assumed that grammars of roughly equivalent power and sophistication had been discovered for both language and music, so that some central psychological findings could be introduced. I have now to confess that, to my knowledge, there have been very few attempts to produce full-blown generative grammars for any significant corpus of music, even in outline. In what follows I shall discuss the most significant psychologically oriented work in this area in order to help us understand what kind of structures we use to mentally represent music. This will bring to light some similarities with language, but significant differences too.

2.5.2. *Syntactical structures in music*

In attempting to produce a musical syntax, an important question to be answered is '*what* body of music do we wish the syntax to account for'? The answer to this question is not as clear cut as the same questions asked of language. Most people have only one language at their disposal, whose grammar is fairly stable over long periods of time. The English language is delimited as containing all utterances which the majority of English inhabitants judge to be acceptable and meaningful. In contrast, the forms and styles of music with which a given person may be familiar can be very diverse. Musical forms change rapidly, and there is heated discussion within our culture about what does and does not count as acceptable music. It is interesting to speculate on the reasons for this difference. One possible reason is that the communicative functions of language favour unity and stability. Syntax is a vehicle for communicating knowledge about the world, and given that the world remains the same sort of place and human concerns remain the same, there seems little to gain and much to lose by diversity and rapid evolution of syntax. Art music, in contrast, has no such clearly defined function. Syntax becomes, in itself, an object of aesthetic awareness, and the pressures for novelty invite diversity and change. It is arguable that music shows the greatest stability in cultural contexts where it is the vehicle for some non-musical activity (the recounting of verse, ritual, etc.).

The most cautious approach to musical syntax would be to start from a particular small sub-area in music, say the works of a single composer, and attempt to discover a grammar adequate for this corpus. The next step might be to extend the domain of the grammar by discovering if other compositions or other composers conformed to it. In this one might be guided by historical and social factors (looking at composers who lived at the same time and were subject to the same sort of influences) and also by the subjective judgements of experienced listeners (judgements of which types of music sound most similar). On the other hand, it is commonly claimed that very large bodies of music share certain aspects of syntax. If this is so, such aspects should be given the greatest prominence. A piecemeal approach to small areas of music can, arguably, obscure wider patterns (e.g. basic features of harmonic, melodic, and rhythmic construction which are common to the vast bulk of tonal music). I shall begin with some work which takes the former, cautious approach, and then move to wider consideration about tonal music as a whole.

Sundberg and Lindblom (1976) have written a complete generative grammar for eight-bar melodies which all bear a family resemblance to a set of Swedish nursery tunes written in the late nineteenth century by Alice Tegner. These tunes are familiar to, and sung by, most Swedish children today. The outline of this grammar is given in Fig. 2.9. It resembles the generative phonology of Chomsky and Halle (1968) in two respects. Firstly, the basic grammatical structure is an hierarchical tree. Secondly, integral to the tree is a 'prominence contour'. In speech, such a contour is used to assign stress, timing, and intonation to a sentence. In this music grammar, the contour is used to generate appropriate chords and durations.

The structure of the constituent tree is given in Fig. 2.10. It is completely symmetrical and composed by binary subdivisions of each node. So, each phrase divides into two equal sub-phrases; each sub-phrase divides into two equal bars; and so on. It is noteworthy that the structure is *metrically* based (in contrast to Schenker analysis where the fundamental structure is *harmonically* based).

The prominence contour is derived from the tree by assigning left elements priority within each foot, but right elements priority within larger sub-units. The contour derived by Sundberg and Lindblom is given at the bottom of

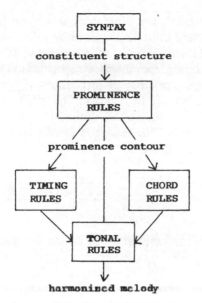

Fig. 2.9. Outline of Sundberg and Lindblom's (1976) grammar for nursery tunes.

Fig. 2.10. The numeral 1 indicates an element with the highest prominence. Elements with equal numbers have equal prominence.

The next step is to generate separately a rhythmic pattern and a chordal progression from the prominence contour. Rhythm is generated by a set of obligatory and optional rules. The most important of the obligatory rules is that no note may begin on an element *following* an element of the highest prominence. In this example, the very last element cannot contain a new note; and the penultimate element will carry the last note of the melody. Then there are other optional deletion and addition rules, with certain repetition restrictions (e.g. the second four bars must repeat the rhythm of the first four bars).

The chordal derivation rests on two main principles. Only notes with prominence of 4 or greater (i.e. 4, 3, 2, or 1) may introduce new chords; and

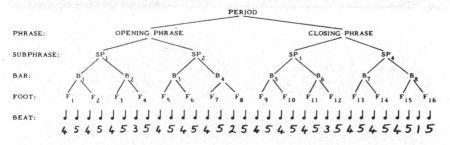
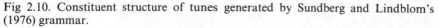

Fig 2.10. Constituent structure of tunes generated by Sundberg and Lindblom's (1976) grammar.

certain sequences of chords are obligatory at certain points (e.g. the final chord must be a tonic and must be preceded by a dominant).

The actual notes of the melody are then generated. Notes at points of high prominence must be chosen from the chord specified at that point. Elsewhere, passing notes and suspensions may be introduced. Examples 2.11–2.16 show six melodies. One was written by Tegner. The other five were produced by the grammar, the choice among the optional alternatives being made at random on each occassion. The reader is invited to try and spot the 'real' Tegner melody before reading on.

Ex. 2.11.

Ex. 2.12.

Ex. 2.13.

Ex. 2.14.

Examples 2.11–2.16.
Tunes produced by Alice Tegner or Sundberg and Lindblom's grammar (1976).

It is Sundberg and Lindblom's claim for the melodies generated by their grammar that 'the general reaction of Swedes listening to these melodies informally is that they are similar in style to those by Tegner.' Whilst this is hardly a rigorous proof of the adequacy of the grammar, the work demonstrates that music with a definite style can be generated from a small set of completely definite grammatical rules. The rules could, no doubt, be improved. For instance, I find it hard to believe that the repetitions of the same pitch in Example 2.12, or the intervallic leap between the second and third bars of Example 2.11, are characteristic of the idiom. However, there seems no principled reason why further restrictive rules could not eliminate such occurrences. The important feature of any such grammar is that major decisions are context-determined. They are governed by an overall structure represented in the constituent tree and the prominence contour derived from it. The psychological implication is *not* that Tegner composed her tunes by running through these precise steps in her mind. Rather we would wish to say that her compositional procedures incorporated the structures and restrictions inherent in this grammar *in some way*.

Of the examples given only 2.15 is, in fact, genuine Tegner. The structure of Sundberg and Lindblom's grammar affords no easy answer to the question of which rules characterize Tegner's music alone, and which are characteristic of wider bodies of music. Perhaps the best way to tackle this question is to consider each of the three traditional features of music—harmony, rhythm, and melody, in turn.

2.5.3. *Harmony and tonality*

If one consults any standard textbook on harmony, one finds that it contains a large set of prescriptions for the sequences of chords that are or are not permissible in tonal music. These are not generative rules; rather they allow one to check whether a given sequence conforms to them. The rules specify, not actual notes, but chords within a key. Thus, for instance, it might be stated that a piece of music must terminate with a tonic chord. In order to check out whether this type of rule is being obeyed by a particular sequence it is, therefore, necessary to determine what key the music is in. A key is specified by a particular scale (e.g. G major; containing the notes G, A, B, C, D, E, and F sharp) and an assignation of functional names (tonic, dominant, etc.) to the members of that scale. The notion of a key also contains the idea that the *tonic* is the fundamental or central note in relation to which all other notes are characterized.

The concept of a key raises two psychological questions. First, in virtue of what is the note C in the set (C D E F G A B) heard or understood as central? Why is it not E or F that has this centrality? Although there exist simple rules for assigning a tonic to a scale (e.g. it is the note preceded by three whole tone and one half tone scale steps when the notes of the scale are arranged in asending order) such rules do not *explain* the psychological centrality of the tonic. Secondly, how does a listener determine which note is the tonic of a musical sequence on first hearing? One possible procedure would be to examine the opening measures to enumerate all the different notes contained there, putting these notes in scalar order to discover what scale was present, and so determining the tonic by the application of a rule like the one given above. Unfortunately there is much music where we can easily hear a tonic, but where there are too few different notes in the opening measures to specify a single scale uniquely, or where the measures contain a set of notes that does not come from any single scale. Two examples from Bach's *Well-Tempered Clavier* demonstrate this point well. Example 2.17 shows the opening two bars of Fugue 15 (Book 2). Only three notes are present (excluding octaves), but most listeners will easily identify the fourth note (G) as the tonic (and not the D or B). Example 2.18 shows the opening bar of Prelude 20 (Book 2). It contains all 12 notes of the chromatic scale yet listeners will identify the key as A minor without difficulty.

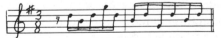

Example 2.17. From J. S. Bach, *Well-Tempered Clavier*, Fugue 15, book 2.

Example 2.18. From J. S. Bach, *Well-Tempered Clavier*, Prelude 20, Book 2.

A theoretical framework in the context of which such problems may be elucidated has been provided by Longuet-Higgins (1972, 1976, 1978). In this theory every note of a composition is assigned a coordinate in a three-dimensional psychological space by a listener. In the first dimension (x) a move of $+1$ raises the pitch of a note by a perfect fifth (pitch ratio 3:2). In the second dimension (y) such a move raises the pitch by a major third (5:4). In the third dimension the octave (2:1) is the unit. For expositional purposes we may ignore the third dimension under the principle of octave equivalence and represent tonal space in a two dimensional form (see Fig. 2.11). The third dimension can be thought of as extending out of and below the page, all notes with the same name in the various octaves being 'stacked' above or below the note shown. Within this space a key is a bounded sub-space. In Fig. 2.11 the space of C major is bounded by the solid line.

major 3rds	B	F#	C#	G#	D#	A#	E#	B#
	G	D	A	E	B	F#	C#	G#
$\hat{y}$	Eb	Bb	F	C	G	D	A	E
	Cb	Gb	Db	Ab	Eb	Bb	F	C

x -----> perfect 5ths

Fig. 2.11. A representational matrix for tonal music. From Longuet-Higgins (1978).

It is of note that, taking C as the origin, all other notes in the scale can be reached in a maximum of two moves (either one move of a fifth and one of a major third, or, in the case of C–D, two moves of a fifth. If we take any other note as the origin the number of moves increases (e.g. it takes four moves to get from A to D). So, a mental representation of this sort accounts in a direct way for the *centrality* of the tonic. It has the closest average distance from its fellow scale members than any other note.

Another feature of note is that the fundamental chord of tonal music, the major triad, can be obtained by taking any note together with its next highest neighbours in the x and y dimensions. The triad thus comes out as a compact L-shaped representation in the space. Whenever chords of this kind are encountered they are strongly suggestive of particular tonalities. The C–E–G triad is to be found within three keys only, and these keys can be visualized by sliding the key 'box' to the left or the right by one step (giving either F major or G major). Some chords are even less ambiguous than this. The dominant seventh chord (G–B–D–F) can be accommodated only within C major. If the key frame is shifted in any direction, one or more of the notes falls outside it. This reflects the fact that, in traditional tonal harmony, the dominant seventh has very strong key implications. In contrast there are some chords which cannot be fitted into any key 'box' (e.g. C–E–G sharp, the augmented fifth; or C–E flat–F sharp–A, the diminished seventh). This is reflected in the fact that these chords do not have key implications, at least in isolation.

A further feature is that notes get multiple representation in the space. For instance, as well as the A in the C key-frame, there is another A just to the right of it. This feature reflects the musical insight that the same note can fulfil different tonal functions in different contexts. Consider the phrase in Example 2.19. Here, given a starting key of C, the A could be *either* part of an implied subdominant chord (F–A–C) in the key of C leading, via a plagal cadence, back to the tonic C, *or* part of an implied dominant chord of G major (D–F sharp–A) leading to a modulatory perfect cadence into the key of G. Longuet-Higgins' claim is that, in listening to an excerpt like this, we have to decide which tonal interpretation to give the A before we can represent the excerpt in tonal memory (or at least acknowledge the ambiguity and hold both readings until further information allows us to choose one of them). The use of equal temperament tuning on many instruments increases the possibility for ambiguity, for then C natural, D double flat, B sharp etc. are all represented by the same sound. Any note played on the piano has multiple ambiguity (in isolation). Listeners generally decide on a single tonal interpretation for a note by taking into account the context in which it appears, i.e. the ordering of the musical elements. This is equivalent to saying that the listener is sensitive to syntactical considerations.

Example 2.19.

Some of these considerations may be quite simple. For instance, all other things being equal, a listener will choose a tonal interpretation for a note which places it close to preceding notes in tonal space. In other words, he operates within a restricted 'window' of tonality which changes position only slowly. Another principle could be to choose an intepretation which preserves the current key frame rather than one which shifts it. Most listeners will hear Example 2.19 as remaining in C major, rather than modulating to G. They choose the intepretation of A which preserves the initial key. If, however, we write out two alternative chordal accompaniments (Examples 2.20 and 2.21) we can disambiguate the phrase. The appearance of an F sharp in Example 2.21 'forces' the listener to shift the key frame to G major. In general, the fuller the accompaniment to a melody, the less possibility for tonal ambiguity there is. This does not mean, however, that composers are advised to 'flesh out' implied harmonies all the time. Ambiguity is, in itself, a very important compositional device. I cannot systematically describe the myriad types of

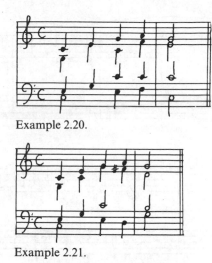

Example 2.20.

Example 2.21.

harmonic ambiguity found even in classical compositions, but here is one simple and beautiful example from Beethoven's Piano Sonata (Op. 14 No. 1). Example 2.22 gives bars 98 to 106 of the last movement. The music is firmly in A major at this point. Taken in isolation, the four-note figure which opens the excerpt (and which recurs in repeated crotchets four bars later) is harmonically ambiguous. The context will, however, suggest to many listeners a move from the chord of A to the chord of D (via an augmented fifth on A). This interpretation in confirmed by the chord in bar 100. This creates a strong expectation that the harmonic pattern will be repeated in bars 103 to 104. The first note of 104 will be heard as an E sharp awaiting resolution upwards to F sharp as before. But then comes the chord of B flat (!), taking the music firmly into the key of F major and forcing interpretation of the preceding two notes as intiating a movement into F. Both the original tendency to interpret as E sharp and the surprise which causes the reinterpretation as F are part of Beethoven's intention. The passage would lose all its dramatic power if an accompaniment such as that in Example 2.23 had been provided. This would have prepared the listener for a transition to F major, and the crucial moment of surprise would have been lost.

In this, and all other examples of musical ambiguity, there is no single syntactical structure. Rather, we have two possible structures, each of which the composer intends to be construed by the listener at different times. The rules for the introduction of ambiguity, if rules there are, lie outside the set of rules which describe legal moves within tonality. When psychologists and others talk of a musical syntax they are usually talking of rules for the construction of music which is intended to be *un*ambiguous (such as Tegner's nursery rhymes). We return, therefore, with caution to our earlier question—how to determine the key of compositions from their opening measures (Examples 2.17 and 2.18). A composer may not always wish for us to solve

Example 2.22. From Beethoven, Piano Sonata Op. 14 No. 2, last movement.

Example 2.23. Alternative harmonization for Example 2.22.

this particular problem easily. Although it would be generally true to say that tonal melodies tend to start on a note of the tonic chord, and therefore a listener would be trying to 'fit' a tonic harmony at the soonest opportunity, there is no guarantee that melodies will not be written which start on other notes. In Example 2.17 the rapid establishment and maintenance of a G major chord strongly suggests G major, and in Example 2.18 the emphatic bass line establishes A as the tonic immediately, although the chromatic writing then does its best to dissuade the listener from his certainty. But what of the F sharp major Fugue of Book 2 (Example 2.24)? This starts resolutely on an E sharp, which is no part of the F sharp major chord. Arguably, what allows such a strong sense of F sharp major here is the trill on the first note. This evokes the leading-note to tonic trill which characterizes the final cadence of many pieces of the period. So Bach may have been relying on listeners' ability to recognise this very distinctive figure to determine the tonality.

Example 2.24. From J. S. Bach, *Well-Tempered Clavier*, Fugue 13, Book 2.

How may we sum up this brief discussion of harmony in tonality? Generative grammars, such as Sundberg and Lindblom's (1976), written for a small corpus of tunes, allow further tunes in the same idiom to be produced. What they lack is reference to any principles in virtue of which the rules may be understood. The purpose of theorists such as Longuet-Higgins is to make general postulates about the way in which listeners represent large bodies of music. They can explain why it is that much music seems to operate within certain constraints, but they also help us understand the effect of music which strikes the ear as tonally ambiguous.

2.5.4. *Rhythm and metre*

The structure underlying the rhythm of a piece of music is often a metrical tree of the sort depicted in Fig. 2.10. The simplest type of structure involves a regular pulse, so marked that every nth occurrence (usually 2, 3, 4, or some simple multiple of these) is stressed. A stress marks the beginning of a metrical unit, which is notated in much music by the use of bar lines. Sometimes the tree has several nested levels (as in Fig. 2.10) but I will concentrate here on the rules which prescribe possible rhythmic structures *within* a single bar. As with harmony, the most fruitful discussions of rhythmic syntax have occurred in the context of the problems facing a listener trying to identify rhythmic stress from a sound pattern. How does he work out which notes are principal stresses? If a listener is presented with a set of equally spaced, equally loud notes of equal pitch (Example 2.25) there is no way in which any rhythm may be said to be present (although the listener may *impose* some rhythmic grouping of his own (Woodrow 1951). To communicate an intended rhythmic interpretation, the primary stresses must be marked in some way. One method of doing this involves variations in intensity. In the absence of other information a stressed note should be louder than its neighbours. Thus, Example 2.26 gives a strong indication of a quadruple metre, each loud note marking the start of a new bar. On instruments where dynamic change from note to note is not possible (e.g. organ) analogous ways of indicating stress are available through articulation and phrasing. For instance, the first note may be held for the full length of its duration (tenuto) whereas the other notes are released early (staccato), as in Example 2.27.

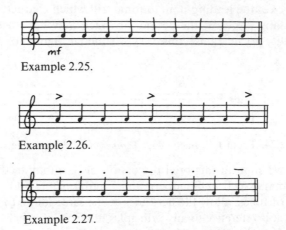

Example 2.25.

Example 2.26.

Example 2.27.

This general class of marking procedures I shall call 'performance markers' because they rely on the way the notes are played rather than on their specified pitches and durations. I shall discuss them further in Chapter 3 (particularly section 3.2.3). They are analogous to stress and intonation in speech.

A different type of marker is illustrated in Example 2.28. Here the note durations are varied by subdividing the beat or by making a note last for more than one beat. Observation of much tonal music supports certain generalizations about the distribution of note values. For instance, the stressed beat is not usually subdivided, and does not occur within a long note other than at its beginning. Thus, in Example 2.28 we can eliminate beats 2, 6, 10, 14, 15, and 16 as primary stresses, leaving a quadruple metre stressing notes 1, 5, and 9 as the only regular interpretation. In this example, however, some possible barrings cannot be eliminated without reference to the 'empty' beats 14 to 16. This seems rather a long time for a listener to wait before the rhythm can be determined, to say nothing of the memory load imposed by holding so many notes whilst various rhythmic interpretations are tried out. Are there other features of the structure which could be used to make an earlier judgement? One possible strategy is to look for repeating patterns, on the assumption that a rhythmic pattern will fall at the same position within a bar on its two occurrences. The distance between two patterns will then be a whole bar or a simple multiple of one bar. On this principle, the repetition of the crotchet + quaver + quaver pattern in Example 2.28 limits us to a duple or quadruple metre because a triple metre would inevitably involve the pattern falling at a different position within the bar on its two consecutive occurrences. Even this strategy, however, does not help the listener decide

Example 2.28.

Example 2.29.

Example 2.30.

between the two quadruple barrings given in Examples 2.29 and 2.30. Here, it is only the absence of a new note at beat 14 which is decisive in favour of 2.29.

Another strategy which allows an earlier decision involves the search for dactylic groupings. A dactyl is a figure where one note is followed by two of half its duration (e.g. crotchet followed by two quavers). A recursive parsing based on this grouping can sometimes yield an appropriate barring quite early. Applied to Example 2.28 the procedure would search for the first dactyl to be encountered, duly identifying the first three notes as such. This dactyl would then be considered as a unit (effectively by replacing the three notes with a single note of their summed durations, a minim). The sequence is thene searched again from the beginning for a dactyl, and the procedure identifies the initial minim together with the following two crotchets as a superordinate dactyl. Once again, the dactyl is replaced by a single note, a semibreve. At this point, the procedure can find no further dactyl involving the first beat, and moves on to consider the fifth beat. Acting on the assumption that the beginning of a dactyl marks a stressed beat, this procedure identifies beats 1 and 5 as primary stresses.

Of course, very little music contains passages which remain at a single pitch for any length of time, and a further possibility for determining rhythm rests on the tendency of much music to contain repeating pitch patterns. Although the notes of Example 2.31 are all of the same duration the listener experiences a sense of triple metre because the pitch pattern repeats itself in transposition after every three notes. This effect can be heightened by emphasising the pitch separation of the first note in each group as in Example 2.32. For a fuller discussion of these and other strategies of rhythm recognition, see Steedman (1977) and Longuet-Higgins and Lee (1982).

The difficulty with proceeding from plausible strategies like these to a grammar of rhythm is that composers arguably use their knowledge of listeners' likely strategies to support music which is neutral with respect to,

Example 2.31.

Example 2.32.

or even violates, the rules which the strategies imply. For instance, one may postulate a principle of consistency with regard to the way in which listeners ascribe metre to a piece of music. If a sequence begins with strong cues to a certain metre, the listener is likely to maintain that metre as an interpretational aid for some time, even in the absence of further strong cues. Thus, the composer may write music which would be 'without metre' if heard in isolation, but which acquires a particular interpretation in a listener's mind by extrapolation of the preceding metre. A good example of this is provided by Bach's Organ Fugue commonly known as the 'Gigue Fugue'. It gets its nickname from the unmistakeable triple metre strongly implied by the first eight notes of the theme (Example 2.33). Then follows a string of quavers. There are certainly no durational cues to metre here, and indeed, the repetition of note 9 by note 11 might be taken as a counter-suggestion of duple metre. Nonetheless one experiences a strong sense of triplet grouping 'carried over' from the opening. Elsewhere, the use of syncopation takes this idea one step further by placing an apparent stress in a place where the previous metre would not predict it. If the syncopation is to be heard as a syncopation (and not as a change of metre) then we must look to the listener's reluctance to alter the inferred metre (and the composer's exploitation of this reluctance) rather than to rules for generating sequences from a rhythmic 'tree.'

Example 2.33. Adapted from J. S. Bach, Gigue Fugue for organ.

As with harmony, one must acknowledge that it is often the composer's intention to thwart or puzzle the listener with rhythmic ambiguities. Take, for instance, the opening of the last movement of Beethoven's Piano Sonata in G (Op. 14 No. 2) given in Example 2.34. Despite the barring, the effect of this sequence, up to beat 9, is to suggest the duple metre shown in Example 2.35. This grouping is suggested by the dactyl groups, particularly the superordinate dactyl formed by beats 4, 6, and 7, but the interpretation runs into trouble at beat 10 (where a subdivision of the beat is not expected) and is strongly challenged by the absence of a new note on the supposed primary

Example 2.34. From Beethoven, Piano Sonata in G, Op. 14 No. 2, Last movement.

Example 2.35.

Example 2.36. From Beethoven, Piano Sonata in G, Op. 14 No. 2, Last movement.

stress at beat 12. In this case the listener has no real way of settling for one particular interpretation of the rhythm, but it would destroy the point of the music for the pianist to thump out an accent on the first beat of each bar. The uncertainty is all part of a mischievous 'catch me if you can' first subject, full of abrupt stops and sudden flurries of activity. All manner of uncertainties are only resolved finally in the serene and rhythmically unambiguous second subject (Example 2.36).

These considerations lead us to some fundamental restrictions on the way we postulate a grammar of music to be *used*. In language we can usually assert that both speaker and listener *abide* by the grammar, and that the speaker's intention is normally to provide unambiguous utterances which the listener will interpret as the speaker intends. In music the composer abides by grammar in a much looser sense. He may certainly know of its existence, and how to write unambiguous music using it, but he also stands outside the grammar in a way that the listener may not. He anticipates the strategies that a listener in his culture will use to structure his or her experience, and seeks to thwart these strategies in interesting ways. Thus, any shared grammar does not *generate* the compositions. Rather, its existence is a major consideration in determining the nature and degree of freedom the composer can exercise to transform and extend musical style. Put simply, if a composition is totally generated by a grammar it is likely to be dull; if it breaks rules in an unmotivated way it is likely to be unintelligible.

The best linguistic analogy for musical composition is not so much the utterance of a novel sentence as the utterance of a non-sentence (as in a poem) which, by virtue of the utterer's appreciation of his listener's linguistic apparatus, has significance for the listener.

2.5.5. *Melody*

Many of the constraints on melody are dictated by the requirement that the melody be capable of communicating harmonic and rhythmic structure to a listener. This is the reason why Sundberg and Lindblom's grammar generates the melody *after* the harmony and rhythm have been determined. It would be oversimplistic, however, to suppose that composers conceived harmony and rhythm prior to melody in all cases. Although a composer may sometimes be constrained by harmony and rhythm (e.g. 'I need to get from D major to A major in four bars') there are times when he may well allow harmony and rhythm to be derived from a melodic idea. The claim that rhythm and harmony are syntactically prior to melody does not rest on observations about the composing process (of which more in Chapter 4). It rests rather on observations about the musical *product* and its effect on listeners. Firstly, the number of different melodies within an idiom is much greater than the number of harmonic and rhythmic sequences common within the idiom. There are many cases where very different melodies are supported by identical harmonic progressions, but rather few cases where very different harmonies support identical melodies. Secondly, it makes some sense to talk of harmony without melody, or rhythm without melody, but very little sense, at least within the tonal idiom, of talking about melody without harmony or rhythm. When listeners hear a melody, their processing of it normally involves the attempt to retrieve implicit harmonic and rhythmic structure. Representing the melody to themselves *means* recovering this structure. In contrast, a chord sequence can be heard without any attempt to recover an 'implicit melody'.

Melody, thus, represents the level of the greatest differentiation in music, the level at which our evaluative and critical faculties are most immediately engaged. It is the aspect of music which is nearest to the 'surface', and that which, for most listeners, most immediately characterizes the music. Our appreciation of a 'great' melody rests partly on our appreciation that a composer has a great many options when generating a melody even if harmony and rhythm are determined. His choice becomes memorable when it is sufficiently different from anything we might have thought of, or heard before, and when we appreciate some particular rightness or fittingness about the choice. A syntax for melody should not aspire to formalize greatness.

What it can do, perhaps, is specify the permissible options in a way which makes clear just how formidable the composer's task is to select from among them.

Let us, then, take a very simple harmonic and rhythmic framework as an example, and examine the kind of rules which would allow us to derive acceptable melodies from it. Example 2.37 gives the rhythm and harmony that our melody must 'carry'. We may imagine this to have been generated by the application of a context-sensitive set of rules such as those of Sundberg and Lindblom discussed in section 5.2 of this chapter. A first rule of melodic construction which we might wish to consider is:

1. A note may be chosen from the chord of the implied harmony at that point.

If we suppose that we are in the key of C major, then this rule allows any note in the first and fourth bars to be C, E, or G, and any note in the second and third bars to be G, B, D, or F (dominant seventh chord). Even if the choice of notes is confined to a single octave this rule allows 2 985 984 distinct melodies. Examples 2.38 and 2.39 are just two of such melodies. Examination of published melodies rapidly demonstrates, however, that Rule 1 is too restrictive for many melodies, because they contain notes outside the harmony at a given point. Consider, for example, Verdi's famous 'La donna è mobile' from his opera *Rigoletto* in which the precise pattern of Example 2.37 is repeated twice (see Example 2.40). There are five notes (asterisked) which Rule 1 does not allow. To accommodate these notes we need at least two more rules:

2. A note may be inserted between two adjacent notes of a given chord if it forms a scale step with one or both notes (passing note).
3. Two occurrences of the same note may be replaced by a pair comprising that note preceded by one a single scale step higher (*appogiatura*).

The derivation of the melody from these rules can be illustrated in stages. Example 2.41 shows a melody derived by Rule 1 alone. Example 2.42 shows the modifications introduced through Rule 2, and Example 2.43 the form achieved after selective application of Rule 3. Notice that there is still one note (asterisked) which does not conform to the Verdi melody. Is there yet another rule which we should introduce to account for this? Maybe there is; but we should also allow for the possibility that Verdi deliberately breaks formal rules for some particular reason. In this case such a reason is not hard to find. The melody breaks down quite naturally into two-bar segments (each with identical rhythm). The second segment (bars 3–4) is an exact repetition of the first segment transposed down a scale step. Clearly Verdi has it in mind that the fourth segment (bars 7–8) should be a similarly transposed version of bars 5–6. If. however, the transposition were to be *exact*, we would get Example 2.44 which leaves the three final notes

Example 2.37.

Example 2.38.

Example 2.39.

Example 2.40. From Verdi, 'La donna e mobile' (*Rigoletto*).

Example 2.41.

Example 2.42.

Example 2.43.

Example 2.44.

Example 2.45.

unaccounted for under the three rules we have so far. Verdi's 'compromise' is to slip the last four notes down by a tone. This preserves the contour (i.e. the 'up', 'down', or 'same' relationship of adjacent notes) of the previous segment, and, additionally, imitates in bar 7 the melodic shape of bars 2 and 4. This mixture of imitation and slight deviation from exact repetition, together with the mild discord of the 'discrepant' last note of bar 7, gives the melody interest. A less imaginative composer might have provided a stricter, more 'correct' solution (e.g. Example 2.45).

If there are simple rules of melodic construction of the sort outlined above, then I believe we must conclude two things about them. Firstly, we will find composers breaking these rules from time to time when they consider some other organizational principle to take precedence. Secondly, these rules allow such a vast number of options that the art of composition consists in developing motivated ways of restricting the options. Because the 'search space' is so large, and because there are so many relevant musical properties which could influence compositional choice, composition seems normally to involve the establishment of provisional goals and the application of heuristic procedures for attempting to achieve them. Such procedures do not formally resemble the steps of a generative grammar, and we shall examine their nature in Chapter 4.

2.5.6. *Pattern and structure*

Although rules of harmony, rhythm, and melody provide much in the way of detailed moment-to-moment restrictions on musical sequences, they do not account for many larger-scale aspects of musical structure which arguably fall within the realm of musical syntax. The most general of such aspects is probably *repetition*. Exact repetition can occur on many levels. The same melodic fragment can be repeated (Bach's French Suite No. 5 in G, last movement, Example 2.46), as can an accompanying figure (Alberti bass as in Mozart's Piano Sonata in C, K. 545, 1st movement, Example 2.47). On a

Example 2.46. From J. S. Bach, French Suite No. 5, last movement.

Example 2.47. From Mozart, Piano Sonata in C (K. 545), first movement.

larger scale, the same phrase may be repeated (e.g. the typical A–A–B–A song form) or a whole large-scale portion (e.g. the exposition of a classical sonata form movement). Equally often, however, the repetition is not exact. Pitch transposition of melodic material is common. Other forms of repetition with change include inversion, augmentation, contraction, segmentation, and retrogression. Sonata form and many later compositional forms make multiple use of such transformations to extend and develop thematic material. Simon and Sumner (1968) have shown that many important characteristics of musical patterning can be captured by simple formalisms involving the operators SAME and NEXT applied to the major dimensions of musical sound. They take, as their example, the Gavotte from Bach's French Suite No. 5, and show how the first four bars can be almost completely described in terms of repetitions of elements contained within the first bar.

Whilst accepting that such patterning is integral to music, I believe that it is necessary to claim that it cannot, on its own, give a full account of the structure of a musical composition. I can, perhaps, illustrate this point by two analogies. The first is an architectural one. A curved masonry arch, such as might be found in an old church, contains several examples of patterning. For instance, the curvature of each brick may be slightly greater than that of its neighbour, whilst retaining enough similarity of shape to appear a fitting next member of the sequence. Repetition and transformation are there, but when we ask why *that* transformation is chosen, and how much transformation is required, we cannot answer the question by recourse to a formalism which describes each transformed element in terms of its predecessors. Rather, we must see what the overall function of the *set* of transformations is: to provide a self-supporting bridge of a certain shape. There is, of course, the possibility that some aspects of pattern (say, decorative carving on the masonry) are irrelevant to this level of structure, but typically, such decoration will, in some way, be *governed* by the structure (e.g. the decoration maintains a constant relation to the line of the arch).

A second analogy comes from graphic art, as exemplified by the work of M. C. Escher. In many of his drawings, a basic technique of patterning is easily discernible. Escher uses ordered series of shapes, each one of which is slightly different from its neighbour, so that as one's eye moves across the picture, subtle and disturbing metamorphoses are experienced. And yet, what makes these pictures compelling is not so much the transformational technique as the end-points which Escher uses these transformations to travel between. A drawing describes a journey with a beginning and an end, and structurally the outer destinations *control* the inner transformations. We are engaged at two levels; the technique fascinates, but a major cause of the fascination is the way the technique is used to arrive at the various significant forms.

And so it is, I believe, with music. Music uses patterning to achieve structural goals; it also uses patterning to engage the listener with decorative detail, but the structural coherence of a piece of music is not to be found solely *within* the principles of patterning. These principles do not have starting points and goals built into them. They can be applied over and over again to any musical idea whatever, so that an indefinitely long piece of music could be produced (just as, using Escher's techniques, an indefinitely large drawing could be produced). Schenkerian concepts offer one possible basis for goal-directed structure, with the concept of a harmonic journey from the tonic which returns back there in the end, but clearly, any fully adequate characterization of goal structure is going to be complex and multidimensional. The fact that it is relatively easy to understand and characterize the small-scale techniques of repetition and transformation which operate within short musical segments, whilst it is extremely difficult to characterize the factors which give a work an integrated and directed form, probably explains Schenker's belief that it takes a genius to produce an extended piece of music with a unified and motivated structure.

A common implication of several aspects of musical syntax we have dealt with is that they are best understood as relating to propensities of *listeners* to infer particular underlying structures from note sequences rather than to the generative processes of *composers*. Recently, Lerdahl and Jackendoff (1983; also Jackendoff and Lerdahl 1982) have extensively followed through the implications of this observation by offering a set of grammatical rules which attempt to account systematically for the way in which listeners assign structural prominence to the various elements in a musical composition. They have, in effect, proposed a formal system for *analysing* a given musical sequence. Their rules can 'cope' with ambiguity because they incorporate a set of independent strategies for grouping musical elements. The final interpretation assigned by a listener will depend on the weight he or she gives to the various strategies, and on whether their effects are to reinforce or contradict one another. Their theory is too recently published to evaluate in detail here, but it promises to be a major contribution to this topic.

2.6. Musical semantics

It is a significant fact about language behaviour that people almost never remember what they read or hear in *verbatim* fashion. Not only does recall paraphrase the original, but it also contains many inferences about information not present in the original. Take, for instance, the following short story:

> Jill was invited to Jack's birthday party.
> She wondered if he would like a kite.
> She went to her room and shook her piggy bank.
> It made no sound.

A typical recall might produce something like the following:

> Jill was going to Jack's birthday party.
> She wanted to buy him a kite.
> She went up to her room and shook her piggy bank.
> There was no money in it.

Such a recall, although we might wish to call it accurate, is heavily laden with inference. For instance, it is possible that the reason why Jill's piggy bank made no sound was that it was full of bank notes. It is also possible that Jill's wondering about Jack's wants was a passing thought, and that she had no intention of buying him anything. These alternatives do not normally occur to us, because we bring knowledge to bear on what we hear; knowledge about birthday parties, the financial circumstances of little girls, and much else. The thrust of recent evidence (see, for instance, Sandford and Garrod 1980) is to suggest that people make these inferences during reception of the message, and that their aim in doing so is to build up an internal model of the portion of the world referred to in the message. Although it is possible that given information can be marked as such and held separate from inferred information, the evidence suggests that it is remarkably difficult to do this. When it is possible to check the verbatim record of some real-life conversation, it is found that even people claiming to have excellent memories for what other people say, and testifying under oath, deviate grossly but systematically from what was actually said (see Neisser's analysis of John Dean's 'Watergate' testimony, 1981).

The implication of this type of evidence is that people recode linguistic information into semantic information. The 'meaning' of a sentence for a listener is, roughly, what he adds to his model of the situation being described as a result of hearing the sentence. This addition allows him to do a number of things. One of these *may* be to reproduce what he received, but this is by no means a necessary, or even important, consequence (we can imitate speech that has *no* meaning for us). Other things may include taking some appropriate action (as in response to 'you have left your car headlights on'), representing the information presented in some other mode (as in drawing a picture of 'the red brick is beneath the green brick'), or experiencing some significant emotion (as to 'your grandmother died today'). From a psychological point of view language is, in some sense, a substitute for sensory experience. We respond to being told that our headlights are on in the same kind of way as we would if we saw them to be on. Contemporary theorists account for this equivalence by saying that the two inputs have equivalent effects on our mental representation of the world.

The principal issue in musical semantics is whether we can establish analogous equivalences between music and some essentially non-musical phenomenon. Does music cause psychological effects which can be caused by other means, and does it do this in a systematic way?

The first position we might consider is that music simply has no semantics. On this view, music is psychologically self-contained, a separate species of psychological activity for which unique modes of representation have been developed. The suggestion, discussed earlier, that people represent music in a tonal space such that notes are assigned harmonic functions within keys, is certainly different from any suggestion psychologists have made about cognitive representation in other spheres.

Clearly, there is much in musical behaviour which can be accounted for by considering musical representation to be a closed sub-system with no essential links to other cognitive domains. This system merits study, is the principal topic of discussion in this book, and is the subject of the most prominent research initiatives in the area. However, I believe that the available evidence forces us to accept that there is some 'leakage'. Musical experience *is* translated into other representational modes. Consider, for example, the case of someone who has just listened to a performance of a long and complex symphonic work. It is quite possible that he or she cannot recall a single theme from the work (I have often been in this situation myself), yet he or she certainly remembers *something* about the work, and can make some appropriate response to it. When this response is expressed in words it characteristically contains remarks about the substance of the music which are neither descriptive ('it was loud') nor reactive ('I liked it') but embody an attempt to *characterize* the music through metaphor ('It had the feeling of a long heroic struggle triumphantly resolved'). It seems less significant that people often disagree about their characterizations than that they nearly always have *some* comment to offer. This is not an arbitrary reaction, but a genuine attempt to describe some real thing or experience. For a great number of us, then, music has extra-musical meaning, however intangible.

What is it that makes music have meaning for us? One possibility is that it *mimics* the sounds which occur in extra-musical contexts. There is a great deal of music which employs mimicry to considerable effect (woodwind 'birdsong' to suggest a pastoral scene, glissandi violins to suggest the howling wind of a storm, and so on). Our recognition of these meanings requires only the knowledge of the appropriate extra-musical sounds. Other music employs *symbolic* reference to an extra-musical event. In opera, for instance, if a particular theme is associated with each appearance of the hero, then it might be used to signify that, in his absence, the heroine is thinking of him. Sometimes music can be *programmatic*, aiming to illustrate a given story. In Dukas' *Sorcerer's Apprentice* there is a bizarre moment when the music suddenly stops; then out of the silence bass instruments take up the first few notes of the main theme one after another, haltingly at first, but gradually increasing in speed and intensity. This corresponds to the moment in the story when the desperate apprentice, unable to undo his spell, chops the relentless water-carrying broom into small fragments. For a moment he thinks he has solved his problem, but then, to his horror, each fragment rises, one after another, to continue its task, compounding his folly.

In all the above cases the composer has set out to depict a definite set of world events through music, and it is easy to understand how it is done.

Unfortunately, very little music has such explicit extra-musical reference, and even in that which does, its reference does not exhaust its significance. If the sole aim of such music were reference, one might as well have a sound recording of the event referred to. Musicial reference is special because the music 'makes sense' even if the reference is *not* appreciated by a listener. A referential passage nearly always serves a double function: it points to an external event, but it also forms part of the thematic structure of the piece as a whole. It is a well-formed segment of the music quite independently of its reference, and one of art of composition consists precisely in finding passages which are capable of serving this double function.

What, then, of the vast bulk of music, which does not have meaning in the specific sense outlined above? One of the most popular suggestions is that musical sequences somehow denote, or stand for, certain emotional states. Deryck Cooke (1959) has presented one of the most fully worked out versions of this thesis. He argues that the intervals of the diatonic scale suggest different emotional qualities (e.g. major third—pleasure, fifths and octaves—neutral) and goes on to isolate several basic melodic combinations of these intervals which seem to recur throughout tonal music. For instance, there are many melodies which start on the dominant of a minor scale, then rise over the tonic to the third of the scale, before falling, possibly via the super-

TABLE 2.1

Composer	Approximate date	Words (English translation)
Dowland	1612	When the poor cripple by the pool did lie
Bach	1722	Flow my tears in floods of weeping
Bach	1729	Have mercy on me, O Lord
Bach	1731	I am weary of this world
Mozart	1791	Day of bitter lamentation
Verdi	1873	Day of bitter lamentation
Schubert	1823	Life flows away like the waters of a river
Schubert	1827	(The jilted lover bids farewell to his faithless sweetheart)
Verdi	1852	Farewell to the past, to the fair smiling dreams
Wagner	1853	(He who wishes for the power of the Ring must renounce love)
Mahler	1883	The unhappiest day of my life
Mahler	1884	Goodbye to all I ever loved
Britten	1944	We planned that their lives should have a good start

tonic, to rest on the tonic (Example 2.48). Of this motif Cooke says: it 'conveys the feeling of a passionate outburst of painful emotion, which does not protest further, but falls back into acceptance—a flow and ebb grief. Being neither complete protest nor complete acceptance, it has an effect of restless sorrow'. In support of this, and his other analysis, Cooke collects together an impressive array of supportive examples from all periods of tonal music. The most telling of these are, perhaps, taken from vocal music, where we have some independent evidence from the words concerning the emotional mood. For Example 2.48 Cooke gives fourteen examples, all from vocal music, summarized in Table 2.1.

The ubiquity and stability of such motifs is impressive, even if it is all too easy to accuse Cooke of picking his examples to support his case. Counter-examples are not immediately damaging to the thesis, because melody is only one of the dimensions along which composers may signify emotion. Rhythm, tempo, orchestration, and dynamics are all capable of modifying the meaning. It is quite clear that Example 2.48 would have different emotional connotation when entoned fortissimo by the entire brass section of a symphony orchestra than when played liltingly by a solo violin. It is not coincidental that most of Cooke's examples of this theme are quiet and slow. I believe that Cooke has identified a real and important component of musical meaning with his melodic analyses. As psychologists, however, we need to ask what psychological mechanisms allows these meanings to be comprehended by a listener.

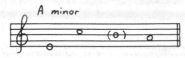

Example 2.48. One of Cooke's (1959) thematic motifs.

One possibility is that the motifs are intrinsically neutral with respect to the emotions and that people acquire their meanings through association with exactly the kind of words that seem to habitually accompany the motifs. Whilst this does not explain why composers should have begun to pair emotions with melodic motifs in the first place, it does seem the simplest explanation for the listener brought up within the existing musical culture. On this argument a listener would have no added difficulty in learning some different pairing of melody and emotion. For instance, it might have been that the emotion paired with Example 2.48 in our culture were paired with, say, a rising major triad in some alternative tonal culture. This is by analogy with the arbitrariness of word-meaning pairings in natural language. We believe that a language like English, where the meanings of 'cat' and 'dog' had been exchanged, would be just as easy to learn and use as the language we actually have. There is nothing about the sound 'cat' as such which makes it particularly suitable to stand for the small feline domestic mammal as opposed to anything else.

Cooke, however, invites us to reject the notion of instrinsic neutrality for music. He argues that certain motifs are more suitable than others for suggesting particular emotions by virtue of the tonal relationships that hold between their members. For instance, positive emotions are suggested by major sequences, especially those involving triads, because such sequences are directly derived from the early members of the harmonic series. Similarly, movements away from the tonic, particularly upwards, are suitable for expressing outgoing emotions, whilst movements towards the tonic signify rest or repose. This is because the tonic occupies a central or 'home' position in tonal harmony. What is suggested, therefore, is that the tonal system, as such, offers analogies for the way in which people represent emotions in some 'semantic space', and that these analogies allow a partial mapping of tonal relations onto emotions (Makeig 1982).

The psychological implications of this view are twofold. Firstly, the discovery of analogical relationships between music and emotion should be discoverable, in principle, by anyone who is capable of appreciating the tonal relationships in music and who has a normal understanding of the emotions. Thus, an explicit word–music association is not necessary to come to appreciate emotional meanings in music (although it may, of course, assist the process of acquisition). This helps to explain how so many composers, working in different times and places, seem to have hit upon the same types of melodic forms for the explicit expression of textual emotion. Secondly, it follows that pairings of melodies with emotions *other* than the ones we now have would not be as easy to learn, since they would be working against the 'ready made' analogical relationships inherent in tonality.

Although Cooke's thesis is empirical, it is not easy to know how it could be practically demonstrated. The 'ideal' demonstration would be given by someone who had never been exposed to any word–music associations (through song, etc.) showing culturally 'normal' appreciation of the emotional connotations of music. Such a person would, of course, have to have received otherwise normal musical and linguistic experience. It is unlikely that the conditions for this demonstration could ever be set up.

The research of Gabriel (1978) illustrates the considerable difficulties besetting the psychologist wishing to conduct empirical investigations into the mechanisms whereby emotional meanings in music are transmitted. He played each of Cooke's basic motifs to musically untrained subjects twice. On one occasion the motif was paired with Cooke's emotional characterization of it, on the other by a randomly chosen description from Cooke's set. Subjects were asked to rate the appropriateness of each motif-description pair. Gabriel argued that if subjects were aware of the supposed emotional connotation of each motif, then they should rate Cooke's designated description as more appropriate than the randomly chosen one. The results showed that subjects did not, in fact, distinguish between descriptions in this way. The 'random' description was equally often chosen as more appropriate. Here, then, is an apparent failure to demonstrate any relationship between tonal pattern and emotional connotation. Gabriel's tentative conclusion is that more primitive features of melodies (such as contour) are the principal carriers of musical meaning. Before accepting this conclusion, however, it is worth questioning whether Gabriel's experiment was maximally *conducive* to the discovery of Cooke's melody–emotion links. There are three issues which seem to require consideration.

First comes the question of subjects. It is natural to suppose that, as one becomes increasingly sophisticated musically, one becomes attuned to finer emotional nuance. A hierarchy of emotional cues seems likely, with primitive cues (such as speed and loudness) available at all levels of musical sophistication, and with more subtle cues (such as aspects of tonal relations) available only to those with deeper analytic powers with respect to the music. A common experience among many music lovers (including myself) is a belated appreciation of the emotional diversity and subtlety in the music of a composer such as Mozart. The inexperienced listener may find Mozart pale, insipid, and all vaguely 'jolly', especially when set beside the kalaeidosocopic turbulence of the romantic composers. Closer knowledge of Mozart (and maybe of the emotional world) results in his music becoming richly and sublimely expressive. The ability to 'read' the emotional language of music is an acquired skill, and we should, perhaps, not be too surprised that a group of 'ordinary' subjects do not show much awareness of the finer details of this language.

Second is the consideration of the nature of the experimental stimuli. In Gabriel's study the motifs were presented in musically 'disembodied' form. Each stimulus was a series of equally loud and equally long sine waves following the minimal tonal context of a tonic chord. The justification for this is the wish to hold all factors other than melody constant. There is no real music where melody is the *only* dimension on which two excerpts differ, and so it is impossible to tell which of several differences between two pieces of music is responsible for a difference in emotional connotation. In Gabriel's experiment, any difference in emotional meaning *must* be due to a difference in melodic shape, since nothing else varies. The major criticism of Gabriel's design is that it may have destroyed the conditions under which it is possible for a listener to activate the cognitive mechanisms which mediate between music and emotion. For instance, one may argue that the ascription of emotional meaning depends upon exposure to an extended context in which the crucial melody is embedded. By analogy, in recognition of facial expression we use information from the area of the eyes, but if we see *only* the eyes without the rest of the face, our ability to use this information is diminished. We may need to know where an excerpt comes in the structure of the music before we can interpret it emotionally; or we may need to give it some metrical reading. It would be difficult even for Cooke to hold that *every* occurence of a melodic motif has emotional significance. More likely, it is the portion of a sequence that is highlighted through its position in the musical structure, or its scoring, that carries the brunt of the emotional burden. For these, and other reasons, Gabriel's task is an unreal one. The future task is to find more realistic listening situations which nevertheless allow for the degree of control over the various dimensions of sound which is an undoubted prerequisite of the experimental investigation of response to music.

Third we must consider the nature of the response that subjects are asked to make. The judgement of the emotional meaning of a piece of music is not necessarily an instantaneous thing. It may be only gradually that one comes to the best characterization of the extra-musical themes that seem to be given metaphorical expression through the music. The analogy from language, where we hear a word or phrase and then can instantly access some central aspect of its meaning, is not necessarily the best one for understanding what goes on in music listening. A better analogy would perhaps be the ill-defined process by which we come to appreciate that a particular turn of phrase in a poem has implications which contribute to the meaning of the poem in a way that some putative 'synonymous expression' would not do. To come to this appreciation may require extended mental work during which we give the object of attention detailed and repeated scrutiny. Gabriel's subjects were required to come to a rapid unmediated judgement about the meaning of short musical excerpts. Although music can have immediate emotional impact, there is nothing in Cooke's thesis which demands that it should be the *tonal* element of music which alone carries this impact.

I have chosen to discuss Cooke's ideas at some length because they seem particularly clear and simple. Once we accept the general idea of analogical relationships between music and extra-musical domains, however, the possibility for other ways of expressing meaning are immense. I have already outlined one possible 'meaning' of Schenkerian structures in section 3 of this chapter. Many other possibilties suggest themselves. For instance, one may wish to find in symphonic form some metaphor for human life. The transformation or metamorphosis of theme parallels the changes we experience in ourselves and our ideas. The unification of diverse themes within a coherent structure parallels our attempts to endow our chaotic lives with meaning. And so on. This is, surely, part of the power of music, and this power is possibly enhanced by the manifest lack of practical meaning of the type supported by language. Musical semantics is of a similar type to poetic semantics. This does not mean that either subject is necessarily opaque to scientific understanding, but that we may be mistaken to seek for musical meanings in the same way as psychologists have so far attempted to elucidate the semantics of normal speech.

I would like to end this section by commenting briefly on the work of the noted American musicologist, L. B. Meyer (1956, 1973). He has made a distinction between two forms of meaning in music, *embodied* meaning, and *designative* meaning. Designative meaning is that which refers outside the music to objects or events in the non-musical domain. We have been primarily concerned with designative meaning in this section. Embodied meaning, in contrast, is the significance that a musical passage can have for a listener in terms of its own structure and the interaction of that unfolding structure with the listener's musical knowledge and expectations. The musical structure can create certain expectations (or implications) which it can then either fulfil or thwart. Among those which are fulfilled, some are fulfilled at once, others after a delay. This creates a dynamic flux of tensions and resolutions which can influence the emotional and aesthetic responsese of a listener.

Like Cooke's theory, Meyer's requires that a listener represents the music he hears in terms of the tonal and other formal categories of the musical culture. It is, however, a broader theory than Cooke's, in that it gives an explicit semantic role to large-scale musical structures, whereas Cooke concentrates on small melodic patterns. Meyer's approach also shows how the same melodic pattern could have quite different meanings in different contexts according to whether or not it fulfilled implications of earlier material. Because the theory is broader it is also more difficult to bring into the laboratory, and I know of no empirical research which bears directly on Meyer's central ideas. This is a shame because he is clearly one of the most influential and psychologically well-informed of contemporary musicologists. I shall give some examples of Meyer's notions of melodic implication in Chapter 5, but would recommend Meyer's (1973) book to anyone who is seriously interested in musical semantics.

2.7. Conclusions

I hope that the diverse topics reviewed in this chapter have shown that it is fruitful to consider music in relation to language. It allows us to notice fundamental similarities (e.g. the Chomsky–Schenker parallel) but also highlights differences in an illuminating way. For instance, the fact that categorical perception in music is not so complete and automatic as it is in language raises productive questions for future consideration. What is it about the two systems which makes for the difference? The fact that a generative grammar for music seems to be a less realizable goal than for language forces us to consider the fundamental differences in aim of linguistic and musical communication. In the process, our perception of both domains is sharpened.

The linguistic analogy is neither 'true' nor 'false'. Like all analogies, it achieves a partial fit with its subject. The 'true' element which I would like to emphasize most strongly is the notion that we represent sequences of individual elements by assigning theme roles in abstract underlying structures, some of which, particularly those with hierarchical organization, have strong family resemblance to one another. It is the relationship of elements to one another within these structures, rather than their temporal or spatial proximity that determines whether or not they are psychologically close. In the following chapters we shall not explicitly pursue the analogy further, but we shall find that the aspects of musical cognition emphasized by the analogy have profound and detailed implications for every musical activity we examine.

3. The performance of music

3.1. Introduction

In its broadest sense, performance covers the whole range of overt musical behaviour. A little child's improvised play-song, the humming of a popular melody, participation in corporate ritual such as hymn or folk singing, and dancing to music, are just some of the diverse modes of performance which merit psychological study. In a narrower sense, though, a musical performance is one in which a performer, or a group of performers, self-consciously enacts music for an audience. In our Western culture, such music is often written by someone not directly involved in the performance. The performers *realize* a pre-existent composition.

In this chapter I shall concentrate on performance in this latter narrow sense. There are several reasons why I do this. Firstly, most of the contemporary research is about this type of performance. Secondly, I shall wish to treat instances of performance where the performer is also the originator of the music (improvisation) as a special case of composition, and so reserve discussion of it for Chapter 4. Music of non-literate cultures is discussed in Chapter 7, and some aspects of children's musical behaviour are examined in Chapter 6. Thirdly, in performance of a 'composition', there is an objective record of the composer's intentions, usually in the form of a score. Without such a record we have no easy way of characterizing a piece of music independently of a particular performance of it, and so questions such as how *well* a performer realizes the music become very hard to answer.

There are three main stages of involvement with a musical score at which we can study performance. First is the unpremeditated performance which a musician is capable of providing at first sight of a score. This is commonly known as sight reading. Second are the performances generated over a period of repeated exposure to a score. Usually the aim of such performances is to improve performance until it reaches some criterion of adequacy, because sight reading does not often produce a totally satisfactory performance. This type of performance is known as rehearsal or practice. Finally comes the more-or-less finished product of rehearsal, a polished performance which may well involve total memorization of a score. This we will call expert performance, although it must be pointed out that some musicians can perform much music well without extensive rehearsal. Good sight reading (and indeed, good rehearsal) are forms of expertise in their own right.

3.2. Sight reading

Almost all of our reading of language is sight reading. Unless we are trying to memorize a text or are scrutinizing it for some professional purpose, we tend to read a text just once, and we expect that to suffice for our purposes. In contrast, many musicians find fluent sight reading very difficult, and brave indeed is the performer who would step on to the concert platform with no preview of his material.

Part of the explanation for this difference may be that whilst the fluent sight reading of language is necessary for a full life in our culture, the same is not true for music. Enormous educational effort is expended on getting children to a state in which their language reading is reasonably fluent. On the other hand, it is not necessary for children to be able to sight read well for them to succeed at conventional musical tasks, most of which allow for, even assume, intensive rehearsal. Thus, music sight reading is taught neither so rigorously nor at such an early age as language reading.

There are other factors too. Children are already fluent language users before they learn to read. They are rarely such fluent music performers. Most children learn a new music performance skill, such as playing an instrument, *alongside* learning to read music. This double task can be an intolerable burden which many solve by memorizing each new piece at the soonest opportunity so that their performance does not depend upon their reading ability. The result of this is that some musicians give themselves very little practice at continuous reading. Some modern educational techniques attempt to circumvent this problem by giving opportunity to acquire some performing skill before introducing music notation (e.g. the Suzuki method of violin teaching).

Finally, and perhaps most importantly, there is a sense in which the *criteria* for successful language reading are more lax than those for music reading. For most purposes it is sufficient, in language reading, to determine the practical meaning of the text. Much reading is silent, and even when spoken, often little more is required than the ability to utter the correct words in the correct sequential order. In contrast, music reading requires the execution of a complex response where there is very little latitude for deviations in timing and quality. The only linguistic task whose performance demands would approach the musical task is the recitation, at sight, of some piece of fine literature, incorporating all the nuance of voice, expression, and timing which one would expect from a first class actor.

The question which many musicians ask is 'what makes a good sight reader?' This question includes two separate concerns—firstly, what can be said about the characteristics of the fluent sight reader—and secondly, what must a poor reader do to become fluent? It is an unfortunate but unavoidable fact that a reasonably comprehensive answer to the first question does not necessarily lead to prescriptions for the second. For instance, the finding that fluent readers typically look further ahead than poor readers does not automatically yield the prescription that poor readers should practise looking further ahead. It may well be that increased ability for preview is the result of some other skill, such as the ability to detect pattern or structure in the score, and that simply trying to look ahead will not improve *this* skill. Therefore, whilst it is important that psychologists should try to to make prescriptions about the techniques for acquiring a skill, the enterprise involves many separate and complex issues. I shall discuss some of them in Chapter 6. Here my primary concern will be with the characteristics of performing skill, regardless of how the skill may be acquired.

3.2.1. *Eye movements in reading*

The first overt behaviour in any reading situation is the movement of the eyes over a page to expose succesive portions of the material to central vision. It is only centrally that we have the acuity to register precise details of visual material (although work on language reading, e.g. Rayner 1978, demonstrates the importance of peripheral information in the guidance of eye movements). At normal viewing distances the area of clear vision is a circle of approximately one inch diameter on the page. The mechanisms of the eye movement system operate to give the reader a series of brief 'snapshots' (known as fixations) of such circles. In fluent reading the duration of each fixation is about 250 ms (a quarter of a second) and the eye moves from one fixation to another in a rapid sweep known as a saccade, lasting about 50 ms. The available evidence suggests that we take in visual information only during the static fixations and not during saccade movements.

The question of primary psychological interest is how the reader controls the sequence and location of fixations. The simplest hypothesis we could entertain is that eye movements are controlled by low-level features of the input. For instance, fixations might occur in regular left-to-right order, each fixation occurring a constant distance to the right of the previous fixation so that the complete text is fixated over a complete sequence. Such neat regularity is, however, hardly ever observed, either in language or in music. Instead we find vertical as well as horizontal displacements, leaps which omit significant areas, and varying amounts of backtracking.

It is possible that some of these deviations are simply random movements of a system over which we have imperfect control. However, a large body of recent research on eye movements in language reading leads us to reject this view. Instead, it appears that the irregularities in eye movements are under immediate cognitive control. Take, for instance, the eye movement pattern in the vicinity of a very common word such as 'the' (O'Regan 1979). Typically readers do not fixate a 'the' directly and their saccadic movements over this word are larger than average. It seems as though linguistic knowledge interacts with peripheral information to allow an identification in the absence of a direct fixation. The eye-movement control system immediately responds by 'jumping' over the word it does not require to fixate. This is just one piece of evidence which contributes to the accepted view that moment-to-moment variations in the fixation sequence are motivated by the precise cognitive requirements of a reader at a particular time. The pattern of eye movements thus tells us something about these requirements.

Eye movements in music reading have not received the intensive study that has been given to eye movements in language reading. Nonetheless, the evidence that exists is consistent with the language data. For instance, studies by Weaver (Van Nuys and Weaver 1943; Weaver 1943) on piano readers show that the sequence of fixations is determined by the nature of the music. Piano music is written on two staves, so that it is impossible to view all the notes to be played together in a single fixation; one must fixate first upon one stave, then upon the other. One might imagine that the optimum strategy for reading would be a vertical sweep down (or up) the system, followed by a shift to the right and a further sweep [Fig. 3.1 (*a*)] Weaver found that this pattern was indeed used when the music was homophonic and chordal in nature. When the music was contrapuntal, however, he found fixation sequences which were grouped in horizontal sweeps along a single line, with a return to another line afterwards [Fig. 3.1 (*b*)]. Figures. 3.1 (*c*) and 3.1 (*d*) show examples of fixation patterns obtained by Weaver. Figure 3.1 (*c*) is from a chordal passage, whilst 3.1 (*d*) is contrapuntal.

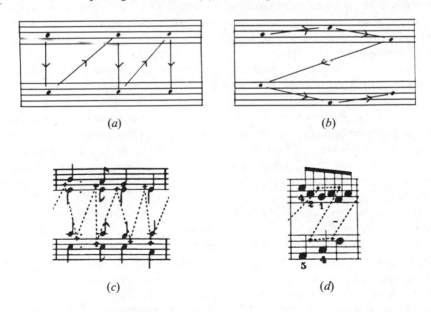

(*a*)   (*b*)

(*c*)   (*d*)

Fig. 3.1. (*a*) Vertical fixation sequence in piano reading. (*b*) Horizontal fixation sequence in piano reading. (*c*) Example of observed fixation sequence in chordal piano music (from Weaver, 1943). (*d*) Example of observed fixation sequence in contrapuntal piano music (from Weaver, 1943).

The general strategy appears to be to identify significant structural units in successive fixations. In homophonic music these units are chords, and so it is necessary to sample both staves in successive fixations. In contrapuntal music the significant units are melodic fragments which extend horizontally along a single stave.

How does such a fixation pattern help the reader? The available evidence suggests that readers require *preview* of structural units in a text if they are to organize fluent and rapid performance. Studies summarized by Shaffer (1976) illustrate this rather well. He examined the behaviour of experienced copy-typists under conditions of controlled preview. Texts were displayed on a computer console. Each time the typist input a character on a keyboard three things happened: all the characters displayed were shifted one space to the left; the leftmost letter disappeared; and a new character appeared at the right of the display. The crucial independent variables were the number of characters displayed at one time, and the number of characters on the screen that had not yet been typed. This latter variable could take any value between a single character and a whole line. It was discovered that if a typist was able to see at least eight characters ahead, performance was indistinguishable from the normal situation with unlimited preview. As preview was decreased, however, performance slowed and became less regular. With preview of eight characters the typing speed was about ten characters per second. With preview of a single letter this dropped to about two characters per second. Shaffer found that it was also possible to slow speed by leaving preview in normal range but manipulating the text. First he randomized word order; this had virtually no effect on performance. Then he randomized letter order within words; this had a highly significant effect, causing speed to drop almost as low as with single letter preview. We can draw quite a firm conclusion from this elegant study. Typists require to preview a whole word, but no more, in order to achieve fluency. It appears that seeing a word in advance allows them to plan a set of partially overlapping hand and finger movements into a single co-ordinated unit.

No-one has yet published experiments with controlled preview in music, although the rapid development of computer music systems (e.g. Tucker, Bates, Frykberg, Howarth, Kennedy, Lamb and Vaughan 1977) makes such studies increasingly more feasible. However, it has been possible to estimate the extent of preview in normal performance by the modification of a technique developed for measuring what is known as the *eye–voice span* in language reading. The technique (as used, for instance, by Levin and Addis 1980, and Levin and Kaplan 1970) involves asking subjects to continue reading out a prose passage *after* the text has been unexpectedly removed. The distance between the word being uttered at the time of removal and the final correct word uttered provides an estimate of the extent of preview. In normal reading situations the eye–voice span of an experienced reader is four to six words. I have modified the technique for instrumental music reading, by asking various instrumentalists to read single-line melodies at sight (Sloboda 1974, 1977a). When the score was removed, proficient readers could produce up to seven further correct notes. If these performers were looking only so far ahead as required to organize fluent performance, then we may conclude, with some confidence, that the units in terms of which fluent performance is organized are not typically larger than seven consecutive notes of a melody. This seems to be true for all instruments tested, and is not a result of constraints imposed by particular instruments.

Of some theoretical importance is the finding that measures of this *eye-hand span* do not always yield precisely the same result. Depending upon the particular note in the melody where the score is removed, the span can be larger or smaller than average. It appears that there is a tendency for span to coincide with a musically defined phrase boundary, so that a boundary just beyond average span 'stretches' the span, and a boundary just before average 'contracts' it. This strongly suggests that phrase boundaries mark the boundaries between effective performance units which tend to be assembled in an 'all or none' fashion. It also suggests that the typical musical phrase is not, in itself, this unit, because most phrases contain more than seven notes. We must suppose that there exists some principled way of dividing a phrase up into smaller units, analogous to words.

Just as in the typing study, manipulating the 'text' gives further clues to the nature of the performance units. When melodies lacked normal harmonic progressions, span decreased significantly. Similarly, obscuring the rhythmic divisions between phrases by the addition of passing notes also decreased span. It seems that the reader subdivides a phrase into performance units in ways dependent on the harmonic and rhythmic structure of the phrase, and that when cues to these structures are obscured, preview is not so useful, and cannot, indeed, be sustained at normal levels.

Comparison of good and poor music readers showed that poor readers have lower spans than good readers (three or four notes) even when the melodies were structurally straightforward. Poor readers seem to behave with 'normal' music rather like good readers with 'obscure' music. If the ability to maintain preview is dependent on the ability to isolate structurally defined units, then poor readers are less capable of doing this, even when the structures are clearly present.

Before leaving eye movements, it is worth commenting that performance units in music, whilst analogous to words in some respects, cannot be very like them. The English language contains a finite number of words, each defined by a set of letters in a particular order. It is quite feasible for a typist to know every one of these words, storing the unique typing pattern for each word in memory. There is no similar agreed 'dictionary' of musical patterns. It is quite possible for a melody to contain a novel combination of notes. On the other hand, there *are* certainly familiar recurrent configurations of pitch and rhythm in many melodies (such as scale and *arpeggio* pitch movements, dactyllic rhythms, etc.) which a reader could learn to recognise as units. Thus, music reading probably involves *some* recognition of frequently occurring patterns, but this is likely to be supported by some more general strategy for organizing groupings of notes which can function even when the patterns are novel. One such strategy would be a grouping according to metre. A metrical unit is like a frame, which can be used to hold and describe a very large number of note sequences. The same frame can be applied repetitively to any metrically regular piece of music, bar by bar. Such units are, of course, easy to find in a score. Bars are marked by bar lines; smaller units are often marked by beams. An efficient 'default' grouping strategy would therefore seem to be—take the bar as the performance unit, unless it contains more than seven notes, in which case take the half-bar. Since musical phrases are normally defined metrically (as well as harmonically and melodically) then the observed 'phrase-boundary' effect would be consistent with such a strategy. Furthermore, a metrical organizer has one extremely useful feature—it incorporates a regular pulse by reference to which finger movements can be targetted, and by reference to which the next performance unit can be 'set up'.

In other words, such an organizer is an aid to fluency and pacing. Suppose, for instance, that the organizer being used is a four beat bar with the internal structure signified by Fig. 3.2 (*a*). Level A represents the whole bar, and, if we set a constant tempo, then the onset of each bar can be timed from a clock operating at this level. Organization of the performance of the subsequent bar can be paced against a countdown of the previous bar. An eye movement sequence must be terminated in time to provide the information for the next unit before the countdown reaches zero. Levels B to D represent a possible way of internally structuring the bar, using a hierarchic binary branching tree down to the quaver level. The bar marker generates timing for half-bar units; the half-bar markers generate timings for beats; and so on. Of course, the reader need not use such a deeply structured organizer as this; he could use a simpler two-deep hierarchy such as in Fig. 3.2 (*b*). Data reviewed later in this chapter (sections 3.2.3 and 3.2.4) favours the notion that experienced performers use an organizer more like 3.2 (*a*) than 3.2 (*b*). However, the general principle shared by any such organizers is that they specify *when* each note in a group should occur, so that the performer can initiate ballistic finger movements by reference to the countdown for each note.

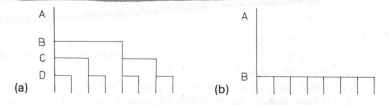

Fig. 3.2. Possible metrical organizers for performance.

3.2.2. *Errors in reading*

Eye movements give useful information about the organization of music reading, but it is the performance itself which provides the most direct evidence of reading behaviour. A crude but nonetheless informative measure of reading performance is what one might call 'notational accuracy'—the extent to which a performer plays the correct notes at their approximate notated values.

In a classic study Pillsbury (1897) demonstrated that experienced language readers are prone to make misreadings which transform wrongly printed words into their correct form. For instance 'internalional' might be seen as 'international'. Under many circumstances these perceptual transformations are unconscious. Readers are not aware of the original stimulus; they believe they are seeing the correctly printed word. The received explanation for this phenomenon is that readers are able to identify words on less than complete information, given their knowledge of the spellings of words. For instance, if a reader of English identifies three letters of a four letter word as W-RK, he should be able to identify the word as WORK. There is no other word in the language that fits the available information.

When people read continuous prose they are even more susceptible to this kind of error than when viewing single words. This is because they now have an additional source of information—context. For instance, the sequence 'She raised her wine glass to her . . .' strongly suggests 'lips' as a continuation. It may not be necessary for someone to actually 'read' the word in order to 'see' it. In normally constructed text, such 'seeings' are usually correct. It is when text incorporates the unexpected that trouble can occur. The phenomenon of *proof-reader's error* is well known to psychologists (Vernon 1931). This is the failure to detect spelling or typing errors when scanning through a typescript. The proof-reader makes unconscious inferences which restore the incorrect words to their correct form, and so the errors are not detected.

By deliberately manipulating texts and introducing errors we can learn something about the nature of the inferences which expert readers make. For instance, readers are more likely to spot misprints if they occur at the beginnings of words than elsewhere (Haber and Schindler, 1981; Sloboda, 1976b). People are more likely to overlook spelling errors which are visually similar to the correct form (Healy 1980).

Proof-readers' error also occurs in music. Wolf (1976) quotes a striking example of such error from the experience of a professional pianist/teacher, Boris Goldovsky:

A student whom Dr Goldovsky describes as 'technically competent but a poor reader' prepared a Brahms *Capriccio* (Op. 76 No. 2) which she brought to her lesson. She began to play the piece through but when she arrived at the C sharp major chord on the first beat of the bar 42 measures from the end, she played a G natural instead of the G sharp which would normally occur in the C sharp major triad. Goldovsky told her to stop and correct her mistake. The student looked confused and said that she had played what was written. To Goldovsky's surprise, the girl had played the printed notes correctly—there was an apparent misprint in the music.

This misprint occurs in most standard editions of Brahms' piano music. It appears, therefore, that many hundreds of musicians had never noticed the misprint. Goldovsky proceeded to test skilled readers by telling them that the piece contained a misprint which they were to find. He allowed them to play the piece as many times as they liked and in any way that they liked. None of them ever found the mistake. Only when he specified the bar in which the misprint occured were most readers able to spot it.

It is easy to understand why this misprint was so hard to detect. But for the misprint, the bar in which it occurs is an almost exact transposition of the previous bar. The underlying harmonic movement is the very common V–I (from G sharp to C sharp) over a C sharp pedal. In addition, the notation in the previous bar has already 'set' the G as a sharp. There are thus multiple and powerful cues for a knowledgeable reader to interpret the crucial G as a sharp (see Example 3.1).

Example 3.1. Bars 76–78 from Brahms, Capricio, Op. 76, No. 2. Reprinted by kind permission of Peters Edition Limited, London

What is important to note about this story is that it was a relatively *poor* reader who was the first to uncover the error. Because she did not have the expectations of more accomplished players she required more information from the score to determine her performance, and so, paradoxically, read more accurately than more accomplished players.

This demonstration, although striking, is anecdotal, and one of my own experiments (Sloboda 1976b) was designed to verify the phenomenon under laboratory conditions. Example 3.2 shows one of the stimulus pieces used in the experiment. It is by the eighteenth-century composer J. Dussek. The musically literate reader is invited to attempt a sight performance of the piece (preferably tape-recording it for subsequent examination) according to the following instructions, which approximate to those given to my experimental subjects: 'Please sight read this short piano piece at your own pace. Attempt to play exactly what is written, but do not stop if you make an error. Do not extensively preview the piece but start playing within five seconds of looking at the page. You may begin now.'

The stimulus materials were prepared by taking little known keyboard pieces by minor classical composers and rewriting them with deliberate notational errors. The errors had two characteristics. Firstly, they involved a shift in the notated pitch of one step on the stave, leaving all other features (accidentals, rhythm, etc.) unchanged. Thus a notated quaver on B flat might become either a quaver on C flat or on A flat. This had the consequence that the visual appearance of the error was very similar to that of the original. Secondly, they were chosen to be musically inappropriate in their contexts. This could be either by creating a dissonant harmony or by violating normal melodic progression. The errors were judged as 'blatant' by musicians. This is particularly important since there are no definite dividing lines between what is acceptable in music and what is not. There is always a grey middle area where the unexpected may in fact be a legitimate violation of norms which extends and transforms style rather than simply being a mistake. The errors chosen for this experiment were well outside such grey areas. They were downright wrong.

The results of the experiment were quite clear. All subjects tested showed 'proof-reader's error'; that is, they played some altered notes as they should have been rather than as notated. This was even though no subject was familiar with any of the test pieces, and in spite of the fact that every subject 'tumbled' the point of the experiment by noticing *some* of the deliberate errors.

Example 3.3 identifies the 'misprints'. The notes which I altered are ringed. It can be seen that the errors are distributed equally between upper and lower staves. They are also distributed within musical phrases. One third of the errors occur at the beginning of a phrase, one third in the middle, and one third at the end. Table 3.1 shows the proportion of altered notes which were restored to their originals by the subjects, for each stave, and for each position within the phrase. The data for the upper stave (containing the primary melodic material) are strikingly similar to those obtained with words. Alterations in the middle of phrases are more likely to be restored than those at beginnings or ends. We may, therefore, argue that phrases form psychologically effective units such that the reader's attention is concentrated on the material occurring at phrase boundaries, and that some form of inference allows the reader to economize on input from intermediate positions.

A further striking feature of the results is the pattern of errors in a second performance of the test pieces that subjects made. As one might expect, their performances improved, as shown by a significant drop in the total number of performance errors. This shows that they had learned something about the pieces from their first performance. However, the proportion of proof-

Example 3.2. Material from Sloboda's (1976b) sight reading study.

readers' errors did *not* decrease. On the contrary, it *increased* slightly. This suggests that, as they gained a firmer hold on the structure of the pieces, they became *more* likely to infer the expected notes. Clearly, at this early stage in learning, subjects were beginning to store the music, not only in terms of individual notes, but also in terms of higher-order structures. This ability is clearly a hallmark of skilled reading.

It is relevant to ask whether musical proof-reader's error occurs for other performers than pianists. Keyboard music presents particular difficulties precisely because it is on more than one stave, and because several notes are often to be performed simultaneously. Most other instruments are capable of playing only one note at a time, and the music is presented on a single

TABLE 3.1

Number of errors on altered notes at each position in phrase

Subject	Beginning	Middle	End
	Upper stave		
A	7	19	12
B	5	10	4
C	2	16	6
D	4	10	6
E	7	10	9
.F	5	8	7
G	7	20	7
Mean	5.3	13.3	7.3
%	23	62	34
	Lower stave		
A	7	7	6
B	5	7	4
C	12	11	9
D	8	8	5
E	8	10	6
F	9	10	9
G	14	12	7
Mean	9.0	9.3	6.6
%	42	43	31

stave. The 'real time' demands are, therefore, reduced, and inference may be less necessary. This issue has not yet received experimental investigation.

Because it is relatively difficult to induce errors in normal skilled reading, many language investigators have degraded the visual stimulus in some way to make perception more difficult. The most fruitful way of doing this has been to expose portions of text for very brief durations, less than a single fixation. By varying the exposure duration we can learn something about the time-course of information pickup.

I have applied this approach to music in a series of experiments (Sloboda 1976a, 1978) where varying numbers of pitch symbols were displayed briefly on staves for subjects to write down. The advantage of this technique is that

Example 3.3. The material of Example 3.2 with altered notes ringed.

it allows comparison between musicians and non-musicians, since the pitch transcription task is one which non-musicians can easily carry out as straight-forward visual copying. Figure 3.3 gives examples of the kind of stimulus material used. Subjects were supplied with blank staves on which to write their responses, which they were allowed to do immediately after the end of the brief exposure. Exposure durations varied from 20 ms up to 2 s.

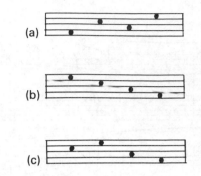

Fig. 3.3. Examples of stimulus materials used by Sloboda (1978).

At the briefer exposures (up to 100 ms) both musicians and non-musicians were very poor at recording the position of notes accurately. They were rarely able to record more than one note correctly. However, when forced to guess all the notes in a display, musicians were significantly better than non-musicians at retaining the approximate *contour* of the original. If one note was higher than its left-neighbour in the stimulus then it tended to be recorded as higher in the response, even though it may not have been placed on the correct stave-line. The ability to retain contour was particularly good when the contour of the original was a straight ascending or descending line [Fig. 3.3 (*b*)] or contained only one change of direction [Fig. 3.3 (*c*)].

We may suppose that durations below 100 ms are just too short for the visual processing mechanisms to gain accurate positional information about the notes, but that more global information about the shape of the note contour is available. This accords with data from other visual experiments (e.g. Massaro and Klitzke 1977; Navon 1977). What is of particular interest here is that the ability to use contour information seems to depend on musical experience. The music reader seems primed to store information about scale or *arpeggio*-like patterns in particular, and this suggests that such information is used in normal reading. This may be because such patterns are usually associated with a stereotyped finger and hand-movement pattern, so that rapid early identification allows advance motor planning. If one can accurately identify just the first note of such a pattern, and one has some contextually supplied knowledge of the harmonic structure at that point, then identification of the contour may be enough to uniquely specify the required action.

As the exposure duration was increased, both musicians and non-musicians increased in their ability to record the notes accurately. However, non-musicians' performance peaked at about three notes, whereas musicians were able to record six notes from a single exposure. This difference remained even at exposure durations of 2 s when there could be no *visual* problems for either group. The superior performance of the musicians is due to their superior *retention* of the stimulus material. They have means of coding and

1. the chess board

storing the notes (as music) not available to the non-musicians, who have to remember the stimuli as purely visual patterns.

A partial clue as to the nature of the musicians' coding comes from an experiment by Halpern and Bower (1982). Using a similar technique to mine they varied the harmonic structure of the stimuli. Half of their stimuli were 'good' melodies, following normal rules of harmonic and melodic progression. The other half were 'bad', designed to violate as many musical conventions as possible. They found that musicians performed better with 'good' melodies than with 'bad', but that non-musicians showed no difference between the two types of melody. Clearly, music-specific knowledge was responsible for the advantage enjoyed by 'good' melodies with the musicians. These melodies could be coded into higher-order structures, thereby reducing memory load. However, even on the 'bad' melodies musicians retained a large superiority over the non-musicians. So structure is not the whole story. In my own experiments, many of the stimuli were randomly generated, and so 'bad'. This did not prevent musicians from showing massive superiority over non-musicians. This is rather different to the outcome in Chase and Simon's (1973) classic chess experiments. Here, masters reproduced 'bad' chess configurations as poorly as novices.

One possible reason for this difference is that the music stimuli are far simpler than the chess stimuli. They contain fewer elements distributed over fewer possible positions. Each pair of adjacent notes will have some musical meaning *whatever* their positions. A random sequence of six notes can always be represented as three pairs of notes, each encompassing a common musical interval, so that it is always possible to impose *some* musical structure on the sequence. Another reason concerns differences in experience at the specific task. Although chess masters have undoubtedly spent longer looking at chess positions than have novices, they probably have not had more practice at recording chess positions from memory. In contrast, skilled music reading involves the continuous performance of short sequences of music from memory, and musicians have developed specialized mechanisms precisely for this task that novices will not possess. One could predict that if a chess master devoted considerable effort to developing memory reproduction skills for chess positions, he would soon develop superiority over novices even for 'random' boards.

what mechanisms?

3.2.3. *Expressive aspects of sight performance*

Although errors of reading can reveal something of underlying psychological processes it is often difficult to induce skilled performers to make *any* errors without experimental intervention. By error, in this context, we mean a performer playing the wrong note or making gross errors in timing and rhythm. If skilled performance is error-free, how can we get behind such performance to understand the psychological mechanisms which control it?

One possibility is to ask skilled sight readers what they do. Wolf (1976) interviewed four expert sight-readers, and although they produced some insightful remarks it is hard to know whether these remarks are more than informed rationalizations about largely unconscious and automatic processes. For instance, they displayed uncertainty about how much music they took in at a single fixation, or how far ahead they looked. One performer, when asked what problems he experienced in sight reading, simply replied 'for me personally, there are none.'

A different approach, pioneered by Seashore (1938) but first applied to sight reading by Shaffer (1980) is to record accurately the microstructure of a performance; the minute variations in touch, timing, and intensity that characterize any human performance. In some cases, these variations may be relatively uninteresting; random fluctuations due to noise in the system (such as limits in the acuity of feedback mechanisms, muscular tremor, lapses of attention). In other cases, however, the variations can be shown to bear systematic relation to structural features of the music.

This is particularly important to our understanding of sight reading in situations where there are no explicit instructions in the score to make variations in touch and timing. Consider a Bach fugue, for instance. Bach generally supplied no dynamic markings, touch, or phrasing instructions. The only explicit information given, in addition to the notes themselves, concerns the tonality (signalled by the key signature) and the metre (signalled by the time signature and the barring). It would be quite inappropriate, however, for a performer to consider that each note should be played in the same way. Such a 'dead-pan' performance, whilst technically error-free on our prior definition, would not be considered musically effective.

Even inexperienced performers soon become aware that their performance must be expressive. Too often, though, this can mean a haphazard application of timing and intensity changes plastered at will over the music. One simple test of how principled a performer's expressive playing is is to ask him to provide two consecutive performances of a relatively unfamiliar piece. If he is able to provide very similar expressive changes on the two occasions, in the absence of explicit score instructions, then we can infer the existence of some rule-based system for assigning variation to his performance. We can rule out the possibility that such performance details simply demonstrates good memory for the details of the first performance. As Shaffer (1981a) argues,

the pianist could not memorize this amount of detail: musicians are no better than anyone else at remembering arbitrary analogue information, and Eric Clarke, at Exeter, has demonstrated this by asking pianists to reproduce short melodies they hear, containing timing deformation in a single pair of notes. Almost inevitably the pianist bends the deformation in the direction of a notatable rhythm. Hence the pianist playing Bach could only make consistent use of expressive variation across performance by having an expressive grammar with which to construct the variation according to features in the music.

Shaffer has provided evidence from two consecutive performances at sight of a Bach fugue (*Well-tempered clavier*, *Book 2*, Fugue 7) by an experienced pianist. A grand piano was linked to a computer in such a way that information about the precise duration and intensity of each note played could be stored (for details see Shaffer 1980). The subject had not played this particular fugue for many years; and following the first performance he was asked to play the fugue again with no instruction to play it the same or different. Shaffer found similarities in expressive performance at many levels. For instance, *within* bars the ranked intensity of individual notes tended to be the same for the two performances. Some notes were given accents on each performance even though the score did not specify this. On a larger scale, increases and decreases in the duration of bars showed a remarkably similar pattern.

What type of rules govern the assignment of expressive variation? Long-term variations, such as gradual changes in speed or intensity, are directed by relatively large-scale aspects of musical structure which often require the performer to appreciate and remember thematic landmarks in the music. For instance, a sequence repeated at increasingly higher pitch can signal the approach of a climax, and an appropriate response is often to increase the intensity for each repetition of the sequential pattern. This requires the reader to spot the pattern, and then visually recognize that what is about to be played is a further continuation of the pattern. At the other extreme, variations occuring within a bar (especially at the beginning of a piece) are unlikely to be determined by the large-scale structure of the piece, and so do not rely on an appreciation of this structure. The variations are linked to the microstructure of the music, the relative importance of the various notes within a bar. One fundamental aspect of this microstructure is the metrical organization, and it is on this aspect that I wish to concentrate.

As discussed in Chapter 2, section 5.4, there are two ways in which a listener can determine the rhythmic parsing for a section of music. On some occasions the patterning of pitches and durations suggest a particular grouping, so that if the performer plays the correct notes for the correct approximate durations, the metre can be determined. On other occasions, however, the patterning of the notes will not suggest a single interpretation, or may even be misleading. An example which caused me some perplexity on first hearing is the opening of Bach's *Clavier Concerto* in D minor (Example 3.4). I took the first two notes to be an upbeat, giving notes 3 and 7 as the major stresses. This intepretation is consistent with the rule that long notes generally denote major stresses. Of course, the correct parsing puts the

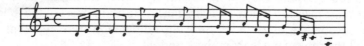

Example 3.4. From J. S. Bach, Clavier Concerto in D minor, First movement.

major stresses on notes 1 and 6. I believe that the only way to guarantee that a listener parses this correctly on first hearing is for the performer to make appropriate expressive variation of a magnitude sufficient to overcome the tendency of a listener to mis-parse.

Using Shaffer's laboratory, I have recently attempted to provide evidence about the use of metrically related variation in piano sight-performance. The basic technique was to present a metrically ambiguous melody under two notational conditions in which bar lines and beams were shifted along the melody, keeping note values and fingerings the same (see Examples 3.5. and 3.6). This is a crucial control, because observing the performance of a *single* notated melody would not be enough to demonstrate that variation was related to notated metre. It might also relate to the precise patterning of pitches and durations, and the fact that different notes use different fingers, etc. In this paradigm we have two melodies whose note and finger patterning are precisely the same. All that differentiates them is the positioning of metrical stress. Therefore, systematic differences in expressive variation *must* be a result of the shift in metre.

Pianists were asked to provide five faultless and similar performances of each of Examples 3.5 and 3.6 at sight. These examples were embedded in a larger number of short melodies, and no subject noticed the fact that the two melodies were, in fact, identical. Each set of five performances represented the spontaneous response to each melody in isolation.

Examples 3.5. and 3.6. The melodies used in Sloboda's (1983) study.

A note-by-note analysis of the differences in timing and intensity (see Sloboda 1983, for full details) showed there to be many significant differences between the performances of the two melodies. For instance, five out of the six pianists played the first bar of Example 3.5 in such a way that note 5 was more legato than its predecessors. In Example 3.6, however, note 5 received no special treatment. This is one example of what emerges from the data as a 'half-bar' effect. The subjects used a variety of devices to differentiate the note immediately following the half-bar (and so falling on the third beat) from its predecessors. These were essentially either an increase in intensity, or an increase in legato touch, or a slight delaying of the onset of the following note, or a combination of these. Individual differences were apparent in the nature of the choices made from these options.

The devices discovered will be of no surprise to performing musicians, corresponding roughly as they do to notions of *accent*, *slurring*, and *tenuto*, respectively. However, the fact that pianists can deploy these devices at sight shows that they are cued rapidly and fairly automatically from a first inspection of the score. Since there are no explicit notational cues which mark the half-bar, the performance variations must arise through some analysis of the notes which assigns them to structures in which the third beat of a four-beat bar achieves special prominence. Of course, the first beat of each bar is also given special treatment in performance, but there is an explicit notational cue here, the bar line.

These preliminary data leave us a long way from understanding the total process by which metrically related variations are assigned to a performance. The main problem is that a performer does not mark every stress, and when he does mark it he makes a choice from the available options, as well as deciding on the *magnitude* of the variations he chooses. We may suppose that individual performers develop 'styles' so that one makes more use of touch variation, another of intensity variations, and so on. Highly proficient performers may even be able to alter performance style at will within certain limits.

There is also the question of relating performance to perception. Expressive features of performance are useless unless they can be detected by listeners. Similarly, it is pointless to expend energy on achieving levels of performance accuracy (for instance, in timing or tuning) that cannot possibly be appreciated by listeners, because the performance resolution is much finer than the discriminatory powers of listeners. This area is one in which little research has been carried out. The principal problem is that one cannot simply use data from standard psychophysical measurements to make prescriptions for performers. Under 'ideal' conditions a listener may, indeed, be able to detect certain small differences in timing or tuning, but in the welter of a complex musical event discrimination may be much poorer. Experienced performers soon come to realize just how much they can 'get away with' in live performance. I have often been amazed, when listening to a recording of my own performance, just how unnoticeable were errors which, at the time of performance, struck me as catastrophic. Indeed, part of the art of sight reading is knowing which parts of the music will not be salient for a listener. One learns how to create an impression of accuracy in a performance that is actually far from faithful to the score.

We may view the process of assigning expressive variation at sight to comprise three major stages. First is the formation of a mental representation of the music, from examination of the score, which identifies features to be marked expressively in performance. For instance, a four-beat bar such as that depicted in Example 3.7 may be represented as two equal sub-units nested within the bar. To respond appropriately to a rising sequence such as that depicted in Example 3.8 more complex representations based on pitch and tonality need to be computed. The three-note pattern which repeats itself

That another performance in
a program that correspond to performance

how it would be interesting to design a
metrical pattern
(This matter over Emch manner

Example 3.7.

three times at higher pitch suggests increasing intensity through A1, A2, to
A3. A tonal representation of the scalar and cadential approach to the tonic
will place B as the culmination of the sequence, and so suggest an intensity
climax at B. The elements A1–3 and B also have internal metrical structure
which, if represented, can provide the basis of expressive variation *within*
each element. Since the first note of each element falls on a major stress
within the bar it could be marked by a greater intensity than its neighbours.
A possible intensity contour that could be derived from computing these
multiple representations (scalar, tonal, and metrical) might be:

312 | 423 | 534 | 64445

where the numbers represent positions on an ordinal intensity scale. It is, of
course, possible to represent a melody on only one of these dimensions and
still produce *some* expressive variation. The dimensions can be computed
independently. For instance, someone who computes only a tonal representation might assign the following intensity contour:

333 | 444 | 555 | 66666

whereas someone computing only a metrical representation might assign this
intensity contour:

423 | 423 | 423 | 42223

There are, of course, further levels of representation which would take us
beyond a single phrase such as Example 3.8 to place it in relation to other
thematic material in a longer piece. Still confining ourselves to intensity
variation, we may want to set the overall level for the phrase with respect to
what has gone before or what is to follow. Let us suppose, for instance, that
Example 3.8 was preceded by an identical two bar phrase in a longer piece.

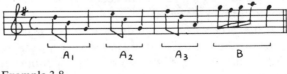

Example 3.8.

We might, then, wish to represent Example 3.8 as an 'echo', in which case
the entire four bar section might be assigned the following intensity contour:

645 | 756 | 867 | 97778 / 312 | 423 | 534 | 64445

in which the calibration for the second phrase is reset three intensity steps lower than the first.

We may hold it as a working hypothesis that the smaller the amount of music a reader has to preview to discover the cues for a particular representation, the more likely it is that the reader will form that representation. In much music, preview of one bar is the maximum required to form an appropriate metrical representation. The important metrical groupings fall within a bar's span. On the other hand, tonal progressions can span many bars, so that preview becomes less possible, and accurate prediction becomes the only way of making the right expressive decisions. As a performer becomes increasingly familiar with an idiom such prediction is increasingly possible, but all performers will experience times when they take a 'wrong view' of a piece of music peformed at sight. For instance, one may believe that a particular cadence is the resolution of a section, and so emphasize it through *crescendo* and *allargando*, only to discover that it is the penultimate cadence of the section—by which time one has 'spent one's last ammunition.'

The second stage in the expressive process involves gaining access to a 'dictionary' of expressive variations which are accepted as effective in communicating the structural markings which have been identified. In other words, we must assume a mutually agreed 'language' of expression between performers and listeners. It is possible that part of this language is based on relatively primitive mechanisms of auditory grouping in temporal sequences which all people share. For instance, a note which is louder than its neighbours will, all other things being equal, be heard as separate from them. Some of these mechanisms are discussed further in Chapter 5.2. Other aspects of the language are culturally determined, and depend on the shared musical experience of performer and listener (for instance, the use, in classical music, of an *allargando* to signal the final cadence of a movement). Paradoxically, it may be this second type of variation which is easiest for a performer to learn and apply, because it *is* a self-conscious product of a culture to be explicitly identified and talked about.

On the other hand, the small-scale moment-to-moment variations which make performances 'alive' are not so easy to describe. In listening to a master performer we experience his grasp of the *structure* of the music (i.e. we are enabled to form a representation of the music resembling that which dictates his performance) but we tend to lose the information about the precise means by which the form is conveyed. As we noticed earlier, people are very bad at remembering analogue information. In terms of metrical information, we may experience a very keen sense of metre through a good performance but be quite unable to say *why* the performance made the structure so transparent. This phenomenon is not confined to music. We find it anywhere that performing expertise is involved. A master can reveal to us the dramatic impact of a difficult monologue that is just dull and wordy in the hands of a lesser actor; but the general listener appreciates only the power of the interpretation, not the precise means by which the power is achieved.

Performing expertise first requires analytic listening powers of a developed kind so as to be able to 'latch on to' the minute timing and intensity variations that make a master performance and then *imitate* them. In my own experience, and that of many musicians, there is no really satisfactory way of *describing* expressive variations in a way which allows one to incorporate them into one's own performance. Expressive techniques are passed from one musician to another by demonstration. That is why master musicians are nearly always passionately interested in hearing the performances of other masters. It is why good teachers *have* to be, in my view, good performers. I can recall occasions when my own teacher taught me more by *playing* the passage under discussion than by talking about it for many minutes.

If, however, performing expertise requires listening expertise, we are left with the problem of what allows a person to listen to, and store the kind of detailed information that most of us find so difficult to retain. As an instrumental teacher I have noticed very great differences between even quite young children in the ability to notice expressive variation in the performance of others. For many learners, teaching by demonstration is useless simply because they do not appear to pick up what is being demonstrated. Others are capable of immediate and accurate imitation and retention. I view this ability as one of the best predictors of high levels of musical achievement. It is unfortunate that the cognitive bases for it are not well understood.

The third stage in the process is what has often been referred to as 'motor programming'. This is the setting up of a sequence of commands to the performing muscles which will reveal in sound the expressive devices selected from the 'dictionary'. There are two important features of fluent behaviour which a theory of motor programming must account for. One is the fact that elements in a motor sequence overlap in time. When, for instance, a performer executes a scale passage, the second finger must already be moving towards its position before the first finger is released. Because the degree of temporal overlap is variable (depending, among other things, on the speed of performance), the second movement cannot be initiated on the basis of some cue from the first movement. This is one of the classic problems of serial behaviour outlined in Lashley's seminal (1951) paper, which has greatly influenced current thinking. The second, related, feature is that fluent motor behaviour results in specified *goals* being achieved rather than specified movements being carried out (Shaffer 1982). In terms of piano playing the goal of motor programming is to ensure that a particular note is begun at a particular time and played with a particular loudness. This will be achieved by different *movements* depending upon the preceding hand position and also by what must follow. Expert pianists may use different fingerings on two consecutive performances of a passage, yet achieve precisely the same sound each time.

These features emphasise the fact that skilled human performance is seldom a rigid movement sequence where each movement is triggered in an inflexible way by the preceding movement, and forces us to realize that performance is the result of an interaction between a mental *plan* which specifies features of the intended output and a flexible programming system 'which has learned through experience to compute the patterns of muscle contraction that will achieve the goal (of producing the specified output) over a broad range of starting conditions' (Shaffer 1981b, p. 331).

This conceptualization accounts for many aspects of musical performance. For instance, it makes sense of the phenomenon of knowing exactly what a passage of music played at sight *should* sound like, but being unable to negotiate the correct notes. In this case the performer has formed an adequate plan of the music he is playing. In terms of my three-stage division of the process he has successfully carried out the first two stages; forming a structurally based representation of the music; and assigning expressive variation to elements of the representation by reference to an expressive 'dictionary'. The failure comes in getting the hands to do what he knows they should do. A common cause of this in my own experience of piano playing is miscalculation of an unfamiliar leap, or 'running out of fingers' in rapid passagework. At such points the expert sight reader can invent a new plan, consistent with the structural context, which he *is* able to program, so 'covering' his error with a plausible alternative.

The dissociation between plan and program also allows us to understand something which many teachers identify in their (otherwise musical) pupils as a 'failure to listen to themselves'. This typically occurs when a teacher criticizes a pupil for failing to make an expressive variation in a case where the pupil is convinced that he *did* make the variation. What could be happening here is that the pupil has formed a plan of the music where a particular note sequence is marked for expressive variation, but that the motor programming does not take account of the marking (or takes insufficient account for reliable auditory detection). The pupil bases his judgement that the expressive variation has occured on the basis of an internal monitoring of his *plan*, whereas the teacher is monitoring the *output*. The inability to monitor one's performance at the level of expressive detail is quite common, and not confined to music. Many people are unpleasantly surprised when they experience recorded versions of their own verbal or motor behaviour.

Finally, the dissociation helps to explain why two quite separate activities are necessary for the acquisition of high degrees of musical skill. On the one hand, a performer needs to listen to, analyse, and discuss, much music. These activities allow him to be able to represent music more fully; and provide him with richer plans. On the other hand, he also needs to indulge in many hundreds of hours of practice at his instrument. To a certain extent, the precise nature of what he plays is not important so long as it presents to the motor system the whole range of ballistic problems which will be encountered in the musical repertoire for his instrument. Only such practice will expose the motor system to the 'broad range of starting conditions' that will allow the system to build up effective computation routines for solving programming problems rapidly and accurately in new situations. The pedagogic use of scales and studies has, therefore, a very sound psychological basis. They ensure that the learner is exposed to the whole range of programming problems in a systematic way.

The two types of activity described here can, of course, be carried out entirely separately, and this accounts for the existence of two common 'types' of musician. The first type is the musician who can play relatively simple music with the utmost sensitivity and has a profound critical appreciation of other people's performances, but falters when high levels of speed or fluency are required. Such a person tends to spend a lot of time involved with music but neglects systematic practice. He has a highly developed skill for representing musical structure, but his motor programming is inadequate to convert representations into sound. The second type is the musician who can tackle the most demanding pieces in the repertoire from the technical point of view, but often performs them insensitively. Such a person tends to spend hours each day at his instrument, diligently attending to scales and other technical exercises, but neglects to deepen his understanding of music through analysis and critical listening. He has a finely tuned motor programming system but possesses impoverished peformance plans on which the system can act.

The master musician, of course, combines excellence in both these separate skills. Fluent sight reading is, it can be argued, a prime example of a skill which demands both these sub-skills. One needs a high degree of representational skill to be able to rapidly construct an appropriate performance plan on the basis of visual information where relevant structural cues are often only implicit, and one needs a high degree of motor programming skill to be able to assemble a fluent motor sequence at an appropriate speed. If a selection panel for some instrumental award had only five minutes in which to examine each candidate, then I believe there are good arguments for devoting the whole of that time to an observation of a candidate's sight reading performance. There can be few tasks which demand as complete a musicianship.

3.3. Rehearsal

Most musicians probably expend the majority of their musical time and effort on rehearsal. The nature and quantity of rehearsal carried out is, therefore, likely to be the most important determiner of performing skill. However, we know almost nothing about the precise ways in which musicians of differing skill go about their rehearsal. The undoubtedly useful and insightful pedagogical literature (e.g. Buck 1944; Hughes 1915) is largely built upon informal observation and personal experience. From this wide body of experience we can glean certain generalizations. Firstly, many novices find it difficult to rehearse in a productive manner (i.e. one that significantly improves performance). Their principal strategy seems to be to simply play through a passage again and again, hoping, as it were, that the mistakes will be 'ironed out'. Teachers and expert performers insist that more is required. Troublesome sections must be 'taken to pieces'. Secondly, experts insist that secure knowledge of a piece of music involves forming multiple representations of it. One of the principal problems facing moderate performers is the dissociation of the performance sequence from full conscious control. Each short section is cued by association from the preceding section so that when something goes wrong the performance cannot be rescued; memory simply 'dries up'. As a teacher, I have noticed that pupils often can gain entry to a memorized piece only at certain points. If they are stopped for discussion, they have to go back to one of the entry points to continue the performance. In contrast, experts insist that full knowledge of a piece of music entails the ability to start in at any point at will. The conscious mind should know what is coming next independently of what the fingers are doing. Achievements which experts advocate as a guarantee that a piece is properly learned include the ability to think a piece through away from the instrument, or to write it out from memory. Thirdly, most teachers acknowledge that rehearsal is transferable, so that each piece rehearsed lessens the rehearsal requirements for future pieces. Conversely, there are times when intensive rehearsal of a single piece fails to yield significant improvements. Some limit or bottleneck is reached which can only be overcome by moving on to other pieces and returning to the troublesome piece some months, or even years, later.

I wish to concentrate the substantive portion of this section around a study by Gruson (1981) which is, to my knowledge, the only recent attempt to look at musicians' rehearsal behaviour in a detailed way. Her subjects were forty piano students taking individual lessons and three professional concert pianists. Their experience was roughly assessed by noting the level of achievement on the local examination board's grading system. There are ten grades in this system which would bring a performer up to the level of proficient amateur, and each grade represents roughly one year's work on the instrument. The level of experience of the professionals was, of course, way off the top of this grading scale. Each subject was given three novel pieces, consistent with his or her grade level, to practise for 30 minutes. An audio-tape recording was made of each practice session; and then each recording was scored according to a detailed observational scale (devised by Joseph 1978). The choice of pianists as subjects was arbitrary. We have every reason to suppose that their general practising strategies are typical of musicians.

Taking all subjects together, Gruson found that uninterrupted playing accounted for about one quarter of the total practising time. The other most frequent occurrences were, repeating a single note (16.9 per cent), repeating a bar (16.7 per cent), slowing down (16.0 per cent), and errors (14.3 per cent). Of these behaviours, two (repeating a single note, and making errors) are specifically warned against by many teachers as counterproductive. Repeating a single note is unhelpful, it is argued, because the aim of rehearsal is to build up fluent integrated performance units of several notes. Errors are unhelpful because they tend to reinforce inappropriate motor patterns; the ideal is to start by playing so slowly that errors are never made. At the other end of the scale, certain advocated rehearsal techniques almost never occurred among this group of subjects. Playing with hands separately occurred only 0.97 per cent of the time, and repetitions of sections larger than the bar occured only 2.6 per cent of the time.

To examine the differences in rehearsal behaviour between pianists of different levels Gruson performed two analyses. First she calculated correlation coefficients between the incidence of each behaviour category and skill level. There were four significant positive correlations. These were behaviours which increased in frequency with increasing skill. They were: repeating a section larger than a bar ($r = 0.72$), playing hands separately ($r = 0.49$), verbalizations ($r = 0.37$), and time spent practising each piece (as opposed to playing something other than the music, stopping, etc., $r = 0.40$). The verbalizations included particularly self-guiding statements like 'slow down', 'I made a mistake, I'd better try again'. Three behaviours showed significant negative correlations; that is, they decreased with skill. They were: making errors ($r = -0.31$), repeating single notes ($r = -0.31$), and pausing for more than two seconds ($r = -0.31$). These results show that conventionally advocated rehearsal techniques increase in frequency with increasing skill, whilst non-advocated techniques become less frequent.

Gruson's second analysis used discriminant function analyses to determine which combination of practising behaviours could most parsimoniously discriminate students into three groups corresponding to apprentice (grades 1 to 8), senior student (grade 9 to diploma), and professional. This gave broadly similar results to the correlational study, and yielded repeating sections as the most reliable discriminator. Seventy-nine per cent of the subjects could be accurately classified on the basis of their use of this single behaviour. Gruson's hypothesis is that the increased use of repeating sections indicates an increased awareness of the structure of the music to be learned, where the sections repeated are isolated as significant units. The breaking down of the music into appropriate units becomes an aid to memorization and the construction of a fluent performance. For this hypothesis to be fully corroborated, we would need to see whether the sections repeated could, in fact, be isolated on *a priori* musical grounds.

Gruson's study had a second stage in which she asked a subset of her subjects (grades 2 and 6, and diploma students) to continue practising the pieces over ten sessions. This was in order to see whether continuing experience with a piece of music altered the way in which it was rehearsed. On the whole, she found few changes at any level of skill. The subjects seemed very consistent in their rehearsal behaviour, so that those behaviours which discriminated between them on the first session (particularly repeating sections) still discriminated between them on the tenth session. It looks as though skilled pianists have a repertoire of rehearsal strategies which serve them well right through the acquisition of a new piece; the less skilled are equally consistent in adopting strategies which may not be so advantageous. Gruson concludes that the major influence on rehearsal behaviour must be the experience gained from 'many hours of practising a wide variety of music pieces'. On the most cautious calculation 'many' must mean 'thousands' at the very least.

Gruson's study clearly leaves many questions unanswered. For instance, we do not know whether the differences in rehearsal strategy actually make the rehearsal more effective. It would be interesting to elicit trial performances after the first and last practice sessions. If the strategies of the experienced players are more effective, then we would expect them to show a greater improvement between the first and last sessions than the beginners. Another difficulty with the study is that age is confounded with experience. The beginners tended to be under the age of eleven, whilst the professionals were all over twenty-five. Some of the observed differences might be due to age changes in general cognitive strategies rather than specific musical experience. A study is needed where the different skill groups are matched for age. None the less, Gruson's study is a pioneering example of the kind of work which urgently needs to be done if we are to gain further insights into the acquisition of performing skills.

3.4. Expert performance

Expert performance demands a large number of sub-skills. Each of these sub-skills merits psychological investigation, and some of them have received considerable psychological study. There are specific technical skills such as vibrato in string playing and singing (Clarkson and Deutsch 1978; Seashore 1938), hand independence in piano playing (Shaffer 1981b), dynamic control of wind players (Patterson 1974), synchronization in ensemble performance (Rasch 1979), and so on. But clearly the expert is more than someone who possesses these several skills. He achieves his expertise through the simultaneous deployment of all these skills in a sustained fashion, and in a manner subservient to the overall structure of a musical composition.

As a teacher I find that one of the greatest stumbling blocks for many pupils is the requirement to attend to several dimensions of musical experience simultaneously. A pupil may be quite capable of playing a passage with appropriate dynamics, but when asked to add some phrasing then loses dynamic control, and when asked to make some third adjustment loses the other two features. Each skill is present, but to utilize it precludes significant attention to other aspects. We may express this in traditional theoretical terms by saying that each skill requires allocation of attention from a limited 'pool' of attentional resources. Somehow, the expert has managed to escape these limits. It is usually held that the expert has no more attentional resources than anyone else; rather, each skill requires little or no attention for its execution. It has become 'automatic'. In the following section I shall try to unpack some of the implications of this for music performance.

If a performer is able to perform a particular piece of music expertly, then we would be most surprised to discover this to be the *only* piece he could play. This is because we rightly assume that some of the skills displayed in the particular performance are *general* skills, learned through the performance of previous pieces of music, and applicable to future works. These skills are *used* in the learning of a new piece, but they are not significantly altered through the learning of a single new piece. The expert performance of a given piece of music is the result of the interaction of specific knowledge of this piece alone with general knowledge acquired over a wide range of musical experience. This point is worth making since for most performers it will be the *specific* problems of a particular piece which will dominate their concerns. It is therefore easy to forget that specific activities arise from, and build upon, a vast storehouse of general musical knowledge. What distinguishes the expert from the novice is the extent and availability of this knowledge.

Example 3.9 is a simple excerpt around which we can base a discussion of some of the elements of expert performance. What would be involved in arriving at an expert performance of this? Perhaps the first thing to discuss is the role of memorization, since many expert performances are indeed from memory. It is clear that memorization of a piece is a performing advantage since it frees the performer's eyes from the score and guarantees the availability of information about what is to come next. Although the job of memorization is to hold the specific sequence of notes which makes *this* piece unique, there are clearly general skills involved too. These general skills can be demonstrated by considering the additional problems posed by trying to memorize Example 3.10. Although the two excerpts have the same key, metre, and number of notes, Example 3.10 presents more difficulty because its parts are less familiar, and because the principles of construction or patterning are less straightforward. It is easy to give a concise description of

Example 3.9.

Example 3.10.

Example 3.9 such as 'a rising major scale of one octave, tonic to tonic, followed by a descending arpeggio in the same octave', etc. In contrast, it is hard to think of a description of Example 3.10 which would be more concise than an enumeration of the notes.

An important skill of memorization is the ability to encode music in terms of familiar groupings and structures. Sometimes the structure is 'hidden' and adequate performance can be achieved only when the pattern is discovered. An example from recent personal experience comes in the piano part of Samuel Barber's song 'Sea-snatch' (Op. 29 No. 6). Example 3.11 shows bars 7–9 of the piano score. I made no headway with this at all until I realised that the right hand repeats the same four-chord sequence four times (at different octaves, and minus the very last chord). Having then applied the same fingering pattern to each of the four sequences, practice rapidly improved performance. The principal reason why I did not see this pattern at the outset was the irregular beaming which visually grouped the chords within each bar, breaking up the repeated groups whose discovery was essential to my performance.

Example 3.11. From Samuel Barber, 'Sea Snatch', Op. 29, No. 6. Copyright © 1954 by G. Schirmer, Inc. Used by permission.

On other occasions the need is to find a familiar structure to which the current music can be *related*. We may remember an unusual chord as a more familiar one with something added or taken away, or an unusual melody as a scale passage with an interruption. In music of any length it is possible to use earlier events within the music to assist memory of later ones. Sometimes the same music is repeated exactly, but even when transposed or transformed, the earlier music provides a framework for economical coding. Teachers will often have had the experience of a pupil who despairs of learning a long movement until it is pointed out to him or her how fingerings worked out for one passage can be adapted for other similar passages. Sometimes learners fail to notice that two distant passages contain identical notes and so need only be learned once.

Considerations like these suggest that effective musical memory depends upon the ability to represent music in terms of groupings of notes which can be related to familiar stylistic patterns and structures, and also to other sequences within the same piece. This does not necessarily mean that these groupings will be at the forefront of consciousness during a highly polished performance from memory. Aspects of small-scale structure can become subsumed into larger performing units which are not 'analysed out' on every occasion. Taking the excerpt from the Barber song again, I found that as my fluency improved I no longer had to consciously *think* of the music in groups of four in order for my fingers to do what was required of them. Gradually the whole section became a single fluent statement, although I could impose the subdivisions on it if I wished. Most performers find that there comes a time when they can play through a well-learned piece completely on 'auto-pilot', devoting their conscious attention to something else. This experience, which some musicians describe as 'floating', and in which the hands seem to have a life of their own, is certainly an exhilarating one. It may, however, have its dangers in public performance. Unless one is supremely confident it is hard to refrain from asking oneself 'do I know what is coming next?' and panicking if the answer appears to be 'no'.

More modest examples of 'floating' underlie practically every example of skilled performance. Take Example 3.9 again. It should be within the capacity of any skilled musician to look at this for a few moments and then give a fluent performance on an instrument. A pianist, for instance, will choose an appropriate fingering. This is not a trivial matter since the options for fingering are many. The art of fingering consists in choosing a sequence which will allow legato where the music requires it and which will leave the hand in such a position that notes to follow are within its compass. There are several legitimate solutions to Example 3.9, but a very common one will involve starting on the right hand thumb (call it 1), following with 2 and 3, and then tucking the thumb under the hand for the C, continuing 2, 3 ,4 ,5, up to the G, and returning down the arpeggio with 3, 2, 1.

This is a good fingering for several reasons. Firstly, it allows the first bar to be played legato. In allegro vivace a semiquaver passage is unlikely to be executed with precision unlesss adjacent fingers are used wherever possible. Continuous legato playing up or down a scale is possible because of the opposition of the thumb to the other fingers. In this example, the thumb can be sliding rightwards under fingers 2 and 3 so that it is in position to play the fourth note on time. Secondly, the fingering allows top G to be played with the fifth finger, so allowing an easy reverse of movement down the octave without change of hand position. Finally, it allows the thumb to fall on the second beat of bar 1, so providing the opportunity for using its extra strength to accent the note if required.

Although there exists this explicit rationale for a particular fingering, most experienced pianists will find themselves playing these fingers without conscious choice. Their hands just seem to 'fall into place'. When pianists talk of music which 'lies well under the hands' they are, in part, reporting that many fingering problems are soluble at sight in this effortless way. They tend to agree about the music of which this is true, reflecting their common experience with a musical/pedagogic literature. Most performers in our culture receive intensive exposure to the classical and romantic repertoire where scales, arpeggios, and diatonic triads form a very large part of the substance of most compositions. The fingering problems associated with these features will have been solved many times in a performer's career, and it is not difficult to see how a relatively simple set of heuristic rules could provide adequate solutions to a large number of these problems. The observation of musicians' fingering sequences and the modelling of the heuristic strategies which could underlie them seems a particularly tractable and worthwhile area of study in which there is, at present, to my knowledge, no significant work.

Because ease of fingering does relate to past experience, most musicians will have had the experience of coming to a new composer or idiom whoses writing seems at first difficult to perform, but after moderate exposure becomes easier. The piano music of Olivier Messiaen, for instance, often seems unperformable to classically trained pianists who encounter it for the first time. It contains none of the traditional scales and arpeggios, and most of the chords are unfamiliar. However, after learning several pieces it becomes possible to recognize typical chord structures and sequences whose fingering problems are closely related to one another. Gradually, solutions become available without conscious effort.

A substantial objection can be made to this line of reasoning. Surely, one may argue, an expert performer who plays something from memory will have solved his fingering problems during the rehearsal stage and will have settled upon a definite fingering which he memorizes along with the notes. Whilst agreeing that this is possible, and may sometimes happen, I would wish to argue that expert performance is often characterized by the fresh reconstruction of performance parameters such as fingering on every occasion. I have several reasons for believing this. One is that expert performers are often prolific, of their nature and of necessity. By this I mean that an expert performer can learn a new piece to concert standard very quickly, and can have many pieces in repertoire concurrently. The argument from economy suggests that he will only learn what new information is needed to perform the new piece, using his general musicianship to supply the rest. This will, perhaps, be particularly true of orchestral players, accompanists, and exponents of new music. There is just not the time to learn each piece to the level of complete 'floating'.

A second reason concerns the existence of variability between different performances of the same piece by the same performer. The reason that it is worth going to live music performances is that each performance will be different. Regular concert-goers will talk of a performer as being 'particularly inspired' on one day, 'detached' on another, and so on. Doubtless, some of this talk is not due to anything the musician does, but the phenomenon is too omnipresent for it to be all in the mind of the listener. Musicians themselves are aware of times when their performances 'reach new heights' or 'fail to come alive'. If all aspects of a performance were predetermined in a memorized plan, such variability would be inexplicable. If, however, many performance decisions are made anew at each performance, then it becomes easier to understand performance variability. Of course, such a process does not necessitate variability. A performer could make the *same* decision each time. Variability, therefore, also implies some *optionality* in whatever system it is that controls the construction of a performance. Such optionality is indeed highly probable when we are dealing with complex patterned material like music. Such material often displays structural ambiguity; that is, it can be grouped in different ways if different principles are invoked (rhythmic, harmonic, melodic, etc.,) or a given element can be serving a double function with respect to surrounding elements (see Chapter 2, section 5.4). Performance, on the other hand, is unambiguous—one has to assign definite values of loudness, timbre, and duration to each note. On one occasion a performer may choose performance parameters which emphasize a note in virtue of its rhythmic importance. On another occasion he may choose a less emphatic performance in virtue of the subsidiary harmonic function of the note.

Expert performance is also characterized by what commentators often call grasp of the large-scale structure or 'architecture' of a composition. One factor which may contribute to this grasp is the internal consistency of a performance. In much music we would expect to find the same theme performed in the same way on each of its occurrences through a movement. For instance, if we choose a given articulation for the first entry of a fugue, subsequent entries should have similar articulation (unless there is some principled reason for change). Inexpert performance is often characterized by inconsistency. The way a theme is played on subsequent occasions is likely to be determined by local contingencies. In a fugue, for instance, it is relatively easy for a keyboard player to give attention to the articulation of the first entry, because it is unaccompanied. A subsequent entry may comprise one line among two or three to be performed at the same time, with all the fingering problems this poses; and articulation often suffers as a result.

Over a longer time scale expert performance is characterized by control over the progression of speed and dynamic. It is not a trivial achievement to keep a piece at the same speed throughout, or to return to a starting speed after variation. The marshalling of dynamic resources to arrive at a climax at precisely the right musical moment is similarly hard to achieve. Unintentional 'drift' in speed, mismanagement of *crescendi*, reaching a maximum too soon or too late: these are commonplace faults of inexpert performers, and well known to any teacher.

There is almost no scientific work on the features of large-scale performance which contribute towards a listener's judgement of expertise. A notable exception is the work of Shaffer (1981b) on timing, and we may use his study as an example of the direction that such work could take. He recorded piano performances of classical music in such a way that the time intervals between successive notes could be accurately measured. It was then possible to examine the variability of timing in some detail. Of particular interest was the *covariance between note durations*. Two quantities covary positively if they tend to increase or decrease together. In a smooth *accelerando*, for instance, the durations of notes near to one another in time should covary positively. Notes at one point in the sequence tend *all* to be faster or slower than notes at other points. In contrast, two quantities covary negatively if one decreases as the other increases. Shaffer's data show that in expert metrical performances of Bach and Bartok the durations of adjacent notes tended to covary negatively. This suggests the operation of a compensatory mechanism such that if one duration is shorter than an envisaged ideal, the next note is given a longer duration, so that the *pair* of notes has a duration close to the intended ideal for that pair. This means that some monitoring and timing is taking place at a level above that of the individual note. An oversimplified, but generally correct, conclusion to be drawn from Shaffer's rather complex data is that timing in expert performers operates hierarchically. The performer generates a pulse which specifies the start of a *group* of notes (be it a bar, beat, or whatever) and then uses learned procedures for timing notes within the group. Clearly, the likelihood of timing 'drift' will be reduced if the performer can operate with such a pulse. One may hypothesize that inexpert performance is characterized by an inability to maintain performance with reference to a pulse. Rather, timing is determined locally by procedures for halving or doubling preceding durations, or for playing common rhythmic patterns. Unfortunately, Shaffer did not compare his expert performers with non-experts; but one informal observation supporting the notion of a deficiency in pulse control is the inability of many inexpert musicians to count out a steady beat whilst playing music where the beat is variously subdivided. This is similar to Ibbotson and Morton's (1981) finding that non-musicians are less adept at a particular tapping task than are musicians. The task entails tapping a steady beat with one limb whilst tapping a rhythm with the other. Curiously, the ability to do this seems to depend partly upon the combination of limbs used. Most people can tap a beat with the left hand against a right hand rhythm, but not vice-versa.

The reader will have noticed a concentration on piano performance in this chapter. This is partly because I am a pianist myself, and have the greatest awareness of performance issues on this instrument. It is also because most of the available research uses pianists. To what extent are the principles isolated for piano performance applicable across the whole range of musical instruments? At the highest level I would wish to claim a degree of generality for the observations made in this chapter. The influence of structure and patterning on the construction of performance plans and motor programs arises from the nature of tonal music and its psychological representation, and not from the nature of the instrument which realizes it. At a lower level, however, the technical and expressive problems presented by the various instruments are very different. Pianists escape a whole set of problems concerning pitch, intonation, and timbral modulation, which face string players, singers, and wind players. The means whereby performers achieve control over pitch and timbre are not well understood, although there is some evidence for the existence of a homeostatic feedback loop which allows performers to make micro-adjustments to pitch so as to keep it in line with an intended pitch (Deutsch and Clarkson 1959).

Modulations of pitch and timbre are not simply 'problems' to be overcome. They are part of the expressive repertoire of music. Spectral analysis of natural sounds produced by, for instance, professional horn players show that, during a single long note, there is not just one typical 'horn spectrum' but as many as 30 or 40 different spectra at different times, which give rise to the aural impression of a 'living' sound. If a computer-synthesized horn uses only one spectrum for the whole duration of a note (leaving aside the initial attack portion as a separate problem), the resulting sound is completely flat and 'un-horn-like'. Furthermore, performers can *control* pitch and timbre modulation to achieve expressive variation related to the musical structure, just as pianists use timing and loudness variations. Researchers since Seashore (1938) have made inroads into the measurement of the dimensions of these variations, but little attempt has been made to account for the control structures which *assign* variations in the service of musical communication. Sundberg's (1978, 1982) preliminary work with singers is a notable exception.

The research of Rasch (1979) is one of the few recent examples of work with instrumental performers other than pianists. He was concerned with *synchronization* between three independent performers in string and wind trios. His professional subjects played classical pieces from their repertoire, and the relations between the onset times of notionally simultaneous sounds were examined. One finding was that the violin lead the other instruments in the string trio by some 4–8 ms on average. This may have implied an intentional strategy which 'highlighted' the main melodic instrument. However, the 'scatter' of asynchrony was quite high, and the mean asynchrony between any two instruments was between 30 and 50 ms. This suggests an error component which would be consistent with a homeostatic timing mechanism which kept on target by corrective overshooting and undershooting adjustments. Interestingly enough, these asynchronies mostly went unnoticed by listeners. The performances of the professional ensembles gave the impression of perfect synchronization. This is somewhat surprising, since in ideal experimental conditions (e.g. Hirsh 1959) subjects can easily judge which of two sounds separated by 20 ms came first. This is one piece of evidence which confirms my earlier remark that we need to examine perceptual acuity in real music contexts rather than generalize from the result of 'ideal' psychophysical studies. There are several possible reasons for Rasch's finding. One has to do with the fact that the different instruments occupied different 'pitch streams' (see Chapter 5.2).

Rasch has also shown that perfect synchronization actually impairs the ability of listeners to identify the component notes of a chord, so that a small degree of asynchronization contributes to the perceptual clarity of the separate lines. This is a reason why some computer-synthesized polyphonic music lacks the contrapuntal clarity of live performances. Advanced programs incorporate a timing 'jigger' to better simulate live sound.

Finally, Rasch discovered a small number of relatively large onset difference times in his data (i.e. from 100 to 200 ms). These *were* clearly audible to listeners. It is possible that these were technical errors, but we must be open to the possibility that some of them were *intentional* timing deformations related to the musical structure. We cannot, however, know this for certain without controls of the sort imposed by Shaffer (1981b) or Sloboda (1983). For instance, intentional variation should be repeated in a second performance.

Although the literature on expert performance is sparse, it is possible to state with some certainty what the principles underlying such performance are, albeit at a level of some generality. Firstly, we see the existence of knowledge of large-scale groupings or patterns within the music which control performance. In many instances this control is hierarchical; parameters which apply to a larger grouping determine the settings for elements within the group. In contrast, inexpert performance is typically controlled by the superficial characteristics of the musical 'foreground'. Secondly, hierarchical control is supported by highly flexible procedures for solving local problems. These procedures operate rapidly, and often without the need for conscious monitoring. The inexpert performer cannot exercise higher-level control because his resources are fully committed to managing the solution of these immediate local problems. Thirdly and finally, the expert has the means to adequately monitor his own performance and take corrective action before he deviates too grossly from plan. Adequate monitoring is not so much a question of listening as of knowing what to listen for. There must be a clear representation of the intended sound if appropriate adjustments are to be made to the actual sound. It is probable, though, that what allows expert performers to make feedback adjustments so effectively is that they are not dependent on consciously monitored feedback at all times and levels. An important feature of skilled motor programming is the ability to operate relatively independently of conscious feedback. Thus, a performer can choose how and when to monitor his performance, knowing which aspects can be safely left to learned programming procedures. For a fuller discussion of experimental work on feedback in performance the reader is referred to Sloboda (1982), which also contains a brief account of social and motivational factors in music performance, which fall outside the scope of this book.

4. Composition and improvisation

4.1. Introduction

In the previous chapter we examined how performers go about the task of realizing in sound a pre-existing composition, either held in memory or specified by a score. We now turn to the creative process itself, whereby new pieces of music are generated.

There is a vast body of literature on the musical compositions which figure prominently in our art culture, but most of this deals with the product of composition, not the process. Even critical analysis, which, according to Meyer (1973), 'attempts to understand and explain the choices made by a composer in a particular work' (p. 18), is concerned more with the musical relationships evident in the finished product than with the moment-to-moment psychological history of the genesis of a theme or passage. The analyst may assert that a theme has the structure it does because it was the composer's intention to create a particular balance, or a particular contrast. He cannot, however, say whether this intention ever figured *directly* as a goal in the compositional process. The theme may have arisen as the result of some unrelated strategy, retained because of the subsequent *discovery* by the composer that it did, in fact, possess a quality of balance or contrast that recommended it. It is also possible that certain features of a composition highlighted by critical analysis were no part of the composer's intention, conscious or otherwise. In a system of inter-related sounds as large as, say, a symphony, there are bound to be some relationships discoverable by analysis which were neither noticed nor designed by the composer.

How, then, are we to gain psychological insight into this central and fundamental musical process? It seems to me that there are *four* possible methods of enquiry. First is the examination of the history of a particular composition as displayed in the composer's written manuscripts. Sketches and notebooks, if datable, can show how a composition grew and changed over the time during which it exercised the composer's mind. Some composers. such as Beethoven, made sketches which were returned to and re-moulded over periods of years. Even where sketches do not exist we can sometimes discover something about the compositional sequence from the final manuscript. For instance, we shall see that differences of ink in Mozart's orchestral manuscripts show that he often wrote out the melody and bass line of entire sections before returning at some later date to 'fill in' the harmony lines.

Second is the examination of what composers say about their own compositional processes. Many composers have been reluctant to do this. However, a few have tried to say in a general and retrospective fashion what happens when they compose.

Third is the 'live' observation of composers during a session of composition. This requires a rare degree of co-operation from a composer and, to my knowledge, there is only one published example in the psychological literature (Reitman 1965). During such a session one can observe the notes written down, their sequence and grouping in time. In addition, one may obtain concurrent comment from the subject about what he conceives himself to be doing. It has become usual when observing problem solving behaviour of many sorts to ask the subject to 'think aloud', supplying what is known as a 'protocol' for subsequent analysis.

Fourth and last is the observation and description of improvisatory performance. This is the special case where the composer is also the performer, producing a novel musical statement without premeditation in a public context. One may argue that improvisation reveals more of psychological interest than does a score. The improviser has fewer opportunities to cover his tracks. However, the constraints of improvisation—immediacy and fluency—make it likely that there are processes which improvisation and composition do not share. Indeed, it would be very unwise to assume that all composers or all improvisers go about their art in the same way. The most superficial reading of the musical literature provides abundant evidence that different practitioners habitually go through very different mental steps to arrive at a finished composition. As Neisser (1983) has succinctly expressed it, 'practise does not make all practitioners alike, it just makes them all effective'.

My intention in this chapter is to say something about what each of these four methods can contribute to psychological understanding, with illustrations, where possible, from the musical and psychological literature. I shall be highlighting two facets of the psychological activities involved. One is the persistent occurence of superordinate structures or plans which seem to guide and determine the detailed note-by-note working out. The other is the degree to which these plans can, particularly in composition, be rather provisional. They can, for instance, be changed in the light of the way a particular passage 'turns out'. The reader should be warned that composition is the least studied and least well understood of all musical processes, and that there is no substantial psychological literature to review. Whilst I hope to retain an empirical spirit in what I say, it is more probable here than elsewhere that my story will be inadequate, or simply wrong. I am emboldened to proceed only because of the absolute centrality of this aspect of musical cognition.

4.2. Manuscript evidence

4.2.1. *Sketches*

A sketch is an incomplete or preliminary draft of a work (or part of it) which was written prior to the final manuscript. Composers have differed in the extent to which they made use of sketches, particularly in the extent to which they were prepared to commit early ideas to paper. The sketches of many composers are nearly complete drafts of the final version, requiring little or no radical revision. Many of the extant sketches by Mozart, Haydn, and Schumann, for instance, display this 'finished' quality (Forte 1961). Beethoven, on the other hand, was a prolific sketch writer, filling many notebooks with fragments and sections which show considerable difference from the finished work. He often worked on a particular composition over a period of years. For instance, a first sketch of the opening theme for Op. 111 is found in a notebook which predates the final version by almost 20 years.

This feature of Beethoven's compositional life has led some commentators to an over-romanticized view of Beethoven as a tormented genius struggling with intractable raw material to mould it into the service of higher art. Early commentators on the sketches offered them primarily as *moral* comment on the character of the composer. Johnson (1980) sees the classic transcriptions and commentaries of Nottebohm (1887) as concerned with 'portraying the demonic opposition [. . . of the raw musical material] and leaving us to marvel at the spiritual power which eventually subdued it' (p. 4).

Our concerns are rather different. We must ask whether the sketches are capable of revealing anything about the cognitive processes which led to the genesis of particular works or passages. How did an initial idea come to the composer; what types of transformations and combinations were applied to the original ideas; what goals were being worked towards; in virtue of what were initial sketches rejected as unsatisfactory?

Johnson (1980) argues that musical analysis of the sketches has not yielded any fresh insights into the finished compositions. He identifies two principal reasons for this. One is the overdependence by modern musicologists on prior analysis of the finished work, and the assumption that it alone has the well-formed structure prescribed, for instance, on a harmonic level by Schenker (see Chapter 2). The sketches then tend to be branded as failed experiments—themes which go places that Beethoven didn't want. For us it would, perhaps, be more fruitful to consider the sketches as signs of competence, necessary and enabling resources for the compositional process. As psychologists we seek not so much fresh insights into the finished composition as fresh insights into the *means* by which a composition is finished.

The second reason for lack of progress is identified by Johnson as a deep pessimism among musicologists about the possibility of understanding the compositional act. He quotes Kramer (1973) as symptomatic of this attitude:

'The creative act is mysterious . . . It is an act so complex, motivated by so many impulses—as remote and impersonal as the entire web of knowable history, and as remote and intensely personal as the sum of one man's experience—that the material evidence (records of the act) are little more than occasional memos of a deeper, continual process' (pp. 516–17). Whilst Kramer is undoubtedly right, he describes conditions which appertain to many, if not most, processes of psychological interest. Psychologists, and indeed most other scientists, are used to operating in such situations. Progress is possible because there are ways of achieving a partial understanding of a system on quite restricted data.

Let us, then, take a small example from Beethoven's sketch books which illustrates the potentials and problems of sketch study. I choose the sketch of the first movement of the Opus 10 No. 3 Piano Sonata (Example 4.1) from

Example 4.1. From sketch of Beethoven, Piano Sonata, Op. 10, No. 3. First movement. Transcribed by Johnson (1980).

the Fischof Miscellany (transcribed by Johnson 1980; F45V, 1) more or less at random, but because it is reasonably extended, and shows many typical features of his sketches.

The first problem is to know the time scale of the composition of the sketch. Changes in paper, ink, or writing style, could signify a long break in the compositional process; but shorter breaks are of psychological interest too. For instance, what happened in this sketch on line 1 where five bars are crossed out? Were these bars the result of a compositional 'slip of the pen' noticed immediately and corrected, or do they represent a genuine first attempt which was then perceived as unsatisfactory, to be followed by more compositional thought? I believe we have some reason to prefer the latter explanation. The sketch as a whole reveals several clear musical features: first the repeated use of the descending four-note scale from the tonic D as a thematic motif; second the use of the four-bar phrase as the basic musical statement; third, the use of classical sonata form as a large-scale structure.

We can take these three features as constraining what was written, either before pen was set to paper, or very shortly after writing began. Both versions of the first phrase lead the music upwards from a tonic D harmony to the dominant A. In the first (deleted) attempt a simple ascending scale is used. In the second attempt the first half of the ascent is arpeggiated, taking the melody up to F sharp before descending by way of G sharp to the A. The two versions are not similar at a superficial level, but they do honour the constraints outlined above, as does the final version of the theme (Example 4.2) which is different from both sketches. We will never know precisely what motivated the rejection of the two sketched themes in favour of the final version, but the sketches provide compelling evidence that successive solutions were generated within the limits set by initial constraints or plans. Whatever alternative was generated, it had to leave the initial thematic motif intact, and had to move from a D harmony to an A harmony in four bars. We see in this sketch a persistent harmonic and rhythmic plan, albeit provisional, for the *structure* of the section, within which melodic alterations could be made.

Some aspects of such a plan are, however, provisional. This is clear when we examine the final version (Example 4.2). Here we discover that, after the first phrase, Beethoven abandons the strict four-bar phrase scheme. The next three phrases each have *six* bars, so as to produce an asymmetric first subject section of $4 + 6 + 6 + 6 = 22$ bars. This unconventional scheme makes the first section musically novel, although stretching rather than abandoning the original conception. The harmonic movement of the first subject section and the phrase structure of the B minor bridge passage are preserved.

In sum, then, structural similarities and contrasts between the sketches and the final version suggest a hierarchy of constraints within which Beethoven was operating. He was making successive attempts at 'filling in' a structure which, in certain respects, was already specified in his mind. We

Example 4.2. From Beethoven, Piano Sonata, Op. 10, No. 3, First movement. Copyright © G. Henle Verlag, Munchen. Reproduced with permission.

see, however, that some initial constraints (such as the four bar phrase structure) were abandoned during the compositional process in the service of some newly discovered goal.

A second problem for us to consider is the extent to which significant compositional thought takes place at times when the composer writes nothing. When comparing two consecutive sketches it is unwise to assume that they are close neighbours in the compositional process. They may be separated by extensive unwritten compositional thought. In Beethoven's case this is particularly likely in view of one of his own remarks from a written conversations with Louis Schlosser in 1822 (Hamburger, 1952; reprinted in Morgenstern 1956):

I carry my thoughts about with me for a very long time, before writing them down . . . I change many things, discard others, and try again until I am satisfied; then, in my head, I begin to elaborate the work in its breadth, it narrowness, its height, its depth and, since I am aware of what I want to do, the underlying idea never deserts me. It rises, it grows, I hear and see the image in front of me from every angle, as if it had been cast, like sculpture, and only the labour of writing it down remains, a labour which need not take long, but varies according to the time at my disposal, since I very often work on several things at the same time.

This passage confirms what we deduce from the sketches, that a distinction can be made between the basic idea and the detailed note-by-note working out. The former is present in the mind over a longer time span; the latter is subject to repeated experiment.

A third problem concerns the extent to which a sketch means for an outsider what it means for the composer. It can be argued that the purpose of writing a sketch is to be able to remind oneself of a musical idea that one must lay aside for some time. It is an *aide memoire*, not a full record. A composer may use cryptic or skeletal signs in the knowledge that these will be sufficient to retrieve the whole idea. In Beethoven's case, sketches are often confined to a single melody line without harmony or counterpoint. It would be extremely unwise to imagine that Beethoven thus *conceived* of a melody before assigning it a harmonic or contrapuntal context. Rather, we should conclude that Beethoven wrote this much only, knowing that he would be able to retrieve or generate afresh the remainder from examination of what he had written. A teacher's lecture notes are personalized in a similar way. They allow him or her to retrieve what was in mind at the time of preparation, but there is no guarantee that a colleague would reconstruct the same lecture from the notes.

There is neither time nor space here to enter into an exhaustive study of sketching processes in different composers. It is a lengthy task in which significant musicological and psychological effort is still|required. However, it is never wise to confine even preliminary remarks to one case. As a comparison I now turn to something from a completely different period and style—the sketches that Stravinsky made for his *Rite of Spring*. A collection which comprises about four-fifths of all the sketches for this work is now reproduced, with commentary by Robert Craft (Stravinsky 1969). In Stravinsky's case there is little need for transcription since the original is highly legible in most places.

There are some instructive comparisons we may make with Beethoven's sketches. Like Beethoven, Stravinsky very often records a mixture of ideas on the same page—sometimes successive workings out of the same material, sometimes different material. Secondly, also like Beethoven, he does not stick to the chronology of the final work, but jumps forwards or backwards in sequence. Thirdly, like Beethoven, many of the sketches are skeletal—a single melody line, a chord sequence, a rhythmic pattern: rarely does one find a full orchestral score. Once again the sketches seem to act as *aides-memoires*, recording the themes and ideas from which the rest can be reconstructed at a later date.

Stravinsky differs from Beethoven as well. Whereas Beethoven's sketches use predominantly the single melodic line, a great number of Stravinsky's sketches depict several simultaneous strands. The chord structure is often fully specified, together with the main contrapuntal elements, and a preliminary indication of how the parts should be disposed among the orchestral instruments. These differences are not surprising in view of the profound differences in style and content between the music of the two composers. In his early and middle periods, at least, Beethoven worked within a conventional harmonic and formal framework. The 'rules' of diatonic harmony and sonata-form were well known. Within this framework, the melodic element became both the main individuating factor of a particular work, and also the main determining factor for the other features. Someone conversant with the classical style could, without too much difficulty, reconstruct a plausible sonata movement from the melody line alone (indeed, this kind of task is often used as a pedagogic exercise). Stravinsky, however, was working within a set of constraints whose bounds were much less well defined. His use of tonality was novel, both in terms of the immediate harmonic effects he created and also in terms of harmonic movement. For a full analysis of Stravinsky's musical style the reader is referred to Forte (1978). Suffice here to say that in this work Stravinsky was forging a new style with respect to the prevailing musical culture and also extending his *own* style. In such a situation it becomes likely that Stravinsky *needed* to capture more of the textural detail in his sketches. Such detail was sufficiently novel to constitute the *essence* of the composition, not something which could be reconstructed from a single line.

Another difference between Stravinsky and Beethoven concerns the number of preliminary sketches made before something approaching a final version was produced. Stravinsky made, on the whole, considerably fewer sketches than Beethoven. We may often observe single sketches of a few ideas which are then combined into a contrapuntal whole on the same page. The ideas themselves are often unchanged from the first sketches. Subsequent sketches show their combination and extension rather than their transformation. When transformations do occur, they are often radical and bold, leaping to the final version without any notated intermediaries. Craft draws attention to one striking example of this on p. 35 of the sketches (Example 4.3). The page is headed 'Dance of the Earth' and at the bottom we find a sketch which is essentially the final version of the first statement of the main theme of this section. Above it are four melodic fragments. Three of these arer quite clearly incorporated into the final version; but the very first sketch appears, at first, to be quite anomalous. It is a simple folk-like chorale in consecutive thirds which does not appear in the section, or anywhere else in

Example 4.3. Page 35 of Stravinsky's sketches for *The Rite of Spring* (1969). Reproduced by permission of M. F. Meyer.

the work. Despite its unfamiliarity, Craft convincingly argues that it is, in fact, the point of departure of the genesis of this section (given in the final version piano duet arrangement in Example 4.4). He writes:

We discover, first, that the composer translates the melody from the top to a middle voice (second stave of the piano score in Example 4.4); second, that he forms harmonic aggregates from it, superimposing the notes as if they were *appogiature*; third, that he exploits its whole tone context—the harmonization in major thirds—in an ostinato bass-figure with the F sharp (rather than the C) as the root tone; and fourth, that he renovates the rhythm (p. xxiii).

Example 4.4. From Stravinsky, *The Rite of Spring*, Dance of the earth. Piano duet version. Copyright © Boosey and Hawkes Limited, London. Reproduced with permission.

This is not an isolated example, and Craft uses the sketches to postulate a basic compositional technique for Stravinsky.'Many of the composer's first notations were simple folk-like melodies which he transformed by a number of face-lifting devices including changes in note order, the extracting of essences, and the grafting of new rhythms and characters of tempo.' It is only the existence of these apparently anomalous folk melodies side by side with their transformed versions in the sketches that allows us this unique insight into Stravinsky's compositional processes.

We may ask what allowed Stravinsky to jump from first idea to radically transformed final version in one step? It is unwise to assume that Stravinsky had a surer technique, or that the transformations he used could be applied with less extensive cogitation than Beethoven. The probable difference between the two composers is the time scale over which each was prepared to let an idea develop. Beethoven kept themes with him for several years. He needed to notate intermediate versions while he moved on to other things. Stravinsky, however, moved from initial conception to final theme over a much shorter time span, during which he worked on few other sections, and certainly on no other compositions. We know, in addition, that he composed at the piano (Stravinsky 1936, p. 14). It is plausible to suppose that ideas intermediate between initial and final versions were tried out on the piano, modified, and discarded, without any need for notation. The time scale was short enough for the whole process to be kept in mind until the final version. The structure of the work—short, contrasting episodes—would help such a strategy. At one level, each small section of 20 or 30 bars could be composed as a self-contained entity.

It is worth commenting, as Craft does, that many of the initial folk-like melodic fragments share common characteristics; such as single step movement up and down the scale, a slightly obsessive character brought about by repetitions of single notes or short motifs, harmonization in parallel thirds, etc. Such similarities lead one to suppose that there is a central core of thematic ideas to which Stravinsky returned again and again for his basic compositional material. It is this thematic unity at the heart of diversity which helps to make the work one of the most powerful compositional achievements of the twentieth century.

4.2.2. *The final manuscript*

It is clear that the study of sketches can, despite all the difficulties, provide some valuable insights into the compositional process. As mentioned earlier, however, not all composers have left sketches. Some composers write very little prior to the final draft. This, together with remarks attributed to such composers as Handel and Mozart has led, in some quarters, to a view of their composition as a form of dictation from inspiration, where the sounds of a work parade themselves fully formed in the imagination—the composer's task being simply to capture them with the pen. And so, composers of fluent inspiration, such as Mozart, are contrasted with composers such as Beethoven who had to do conscious work on their material, as their sketches show.

This division of composers into two classes is, I believe, a gross oversimplification based on an erroneous equation of sketching with conscious compositional effort, and on inadequate attention to the details of what composers say about their own compositional processes (see section 3 of this chapter, to follow). Beethoven's comment already quoted on p. 107 asserts that there was much compositional effort before anything was committed to paper, even though he was a prolific sketcher. Also, the evidence we have of how composers such as Mozart wrote out their final manuscripts is inconsistent with a 'dictation' hypothesis.

It is a little unclear what the constraints of 'dictation' are, but we may start by assuming the constraints that exist in 'real' dictation, where a musician is required to notate an unknown passage played or sung to him by someone else. In this case, the length, speed, and complexity of the passage will be crucial to success. The subject will be engaged in a struggle to 'keep up' with the music, missing out fast passagework and complex harmony whilst making some attempt to get down the more straightforward and slow-moving sections. Clearly, Mozart scores show no evidence of this type of struggle. Perhaps, however, we should loosen the constraints a little. Maybe the composer has control over the speed of 'playback' so that he is able to stem the flow of inspiration for long enough to adequately record all the details. In this case we would expect to see a score written out 'vertically' with each section completely transcribed before going on to the next section. However, recently published facsimiles of Mozart's autographs (for instance, Mozart, 1979) tell a quite different story. It is fortunate for us that Mozart changed ink during the writing out of *Die Zauberflote* ('The Magic Flute'). The second ink used has faded more quickly than the first, so that the passage of time has revealed the writing history. In many of the movements, Mozart's first task was to write out the entire melody and bass lines on the outer staves, leaving gaps for the inner parts. At a later date, using a different ink, he then went back over the score to write out the inner parts.

In order to hold to a 'dictation' hypothesis, this data forces us to postulate some form of storage of the received composition such that Mozart could return to it at will and obtain repeated 'playbacks'. In other words, there would have to be *two* dictation processes: an initial one when the inspirational stream was 'fixed' in memory—a mental process requiring no overt activity; then a series of playback dictations whereby what was fixed in memory became fixed on paper.

Even this story, however, leaves unsolved puzzles. Why, for instance, should Mozart write out melody and bass first? Surely any order of writing out would be as efficient as any other. Suppose, for example, that a playback allowed a single line to be copied. Why not, then, work down the score from top to bottom? Then there is a further puzzling feature of the Mozart manuscripts. There are occasions when, in the first ink, Mozart has filled out the whole score for a few bars. At other points, isolated passages in a few interior parts are written in the first ink. Such points are not musically arbitrary. They consist of linking passages between sections, closing orchestral cadences, important counter-subjects, and other points where interior parts have particular prominence or importance. It seems as if Mozart was anxious to 'fix' these particular passages on paper, perhaps in the fear that they would be less easy to retrieve on another occasion.

We move, then, towards the notion that whatever was held in Mozart's memory was not a simple serial concatenation of notes—some mental tape-recorder which could be turned on or off at will. Rather, it was a structured and sectionalized representation which identified crucial parts within a super-ordinate plan. The first writing allowed Mozart to fix the crucial individuating elements of the composition on paper. These elements would allow the re-construction of the rest even if the overall plan was lost from memory. For Mozart, writing out was not so much dictation as the negotiation, in a planned way, of a highly structured internal representation.

There is, of course, no manuscript evidence which could possibly be per-tinent to the question of a prior 'mental dictation', at least for those com-posers who did not leave sketches. It is entirely consistent with the manuscript evidence that Mozart 'heard' his compositions as once-for-all hallucinations, played for him on an imaginary orchestra by his unconscious mind. The representation of such 'performances' in a structured memory form could well have been the result of a conscious strategy for retaining the details of the hallucination, just as we argued earlier that such strategies were re-sponsible for success in remembering Allegri's *Miserere* (Chapter 1).

Such a picture is, however, profoundly unsatisfactory for a cognitive psy-chologist, because it leaves unexplained the unconscious processes by which a highly structured composition could come to appear, fully formed, in the composer's consciousness. If any composer was, or is, such a 'recipient' of unconsciously formed compositions, then the prospect for analysing and understanding the compositional process are not good.

In fact, when we move on to consider verbal evidence, we will find very few instances where compositional processes are totally inscrutable to the individual concerned. The most convincing case of 'unconscious com-position' on a large scale is that of Rosemary Brown, who claims to receive compositions from dead composers by dictation. The works so produced, mainly for piano, are certainly coherent, and characteristic of the various composers she names. Although she is a reasonably competent pianist who is acquainted with the classical and romantic piano repertoire, she has no formal compositional training. Her verbal reports and her writing technique are consistent with a literal note-by-note dictation process, and, unless she is the perpertrator of an elaborate hoax spanning many years, her compositions provide incontrovertible evidence for the possibility of unconscious com-position on an extended scale. Parrott (1978) reports a first hand observation of Rosemary Brown at work:

I have watched the process many times and have often filmed it. You will know better than I how normal composition actually occurs: I have certainly never seen anything like the process Mrs Brown uses. The music literally flows onto the paper in a continuous stream—sometimes both clefs together, sometimes one first and then the other. And all the time Mrs Brown chats away: 'Not so fast; did you say natural or flat? This G or the octave higher?', etc. And as fast as she can write, so it's taken down.

4.3. Composers' writings on their own compositional processes

To give a flavour of the kind of insight we can gain from examination of composers' writings, I wish to begin this section with four short extracts from the writings of various composers, without comment or identification.

(*a*) It has been my own experience in creative activity that a motive or a two to four measure melodic phrase occurs to me suddenly. I put it down on paper and immediately extend it to an eight, sixteen, or thirty-two bar phrase, which naturally does not remain unaltered, but after a shorter or longer 'maturing' is gradually worked out in definitive form. . . . This work now proceeds at a rate which depends primarily on my awaiting the moment at which my imagination is capable and ready to serve me further.

(*b*) You may ask me where I obtain my ideas (for a theme). I cannot answer this with certainty: they come unbidden.'

(*c*) Whence and how (my ideas) come, I know not; nor can I force them. Those ideas that please me I retain in memory, and am accustomed, as I have been told, to hum them to myself. If I continue in this way, it soon occurs to me how I may turn this or that morsel to account . . . agreeably to the rules of counterpoint, to the peculiarities of the various instruments.

(*d*) The first stage in the composer's work is . . . 'inspiration.' The composer . . . 'has an idea' . . . consisting of definite musical notes and rhythms which will engender for him the momentum with which his musical thoughts proceed. The inspiration may come in a flash, or as sometimes happens it may grow and develop gradually. [In this latter case] the inspiration takes the form . . . not of a sudden flash of music, but a clearly envisaged impulse towards a certain goal for which the composer was obliged to strive . . .

After inspiration and conception comes execution. The process of execution is first of all that of listening inwardly to the music as it shapes itself; of allowing the music to grow; of following both inspiration and conception wherever they may lead. A phrase, a motif, a rhythm, even a chord, may contain within itself, in the composer's imagination, the energy which produces movement. It will lead the composer on, through the forces of its own momentum or tension, to other phrases, other motifs, other chords. . . .

[The composer] is not so much conscious of his ideas as possessed by them. Very often he is unaware of his exact processes of thought till he is through with them; extremely often the completed work is incomprehensible to him immediately after it is finished. Why? Because his experience in creating the work is incalculably more intense than any later experience he can have from it; because the finished product is, so to speak, the goal of that experience, and not in any sense a repetition of it.

These quotes show, I believe, that composers have been capable of providing coherent and articulate accounts of their inner experiences. They span about 150 years, yet contain so much that coheres across the accounts that one has some confidence in taking them to isolate some of the fundamental features of the compositional process and the creative experience. Before we examine the psychological implications of these quotations in detail it may be as well to identify them:

(*a*) Richard Strauss (1949); translated Morgenstern (1956).

(*b*) Beethoven (1822); from Hamburger (1952). This should be read in conjunction with the quote on p. 107, which comes from the same letter.

(*c*) Attributed to Mozart (1789?); from Anderson (1938).

(*d*) Roger Sessions (1941).

I would like to focus on the agreement across accounts about the existence of two stages in composition: the first called 'inspiration' by Sessions, where a skeletal idea or theme appears in consciousness; the second called 'execution', where the idea is subject to a series of more conscious and deliberate processes of extension and transformation. This dichotomy is by no means confined to musical composition, and is to be found in every branch of creative activity, as collections such as those of Ghiselin (1952) and Vernon (1970) show. It is as if the creative artist has a consciously known repertoire of things he can do with basic material, but has no such repertoire for generating the first germs on which he exercise his craft. The inspiration seems almost externally 'given', much as a sculptor may be given a lump of stone of particular shape and texture to work upon. Compositional skill entails the existence of a repertoire of ways of extending and building from the given, by discovering and using its inherent properties in principled ways. It is much easier to discover what composers do with themes, through examination of sketches and writings, than to discover where first themes come from. Analytic writing on musical compositions shows how extended works are built from kernel themes by means of such devices as transposition, augmentation, subdivision and recombination of elements, changes of rhythm, etc. Much of what we identify as compositional style inheres in the habitual ways in which composers modify initial thematic material.

Yet even if a composer is selective in the types of transformation he uses, there is still too much freedom. Anyone can learn 'tricks of the trade' and concatenate them together, but the result can be weak and lacking in integrity. It is clear that skilled composers are very hard on themselves, rejecting many permissible developments as unsatisfactory; but just as they are unable to articulate where inspiration comes from, so they are very unclear about the criteria by which they choose among the available ways of developing a theme.

It seems to me that the choice of the 'right' development may be governed by considerations of large-scale structure and balance, as discussed in Chapter 2. The art of composition lies, in part, in choosing extensions of initial thematic ideas that honour superordinate constraints, often to be formalized in terms of hierarchical structures governing sections or movements. Schenkerian notions of melodic and harmonic movement constitute one way in which such superordinate constraints may be expressed, but doubtless there are others too. We may parsimoniously account for much of the sequence of compositional behaviour if we suppose that skilled composers are often unable to use superordinate constraints as starting points for *generative* processes, but are able to use them to *recognize* satisfactory musical material generated in some other way.

Newell, Shaw, and Simon (1962) have postulated a general theory of problem solving in which they distinguish two classes of process, the first of which they call *solution-generating* processes, and the second *verifying* processes. Typically, solution-generating processes involve the use of heuristics (strategies) for producing candidate solutions. Development of skilled problem solving involves finding better heuristics, i.e. ones which produce fewer bad solutions, and take less time. Heuristics are always less than perfect. They do not guarantee success; and it is arguable that in ill-defined problem solving situations such as musical composition, where the composer is at liberty to change the nature of the problem as he proceeds, algorithms (foolproof solution generators) are of limited value, even if discoverable. Because heuristics are not perfect, there has to be a process of verification whereby trial solutions are tested against criteria for success.

What we are wont to call compositional processes, those events over which composers have greatest conscious control, can possibly be identified as solution-generators in the theory of Newell *et al.* These are the repertoires of ways of 'turning themes to account' by exploiting and transforming their properties in principled ways. The process of judgement, whereby a particular development is accepted or rejected as achieving compositional goals, can be identified as the verification processes postulated by Newell *et al.* It is here where, arguably, testing of a trial solution against higher-order constraints takes place. This process also changes with increasing skill, as a composer develops more comprehensive and large-scale goals. Initally, a young composer may rely on a superficial understanding of the forms of his culture to determine his goals. For instance, he may notice surface features of a sonata form movement, such as the introduction of a second subject in the dominant key. As he grows in knowledge of his medium he may begin to extract the more fundamental principles of harmonic and melodic movement that underlie particular forms. He will understand why the standard features of sonata form usually 'work' musically; but he will also see how and when such features may be dispensed with to produce new forms which also 'work'. The verification is then based on 'intuition' that what has been composed is, in some sense, effective.

Composers throughout the whole of the last two centuries have insisted that the best route to the development of compositional skill is detailed study of Bach and the contrapuntal masters. Composers as varied as Schumann,

Kodaly, and Stravinsky, emphasize, in their different ways, the common principles underlying tonal music of the last 500 years in virtue of which it is fruitful to immerse oneself in the 'old masters'. From this immersion one gains the essential familiarity with the potentials and possibilities of the tonal medium from which one can forge one's own style. Verdi puts the point as succinctly as any (Werfel and Stefan 1942):

No study of the moderns! Many people will think this strange. But today, when I hear and see so many works put together in the way a bad tailor puts clothes together on a standard model, I cannot budge in my opinions. . . . When a young man has gone through a severe course of training, when he has achieved his own style, then, if he sees fit, he can study these works, and he will no longer be in danger of turning into a mere imitator. (From a letter to Giuseppe Piroli, 1871.)

From a psychological point of view we may explain the benefit of such study as forcing the student to concentrate on basic underlying properties of the tonal system rather than on the particular compositional forms which are fashionable in the culture, and which constitute only a small subset of the ways of writing acceptable tonal music.

We may summarize our discussion so far by reference to a diagram of a 'typical' composer's compositional resources and processes (Fig. 4.1). There appears to be a distinction between those processes on which a composer is able to report fairly easily and those on which he is not. For convenience these have been labelled 'conscious' and 'unconscious'. Square-edged boxes depict knowledge or structures that are stored in long term memory. The

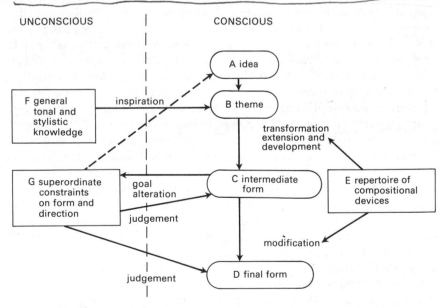

Fig. 4.1. Diagram of typical compositional resources and processes.

Kernal

curved boxes contain the transitory materials that constitute successive versions of a composition as it grows in the composer's mind. The square boxes represent items of long-term knowledge which a composer has built up over the years, and which can be applied to new compositional problems. The lines joining boxes represent processes which transform or use the contents of the various boxes.

Box B represents the thematic kernel that springs 'unbidden' to mind out of the storehouse of thematic knowledge (F). Box A is optionally present in view of the comments (e.g. Sessions 1941) that sometimes a more or less specific idea of the *kind* of music required precedes an actual theme in awareness.

Box C represents the results of applying compositional techniques of transformation and modification (E) to the original theme. Its contents are then judged against criteria of 'rightness' (G) and, if found wanting, are modified until a satisfactory final form (D) is reached. The pathway 'goal alteration' acknowledges the fact that discovered properties of intermediate themes can actually overwrite originally held goals, so that the composition can appear to the composer to generate its own momentum or 'life', almost independently of his will.

It should be emphasized that Fig. 4.1 is not a 'theory' or an 'explanation' of the compositional process, but simply an economical way of describing some of the elements present in composers' accounts of their activities which makes clear the possible relationships between them. A rigorous psychological theory of composition would need to specify the contents of the various boxes and the nature of the transformations operating upon them in some detail.

The most rigorous test of the efficacy of theories in modern cognitive science is the production of a working computer program whose external behaviour mimics that to be explained. No such program has, to date, been written. The few documented programs (e.g. Sundberg and Lindblom 1976) do not attempt to model actual compositional sequences of the type portrayed in Fig. 4.1. In particular, there is no interplay between the generative process and processes of verification. The computer 'gets it right' at the first attempt.

It is also worth noting that in an effective theory of composition, the conscious/unconscious distinction is irrelevant. Both types of process must be fully specified, and it is the internal logic of a process which is of importance. We may suppose that, for different composers, the line dividing conscious from unconscious processes may be drawn in different places. Indeed, the whole issue of individual differences is an important topic of study. It would be oversimplistic to assume that there is only one route to an acceptable composition. A full analysis of such differences is beyond the scope of this book, but a single example illustrates the kind of issue which arises here.

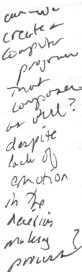

Tchaikovsky, in his letters (Newmarch 1906; reprinted in Vernon 1970), frankly identifies a particular point of failure for him—form:

I cannot complain of poverty of imagination, or lack of inventive power; but, on the other hand, I have always suffered from my want of skills in the management of form. Only after strenuous labour have I at last succeeded in making the form of my compositions correspond, more or less, with their contents. Formerly I was careless and did not give sufficient attention to the critical overhauling of my sketches. Consequently my *seams* showed, and there was no organic union between my individual episodes. This was a very serious defect, and I only improved gradually as time went on; but the form of my works will never be *exemplary*, because although I can modify, I cannot radically alter the essential qualities of my musical temperament.

Translating this into the formalisms embodied in Fig. 4.1, we may say that the route F–B–C–G is strong, but that the G–C and G–A–B routes are not. It is more likely that properties of a theme control the eventual structure rather than a strong conception of the structure exerting control over the thematic process.

Tchaikovsky clearly sees his own compositional process as inadequate, and others such as Hindemith (1952) stress the point that there may be as much separating the master composer from the 'ordinary' composer as there is separating the composer from the novice. Of the themes and motives which form the substance of inspiration, Hindemith says: 'they are common to all people, professionals and laymen alike; but while in the layman's mind they die away unused in their earliest infancy . . . the creative musician knows how to catch them and subject them to further treatment.' This treatment is precisely the moulding, transforming process that we have identified with the B–C–D route in Fig. 4.1. However, Hindemith goes on to claim that 'if only the work involved in reaching this goal really counted, there would be many a genius. The petty composer could do the same, technically, as the real genius did, and he would almost be justified in feeling godlike . . . because he was able to turn his bubbling inner singing and ringing into music, which [the layman] could never do.'

Hindemith then asks what separates the genius from the workaday composer and identifies the mark of the master as 'vision', which concept he explains in the following way:

A genuine creator . . . will . . . have the gift of seeing—illuminated in the mind's eye as if by a flash of lightning—a complete musical form (though its subsequent realization in a performance may take three hours or more); [and] he will have the energy, persistence, and skill to bring this envisioned form into existence, so that even after months of work not one of its details will be lost or fail to fit into his photographic picture. This does not mean that any F-sharp in the 612th measure of the final piece would have been determined in the very first flash of cognition . . . but in working out his material he will always have before his mental eye the entire picture. In writing melodies or harmonic progressions he does not have to select them arbitrarily, he merely has to fulfil what the conceived totality demands . . . The man of average talent may have visions too; but instead of seeing them in the clarity of lightening, he perceives dark contours which he has not the divination to fill out appropriately . . . [He] may manage the few basic rules of construction with all their combinative possibilities pretty well, and yet the highest degree of subtlety, in which each technical item is in congruence with the respective part of the vision, again may be attained only by the genius. There are relatively few masterworks in which this ultimate congruence can be felt.

Hindemith sees the acquisition of compositional mastery as one in which the demands of box G in Fig. 4.1 gain greater control over the compositional process so that the conception (A) exercises greater constraints over the compositional process from the outset. The subservience of detailed working out to a controlling plan or 'scheme' has been proposed as a partial explanation of introspective remarks attributed to Mozart and other composers (Gardner 1980), although it is clear that by 'vision' Hindemith means considerably more than the ability to plan a composition according to some stock structural formula (such as minuet and trio, rondo, or sonata form). He is referring to some underlying thematic and harmonic unity which transcends particular forms.

In the light of Hindemith's comments it becomes easier to understand the achievements of someone such as Rosemary Brown. We may see that she has grasped some of the rules of construction used in the music of classical and romantic masters. The compositions she produces are, however, mainly of simple episodic form, and lack the organic mastery sometimes achieved by the composers she claims to transmit. She is a good, albeit, unconscious imitator of surface styles. But for the total insulation of her compositional processes from her awareness she would be as little worthy of note as the countless unmemorable imitators in every sphere of creative endeavour. There is no evidence of the 'vision' that her composers had in such abundance in their lives.

The general issue of the psychological status of verbal reports has been a central one in cognitive debate. It is obviously naive to suppose that verbal introspections can be taken as true descriptions of mental processes in every respect. Nisbet and Wilson (1977) draw on a wide body of evidence in support of the view that, in many cases, people attempting to report on their cognitive processes do so not on the basis of true instrospection, but on the basis of *a priori* theories about plausible causes and effects. They reconstruct, in a more-or-less rational fashion, what they infer *should have* gone on to produce the results of cognition. Nisbet and Wilson's evaluation of the literature on creative processes leads them to the conclusion that

creative workers describe themselves almost universally as bystanders, differing from other observers only in that they are the first to witness the fruits of a process that is almost completely hidden from view. The reports of these workers are characterized by an insistence that (*a*) the influential stimuli are usually completely obscure—the individual has no idea what factors prompted the solution; and (*b*) even the fact that a process is taking place is sometimes unknown to the individual prior to the point that a solution appears in consciousness.

Whilst it it true that *some* compositional processes seem obscure to consciousness, the material reviewed here suggests that Nisbet and Wilson's conclusions may be too sweeping. There are many aspects of the process which are open to conscious inspection and control. Furthermore, the insistence by many composers that there are processes that they cannot report upon encourages us that they are *not* 'telling more than they know'; that they are really attempting to describe the phenomenal experience *without* inference.

Ericsson and Simon (1980) argue that Nisbet and Wilson are overly pessimistic about the degree to which we can treat verbal reports as reliable indicators of cognitive processing. They point out that reporting verbally on introspective data characteristically means *remembering* a past sequence of events. The distinction between what can be reported and what cannot is not necessarily one between conscious and unconscious processes, but may be one between what can be readily recalled and what cannot.

They cite evidence which suggests two conditions under which material that has been the object of focal attention may not be recalled: cases where a solution is reached in a single step without intermediate or partial solutions; and cases where a process or a product is transient, being held in focal attention for only a brief moment before being superseded by new material. They argue that these factors are 'adequate to account for the phenomena of sudden insight that are the subject of so many anecdotes in the literature of creativity.' The studies cited in support of sudden insight are based on 'retrospective accounts of purportedly real creative acts, often reported many years after the event'. Ericsson and Simon's view is supported by evidence from studies where subjects were asked to introspect *whilst* solving the problem (e.g. Bulbrook 1932; Durkin 1937; Henry 1934). They argue that studies such as these show that the progress to solution was either gradual or determined by trial and error. No additional unconscious processes were required to be postulated.

A related cause of memory failure is concerned with the fact that the thought processes preceding 'inspiration' are often diffuse, unplanned, and undirected, and may be interspersed with other cognitive tasks which form the prime focus of attention. Although such unstructured thought is difficult to recall, there is evidence (e.g. Klinger 1971) that it is not unconscious. If people are asked to verbalize their processes *at the time* they are able to do so; but memory for the events fades very quickly.

No-one would wish to deny the immense complexity of the processes involved in musical composition. The arguments of Ericsson and Simon are simply a reminder that we may be making life too difficult for ourselves if we succumb fully to the prejudice of the contemporary psychologist against using verbal reports as data. With a clear understanding of the conditions under which they tend to be unreliable, we can proceed to a relatively free use of this vast storehouse of psychologically relevant data. The thrust of Ericsson and Simon's argument is that we will gain the most detailed and accurate picture by examining verbalizations made *concurrent with* the act. It is to such data that we now turn.

4.4. Observations of composers at work

This section is based on two observations. One is reported by Reitman (1965) and involved obtaining a verbal protocol from an unnamed composer who was set the problem of writing a piano fugue (Sanchez and Reitman 1960). This yields a number of insights, but has inadequacies too. The complete protocol is unpublished, and there is no record of the concurrent musical protocol, the notes tried out at the piano and written down. Accordingly, the second observation is one made on myself as I composed a section of a work for choir and organ. As I worked on this section I wrote down as many of the steps of my thought as I could capture, alongside the relevant musical notation.

4.4.1. *Reitman's protocol of fugue composition*

To specify a fugue is to specify certain features which the final composition must possess. A strict fugue contains two or more independent contrapuntal voices which enter, one after another, with the statement of a single theme. The entry of the second voice is accompanied by new, contrasting material in the first voice which constitutes a 'counter-subject'. When each voice has entered, the music develops through the segmentation and recombination of the thematic elements in various ways; towards the end of the fugue one normally finds some dramatic intensification of the texture, through harmonic and dynamic climax, through the overlapping of thematic entries in the various voices (stretto), and other conventional devices. The prime constraints on a fugue are that each voice should possess some continuity and individual coherence, and that there should be a minimum of free writing where the voice material is not derived from the theme and counter-subject material (see Bullivant 1971).

A composer's problem, when working in any medium, is to set additional constraints over and above those loosely specified by the compositional type. There are an infinite number of possible fugue themes and possible fugues. The composer clearly cannot search through all possible themes in an unprincipled way. He must, in technical terms, 'reduce his problem space'. We find, in Reitman's protocol, evidence of external constraints operating, such as the need to find something which fits under a pianist's hands. When attempting to compose the countersubject the composer says: (erasing) 'I think we'll abandon the idea of the enlarged syncopation to get away from repetition of the theme . . . and try to do something more pianistic.'

Probably more important than such constraints, however, are those *internal* constraints generated by what has already been composed, following some general principle of consistency or balance. Throughout the protocol, observations such as 'I'm playing through measure six to try and get my ear attuned to that kind of material' are common. It seems that the composer is attempting to discover initially unnoticed properties of what he has already composed to help him generate ideas for continuing. He is indulging in what Reitman calls 'after-the-fact adoption of a convention which is consistent with what has already been done'.

There comes a point in some compositions where the constraints, external or self-imposed are so many that the element of search or choice seems to be reduced or removed altogether. Towards the end of his protocol the composer calls out '*Voilà!* From here the ending is quite obvious, and there's no problem. This is the solution . . . The structure of the piece is solved now . . . I don't think it can miss.' It is a universal phenomenon of expert mental life that points occur in a problem-solving process where one 'turns onto a familiar road' traversed so many times before that the novelty and challenge of the particular problem disappears. Such points depend, of course, on the expert knowledge of the problem solver, and may be undetectable when reached by a novice working on the same problem.

I am a moderately poor Bridge player, and, sitting at the tables of the mighty, have often been astonished when, three or four tricks into a hand, the declarer lays down his hand with the claim that 'the rest is obvious'. This is followed by some explanation of his intentions of play, to which the others at the table immediately acquiesce; and I am left trying confusedly to follow what seems so obvious to the others. My self-esteem is only somewhat restored by the observation that sometimes such a declarer is wrong. A keen opponent says, 'I'm sorry, but do you mind actually playing that out?' and the unlucky declarer discovers some unforeseen twist of card distribution or tactic which undoes his strategy. The same is true of music composition, and Reitman's composer had the insight to add 'of course, you never can tell until you get to the end; it's always dangerous . . .' Some unforeseen conflict between the various constraints adopted may prevent any satisfactory ending from being found.

When multiple constraints build up over the course of a composition, it can become impossible to find ways of progressing which honour all the constraints. In such situations the protocol reveals the composer temporarily dropping some constraints, producing continuations which honour only some of the features defined earlier. He then readjusts in one of two ways: he either modifies the new material so as to bring it back into line with earlier constraints; or he may change the constraints. Thus, at one point the composer ignores all attributes of a pair of melodies except the arrangements of harmonic intervals they form, ignoring the rhythmic aspect to generate a continuation.

What we are unable to do from the brief set of selected fragments presented by Reitman is to get any idea of the detailed *musical* working out of the general principles of problem solving which emerge with clarity. There is no opportunity to experience the music that the words are about. Accordingly, the next protocol gives some of the crucial musical material in addition to the words.

4.4.2. *A self-generated protocol of choral composition*

A few autobiographical details are necessary to set the context. I conduct a small amateur choir, and some years ago I decided to try and write something for the choir, taking up again a compositional interest that had absorbed me in early adulthood. My compositional style might best be described as 'twentieth-century English church' as exemplified by such composers as Herbert Howells. The style is traditional, placing great emphasis on melody, counterpoint, and a strongly tonal harmonic framework. I came to this work with a cluster of general constraints: the work must be learnable by an amateur choir; it should be for four voice parts plus organ accompaniment; it should conform to my general style—I was not deliberately intending to transform or extend my repertoire of compositional devices.

I chose to write a setting of Psalm 92, in English translation. The psalm has five verses, and the general mood is vigorous, joyful, and triumphant ('The Lord is king, with majesty enrobed'). The demands of contrast suggested to me that the third verse could take a more serene setting, and so a vague three-section notion was born; an initial vigorous setting of verses 1 and 2; a restful slow section for verse 3; returning to a triumphant close for the last two verses.

My initial compositional effort got me to the beginning of the last line of verse 2, and then I became blocked. My initial idea for the words 'From all eternity, O Lord, you are' seemed to lead nowhere, and I abandoned the project for at least a year.

It was some months after this abandonment that I first developed an explicit interest in the process of composition. When I returned to the task of completion in the summer of 1981 it occurred to me that it would be of interest to capture some of my compositional steps in a protocol. At this stage I was relatively naïve with respect to the literature reviewed in this chapter, and I had few preconceptions about the kind of thing such a protocol would show.

The protocol begins at bar 27 of the composition, where the abandoned theme was sketched in. Example 4.5 shows the score from bar 21 through 29 as it stood when I began. Since the protocol is fairly short, it can be given in full, with commentary and musical examples. The protocol is in italic type; comments and explications follow each segment of protocol in normal type.

Example 4.5.

I should add that the original written protocol is highly cryptic, using personalized abbreviations and deviations from grammatical usage. The version presented here is as literal a translation into grammatical English as possible.

A. *How am I to continue at bar 29? The next verse is going to be quieter and slower. A theme is needed for 'From all eternity'. The tentative one where composition broke down before didn't seem right, partly because it was over too quickly.* This initial passage can be seen as a statement of the problem to be solved, and the setting of two immediate constraints. There was a general need to 'wind down' from a rather extrovert and 'busy' texture into something more easeful for the next verse; and a particular need to find a theme for the last line of verse 2. Lengthening the vocal phrases, which up till now had been short and separated, could be one way of introducing the required 'easement'. These constraints, however, were not yet specific enough to suggest actual notes.

B. *I decide to progress the accompaniment so that it slows down. It occurs to me that the word 'eternity' can be represented by a repetitive circular motif. We already have a circular four-note fragment in bars 23–27 (Example 4.6). So I try to use it to slow down (Example 4.7). The writing of bars 27–33 then becomes routine. A B flat is added at bar 33 on the intuition that harmonic movement is needed by now.* The vocal theme for 'Your throne has stood firm' is a rather self-contained 'closed' phrase. It did not have implications for any particular continuation to me. The accompaniment is, however, much more flowing and open ended at this point. To overcome the 'block' in the vocal material I decided to develop the accompaniment in the hope that this would, in its turn, suggest what the voices might do. The word 'eternity' suggested the possibility of a repetitive cyclical motif, and the accompaniment happened to contain such a motif, introduced at bar 23 for reasons I have now forgotten. It consists of a falling four-note scale, which returns to a higher note to fall again and again (see Example 4.6).) I seem to have decided

Example 4.6.

that the passage from bar 27 to 33 should be harmonically static (over a dominant G pedal). The task, then, was simply to repeat the falling motif over and over, at the same pitch, but with a spacing out and slowing so that from bar 31 there is just one cycle per bar (Example 4.7). Once the problem

Example 4.7.

had been narrowed this far, I was able to compose fairly mechanically, thus the comment that this section is 'routine'. The full organ part for bars 27 to 33 is given in Example 4.8.

At bar 33 the problem was perceived as one of maintaining interest whilst continuing with the repetitive melodic material. The solution that occurred to me was to alter the tonal implication of the G pedal by adding a B flat in the harmony, suggesting a reinterpretation of the key as tending towards F major.

C. *Now I leave the accompaniment and return to the voices. The basic rhythmic pattern of the earlier, unsatisfactory theme (Example 4.9, bars 27–28) seems right, but it needs slowing down. The rise in pitch is right too, but it needs to be less extreme. If we incorporate alternate rising fourths and falling thirds (Example 4.10) that produces a coincidence. Starting where I feel it to*

Example 4.8.

- ter - ni - ty   O Lord

Example 4.9.

Example 4.10.

be right (bar 31) it comes out on B flat at the same time as the accompaniment (Example 4.16, bar 33). In this rather condensed section of protocol the accompaniment is now left. It provides a suitable bed over which new voice material can be added. The first, unrecorded step was to delete the abandoned voice entries in bars 27 and 28 (Example 4.5) so that by bar 29 only the organ was sounding. Clearly, I liked the basic rhythm of the abandoned theme, and its ascending pitch direction: but the speed of the rhythm and the rate of pitch rise were both too fast for the intended 'easing up' role that this theme had to fulfil. The first modification that occurred was to double the duration of the dactyl pairs (from Example 4.11 to Example 4.12). The second modification was to allow *alternate* notes to carry the pitch rise, with intermediate notes dropping back below (changing from Example 4.13 to Example 4.14). I cannot be sure why I chose the interval of a rising fourth at this point. It is possible that I was looking back to earlier thematic material to find some grounds for consistency. The very opening theme of the work, in fact, contains two germinal elements; ascent by rising fourths, and a falling scale of four notes (Example 4.15).

The 'coincidence' refers to the happy discovery that when I started the

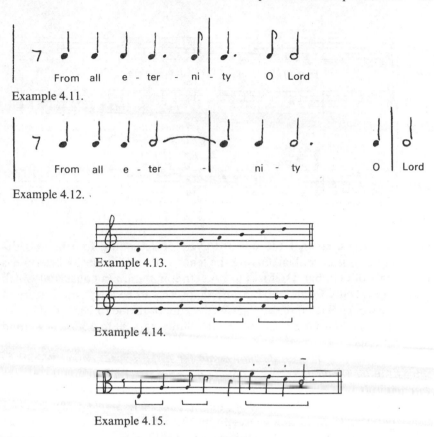

Example 4.11.

Example 4.12.

Example 4.13.

Example 4.14.

Example 4.15.

first vocal entry on D in the soprano line at bar 31, which, for reasons now lost to me, seemed the right time and note to start, the theme's already determined structure led it to B flat at precisely the point at which I had already decided to introduce a B flat in the accompaniment (see Example 4.16). This seemed to act as a confirmation that I was 'on the right track' at this point.

D. *The soprano theme finishes on C (bar 33), but I want that repetitive upward movement to continue. I will have to give the theme to another voice an octave lower. My first thought is to follow on, starting in bar 34. My second thought is to start in earlier (bar 33) and grow on out of the soprano ending. That works for the tenor voice.* The organ harmony at bar 33 is unresolved (see Example 4.8) and so this creates the feeling that the music is still moving towards a point of resolution. I experienced a strong sense that the upward movement started by the soprano voice should continue, but in a way that brought in another voice. The first thought was to start a lower voice in an imitation of the soprano in bar 34. This was discarded almost immediately in favour of an overlapping join in which the lower voice starts before the

Example 4.16.

soprano finishes, so that the upward cycle of ascending fourths and descending thirds is unbroken. Giving the tenor voice a C at bar 34 determines a start note of G in bar 33, if it is to be a strict imitation (a constraint which I did not explicitly formulate, but one that seems to be a stylistic feature of the whole work). Such imitation allowed the tenor theme to be copied out to the F at the end of bar 35. Example 4.16 shows bars 30 to 35 as they stood after this stage.

E. *It would be boring to do that again for a third vocal entry. Would an entry fit in the rhythmic spaces, to make a sort of 'stretto'? I experiment with different interval separations. A bass part entering a fourth lower than the tenor seems to work quite well, so fit that in up to bar 36 (Example 4.18).* It seems clear that I was constraining myself by the relatively strict contrapuntal requirement that each of the four voices should enter with the theme in sequence. My problem was, thus, how and when to bring in the next voice? I decided that it would be uninteresting to generate entry three in relation to entry two by direct analogy with the relation of entry two to entry one. Instead, I conceived of an earlier entry which allows for rhythmic interplay (Example 4.17). Once this was decided, it remained only to choose a pitch

voice 2 (tenor)

voice 3 (bass)

Example 4.17.

for entry three. The protocol suggests extended trial-and-error experimentation at the piano here (I always compose at the piano). Eventually I chose a bass entry on D as harmonically appealing, and wrote that out routinely to bar 36 (see Example 4.18).

F. *What happens to the accompaniment now? In experimentation I discover*

Example 4.18.

that a drop to F in the bass fits with the voice parts quite well at bar 35. I carry through a tied B flat from bar 33 to 34, repeat bar 32's left hand descending scale in bar 34, and tie the middle C in bar 33 through to 34. By rule, the tenor D in 34 should carry through to 35 as well as the tied treble notes. Does this sound a bit messy? In bar 35 we certainly cannot repeat the FEDC figure, because the voice parts have shifted to an E flat key space. Perhaps this is the time to stop the pattern, and let the tenor D go down to C. I try it. Now we have a totally static accompaniment (Example 4.19, bar 35), so we must look to the voices to see how this might develop.

Example 4.19.

This section of protocol offers the most detailed comment so far, relating, as it does, to the composition of just over one bar of material for the organ. It was clearly a difficult and crucial moment for the direction of the music. The main problem was that there seemed no way of stopping the accompaniment just going on and on with the pattern established in bars 31 and 32. However, the voice parts were moving into remote harmonic regions, and so the accompaniment had to change somehow. The first decision was, then, to abandon the G pedal and drop to F at bar 35. The second decision was to abandon the repeated scale passage. The pattern established during bars 30 to 34 was that the last note of the scale passage should be tied over to the first beat of the next bar (see Example 4.8). If the left-hand passage at bar 34 is written according to this rule (repeating bars 32 to 33) this results in a tied D in bar 35. The chord produced by this (organ F, D, B flat, C; bass G, tenor E flat) was heard as unsatisfactory. It contained too many dissonances. By breaking the pattern and dropping the D to a C the chord was simplified and suggested as partial resting point. This suggestion was confirmed by the 'test' of putting a continuation of the right-hand scale pattern in bar 35 (F, E, D, C, as in bar 33). This created an unpleasant dissonance between the E flat in the vocal line and the organ E which was instantly rejected as a possibility. So, I was left with a simple unmoving chord at bar 35 (see Example 4.19) with no obvious implications for continuation. I returned to the voice parts to find the key to further development.

G. *I must bring the soprano voice in with the theme. I imitate the bass entry in relation to the tenor, so start on A flat in bar 35 (Example 4.20). If I follow strictly, this gets to D flat and G flat at bar 37. This is too harmonically remote, so I cheat and give D and G. Now that's four entries, but I have a feeling that this 'stretto' must be maintained for a while without working higher in pitch. How about taking the organ off at bar 35 or 36, then bringing it crashing in with some sort of perfect cadence later? Key? Who knows?* Here we find the completion (in principle) of the choral entries. I suspect that the fourth entry was given to the soprano rather than the alto because of its high tessitura. The soprano voice enters at bar 35 with the same pitch and time relations to the bass voice (at a suitable octave) as the bass has to the tenor. Once again, this pattern of successive entry can be repeated indefinitely. However, unlike the accompaniment at bars 30 to 35, there is a continual upward motion of pitch, and a movement round the circle of fifths in key, one step for each new entry. I seem to have wanted the continuing contrapuntal texture, but without further harmonic movement, so I was led to break my self-imposed constraint that the entries should be exact imitations. In bar 37, the soprano theme was shifted down a semitone from what it 'should be' so as to break the continuing movement round the circle of fifths (see Example 4.20).

At this point, an idea of the form of the next few bars presented itself in vague form. The organ stops, leaving the voices alone, intensifying the 'stretto' up to some climactic cadence, which is marked by the re-entry of the organ, fortissimo. Now there was a goal to control the next few bars, but, as yet, no idea of the final tonality.

H. *I notice that the vocal theme is four bars long, so it should be possible to bring it in each bar in a new voice* ad infinitum. *I bring the alto in at bar 36 on an E flat (same relationship to preceding voice as before). Then the tenor comes*

Example 4.20.

in on A in bar 37, the bass on E flat (no—we get an unwanted A flat). I try
entering on F—this seems to work. I write out the bass part to bar 40. How do
we fill in the soprano and alto whilst the bass is finishing? Repeat 'you are'
more insistently, off beat with other parts (bars 39 to 40). It is not until this
fairly late stage in working with the vocal material that I noticed the theme
to be four bars long, deducing that it could, therefore, fit into an indefinitely
long pattern where a new entry comes in once per bar in a different one of
the four voices. This allowed the routine writing out of three more entries;
alto at 36, tenor at 37, and bass at 38 (see Example 4.20). The first attempt

at the bass entry (following the strict pitch relationship to the previous entry already established) yielded an unsatisfactory harmonic result. The scale E flat, F, G, A flat moved too far away from the prevailing tonality, so, once again, I relaxed my constraints and allowed the theme to start on F, remaining in consonance with the other parts.

For some reason, I decided that there should be no further full entry after the bass, so the problem became what to do with the upper voices during bars 39 and 40. Anticipating an imminent climax, I hit upon the idea of taking the last two notes of the theme (ascending fourth) and repeating them with increasing insistence. This led to a chord at bar 41 which, in context, is harmonically unstable, and needs resolution (E flat, G, D). Even at this point, however, I was not clear where it should resolve.

I. *Now the accompaniment comes in at bar 41. I try various bass notes. A sounds well, suggesting a perfect cadence to D major. It is too direct just to go from A to D. I try A, B, C, D ascending. That sounds good.* At this point I was 'fishing' for the right organ harmony by piano experimentation. A bass A was recognized as the right note for bar 41, and I soon found the cadence required (Example 4.21). An elaboration (small intermediate notes B and C)

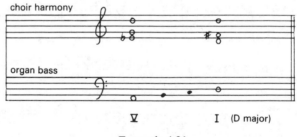

Example 4.21.

soon suggested itself. I now interpret my need for these notes as a prolongation of the unresolved dissonance, screwing up the tension until the very last moment. At this point, only the bass line of the organ part was plotted out.

J. *The choir has to have something on the D major chord (silence sounds wrong). I tighten the screw once more in the soprano with E, A (Example 4.22).*

You are.

Example 4.22.

I now find a choir harmony which fits, especially bearing in mind the E flat in the bass at bar 41 (Example 4.23). I think what sounded wrong here was the unresolved choir chord at bar 41. It needed to be resolved by the choir as

well as by the organ. I thus returned to the immediate choral context to find
something which could be used, and arrived at the idea of moving the
ascending soprano figure of bar 40 up a whole tone, to bring the sopranos to
top A (Example 4.23, bar 43), the highest note in the whole piece, and an

Example 4.23.

integral part of the D major chord planned for the organ. In this way, the
chord of bar 43 becomes a climax, culmination, and summing up of the
whole first section. I notice now, in retrospect, that the total composition has
moved at this point from an opening G major to D major, the traditional
tonic–dominant move of sonata form exposition; and that bar 43 contains
the most emphatic statement of the ascending fourth motif which opens
the piece. All this escaped conscious attention at the time, but, arguably,
contributed towards my sense that this was a 'right' development. The filling
in of the three outer choral parts at bar 43 was a piece of routine harmonization. Example 4.23 gives the final version of the choir parts in bars
41 to 43.

K. *The organ writing is a bit bare in bars 41 to 43. I add a right-hand part
in descending fourths. Bar 44 is a straight D major chord, then the choir motif
of bar 43 is repeated in a more luxuriant way (bar 45). I repeat bars 44 and 45
and this begins to form a flowing accompaniment out of which the next choral
theme begins (Example 4.23). Here the protocol ends.*

The organ cadence, of such climactic importance, required more substance than a bare bass line. The notion of introducing a descending contrary motion line in the right hand must have come easily. As I now write, I notice that the melodic progression D, C, B, A is a slow version of the descending four-note scale which dominated the earlier accompaniment part (bars 22 to 33). The juxtaposition of this motif with the rising bass scale (derived from the opening of the vocal theme of the section at bar 31) makes a kind of grand, final statement of the thematic core of the whole section. In retrospect, the whole compositional process described here can be seen as a search for this crucial cadence. Through the fog of my compositional mediocrity loomed the dim shape of the 'inevitable' Schenkerian I–V movement, begging to be realized, but, at the outset, totally inarticulated. Climactic pivotal moment over, it then became easy to set the scene for my slower middle section. Bars 44 to 50 came quickly, allowing the organ to settle into a gentle rocking accompaniment for what was to come.

Something happened next which is of considerable importance in coming to understand the strengths and weaknesses of a protocol like this. Shortly after I arrived at bar 50, I began on the next section of the composition; but became immediately aware of a difference in the quality of the compositional experience. It was as if I had more urgent sense of direction. There came a wish to capture an unfolding shape before I lost it. As a result, I found myself incapable of continuing with the protocol, and embarked on an intense period of composition which produced the next 35 bars in an uninterrupted period of work.

This is not to say that I experienced a pure 'flow of inspiration'. Rather, it was as if I feared to lose some momentum if I stopped to record my thoughts in words. In retrospective examination of my manuscript, I sense a lyrical, overarching quality about the next section, giving it a unity and repose quite unlike the kaleidoscopic first section. It is in D major, and moves, with few intermediate steps, along the well-trodden harmonic path I–V–I, with a single melodic idea unfolding in the voice parts. I would hesitate to say that this section is *better* than the section for which a protocol exists, but I am quite certain that the compositional strategy was different. There was not the same sense of indecision and search. I was lucky enough to start with a set of constraints which, within the bounds of my compositional style, almost allowed the section to 'compose itself'. It seems probable to me that verbal protocols reveal most of the genuine compositional process precisely when the composer is rather unsure where he is going, and casts around among his consciously held stock of transforming and extending devices to come up with a possible solution. When things go smoothly, the requirement to provide a protocol may well alter, even disrupt entirely, the process one is trying to describe.

Tchaikovsky has expressed well the concentration that is often required when creative activity seems to flow particularly well:

I forget everything and behave like a madman. Everything within me starts pulsing and quivering; hardly have I begun the sketch ere one thought follows another. In the midst of this magic process it frequently happens that some external interruption wakes me from my somnambulistic state: a ring at the bell, the entrance of my servant . . . Dreadful are such interruptions. Sometimes they break the thread of inspiration for a considerable time, so that I have to seek it again, often in vain

(From Newmarch 1906; reprinted in Vernon 1970.)

What general psychological conclusions can be drawn from this protocol? The first is that the protocol and its subsequent explication leave much unsaid, detailed as they are. They do not come near to documenting the rationale for the choice of each and every note. For instance, there are many possible melodic patterns consistent with the constraints I identify for the vocal theme starting at bar 31. Why did I choose the one I did? In retrospect, I can formulate reasons why the theme I chose is better than an alternative such as Example 4.24. The chosen theme (Example 4.15) has more melodic

From all e - ter - ni - ty   O Lord you are.

Example 4.24.

interest (this latter alternative is too repetitive), and it has more harmonic movement (the alternative spans an octave, and, as such, is harmonically rather static). I doubt if I would have consciously entertained this alternative at all. It is as if I was able to choose the *kind* of theme which had musical potential almost automatically. This is reminiscent of observations on other forms of skilled choice (e.g. chess playing; Simon 1979). In choosing moves, skilled players seem to consider fewer unpromising moves than do beginners. My own protocol is littered with unexplained choices. Something is *felt* to be right, or chosen without any justification at all. I take this to be a general characteristic of skilled problem-solving.

A second conclusion is that, at least in my case, the interplay between the discovered properties of previously composed material and some broader conception is paramount. All the way through the protocol I find myself deliberately using some feature of melody or harmony in previously written material as the starting point for a continuation. On the other hand, there are many cases in which superordinate considerations of harmony and structure prescribe changes which modify or overwrite the essentially imitative strategies which generate the first continuations. Just like Reitman's composer, I find myself engaged in trying to characterize what I have already got, so that continuations will be, in some sense, fitting or 'in style'; but I also have shifting, and often dimly perceived notions about the direction of a section which allow me to discern when strict imitation must stop.

Third, because characteristics of previously written material are often discovered some time *after* the writing, but can still be important in shaping future events, I suspect that an important component of compositional skill is a degree of 'trust' in one's medium—a certainty that the habitual processes of generation will yield material which is richer than one first sees, and which, even if initially unsatisfactory, usually contains within it discoverable properties which can be used to profit. This trust is partly engendered by the sheer fact of previously solved problems; but it also has something to do with increasing awareness of the richness of a medium such as the tonal system. There are so many different kinds of relationship which hold between a set of notes that even the simplest theme can become an almost inexhaustible source of discovery. The consequent delight that any creative worker experiences in the sheer fecundity of his medium is, arguably, not simply a pleasant by-product of creative activity, but the essential source of motivation which keeps him involved with his own material through 'blocks' and blind alleys in the creative process. Such delight is amply documented by the practitioners of all sorts of skill; from mathematicians to poets (for example, Poincaré 1924, and Spender 1946; both reprinted in Ghiselin 1952, and Vernon 1970).

In discussing my protocol with fellow psychologists and musicians, the question has often arisen of how one might use such protocols to generate fruitful scientific research into composition. Protocol gathering is a species of natural history, and although it is an essential first step in understanding any complex mental process, it does not, on its own, allow detailed theory building and testing. For this, two lines of attack seem possible. One would be to focus on a simple compositional task, such as the harmonization of a short melody, attempting to specify *all* the cognitive steps which underlie the choice of particular chords by a particular composer. This would naturally lead to some form of computer simulation to test the adequacy of one's theory. Another related possibility would be to take some circumscribed compositional task, maybe the same one as before, and ask a range of musicians of varying ability and experience to carry out the task. By a comparative analysis of the behaviour of the different subjects it might be possible to specify some of the ways in which compositional skills change with experience.

4.5. Improvisation

The keynote of the compositional process seems to be the moulding and perfecting of musical ideas. Although an idea may come spontaneously, unbidden, and instantaneously, its subsequent development may take years. In improvisation, the composer has no opportunity to mould and perfect his material. His first idea *must* work. Is, then, the improviser a different sort of animal to the composer? Is he the musician who, like Rosemary Brown, seems to exert no conscious creative effort in the production of coherent music? The record tells us that this cannot be so; we know that composers such as Beethoven were also master improvisers. The same man that could chisel away at a theme for 20 years could also produce live compositions of extreme accomplishment.

I wish to argue in this section that what distinguishes improvisation from composition is primarily the pre-existence of a large set of formal constraints which comprise a 'blueprint' or 'skeleton' for the improvisation. The improviser can, therefore, dispense with much of the composer's habitual decision making concerning structure and direction. He uses a model which is, in most cases, externally supplied by the culture, and which he embellishes and 'fills in' in various ways. Such models frequently have a recursive sectional form, so that the performer becomes very familiar with the structure of the basic section, which can, to a large extent, be considered independently from other sections. This means that the improviser does not have to be constantly referring back to the detailed working out of earlier sections as, it may be argued, a composer must. He can rely on the given constraints of the form together with his own 'style' to give the music unity.

If we look at one of the forms in which improvisation flourishes, we can see how it helps the improviser to construct his performance. 'Theme and Variations', for instance, is a common form in classical, folk, and jazz idioms. A typical structure is

phrase:	A A B A	$A_1 A_1 B_1 A_1$	$A_2 A_2 B_2 A_2$	etc.
section:	theme	first variation	second variation	etc.

In this structure, the theme is composed of four phrases (typically each eight bars in length). The second and fourth phrases are repeats of the first phrase; the third phrase is different, but stylistically and thematically related to the first. The theme will be characterized by a certain underlying harmonic progression, and this progression will be repeated in each new variation. The improviser maintains interest and momentum by embellishing and transforming the melody and the texture within this repeating harmonic framework. Once the character of the A phrase variant has been determined, the remainder of the variation becomes highly constrained. An improviser can, for instance, 'run off' the last phrase of a variation as a rough copy of the first phrase, whilst giving some advance thought to the construction of the next section.

It will help us to see musical improvisation in perspective if we compare it to a verbal skill which has roughly the same sort of demands, such as the recounting of a story by a skilled story-teller. First, the story-teller has knowledge of a particular set of episodes which constitute the 'plot' of his story. This is similar to the knowledge of a particular melody or chord sequence in music.

Second, each element of the plot contains reference to well-known objects, situations, people, etc., whose detailed characteristics are not necessarily specified in the plot, but which may be used to elaborate and keep the tale fresh on any particular occasion of telling. For example, the plot may specify a character such as a farmer, who, without damage to the plot, can be further specified as old, lonely, jolly, tall, etc. on particular occasions. Minsky (1977) has used the term 'frame' to describe the cognitive structure that is accessed when a word like 'farmer' is introduced. This frame specifies attributes appropriate to the object or situation that can be specified, together with details of limits and constraints on those specifications. For instance, in a folk tale, a farmer will be an adult human being, so it is possible, although not necessary, to specify an age between, say, 15 and 70. Tellers and listeners frequently operate with 'default' values for attributes which are not actually specified. Such values may be chosen to be consistent with earlier information, or may arise from 'stereotypes'. For instance, when a farmer is mentioned, many listeners will assume a middle-aged, rather rough-cut male; and so a storyteller may choose to leave some details unspecified, knowing that the listener will still be able to make sense of the story through shared frames and stereotypes.

In music, we may equate 'frames' with characteristic harmonic or melodic progressions that underlie many different types of music. For instance, cadences are harmonic frames; particular types of melodic movement such as scales, arpeggios, gap-fill or changing note patterns (Rosner and Meyer 1982) are melodic frames. As in stories, many of these frames can be filled quite simply, with a couple of notes or chords, but can be fleshed out with various types of embellishment; passing notes and passing chords, for instance. There are many options for the way in which a musical frame may be filled. Performers and listeners within a culture will know about stereotypic ways of filling in such details. The composer and improviser achieve aesthetic impact by finding novel or surprising ways of embellishing a frame without changing its basic character.

A third feature of stories is their tendency to conform to certain structural specifications. One common type of story is the 'problem–effort–resolution' structure. An initial situation is specified. This situation presents some problem for a principal character or group of characters. They attempt to solve the problem; and this often involves the resolution of intermediate sub-problems. Finally, the goal is reached. Such structures allow both listeners and teller to keep track of the complex internal details of a story by labelling them according to their roles in the familiar structure. When stories do not conform to familiar structural models they are very hard to understand and remember (Bower 1976). The teller can use such a shared structure to pace his storytelling. If he senses his audience losing grip of the plot, he can add explanatory sentences to refresh memory of the position he is at within the structure (e.g. 'now the prince needed to find just one more thing before he would be able to slay the wicked dragon'). Similarly, if the plot seems too simple or bare for his audience, he can go down an irrelevant digressory path, provided that he is able to leave a 'marker' which tells where he is within the main structure.

We can roughly equate story structure with 'form' in music, as exemplified by 'theme and variation' or 'fugue', etc. When such structures are known by listeners, they are able to appreciate the function of present events, and through their anticipation of future constraints they can appreciate the art that produces novel sequences to fulfil the relevant function in the correct time. In jazz ensemble music, for instance, there is often a distinction between a fairly invariant 'chorus' played by the whole group, and a 'solo' where an individual performer is given the opportunity to come to the fore in an improvisatory fashion for a fixed number of bars before leading back into the next chorus. A listener who knows this structure can realize that the solo is about to end, and wonder how on earth the soloist is going to return satisfactorily from his harmonic and melodic excursions in a way that appropriately leads into the chorus. When such a performer does 'get home' in an appropriate but novel way, the listener can derive satisfaction which would be denied to someone who did not appreciate the demands of the structure. Similarly, the performer's own knowledge of the structure allows him to plan excursions whilst retaining markers which tell him exactly when he must arrive at a particular musical event.

In a sense, every act of story-telling that is not a verbatim recall is an act of improvisation. However, such improvisation reaches a peak in feats such as the singing of epic poetry in the Homeric tradition, preserved into the twentieth century among the folk singers of Yugoslavia (Lord 1960; Parry 1971). The singers are often illiterate, yet each singer has a large repertoire of poems (as many as 100), some of which are several thousand lines long and take more than an hour to sing. Parry's observations and recordings show that epic singers composed their songs anew on each occasion. No two performances were the same.

Neisser (1982) summarizes the main features of this epic poetry:

(the songs) show repetition of units at two levels of analysis, known as *themes* and *formulas*. Themes are types of events that occur in many different songs; a council of war, the arming of a warrior, the return of the hero in disguise. The formula, a much smaller unit, is 'a group of words which is regularly employed under the same metrical conditions to express a given essential idea' (Lord 1960, p. 30). The singer may have a dozen formulaic ways to describe daybreak: 'when dawn put forth its wings', 'when it was dawn and white day', or 'when the sun had warmed the earth', for example. When he comes to a part of the action that takes place at dawn he uses the one that best fits the metre and his mood. He knows dozens of themes and thousands of formulas, not from having memorized them but from having heard and used them, as we know the words and phrases of our own language.

This poetry is of special interest to us because it is *sung* and so involves musical improvisation too. The composer and musicologist Béla Bartók had a particular interest in Eastern European folk music, and collaborated with Lord in transcribing and analysing some of the musical recordings made by

Parry (Bartók and Lord 1951). The epic poems were always sung by a man, accompanying himself on the gusle, a one-stringed variety of lute which could provide a few different single notes for a drone-like accompaniment. The sung music was a version of chant. As far as one can undertand the comments of Bartók and Parry, who did not transcribe many of the epic poems, these chants were short simple melodies which were repeated with minor variations in the successive lines of the poems. Bartók was more interested in the shorter 'women's songs' where the degree of verbal improvisation was much less, but where the music was of considerably more complexity. His analysis identified various 'principal tones' which constituted the basic melodic frame for successive verses. The painstaking transcriptions show that a singer would embellish each verse in a different way, and would not use the same embellishments on two performances of the same song. There was much use of interpolations; glides, grace notes, ornaments, and passing notes.

In general, although vocal music is no stranger to improvisatory treatment, purely instrumental music seems to have encouraged more ambitious musical improvisation through the ages. One reason for this is that words constrain vocal music in many respects. A sung melody can be embellished only at the expense of directness of word communication. The 'basic' folk melody usually has only one note for each syllable. If more notes are added, then words must be repeated, or new syllables be created, or existing syllables lengthened and sung to several notes. The second of these devices is apparent in the Bartók transcriptions, where nonsense syllables (e.g. 'Aj' or 'Ahaj') are interpolated between words. Similarly, English folk songs are often embellished with 'fa la' or 'fol de rol', etc. The third device is known as melisma, and is common in many types of vocal music. Excessive use of melisma does, however, destroy the natural metre of the words, and can lead to severe difficulties in understanding them. In Gregorian chant, for instance, it can sometimes take five minutes to sing one sentence; a distortion which can only be tolerated if the words are well known to the listeners.

Although improvisation has flourished in various cultural and historical settings, I shall base the remainder of this section around jazz improvisation. Jazz is a contemporary Western form in which improvisation is paramount. It is a convenient form to study because (*a*) the idiom of most of its styles is derived from popular Western music (in its widest sense), and so is straightforwardly tonal; and (*b*) being contemporary, it can be experienced by any listener with access to a radio or a record player. We can only guess, from imprecise reports of observers, exactly how an improvisation by Mozart or Beethoven sounded. (For some observations on contemporary non-Western improvisatory forms, see Chapter 7).

There are two primary jazz forms; the 12-bar blues and the 32-bar song. The melody is often a 'standard' which is played in a fairly straightforward way to begin with. Repeated improvisations retain the basic harmonic sequence (although with the possibility of varying the harmonic detail); but the *essence* of improvisation, both here and in the 12-bar blues, is in the melodic line. This is partly due to the fact that the prototypical and original jazz medium is the brass ensemble where, because each player can produce only one note at a time, solo performance is necessarily melodic. Jazz piano came later, but it copies features of brass ensemble playing. The left hand typically provides chords and rhythm; the right hand 'plays the solo', carrying a single melodic line which is the focus of improvisatory effort.

All this, though, does not uniquely specify *jazz*. It would be quite possible to produce something perfectly 'Mozartean' using the 12-bar blues frame. What gives a performance its jazzy character are the particular types of melodic, rhythmic, and harmonic devices which form the basic building blocks for larger sequences. Such devices are almost exactly analogous to the *formulas* of epic poetry. They constitute the vocabulary of jazz. However, just as Yugoslav singers do not memorize a dictionary of formulas, so jazz improvisation is not normally learned by arming oneself with a list of characteristic chords and progressions. Jazz is learned through listening intently to other musicians and performing with them. Books and notation are not necessary; many great jazz performers could not read a note of music.

The pianist David Sudnow has performed a valuable service by writing a book which records his progress at learning jazz improvisation (Sudnow 1978). He provides a detailed exposition of his experiences at various stages of his development. In pulling out the principal features of his account, we can reinforce and expand the characterization of improvisation already given in outline.

When Sudnow approached the task of learning jazz he was already a competent classical pianist. The first new thing he learned was the 'anatomy' of typical left-hand jazz chords—practising placing single chords in the various keys of the chromatic scale. This was so that his hand would come to take up the appointed finger configurations rapidly and accurately without hitting adjacent wrong notes.

Second came the task of combining chords into the sequences typically found in songs. This entailed the co-ordinated ballistic movement of arm, hand, and fingers, to negotiate the sequence in a smooth but strict rhythm. At first, much visual monitoring was required, but eventually, common song sequences could be negotiated independently of visual control.

Next, standard (non-improvised) song melodies were combined with their appropriate chord sequences, so that the first statement of the 32-bar song could be given. All this was preliminary to the main task, that of melodic improvisation over a standard left-hand chord sequence.

At the outset, Sudnow did not know how to start nor once started, where to go next. The hand

might as well have gone anywhere, but once it did, there was nothing for it to do, and I discovered from the outset that if you don't know where you are going, you can't go anywhere except incorrectly. The hand has to be motivated to particular next keys to depress, and when there was nowhere for it to go it became totally immobilised, stumbled around . . . (p. 18).

He had no *formulas* to put into play. This was despite much experience of listening to jazz improvisations. He found the improvised passagework of his favourite performers so fast and complex that he simply could not get a detailed, note-by-note grasp of the structure. He reports that 'a three second stretch of play, within the course of an ongoing jazz improvisation (on record) I had listened to for many years, demanded several hours to catch the details sufficiently . . .' (p. 16).

Sudnow's teacher dealt with this problem by giving him some specific formulas. He would say 'with this particular chord you can get a characteristic sound by playing this particular scale.' An example of a chord-scale combination that Sudnow learned in this way is given in Example 4.25. He learned enough of these scales to have one available for each of the twelve chromatic dominant-seventh chords, and became fluent at playing them rapidly, both ascending and descending. At first, he could begin these scales in only one or two places. He reports that 'over the first years of play, nearly every time I played this particular scale, I either started on the F with the thumb (Example 4.25) or on the fourth finger (A) then moving down to the F (Example 4.26). This rigidity in a scale that could, in principle, be started on

Example 4.25. and 4.26. Jazz formulas learned by Sudnow (1978).

any note, was attributed to lack of useable knowledge about what finger to use if starting on other than the familiar note. To start, for instance, on the B natural and move upwards would require a second finger. But Sudnow knew the sale only as a single 'handful'. He knew a start note and the rest 'just happened'. So, in his early improvisation, he would simply find the appropriate scale for a particular chord, varying only the octave in which it was started or the number of notes used.

Gradually a repertoire of characteristic jazz formulas was built up in this way: 'arpeggios to be taken and scales to be linearly played, various "licks" constituted by certain intervallic relationships.' It was at this point that Sudnow tried his chances with a jazz trio at a club. His graphic description makes it clear just how far from true improvisation he yet was:

. . . and now a run for chord A is played, starting near the middle of the keyboard, and rises up, while the pathway I know best for chord B is played starting at the middle also. So that I started going up with a fast, spluttering, and nervous scale course, and the next chord came up and I had to shoot back down to the middle of the keyboard, to get the thing I knew how to do well done for it, and then there was the next chord. . . . An upward-moving line would more or less end when the next chord's sustaining had to be terminated, no matter where it was. Or, in order to get to the next starting place, I would end it a bit sooner, to give myself time to relocate, feeling the upcoming chord as an encroaching presence whose necessity was fixed by adherence to the chord chart of the song . . . so that what the left hand was doing in its pre-set ways was guiding what the right hand was then obliged to do. (p. 37.)

Sudnow continued for a few more years on essentially the same course, adding more and more formulas to the repertoire. Then, one day in the third year of his play, he began to have a different experience with his playing, which he calls 'going for the sounds'. This experience was essentially one of selecting and anticipating *particular* notes in the melodic improvisation. He explains that, up to that point

there was, with respect to the finely textured note-to-note nature of my play, an order that was guaranteed by the path's formal theoretical construction . . . (e.g. a scale) . . . I was not doing note-to-note selectional work. I decided where to start out each run, which run to choose, how fast to play it. But, we may say, no intentionality of aim was given to particular pitch achievments—only these broad 'parameters' received a motivated determination. (p. 39.)

Now, in contrast, Sudnow started to plan particular note effects. He did this primarily by attempting to relate a particular melodic line 'backwardly' to what had been done before, on the previous chord. So for instance, two adjacent chords might be given the realization shown in Example 4.27. Here,

Example 4.27. Imitatory improvisation. From Sudnow (1978).

the second group of four notes is a melodic imitation of the first group.

Previously, Sudnow had only the capacity to respond melodically to each chord as it came up by 'pulling something out of the bag' in respect of that chord alone (Fig. 4.2, stage 1). Now he was able to choose a continuation which both fitted the chord and was similar to the previous melodic fragment (Fig. 4.2, stage 2). This new way of playing led at first to a loss of fluency.

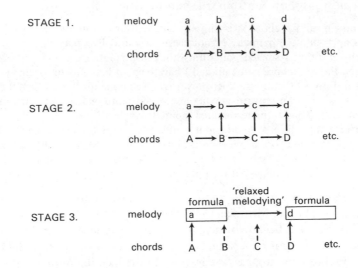

Fig. 4.2. Three stages in the development of David Sudnow's jazz improvisation.

Because the hand was attempting more ambitious things, it more often went wrong. For instance, to transpose a melodic pattern up or down a fixed number of semitones requires different fingering and hand configuration according to the particular black and white note pattern that the new key has. The melodic fragment in Example 4.27, if transposed to start on E flat, has a black–white–black–black key sequence, in contrast to the original all white sequence. This requires a shift in hand shape and, if uncertainly known, entails the possibility of hitting a wrong note. The well learned scale formulas were, however, played impeccably by this stage.

At this stage a typical experience is described as follows:

I would play a figure, go for its repetition, get some way into it, and stumble. To fill what I felt to be the remaining empty space, keeping this jazz going, I would do something quite unrelated to the explicit continuities I had partially achieved. I would accomplish the beginning of a reiteration (transposition, inversion . . . exact duplication, etc.), and then, for example, use up a remaining allotted chord time by taking on any notes that were thereabouts to take. (p. 56.)

Gradually, Sudnow worked towards something more assured and principled to do when the imitation attempt failed. He calls this the 'chromatic way'—and it essentially involves a bunched hand which plays a close set of notes which, although not necessarily composed totally of semitones, would have a chromatic character (e.g. Example 4.28). Such devices 'were afforded potentials for keeping action going in a sector, for making streams of notes,

Example 4.28. Chromatic improvisation. From Sudnow (1978).

for doing a fair amount of unthoughtful, weakly geared aiming for sounds. They allowed sustaining, at the same time, a connective tissue of action within attempts to tie up courses taken with one chord to those taken with the next' (p. 60).

Still Sudnow knew he was not really playing jazz the way he wanted it. It was too 'lungeful', composed of sporadic 'bits' of motivated improvisation joined together by *ad hoc* connections. It was after listening to the jazz pianist Jimmy Rowles (and watching him) that a breakthrough came. Rowles 'sat rather low down and stretched back, almost lazy with the piano like a competent driver is nonchalant behind the wheel on an open road. Still, there was a taking care with the melody, a caressing of it, a giving each place its due. He was never in a hurry . . .' (p. 81).

Rowles' relaxed swaying way at the piano contrasted with Sudnow's own 'frantic' attempts to negotiate fast passagework. Rowles played more slowly, with more attention to the basic melody. In trying to imitate Rowles, Sudnow began to find that

within my practice sessions little spates of that jazz on the records unpredictably showed themselves to me, and then disappeared. No sooner did I try to latch on to a piece of good-sounding jazz that would come out in the midst of my improvisations, than it would be undermined. . . . But there is no question that the hang of it had been glimpsed . . . All prior ways of being seem thoroughly lacking, and the new way is encountered with a 'this is it' feeling, almost like a revelation. . . . For a brief course of time while playing rapidly along, a line of melody would be generated, interweavingly flowing over the duration of several chords, fluently winding about in ways I had never seen my hands wind about before. (pp. 83–4.)

At first, Sudnow was unable to characterize exactly what he was doing in these moments, but gradually he came to realize that it was a sort of 're-leasing' from the rigid formulas which sent him scampering up and down the keyboard, on the basis of a new understanding that 'note choices could be made anywhere, that there was no need to lunge, that usable notes for any chord lay just at hand, that there was no need to find a path, image one up ahead to get ready for a blurting out . . . Good notes were everywhere at hand, right beneath the fingers.' He found

for example, that where it before seemed required to reach for a big path for a chord, foreseeing its location and organizational requirements . . . a single note would do to make melody over the course of several chords' durations. I could take my time in going for a long run, could linger, finding right beneath a non-venturing hand all sorts of melodying possibilities. (pp. 94–5.)

This allowed him to escape the tyranny of a rigid time schedule which had so hampered his earlier attempts. In the old way of playing, each chord was like a starting gun for some new pattern. So, the previous pattern had to get finished in time, maybe breaking off in an unplanned place. Sometimes he would fail to get to the new start in time, so the hands moved unintentionally out of phase, and the next figure would be hurried to get back on schedule. The new style allowed

mobile ways with the terrain such that commitments to arrival times could be continuously altered and shifted about in the course of the negotiations, a steady beat to the song as a whole sustained all the while. . . . It was to permit nonstuttering and nontripping disengagements from the terrain when a saying was not at hand, disengagements that would not make the music stop but would be silences of the music. (pp. 103–4.)

So now, the relation between the chords and the melody was looser; chords would still suggest typical formulas, but maybe a formula could run over into the next chord, then leaving the hand in a position to do some of the new relaxed melodying, taking time to introduce the next formula (Fig. 4.2, stage 3).

Very often a 'wrong note' in an attempt to play a formula could be used to good purpose. Instead of stumbling to correct the mistake, the note could be exploited in a jazz-like way. We see, therefore, an increasing understanding of the potentialities of almost *any* note to be used to effect in jazz. This presumably comes about through the years of experience of exploring the sounds that a keyboard makes. The improviser is relaxed and unhurried because he knows that, wherever he lands up, there are a dozen different ways of getting from there to the next place.

This confidence in the availability of plenty of 'escape routes' is, surely, a hallmark of skill in any impromptu accomplishment. To take a non-musical analogy from personal experience; my profession entails the fairly frequent giving of lectures and seminars to other members of the profession. When I began doing this, I was particularly terrified of the questions session which followed my 'set piece'. I was afraid of many things: not knowing the answer to a question, having some devastating criticism pointed at my work, not being able to put together a fluent reply without preparation. These fears began to subside as (*a*) I realized that I had a natural advantage over my audience; that of knowing the details of my own material, through many months of involvement with it, far better than anyone in the audience, and (*b*) I developed a repertoire of ways of handling awkward or unpleasant questions without faltering or becoming confused. The most important thing in situations like this is not to provide the *best* answer, but to provide *an* answer of some respectability with the fluency and immediacy that signals competence. Now, I usually face a question session in a relaxed and confident frame of mind because I know that I will always be able to find *something* appropriate to say. The jazz improviser can enjoy his improvisation because he knows that there will always be *something* he can play. Within this competence he, like all improvisers, knows that for much of the time he will produce quite ordinary improvisations; but from time to time, according to circumstance of mood and choice, something superlative will come up.

Here, then, is a fundamental difference between improvisation and composition. The composer rejects possible solutions until he finds one which seems to be the best for his purposes. The improviser must accept the first solution that comes to hand. In both cases the originator must have a repertoire of patterns and things to do with them that he can call up at will; but in the case of improvisation the crucial factor is the speed at which the stream of invention can be sustained, and the availability of things to do which do not overtax the available resources. In composition, fluency becomes less important; but it is much more important to keep long-term stuctural goals in sight, and to unify present material with what has gone before.

As we said at the beginning of this section, what absolves the improviser from the task of evaluation and long term planning is the relatively rigid formal 'frame' within which his improvisation takes place, and which dictates the large scale structure of his performances. Because this frame persists over many improvisations, the performer builds up a repertoire of 'things that have worked well in the past'. Commentators on jazz have emphasized that there is often less improvisation on the concert platform than one might imagine. The musician is often 'playing safe' by using improvisatory devices which have worked well in other circumstances, so as to create the best effects he knows how. A so-called improvisation may, in fact, be a carefully planned and rehearsed performance; although there is nothing about the performance as such that would allow us to know this. To evaluate the degree of true improvisation, one would need to ask for two or more performances of the same piece for comparison. This observation is not to denigrate the musicians concerned. Improvisation is still at the heart of their art, but the social and commercial pressures of the concert platform do not encourage the risk-taking that improvisation inevitably involves. For real improvisatory jazz at its best one may have to seek out the late-night backroom informal sessions where, amidst a dedicated and sympathetic audience, experiments that fail, as well as those that reach new heights, may be observed.

As when discussing composition, we may ask how these informal observations on improvisation may lead to more rigorous scientific study of the processes involved. Sudnow's commentaries, for all their merits, were formulated some time after the improvisational acts in question, and at a level of some generality. There is a need for detailed and controlled study of *in vivo* improvisations. Although concurrent protocols could not easily be obtained from an improviser, the next best thing would be an immediate retrospection. By recording an improvisation and then playing it back to the performer, with as many pauses and backtracks as required, we could hope to obtain a detailed record of the conscious decisions involved in constructing the improvisation. Experimental studies also suggest themselves. For instance, one could pre-record simple repeated chord sequences and ask performers of varying ability to provide as many different melodic variations as they can. Effects of the 'stereotypicality' of the chord sequence, or its speed, could then be examined. There is a rich untapped vein of data here which urgently awaits psychological attention.

5. Listening to music

5.1. Introduction

The two musical activities we have considered in detail so far, performing and composition, each entail the production of an externally observable end-product. Performance involves making a sequence of sound-producing movements, and composition involves making a score or some other communicable record. In contrast, listening to music is, in many situations, a passive affair. When I go to a symphony concert or listen to a gramophone record there may well be a lot of *mental* activity, but there is not necessarily any observable physical activity. The principal end-product of my listening activity is a series of fleeting, largely uncommunicable mental images, feelings, memories, and anticipations. When trying to understand what happens during music listening, the psychologist, therefore, is at a considerable disadvantage. In the previous two chapters we used concrete evidence from performances, scores, sketches, etc. to infer something about the cognitive processes that produced them. Such types of evidence provide what we may call 'records' of the music concerned, because they have a detailed event-by-event correspondence with the music. Many, if not most, instances of music listening do not provide 'records' in this sense.

Sometimes there is a specific behavioural activity attached to listening. For instance, one may dance, clap one's hands, or tap one's feet in response to the music. From such behaviour the psychologists may be able to infer something about the listener's ability to derive rhythm and metre from music (see the discussion of rhythm in Chapter 2, section 5.4); but such a response is hardly a *record* of the music. Rather, it is a generalized response to rhythmic characteristics which can be shared by very many pieces of music. By simply examining the response, one would not know *which* piece of music had been heard.

We approach closest to obtaining a musical record when we ask a listener to *recall* what he has heard, as we may do when teaching someone a new song. However, unless the material to be recalled is very short we are in danger of seriously underestimating the amount of musically related mental activity that has taken place. I have frequently been unable to recall details of a long piece of music after a first hearing, even though I was totally engaged with the music while it took place. As when listening to a lecture, or reading a novel, the details of argument and plot may fully engage one's intellect *whilst* one experiences the unfolding of ideas, but they may leave few recoverable traces at the end of the session.

The principal problem facing the student of listening processes is to find a valid way of tapping the moment-to-moment history of mental involvement with the music. As we examine research in the field of perception, attention, and memory in music we shall find that this problem has not really been solved satisfactorily. Most research evades this crucial issue by examining responses to very brief segments of music, made up of between two and twenty notes. Such segments hardly present listeners with the range of patterns and relationships which they must deal with in even the simplest short song.

In defence of such research one may, of course, argue that music is made up of a large number of small fragments chained together, and that music perception is simply a concatenation of a series of perceptual acts on such fragments. If so, however, then all the art of classical composition must go for nothing, because, as has been argued earlier, events quite far apart in time can be intimately connected structurally. Intelligent listening, we may argue, picks up such relationships; it spans large numbers of notes so as to be 'structural hearing' (to use the phrase coined by Salzer 1952). Composers write for listeners, not analysts, and the testimony of many listeners is that they *can* discern the large-scale relationships which analysts characterize.

What we may, more modestly, claim for studies on short musical fragments is that they shed light on elementary listening processes whose results are then used by higher processes about which little is known. In a similar way, students of language perception have discovered a great deal about the way in which listeners deal with isolated sentences (e.g. Fodor, Bever, and Garrett 1974), but these findings do not allow a very clear picture to be formed of how listeners or readers deal with whole paragraphs or books. For that, one has to find ways of observing behaviour in response to the larger units (Bransford 1979; Clark and Clark 1977; Sandford and Garrod 1981).

A further problem hinders our attempts to appreciate the significance of music listening studies. We must distinguish effects which are due to real and abiding features of normal listening from those which are special effects of the experimental task, which may involve activity quite unlike that of normal listening. Let me give a common example. Many studies require a listener to hear two short extracts of music and then to judge whether they are the same or different in some respect. The normal inference drawn from such studies is that if a listener can reliably tell when a particular type of difference is present, then he extracts this information in normal listening, and conversely, if he cannot reliably detect a difference, then he does not extract such information in normal listening. In fact, neither inference is necessarily valid. *Success* at discrimination in the experimental task may be a result of the subject's being able to focus on the dimension concerned for a brief period. This does not imply that he will choose to, or be able to, focus on this dimension in continuous listening where other dimensions of sound also demand his attention. For instance, fine differences in timing or tuning may be noticeable in very short sequences, but be completely unrecoverable in longer ones. *Failures* of discrimination in the experimental task may be due to lack of cues that would be supplied by a more extended context. For instance, we shall see that listeners are often unable to tell short sequences apart when they have slightly different pitch intervals but identical up–down contour. It would be wrong to conclude from this that listeners cannot use pitch interval information in extended listening. It seems that in more realistic listening situations pitch information becomes crucial in discrimination (Dowling and Bartlett 1981).

Another example concerns the degree of familiarity that a listener has with the materials. In most music perception experiments this familiarity is low — the listener is exposed to sequences that he has never heard before. In contrast, real-life listening often involves the repeated hearing of the same material so that its internal structure becomes better and better known. Most serious listeners to music will have experienced times when they suddenly 'see' some new relationship between elements of a well-known piece of music—music that they may have lived with for many years. The experimental literature has told us very little about such processes, although recent work by Pollard-Gott (1983) has shown that subjects change their coding of segments from Lizst's Sonata in B minor after only a few opportunities to listen to the complete work. Briefly, she found that repeated exposure increased the likelihood that subjects would notice 'deep' harmonic or thematic similarities between segments, as opposed to 'surface' features, such as speed or tessitura.

I do not wish to dwell at any further length on the hazards and shortcomings of 'music perception' research. I have put these cautionary comments at the beginning of this chapter because it is a source of great disappointment to me that the one area of music psychology in which research is flourishing should be characterized by a relative insensitivity to the problems of relating research findings to normal music listening. This disappointment is shared by others (e.g. Davies 1979) but rarely voiced in print.

Another factor which prompts cautionary remarks at this point is the 'halo effect' which can surround a body of research which has the credentials of a *paradigm* as typified by Kuhn (1962). A paradigm is signalled by the existence of a set of agreed research problems, a methodology capable of solving them and generating new, but similar, problems, and a group of scientists who interact around these problems. When, as often happens, such a group 'captures' prestigious communication channels, in journals and elsewhere, generating a continuous series of co-ordinated and logically connected research articles, it is tempting to accord the research a significance which is not necessarily justified by its long-term achievments. The history of psychology is littered with forgotten paradigms. Many of them were initially motivated by important and substantial psychological problems, but in the end subsidiary problems raised by the research became the main focus of potentially indefinite elaboration which contributed nothing to the original substantive question. I speak as one who has been seduced by the attractions of paradigm-driven research; and I have dabbled at the edges of a paradigm (Sloboda 1976c, 1977b) which is, I believe and hope, already being consigned to obscurity. I would not wish to go so far as to say that music perception research is unproductive, or to argue that science should proceed in any other way. I would argue, however, that we need to be constantly checking that questions of real musical importance are being asked and answered. It is all too easy to take currently researched issues to be *the* issues of music perception, just because a substantial body of research is *there* in all its solidity, interconnectedness, ingenuity, and undoubted methodological soundness.

If this causes me to stand a little lightly to the current research, mentioning some, but by no means all, of the experimental approaches to music perception, then I must say that I feel happy to do this, not least because there are several very good and fairly exhaustive reviews of experimental work in this area which absolve me from duplicating the effort here. I would advise the reader who is seriously interested in music perception to read one or all of the following: articles by Deutsch, Dowling, Shepard and Ward; all in Deutsch (1982a); and the authoritative survey and bibliography provided by Spender (1980).

5.2. 'Natural hearing': primitive grouping mechanisms in music

The first area of study that I wish to examine relates to a fundamental question about music. This question is: what natural mechanisms and propensities of the human auditory system can determine the way in which we hear musical sounds to be grouped? The principal characteristic of music is that sounds stand in significant relation to one another, not in isolation. For music perception to 'get off the ground' listeners must start to notice relationships and identify significant groupings. At the highest level such groupings will be large and complex, corresponding to formal structures within a work. At the lowest level they will be relatively simple, features of the sound pattern which characterize small groups of notes.

Studies of visual perception have revealed a number of basic and universal grouping tendencies which go under the name of 'Gestalt principles of perception' because they were first given systematic demonstration and formulation by the Gestalt school of psychologists (e.g. Wertheimer 1923). Although visual examples are most commonly cited, these principles can be seen as having application to any perceptual domain, representing as they are held to do, primitive and innate grouping tendencies. It seems that very young children and animals are subject to the operation of these principles as well as human adults (Gibson 1969).

If these principles are innate and universal, then it is possible that they have been incorporated into the brain's way of operating in order to solve perennial perceptual problems faced by living organisms that interact with a natural environment. Some of these problems have been identified (see Sutherland 1973, Hochberg 1974, and Marr 1982, for vision; Bregman 1981, and Kubovy 1981, for hearing). For instance, the principle of 'common fate', which states that elements that move in the same direction are perceived together, allows a solution to the problem of how to identify the elements of a visual scene which belong to a single moving object that may be partially obscured or occluded by other visual elements. This principle explains why an animal which may be perfectly camouflaged against a background whilst stationary becomes instantly visible once it moves. Striking demonstrations by Johanssen (1976) show that conjoint motion of lights fitted to the joints of otherwise invisible humans is sufficient for an observer to reconstruct a percept of them which can not only identify them as humans, but allow a normal observer to make accurate estimates of their age, sex, and actions as well.

Most of the natural mechanisms of visual grouping are motivated by 'action' requirements. They help the organism to orient and move about the environment effectively, to locate and track objects in that environment, and so on. We should expect auditory grouping mechanisms to have their roots in similar requirements. Deutsch (1982b) suggests that a primary function of auditory grouping mechanisms is to assist in the enumeration of sound-producing objects in the environment. Such objects are likely to be of importance because they are other animals (friendly or unfriendly) or because they signal significant change in the environment (e.g. fruit falling from trees).

We may imagine the sounds of a forest at night, a potentially bewildering confusion of overlapping sounds. Yet it is possible to separate and group the sounds. We hear the complex sound-pattern created by the wind rustling in the trees as unified, yet separate from the chirps of insects. And we hear the calls of three birds of the same species *as* three sounds. To each source is assigned the correct 'package' of sounds. Gestalt grouping mechanisms underlie our ability to 'parse' the acoustic environment effortlessly. Thus, Deutsch argues that 'similar sounds are likely to be emanating from the same source, and different sounds from different sources. A sound sequence that changes smoothly in frequency is likely to be emanating from a single source. Components of a complex sound spectrum that rise and fall in synchrony are also likely to be emanating from the same source' (Deutsch 1982b, p. 101). These likelihoods govern the way we group complex sound 'scenes'. The existence of such grouping tendencies is, arguably, one of the happy chances that allows us to hear *musical* groupings spontaneously. Let us look at the operation of some of these tendencies in more detail.

Sound sources usually have definite physical locations, and a possible way of sorting out a complex set of sounds is to group them according to perceived location. One way of locating the direction of an unseen sound source is through the comparison of the sound signals that arrive at each ear. When a sound to the left of a listener is turned on, the first impulses arrive at the left ear slightly before they arrive at the right. The technical term for this time differences is 'onset asynchrony'. Humans, and many animals, have precocious ability to locate an unseen sound source through onset asynchrony. Quite young babies will turn their heads to look in the direction from which a sound has come.

A listener can also locate a steady tone through phase differences between the two ears. Because sound is transmitted through air by a series of air molecules, and because points of maximum compression move outwards from the source at a finite speed (taking about 680 μs to traverse the 23 cm between the two ears), there is a time difference between the energy peak at the two ears which can be detected. In this case, though, the energy differences are small compared to sounds which have sharp onset or offset bursts (known as transients). Therefore, sounds with transients, such as clicks and chirps, are more accurately localized than steady tones. The wise hi-fi salesman uses this fact when demonstrating the power of his stereo systems. Music with percussive elements will give rise to a more compelling 'stereophonic' effect than will the 'smooth' characteristics of voice or string sounds.

There are other problems with grouping by localization. Echoes and reverberations can cause sounds to arrive at the ear from other directions than the source. Also, the auditory system has no way of distinguishing between a single sound coming from directly in front of the face and two identical sounds coming from equidistant sources on either side. For these and other reasons it has been argued that location is a less important grouping cue than *pitch* (see Bregman 1981; Bregman and Campbell 1971; Deutsch 1982b; Kubovy 1981). In nature, sounds coming from the same source over a brief duration will also tend to have the same, or similar pitch. If pitch *does* change it is more likely to be smoothly, or in small steps, than discontinuously or in large steps. Additionally, in nature, perceived pitch and perceived location are often mutually reinforcing; confirming the *same* grouping of sounds.

Man-made sounds, in music and in the laboratory, can deliberately set grouping cues in opposition, creating illusory or ambiguous percepts which demonstrate the relative strengths of the grouping tendencies. A good example of this work has been provided by Deutsch (1975) who played listeners two simultaneous tone sequences through headphones, one to each ear. The two sequences are shown in Example 5.1. The commonest perceptual experience which arose from these stimuli is shown in Example 5.2. Listeners heard all the high tones emanating from the right headphone and all the low tones emanating from the left headphone. Deutsch calls this phenomenon the *scale illusion* because listeners hear the stimulus as two smooth scale passages rather than as the two angular melodic contours which were actually present.

Example 5.1. and 5.2. The scale illusion. From Deutsch (1975).

Butler (1979) has demonstrated that this pitch grouping phenomenon is highly robust. Deutsch used pure tones with headphones, but Butler used real instrumental sounds (e.g. piano) with spatially separated loudspeakers. Even when the notes from one speaker had a distinctive timbre, listeners still predominantly grouped by pitch.

Composers seem to have discovered this phenomenon long before it was brought into the laboratory. The best known example occurs at the beginning of the last movement of Tchaikovsky's Sixth Symphony. Example 5.3 gives the first and second violin parts as played. Example 5.4 shows what most

Examples 5.3. and 5.4. An analogue of the scale illusion. From Tchaikovsky, sixth symphony, last movement.

listeners hear. Those who know the work by ear before they see the score sometimes cannot believe that there has not been a typographical error! The 'illusion' does not require the sounds of the two violin sections to come from the same direction. The perception is still the same when the two sections are on opposite sides of the conductor's rostrum.

It is not totally clear *why* Tchaikovsky chose to write the parts in this way if they are really indistinguishable from the case in which the violins had actually played Example 5.4. It is possible that typical violinists produce subtly different sounds when negotiating an angular rather than a smooth melodic sequence, which would be heard as a difference in texture or timbre.

A less well-known example is to be found in the second movement of Rachmaninov's Second Suite for Two Pianos, Op. 17. Example 5.5 shows a transposed version of the notes played by first and second piano towards the end of the movement. I was recently involved in a performance of this work, playing first piano, and was subject to the compelling illusion that Example 5.6 was being played. This was even though I could see my hand playing two

Examples 5.5. and 5.6. A perceptual illusion experienced in Rachmaninov's suite for two pianos, Op. 17, second movement.

notes, and not just repeating one. It was as if someone had suddenly retuned the lower note I was playing to the same pitch as the upper one. We may suppose that Rachmaninov wrote the parts in this way because it would be difficult for a pianist to repeat the same note in the figuration of Example 5.6 with the kind of speed and dynamic control which the music requires (about six quavers per second with a controlled decrescendo to pianissimo).

In the examples we have considered so far there are two *really* distinct sound sources producing simultaneous sounds. Pitch grouping causes some of the sounds to be mislocated. There are other cases when grouping by pitch (or *pitch streaming* as it is often called) allows a single sound source to be heard *as if* it were two independent sources. Thus, a solo instrument can create an illusion of polyphony by interleaving the notes of two contrapuntal lines separated in pitch. This device has frequently been used by composers, especially in the baroque period. Example 5.7 shows this device at work in the right hand of J. S. Bach's Prelude in G from book 2 of the Well-Tempered Clavier.

Example 5.7. From J. S. Bach, *Well-Tempered Clavier*, Prelude 8, Book 2.

Whether or not the single melodic line is heard as one or two pitch streams depends crucially on the pitch separation and the speed of the component notes. Miller and Heise (1950) presented listeners with a sequence containing two notes that alternated at a rate of ten per second. They varied the pitch separation of the two notes and found that intervals of less than about one seventh of an octave were heard as a *single* stream, whereas intervals greater than this caused the notes to separate out into two independent streams. In terms of the chromatic scale, this means that intervals of a minor or major second produce *fused* percepts which correspond to musical trills. Notes a minor third apart or greater tend to be heard as separate, producing stream *fission*. Van Noorden (1975) has shown that if the rate of alternation is slowed beyond about six notes per second, it becomes possible to hear wider intervals up to an octave as fused to form a single stream. The effect is, within limits, open to conscious control. It is possible to switch one's perception of an intermediate case so that at one time it is heard as a trill or single line, at another time as two independent lines. There seem to be limits, however, beyond which the percept is not open to such switches. Intervals of a tone or less, when repeatedly alternated, tend not to give rise to fission. No matter how slow the speed of performance, they are heard as a single line.

None the less, Example 5.7 suggests a case in which intervals of a tone or less *may* be heard in separate streams. Here, the C at the end of the first bar is heard as belonging to the lower stream, and does *not* fuse with the upper stream of repeated Ds. We may suppose that larger patterning context overrides the immediate factors, so that the repeated Ds are heard as one line, and the rising and falling scale as another. This tendency is accounted for under another principle of Gestalt grouping, the principle of *good continuation*. We may illustrate this by an almost exact visual analogy. In Fig. 5.1 (*a*) the lower dot is seen as forming a group with the two adjacent upper dots. In Fig 5.1 (*b*) it is 'captured' by the lower dots and becomes part of a curved line distinct from the upper straight line.

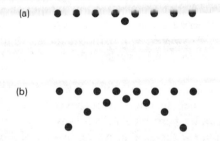

Fig. 5.1. Example of gestalt principles of perceptual organization.

(*a*) The lower circle appears joined to its neighbours (principle of proximity).

(*b*) The circle is 'captured' by the curved sequence (principle of good continuation overrides proximity).

The basic pitch streaming phenomenon demonstrated by Miller and Heise also has a fairly direct visual analogy (as noticed by Kubovy 1981). If two nearby point light sources are switched on and off in alternation in a darkened room, the impression is often of a *single* light moving backwards and forwards between the two locations. This well-known visual illusion is called the *Phi phenomenon*. The likelihood of the two lights being seen as a single moving light is decreased if the speed of alternation is increased, or if the sources are moved further apart. Under these latter conditions one is more likely to see two independent 'flashing' light sources. When tones are substituted for lights, and pitch distance for spatial distance, the Phi phenomenon becomes the pitch streaming phenomenon.

We can suppose that the striking parallel between these phenomena has its origin in the general properties of natural objects which the perceptual system has developed to deal with. Two sounds very close to one another in time but widely separated in pitch are unlikely to come from the same object. Likewise, two visual events very close to one another in time but widely separated in space are unlikely to come from the same object. As the time separation between events increases, however, the possibility of them belonging to the same object increases. A high sound may come from the same animal as a low sound once it has had time to adjust voice register. A light on the left may come from the same object as a light on the right if it has had time to move between the two locations, unseen.

The work of researchers such as Miller and Heise (1950) and Van Noorden (1975) has demonstrated pitch streaming in very simplified perceptual situations. Dowling (1973) extended these studies to more musically realistic stimuli. He took familiar melodies (such as 'Frère Jacques', 'Happy Birthday', etc.) and interleaved pairs of them so that listeners heard note 1 of tune A, then note 1 of tune B, then note 2 of tune A, then note 2 of tune B, and so on. These composite sequences were played at a rate of eight notes per second (four of each tune). Listeners were required to identify the component melodies. Dowling found that recognition of the melodies was almost impossible when they overlapped in pitch. They merged into a single, unrecognizable sequence. However, when the melodies were moved apart in pitch, so that their notes did not overlap, the melodies could easily be recognized.

Dowling found one condition in which overlapping melodies could be recognized. This was when listeners were asked to search for particular named melodies. Melodies perceived in this way were done so with effort, however. They had none of the ease and spontaneity of recognition enjoyed by the pitch-separated melodies. The process was one of active search rather than passive awareness. A visual analogy may again be helpful. Figure 5.2 will be seen spontaneously as two triangles. You do not naturally see the

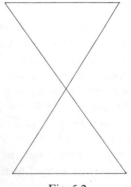

Fig. 5.2.

numeral 7; but if I ask you to *find* a 7 in the figure, you can do so. In the former case, your perception was governed by the spontaneous and largely automatic Gestalt principles of grouping (the 'laws' of proximity, closure, and symmetry being operative here). In the latter case you use prior know-ledge about the shape of a figure 7 to overcome your natural grouping tendencies and achieve a more difficult, less spontaneous, way of seeing the figure.

Dowling also found that unfamiliar melodic patterns (learned by the lis-teners during the experiment) could not be recognized so easily when inter-leaved with other melodies, even when there was pitch separation of as much as an octave. This shows that the use that can be made of pitch streaming is not invariant, but can be helped or hindered by acquired knowledge about music.

This conclusion raises a general question about *all* the demonstrations we have examined in this section. Do they *really* show the natural auditory system at work, unaffected by the musical experience that most of us share? Many of the experiments use materials which make most *musical* sense when grouped by pitch. The grouping could be a result of application of knowledge about likely melodic patterns in music. This argument applies, for instance, to Deutsch's scale illusion. The melodies produced by each sound location are angular, with atypical pitch contours, whereas those arising through the supposed operation of pitch streaming conform to one of the commonest of all melodic patterns, the diatonic scale. Musical knowledge would, therefore, contribute to the tendency to group by pitch. There is, of course, a curious circularity here. It may be precisely *because* pitch grouping is a a fundamental auditory phenomenon that many common musical sequences move within restricted pitch ranges.

None the less, it should be possible to tease apart the contributions of fundamental auditory groupings and musical knowledge. One way of doing this would be to modify Deutsch's (1975) stimuli so that pairs of simultaneous melodies made more musical sense when grouped by location than when grouped by pitch. Example 5.8 shows such a pair. Here, the sequence played to the right ear forms a C major arpeggio/chord whilst that played to the left ear forms a D flat major arpeggio/chord. Each pattern is commonly found in tonal music, and has a strong and simple harmonic structure. Example 5.9 shows the sequence obtained if the notes are streamed by pitch,

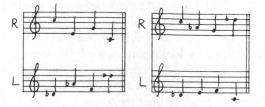

Examples 5.8. and 5.9.

taking the upper note in each pair for the first stream, and the lower note for the second stream. Both streams contain unusual pitch leaps (diminished fifth, augmented second) rather than the smooth scales of Deutsch's illusion, and do not have straightforward harmonic implications. If the tendency to group by pitch is lessened in such sequences, then musical knowledge is implicated in streaming mechanisms.

A second way of determining the part played by musical knowledge in such effects is to look for differences between experienced musicians and novices. If differences exist, then musical knowledge is implicated. This approach has been taken by Smith, Hausfield, Power, and Gorta (1982) who compared musicians and non-musicians on several varieties of the scale illusion. They found that musicians were more likely than non-musicians to stream by pitch, even when there were conflicting cues (such as timbre) suggesting a streaming by ear. They argue for the conclusion that musicians are more likely to expect 'tunelike' stimuli than non-musicians.

The most convincing demonstrations that pitch streaming is a primary auditory grouping mechanism, regardless of musical knowledge or structure are, perhaps, those that require perceptual judgements that have nothing to do with music as such, and point to the existence of pitch streams by implication, rather than because listeners are asked to directly *identify* streams. I will give just one example of such a demonstration. Fitzgibbons, Pollatsek, and Thomas (1974) asked subjects to detect a small temporal gap in a sequence of four tones, the first two of which were high in pitch (2093 and 2394 Hz) and the last two of which were low in pitch (440 and 494 Hz). This sequence (HHLL) was presented with the gap (G) in three possible positions: HGHLL, HHGLL, and HHLGL. In two cases the gap was between notes close in pitch, in the other case (HHGLL) it fell between two notes widely different in pitch. In the former two cases gap detection was nearly perfect, but in the latter case, detection of the same gap was significantly poorer. The interpretation given to these results is that listeners are able to notice time relationships *within* pitch streams more easily than time relationships between different pitch streams. Such relationships are not preserved in the automatic 'parsing' mechanisms which split such stimuli into two independent parts on the basis of pitch.

Such demonstrations provide strong evidence that pitch streaming is a real 'pre-musical' phenomenon, although musical knowledge may interact with and modify its effects. Pitch is not the only 'primitive' cue to grouping. Other cues, such as timbre and amplitude are described by Deutsch (1982b). I do not intend to deal with them in a detailed way here. Rather I would like to conclude this section by looking at some more complex and musically sophisticated ways in which composers can use pitch relationships as the basis for creating dynamic impetus in extended melodies.

This discussion owes much to the theoretical approach to melody outlined by Meyer (1973). According to Meyer, one of the functions of a melodic line is to create *implications* for future events. In earlier writings (Meyer 1956) he used concepts of 'creating expectancies' in listeners, but this is a slightly misleading way of talking. The implications are inherent in the melody itself, by virtue of its structure; such implications may or may not be picked up by a listener and used to form expectancies on a given hearing.

For Meyer, implications are objective features of a melody which create some patterning or direction which admits of continuation. One implication, for instance, of an ascending five-note scale passage on its own is for a sixth note to be added to continue the sequence. An implication of the sequence CDCDCD is that CD should be repeated again; and so on. These are very simple implications. Any interesting melody has multiple (and sometimes conflicting) implications. A composer may not necessarily realize all of the implications of a melodic opening. Some he may not notice, others he may deliberately go against for musical effect. Even those that he does realize in a continuation may not be noticed as such, even by an acute listener. Rather, they contribute to an undifferentiated awareness that this is a good or interesting melody.

There are many devices for creating implications which rely on tonal or rhythmic factors. Here, I want to consider the use of pitch separation alone as an implicative device. Consider the melody which J. S. Bach uses for the F minor Fugue from book 2 of the Well-Tempered Clavier (Example 5.10)

Example 5.10. From J. S. Bach, *Well-Tempered Clavier*, Fugue 12, Book 2.

The opening nine notes contain some quite large pitch separations between adjacent notes. Thereafter, the melody moves in scalar fashion. The ideal performing speed for this fugue is about four quavers per second. This places the melody in the range established by Van Noorden (1975) where intervals of up to an octave between successive notes can be heard either as separating the two notes into distinct streams, or merging them into one, depending upon one's 'set'. So the opening of Bach's melody can be heard as a single unified line; but it has ambiguity—it can also separate out into two lines, an upper one created by notes 1, 5, and 6 (C, D flat, and B flat), and a lower one created by notes 2, 3, 4, and 7, 8, 9 (F and E). On the other hand, the material after note 9 proceeds by scalar steps of major and minor seconds, each note therefore being necessarily perceived as part of a single line with its neighbours. So these semiquaver runs serve as a sort of retrospective 'glue', bringing together the potentially separable lines of the opening notes. A different continuation could, in contrast, have sustained and accentuated the line separation (Example 5.11). Bach's intention seems to have been to create a tension between two potentially separable melodic lines which is

Example 5.11.

then resolved by 'knitting' them together. In Rosner and Meyer's (1982) terminology, the melody has features of a type labelled 'gap-fill' where an unfilled interval is created, then filled through scalar movement.

This is not the whole story, however. Each melodic line of the opening has its own implications which are not realized in the immediately following notes. Each creates a *direction* of pitch movement. The lower line on its own creates an implication for further downward movement (F→ E→). Conversely, the upper line has an implication for further upward movement. The topmost note is C, then D flat; an even higher note is implied. Both these implications are left unfulfilled in bar 2, but they are both realized on the first beat of bar 3: the lower movement through the second fugal entry which drops to middle C; and the upper movement through the simultaneous achievment of top E flat in the first voice, the highest note in the piece so far. This resolution of unfulfilled implications contributes to the sense of closure experienced as the second theme enters, and gives the melody a dynamic forward movement that makes it vital and satisfying. Consider how lifeless Example 5.12 is in comparison, where there is no upper pitch line, and therefore no sense that the final E flat resolves an earlier implication.

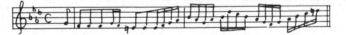

Example 5.12.

A second example of the implicative use of pitch streaming is provided by the principal theme of the last movement of Mozart's Concerto in E flat for Two Pianos (K. 365) given in Example 5.13. Here, the scalar motion of the

Example 5.13. From Mozart, Concerto for two pianos (K.365), last movement.

opening creates a unified melodic line spanning the F above middle C to the B flat below it. The last note of bar 2, an upper B flat, stands isolated from this line by a perfect fourth. In bars 3 and 4, the melody continues in the initial lower register. Arguably, the single upper note creates an implication for further notes in that pitch range. Such implication is only realized in bar

5, where the melody leaps up to this B flat before descending in scalar fashion to bring the melody back to the opening E flat. Bar 5 is, therefore, motivated by what has gone before in a way that it would not be without the bar 2 that Mozart supplied. If we rewrite the first two bars as in Example 5.14, then the pitch leap at bar 5 comes as arbitrary and surprising.

Example 5.14.

My treatment of these examples has been discursive and analytic in the musical sense. However, I have imputed psychological consequences of listening to them which have not been strictly demonstrated. What kind of evidence could we supply that a supposed implication of a melody has actually been detected by a listener? One, rather naîve, approach would be to play listeners the opening parts of melodies, and ask them to provide fitting continuations. For instance, we could compare listener's responses to the first four bars of Example 5.13 with the same four bars as modified in Example 5.14. If they pick up the implication of the high B flat, then Example 5.13 should result in significantly more continuations in a pitch range around that B flat.

I call this approach naîve because it assumes that implication is likely to be detected on a first hearing in a way that could guide conscious choice. It is equally possible that, for many listeners, the implications of a good melody are revealed gradually over many hearings, and that, even when revealed, can be used only to *recognize* fitting continuations rather than to *generate* one's own continuations. Such considerations make it quite likely that no positive results would be obtained with this technique. None the less, something of the sort is clearly worth trying. The only experiments I know to have used a similar technique (Carlsen 1981) involved presenting subjects with simple two-note sequences and asking them to provide plausible continuations. The types of implications that can be contained in two-note sequences are very limited, and hardly begin to tap the range of devices used by real composers. As far as they go, however, Carlsen's results show some evidence for pitch range sensitivity. His subjects showed a marked tendency to choose a third note close in pitch to the second note given. Sixty per cent of all continuations began within a major second of the second note given. It would be interesting to know whether subsequent continuations employed the 'gap-fill' technique, moving back to the first note through scale-like movement, but Carlsen analysed only the first note of each subject's response.

The mechanisms of melodic perception required to notice implications of the type discussed above involve more than can be supplied by the involuntary and immediate processes of auditory grouping. They require *attention* to the salient aspects of a complex stimulus, and *memory* of past events which stand in important relationships to present material. The next two sections deal with these aspects of music listening.

5.3. Attention in music listening

We begin our consideration of attention by returning to Dowling's (1973) experiments with interleaved melodies. We saw earlier that subjects could recognize both melodies provided that they did not overlap in pitch, but formed separate perceptual streams. However, Dowling reports that subjects did not identify both melodies at the same time. More commonly they would identify one of the melodies on a given hearing, and the other on the next hearing. They seemed to be *selecting* either one or the other stream to monitor; but were not able to monitor both streams at once. This result points to the existence of a serious problem in music listening. A great amount of music is polyphonic; that is, it has more than one line of music proceeding at the same time. If we can attend to only one line at a time, how do we ever achieve a full experience of the polyphonic structure?

Pioneering studies on attention to speech (Cherry 1953) have shown that when two speech messages are presented simultaneously it is possible to shadow (verbally report) one of them, but that almost nothing is known about the characteristics of the other message. Thus, for instance, the non-shadowed message may change language, or repeat the same phrase over and over again without the subject being aware of it. These studies, and others like them, have been used to support the notion that our perceptual system incorporates a single, limited capacity attentional 'channel', through which only a small part of our sensory experience can pass at any one time. This mechanism operates like a 'filter' which lets through only material which is defined by some distinguishing sensory feature (like pitch, or ear of entry) at any one time. All other material is lost before it can reach those higher mechanisms which recognize and classify input. Broadbent (1958) provides the classic formulation of such a position.

More recent studies have challenged the 'filter' theory in various ways (Allport, Antonis, and Reynolds 1972; Deutsch and Deutsch 1963; Shiffrin and Schneider 1977; Triesman 1964). For instance, Allport, Antonis, and Reynolds asked pianists to sight-read piano music at the same time as shadowing a prose message played over headphones. They found that performance on both tasks was just as good when carried out together as when carried out alone. Such a finding is incompatible with the filter theory, which would predict that subjects could attend either to the sight-reading input (visual) or to the speech input (auditory) but not to both. An alternative way of explaining attentional phenomena is to propose that processes *may* take place simultaneously provided that they do not use the same kinds of cognitive mechanisms. In Cherry's and other speech experiments, both messages were verbal. In the study of Allport *et al.*, one message was verbal, the other was musical. Each message required a different *type* of processing.

If we examine everyday situations where we are able to do two things at once, we see that most of them have similar properties to the demonstration of Allport *et al.* We can hold a conversation whilst driving a car; listen to the radio whilst doing housework, and so on; but we *cannot* listen to a radio talk whilst reading a book.

What is the relevance of this to music? It suggests that our difficulties in attending to two concurrent melodies are not so much due to an incapacity to take them in as to an incapacity to subject them to the same kind of *analysis* simultaneously. In situations where nothing is required of an observer other than the detection of some simple event, he is capable of monitoring very many simultaneous 'channels', even when only a single sense modality is involved. For instance, Shiffrin and Schneider (1977) report demonstrations that people find it as easy to monitor 49 separate spatial locations for the occurrence of a brief visual event as they do to monitor only one location. It is when some integrative response is required to the material in each channel, such as detecting sequential structure (as in understanding a sentence or recognizing a tune) that problems begin to occur. As Neisser (1983) puts it, 'there is no way to avoid assigning the verb in speaker B's sentence to the noun in speaker A's, with resulting organizational chaos.' When we hear two people speaking at once, what each of them says is an independent message, bearing no necessary relation to the other. Trying to construct the two independent but simultaneous structures yields misleading and unintended results as elements are assigned to the wrong structure. It is hardly surprising that the conventions of normal human linguistic communication are designed to ensure that only one person speaks at a time.

In Dowling's (1973) experiment, the two interleaved melodies could be just as unrelated to one another as two randomly chosen verbal messages. In most contrapuntal music, however, the various lines are *not* independent. They are constructed with skill and care to be related to one another. Each line possesses not only its own 'horizontal' melodic identity (enabling it to stand on its own as a valid musical sequence) but also a 'vertical' harmonic function with relation to the other concurrent lines. At any instant, the simultaneously sounding notes make up a chord which has its own musical identity. The progression of chords found in the piece constitutes the harmonic structure of the music, and this structure acts as a single underlying framework in which the individual lines can be placed. We may hypothesize that this underlying harmonic unity makes it easier to attend to several simultaneous melodic lines. This hypothesis was tested in an experiment (Sloboda and Edworthy 1981) where subjects learned two melodies which cohered harmonically when played in the same key (Example 5.15). After each melody was learned on its own, subjects heard trials where the two melodies were played together. The melodies were always separated in pitch by at least an octave, so that they were easily heard as separate streams. On

Example 5.15. Melodies used by Sloboda and Edworthy (1981).

each trial, one of the melodies contained a pitch error on one of the notes. Subjects were required to say which melody contained the error, and, if they were musically literate, to mark the error on a score.

The crucial experimental variable was the key relation of the two melodies. In condition A the melodies were in the same key. In condition B they were in keys a perfect fifth apart (e.g. C and G.) In condition C they were in keys an augmented fourth apart (e.g. C and F sharp). We predicted that, if harmonic coherence aids simultaneous attention, subjects should correctly locate most errors in condition A and least in condition C. The results exactly upheld these predictions. Subjects were 80 per cent correct in condition A, but only 67 per cent correct in condition C. Condition B gave intermediate results (74 per cent).

How does harmonic coherence aid attention? Our current hypothesis is that polyphonic music is perceived as an ambiguous pattern capable of 'figure-ground reversal.' There are many well-known examples of this. Rubin's 'faces-vase' figure is one of the best known. It oscillates between being seen as a white vase on a black background, and as two black faces looking at each other across a white background (Fig. 5.3). Shape and contour is

Fig. 5.3.

seen as being possessed by the elements which form the figure at a particular time. The background is seen as a contourless occluded surface.

In music we propose that only one melodic line can be treated as 'figure' at any one time. When so treated we may say that this line is being given 'focal attention'. Focal attention allows the noticing of relationships within the melodic line, so that the melody may be recognized, related to previous material, and so on. The other line, or lines, form the background. They are registered, but are not processed focally. Instead, they are fragmented into a series of individual notes which are heard 'vertically' as chords which support or accompany the focal melody. Thus, there are two types of process taking place, melodic processing of the focal line, and harmonic processing of the other parts. Furthermore, each note of the melody being focally processed has a harmonic function which is confirmed by the notes in the other parts, so both the melodic and the harmonic processes contribute to the building up of a unified structural representation for the whole piece.

A diagram may help to make clear the relationships being proposed. Consider a piece of music containing three contrapuntal lines. Fig. 5.4 (*a*) represents the primary relationships noticed when line A is the subject of focal attention. The listener extracts the 'horizontal' melodic relationships between notes in A (represented by double lines) but he does not hear B and C as melodies. Rather, their individual notes are heard as harmonizations for the concurrent note of A, assisting the understanding of the structure of A. Fig. 5.4 (*b*) represents the case where a listener is hearing precisely the same music, but this time giving line B focal attention. Now A and C become background harmony.

How does this formulation explain our experimental results? We suppose that listeners will succeed in incorporating most contrapuntal material into

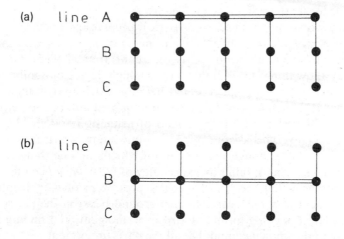

Fig. 5.4. Two different possibilties for focal processing in a contrapuntal sequence.

their representation of the music when the chords supplied by the background parts are familiar ones which support a plausible tonal harmonization for the focal melody. When the two melodies of Example 5.15 are played in the same key, they mutually reinforce a simple and common harmonic structure. Bars 1 and 2 are subsumed under the tonic chord (I), bar 3 subdominant to dominant (IV–V), and bar 4 tonic again (I). With such a conventional progression, the experience of most listeners is that a wrong note 'sticks out like a sore thumb' because it creates an odd and unexpected harmony. It does not matter what line is being given focal attention; the 'queer' harmony is heard. If the wrong note is in the focal melody it will be detected as a deviation from the known melodic pattern. If, however, the focal melody 'matches' the listener's memory of it, then the inference is that the wrong note must be in the other, non-focal melody.

If our explanation is the correct one, then there is a simple prediction which may be tested. This is that when there are *more* than two simultaneous lines, location of wrong notes will become less efficient, even when all lines cohere harmonically. This is because in the case where the mistake is in a non-focally processed line, the listener has to guess at random between these lines. All he will know is that there was a wrong note, creating an odd harmony, which was *not* in the focal melody. By simple application of probability theory we would expect the 80 per cent performance with two lines to drop to 53 per cent with three lines, and 40 per cent with four lines. This prediction is yet to be tested.

Informal support for this prediction comes from a common experience of ensemble conducting. When a conductor is rehearsing a group he will often hear 'something go wrong' but be unable to say with certainty which part went wrong without going back and hearing the section again. It appears that he was focally processing a part which did not go wrong, and needs to redirect his focal attention to locate the mistake.

If focal processing is limited to one part, it becomes pertinent to ask how, if at all, it is possible to justify the claim made by some listeners that they *can* follow all the simultaneous parts of a contrapuntal piece. One factor which may allow things to seem that way is a high degree of familiarity with the individual parts, through repeated hearing. Each part is then so well known that it does not need to be continuously monitored to refresh the experience of its being 'there'. This kind of listening is rather like the experience we achieve when casting our eyes round a familiar visual scene, such as our own room. Although the eye can only focus on one thing at a time, the fact that each glance fulfils an expectancy of what *should* be there allows a real experience that the whole scene is present in one's perception. In familiar music, the 'mind's ear' can dart around between the parts, always knowing what it is going to find at any given moment, and finding it, thus confirming to the knowing mind that all the parts *are* present.

Even if each contrapuntal line is not well known as such, it is also possible

to know a piece very well *as* a melody plus accompaniment (in the case where
the same contrapuntal line has always been the object of focal attention). In
such a case, each chord may be so well known that the listener has the
possibility of *constructing* a non-focal line by picking out a given note from
each chord and integrating a new line. In such cases all the contrapuntal lines
may be *implicit* in what a listener knows, simply awaiting a reorganization
of his knowledge to be made explicit. In such a way may a listener suddenly
realize that the 'accompaniment' of a well-known passage actually has its
own melodic integrity. It is not that there are notes present which he has not
noticed before. It is simply that he has not heard them *as* melody before.

Another way of achieving the impression of total awareness in polyphony
has more to do with the composer's art than with the listener's knowledge.
In the cases discussed so far we have assumed that a note in any one part is
associated with a simultaneously played note in every other part. Whilst this
is true of some chordal counterpoint, such as hymn harmonizations, it is by
no means true of all counterpoint. It is possible to lighten the listening load
considerably by limiting significant events to one or two lines at any one
time. Consider, for example, the counterpoint of the top two lines in no. 18
of J. S. Bach's Goldberg Variations (Example 5.16). These lines (which form

Example 5.16. From J. S. Bach, Goldberg Variations.

a canon) are distinguished by the fact that there is not a single occasion when
notes begin simultaneously in the two parts, although the notes are sustained
in such a way that the two-part texture is continuous. We may argue that
listeners can focally process each melody, by switching from line to line as
each new note is played. Secondly, once one has realized the canonic relationship it is possible to predict the next event in the upper line by reference
to what has just happened in the lower one. This is a quite different situation
to that of Dowling's 'interleaved melodies' experiment. First, the rate of
switching between parts is much less (about one per second rather than four
per second). Second, because of the musical relationship between the two
parts, understanding one part can directly help a listener understand the
other part.

In this Bach example both contrapuntal lines are equally important. In
some cases, however, the composer may quite clearly mark one line as containing the most significant material, with another part relegated to a secondary role where texture may be more important than the precise melodic
sequence. For instance, in the orchestral music of Rachmaninov one often
finds subsidiary countermelodies of a 'busy' scalar nature whose function is
to provide a restless undercurrent to some more salient theme. Although a

connoisseur may come to know every note of such countermelodies, there may be a sense in which this is knowing more than Rachmaninov intended. It is enough for adequate listening that one can detect 'that kind of thing going on' which can be done, perhaps, without too much focal attention, in the 'spaces' between significant events in the primary melody.

If, indeed, focal attention can only be in one place at a time we may move to consider a compositional problem. Is it possible for composers to write music which will tend to direct the focal attention of first-time listeners to the intended part? We ask this question on the grounds that it is not correct to say, for most music, that all parts are equally important for a first-time listener; that he would 'hear the music rightly' whatever part he happened to focus on. This may possibly be true for a fugue; it is not true for a symphony or a sonata. In such works there are nearly always primary themes which must be apprehended, because later transformations and extensions of these themes form the substance of the compositional structure. It would hardly do if a listener focally processed the lower line of Example 5.17 (Mozart's Piano Sonata in C, K. 545) at the expense of the upper line.

Example 5.17.   From Mozart, Piano Sonata in C (K. 545), first movement.

Almost no experimental work relates directly to this question, but it is possible to point out some of the most easily observable 'attention grabbing' devices. First, it appears that, all other things being equal, it is the line with the highest pitch range that tends to be focally processed. When listening to, say, a hymn tune harmonization, many listeners are simply unaware that the lower parts comprise melodic lines. In the vast majority of classical music, principal themes are stated by high-pitched instruments, with lower ones playing subsidiary material. For instance, in string music it is nearly always violins, rather than violas or cellos, which present the principal themes; and in piano music it is nearly always the right hand. Why should this be? One possible contributory factor is that outside lines are heard better because they are *on* the outside and so are not 'surrounded' by other lines. Thus, the highest and lowest lines of a polyphonic texture should be most salient, with inner lines being less salient. We still need a further reason for the topmost line 'winning out' over the bottom line. One possible reason is that high notes in normal musical textures mask one another less than do low notes. 'Masking' is a technical term of psychoacoustics which refers to the detrimental effect the presence of one tone has on the ability of a listener to hear a second tone close in pitch or time to the masking tone (see Moore 1982, for a good introduction to this topic).) The masking power of a particular note may be assessed by varying the intensity of nearby notes to the point when they can only just be heard. This intensity is called the auditory threshold. The auditory thresholds of notes close in pitch to the masking tone are considerably raised by the simultaneous presence of the masking tone. However, as one moves the test tone further away from the masking tone in pitch there comes a point where the masking tone no longer has any effect on the threshold. One hears the test tone just as easily with the masking tone as without it. For any particular tone it becomes possible to estimate its 'critical bandwidth'. This is the frequency range within which it has a masking effect on other tones. Estimates of the critical bandwidth at various frequencies have been provided by Scharf (1970) and others. Table 5.1 shows the kind of results obtained, translating frequency values into approximate musical intervals.

TABLE 5.1
Sample masking ranges of musical tones (adapted from Scharf 1970)

Approximate frequency of masking tone (Hz)	Musical note name of masking tone	Average musical interval from masking tone within which threshold of another tone is raised
110	A2	octave
220	A3	perfect fifth
440	A4 (concert A)	major third
880	A5	major second
1660	A6	minor second

These rough estimates show that within the range of normal music, low tones mask over wider musical intervals than do high tones. In the range of a double bass, two octaves below middle C, tones as much as an octave apart will mask one another. In the range of a piccolo, two octaves above middle C, tones as close as a major second apart will not mask one another. In a thick contrapuntal texture there is real reason, then, to suppose that upper notes are more audible than lower ones. In a reverberant environment, the perception of low notes is also hindered by their greater tendency to persist in the environment after being played, creating a 'muddy' low-pitch noise, which makes lower parts less discriminable. Finally, we have to consider the fact that crucial acoustic information may be carried, not by the fundamental frequency of a musical note, but by its weak upper partials or harmonics. For low-pitched instruments these partials are likely to be masked by the higher pitched instruments, so making them less distinctive. All of this cannot, however, be the whole story, since I at least experience a strong 'set' for the upper line in simple two-part 'staggered' counterpoint where the effects of masking and acoustic environment are not significant (e.g. Example 5.18, Two-part invention in E by J. S. Bach). It seems likely that experience with normal music, where the upper parts are known to be more important, on the whole, has resulted in a learned disposition to attend to the upper voice when there are no strong counter-signals.

Example 5.18. From J. S. Bach, Two part Invention in E.

A second type of characteristic of melodic lines which capture focal attention is a feature which discriminates them from the other lines in some way. Thus, a line may be louder than other lines, or have a distinctive 'solo' timbre. It may introduce change against an unchanging background. For instance, in Example 5.7 we tend to focally attend to the lower pitch stream which moves, rather than to the upper one, which is stationary. For the same sort of reason, the upper line of Example 5.17 invites attention because the lower line simply repeats the same figuration over and over again.

A third and related device is *change* of quality or texture in the focal line. This exploits a natural tendency, sometimes called the 'orienting response', to attend to a new event in a complex environment rather than to familiar ones. One principal way of introducing change is to add a new voice in a distinct pitch stream to a polyphonic texture. Successive entries of a fugue fulfil this condition.

Fourth, we may postulate a principle of 'attentional conservatism' such that a listener will tend to remain with a particular line once drawn to it unless there are strong enticements for him to shift attention. Thus, the composer can increase the likelihood of keeping a listener on the right line by avoiding sudden change in other parts.

Of course, composers rarely use such devices in isolation. An important part may be topmost in pitch, and loudest, and the most novel of the parts. The scientific evaluation of the relative effectiveness of these devices and the precise conditions under which they apply awaits detailed study of controlled musical examples where each attentional device can be manipulated separately.

5.4 Memory in music listening

The way one hears music is crucially dependent upon what one can remember of past events in the music. A modulation to a new key is heard only if one remembers the previous key. A theme is heard as transformed only if one can remember the original version of which it is a transformation. And so on. A note or chord has no *musical* significance other than in relation to preceding or following events. To perceive an event musically (that is, to recognize at least part of its musical function) is to relate it to past events. It is, therefore, important for us to know how good we are at remembering past musical events, and to know what factors assist our memory.

We may begin by considering a very thorough series of experimental studies by Deutsch on memory for individual notes (Deutsch 1970, 1972, 1973; Deutsch and Feroe 1975; and others summarized in Deutsch 1982c). The basic experimental task is simple. Listeners hear two notes, separated by a five-second interval. They are required to judge whether or not the notes have the same pitch. In fact, the notes have the same pitch on half the trials On the other half they differ by a semitone. The interest of these studies lies in the ways in which Deutsch filled the five-second interval. In the basic control condition the interval was silent. Most listeners were then able to perform the pitch judgement with 100 per cent accuracy. In another condition, the interval was filled with spoken numbers, either to be recalled or ignored. In both cases listeners were still able to make the pitch judgement with 100 per cent accuracy. Another, crucial, condition interpolated randomly chosen notes between the two test notes. These interpolated notes were drawn from the same octave as the test notes. In this condition performance dropped to 68 per cent *even though* listeners were instructed to ignore the interpolated notes.

This result shows that intervening notes have a highly disruptive effect on memory for pitch of an earlier note. This is not some *general* deficiency in perceiving or remembering sequences, since the performance was not affected by intervening numbers, even when the numbers had to be recalled. It seems that the effect is specific to pitch.

In further conditions Deutsch discovered that the disruptive effect was greatest when one of the intervening notes was close in pitch to the test notes. Maximum disruption occurred when an intervening note was two-thirds of a tone above or below the first test note. The disruptive effect also generalized across the octave. The same pattern of results was obtained if the intervening tone sequence was shifted up or down an octave.

At first sight, Deutsch's results suggest a very gloomy conclusion about musical memory. Memory for individual pitches seems incredibly poor, if it cannot survive a few succeeding notes. How is it possible to remember notes across structures of symphonic proportions, containing tens of thousands of notes? The general answer to this problem would seem to lie in the opportunities which most music affords for listeners to classify and organize what they hear. Deutsch's sequences were atypical in two respects. They did not confine themselves to the intervals of a common scale (using fractions of a semitone in some instances), and their notes were randomly chosen so that they were not designed to form common musical patterns within the scale framework. To see how musical memory is possible we will have to consider the two aspects of organization that Deutsch's materials violated—scale and sequential pattern—and show how they may be used by listeners to construct representations of music which do not rely on the preservation of precise pitch information.

5.4.1 *Scale*

Within a musical culture such as our own, there is general agreement about the scales from which music is constructed. In our culture the predominant scales are the diatonic major and minor scales. Furthermore, there is general agreement about the absolute pitches which scales should be based upon. This is so that a correctly tuned instrument can be played in ensemble with any other instrument. Thus A4, the traditional 'concert A' used for orchestral tuning is set at 440 Hz. With equal temperament instruments, such as piano, it is possible to set each of the twelve chromatic notes to definite pitches which allow all twelve major and minor diatonic scales to sound 'in tune'.

Given this 'fixity' of musical pitches, the possibility arises that music listeners could learn to associate particular pitches with musical note names. If they can do this, then it is possible that memory could be improved through the recoding of sensory pitch information into verbal information— remembering note names rather than raw sounds.

People with the ability to name individual heard pitches, or accurately sing named pitches are said to possess 'absolute' or 'perfect' pitch (see Ward 1963a, 1963b; Ward and Burns 1982, for reviews). This ability seems to be learnable by anyone prepared to undergo lengthy and systematic training (Brady 1970; Cuddy 1970). However, by no means all musicians have absolute pitch (AP), and a study by Sergeant (1969) shows that, among a sample of 1156 professional musicians, there was a high inverse correlation between age of commencement of musical training and the possession of AP. Almost all musicians who began training before the age of six had AP, but almost none of those who began after eleven did.

An elegant study by Siegel (1974) demonstrates the kind of memory advantage that absolute pitch confers. Her subjects were presented with two notes, separated by a silent five-second interval. These notes differed in pitch by either one-tenth of a tone or by three-quarters of a tone. Subjects were asked to judge whether the second note was higher or lower than the first. Siegel used two types of subject: music students with AP; and music students of an equivalent standard without AP. Siegel found that whilst the two types of subject did not differ in performance on the one-tenth tone intervals, the AP subjects did much better than the non-AP subjects when it came to the three-quarter tone intervals. The AP subjects were able to assign different verbal labels (note names) to the two notes. When the notes were only one-tenth tone apart such verbal coding no longer worked, because it provided the *same* name for both notes. Thus they had to fall back on a 'sensory' coding which the other subjects reported using all the time.

Verbal coding aids retention over longer time spans, as shown in a second experiment where the time interval between the two test notes was varied. The interval was now filled with other random notes at the rate of four per second, making the task very similar to the one in which Deutsch found such poor performance. For the one-tenth tone test interval, performance of both types of subjects dropped very rapidly as the time interval was increased. However, for test intervals separated by a semitone, only the performance of the non-AP subjects dropped. The AP group were just as good after 15 seconds as they were after 5 seconds.

These results not only demonstrate the superior memory performance exhibited by subjects with AP. They also demonstrate the categorical nature of absolute pitch (see also Chapter 2.4). It is not the case that people with AP have finer pitch discrimination than anyone else. They cannot remember pitch within one-tenth of a tone over a five-second silent interval with any degree of accuracy. What they *can* do is assign the pitch to a *class* or *range* of pitches which are given the same name. Within a name category (spanning perhaps 30 Hz in the range of A4) they cannot remember pitch differences reliably. Furthermore, the results show how subjects with this categorizing ability can overcome the disruptive effect of intervening notes demonstrated in Deutsch's subjects, and by the non-AP subjects in this study.

Do these results suggest that people with absolute pitch have the best equipment for listening to and remembering music? If they do, then all of us without AP should, maybe, strive to obtain it. In fact, there are other types of ability which can be even more important in most tonal music. These include the ability to identify musical intervals and key. Of these, more shortly. AP would seem to be most advantageous in situations where music, whilst using the notes of the chromatic scale, violates the normal rules of harmonic and melodic construction, producing unfamiliar intervals and sequences where no key or tonal centre is implied. Much music in contemporary 'atonal' idioms would seem to fulfil these criteria; and those musicians particularly singers, who need to work with such music, have their task made much easier if they possess AP. There are situations, however, in which AP can be a nuisance. Listening to, or performing key-transposed music can be very difficult. The sounds produced are constantly violating expectancies created by one's own prior knowledge of the music or by the printed score. When scales or tunings are non-standard then it is possible to devise experimental tasks in which possessors of AP are actually at a disadvantage, because their categorizations are inappropriate to the task (e.g. Cuddy 1977, reported in Ward and Burns 1982).

Many musicians possess an ability which they prize much more than absolute pitch, and this is often called 'relative pitch'. This is the ability to say what musical interval separates two simultaneously or successively played notes, or to be able to sing a named interval above or below a given starting note. This ability is important because melodic or harmonic identity is conferred on a set of notes through the interval relationships they hold to one another, and not their absolute pitches. A melody can start on any pitch within audible range and still be recognized *as* the same melody provided its pitch intervals (frequency ratios) are the same. This feature of music offers a possible explanation for why it is that relatively few people with the appropriate opportunities learn absolute pitch. When a child is taught a song, he is reinforced for producing the correct intervals, not a particular set of absolute pitches. He hears songs sung at various pitches (e.g. father sings the same song in a lower register than mother) and in general has every incentive to record interval information at the expense of absolute pitch (Pick 1979).

Siegel and Siegel (1977a) have demonstrated that relative pitch improves with training, and that highly experienced musicians can identify intervals reliably, accurately, and independently of stimulus context. Furthermore, musicians report hearing intervals as sounding qualitatively different from one another. Thus, a major third comes to sound not so much 'larger' than a minor third as a different *type* of sound. Each interval acquires its own unique character or colour that makes it unmistakable and not confusable with any other interval. Just as absolute pitch is 'categorical' so is relative pitch. Two notes do not have to be separated by the *exact* correct pitch interval to be heard as a major third, or whatever. Rather, their separations must fall within a *class* of separations about a central point. Categorical perception of intervals was demonstrated by Locke and Kellar (1973; see Chapter 2.4). It has also been demonstrated by Siegel and Siegel (1977b) who asked subjects to judge the magnitude of various standard and non-standard intervals. Although only 23 per cent of the intervals were actually 'in tune' (on just temperament tuning), subjects judged 63 per cent of them to be in tune, judging 'sharp' and 'flat' intervals to be equal in magnitude to correctly tuned intervals. There were even cases where subjects judged a sharp interval to be flat, and vice-versa. In this case it appears that they noticed a mistuning, but were unable to retain the precise pitch information which would allow them to tell whether the interval was sharp or flat. This loss of precise pitch information has many musical uses. For one, it allows the existence of the equal-temperament chromatic scale, which slightly distorts many of the 'perfect' small integer ratios of the harmonic series. These distortions are not noticeable under normal conditions, and provide musicians with the advantage of being able to play music which modulates round the circle of fifths without sounding more and more out of tune; unlike just intonation, where intervals in keys remote from the originally tuned key sound grossly mistuned. A technical discussion of tuning and temperament is beyond the scope of this book, and the interested reader is referred to Barbour (1951).

Just as absolute pitch aids memory under certain conditions, so does relative pitch. Idson and Massaro (1976) have provided one demonstration of this. Subjects were trained to recognize three-note sequences derived by permuting the notes A, C, and D sharp in different orders. The notes were given arbitrary labels (A, B, and C respectively) and subjects were required to identify a sequence as one of six possibilities, ABC, ACB, BAC, CAB, CBA. When they had learned to do this task accurately a 'masking' condition was introduced, where each note of the sequence was followed by an ir- relevant note (e.g. AMBMCM, where M is the masking note). This masking note could be either in the same octave as the test sequence or in another octave. Idson and Massaro found that a same-octave mask disrupted id- entification of the test sequence, but that identification performance remained high if the mask was in another octave. In a second condition, subjects learned to identify not sequences but single notes. There were three notes, each given an arbitrary name (A, B, and C). Subjects learned to say which of the three notes had been presented on a given trial. Then they had to continue the task with various masking notes introduced, as in the first condition. It was found that *any* masking note, and not just one close in pitch to the test note, was highly disruptive of identification.

It is important to note that the first 'sequential' test could be done on the basis of relative pitch information, whilst the second task requires absolute pitch memory. We may interpret the results by saying that interference is more likely to disrupt comparison of present with past notes on the basis of absolute pitch than on the basis of relative pitch. When subjects are looking out for learned pitch intervals or contours they can perform the necessary perceptual and memory operations provided that interfering material does not fuse with the test material into a single pitch stream (see this chapter, section 2). When, however, subjects are trying to hold a particular absolute pitch in memory for comparison with later material, they are disrupted by *any* interference.

Idson and Massaro's experiment involved recognizing a stimulus which, although containing interval information, also retained the absolute pitch of the original. A common occurrence in music is the *transposition* of a melodic theme to a new key within the same piece of music. If we do, indeed, re- member sequences of notes in terms of pitch interval, we should be able to recognize transpositions *as* repetitions of the same melodic stimulus. Ex- periments by Cuddy and Cohen (1976) and Cuddy, Cohen, and Miller (1979) have shown that both musically trained and untrained listeners can dis- criminate true transpositions of three-note sequences from those where one of the notes has been raised or lowered by a semitone relative to the other notes. This ability is, however, greatly affected by the precise nature of the sequence to be transposed. For instance, Dowling (1978) has shown that it is difficult for listeners to discriminate between 'real' and 'tonal' transpositions (see Chapter 2.4). Bartlett and Dowling (1980) have shown that dis- crimination of real from false transpositions is best when the transposition is to a key closely related to the original. Cuddy, Cohen, and Miller (1979) have shown that if the sequence to be transposed is embedded in a tonal context, it is easier to recognize than when in a non-tonal context. All these findings suggest that memory for pitch intervals alone does not account for the way in which listeners deal with tonal sequence.

Much of the evidence points to the importance of establishing a key, or tonal centre, for memorization of melodic sequences. This provides an economical way of representing a melodic sequence in terms of scale steps within a key. An example will help make this clear. Consider the sequence in Example 5.19. Viewed as a set of successive intervals this could be seen as

Example 5.19.   Example 5.20.   Example 5.21.

the ascending sequence tone–tone–tone–semitone. If we consider intervallic relations between non-adjacent notes, we would add minor third (A–C), major third (F–A and G–B), perfect fourth (G–C), augmented fourth (F–B) ,and perfect fifth (F–C). Viewed as components of a scale, however (in this case C major), we could see it as four ascending adjacent intervals of one scale step starting on the fourth degree of the scale. The intervals between non-adjacent notes are then simple multiples of a single scale step. If we hear melodies in this second way, then we can argue that shifts of a melodic contour up or down *in the same key* are likely to be heard as 'the same melody' because a most important aspect of the melody—scale-step interval—is retained. If Example 5.19 is to be described compactly by the notation:

Key: C major
Start: 4
Sequence: +1, +1, +1, +1

then Example 5.20 is described in exactly the same way, except that the start of the sequence is now note 7 of the scale (B):

Key: C major
Start: 7
Sequence: +1, +1, +1, +1

Describing Example 5.20 in terms of its pitch interval relations, however, gives a very different pattern to that of Example 5.19. The intervals between successive adjacent notes are now semitone–tone–tone–semitone. Among the non-adjacent intervals there is no longer a perfect fifth or an augmented fourth, but a diminished fifth is added. The fact that people find such sequences (called 'tonal answers') as similar to the original as 'real' transpositions (which preserve the actual pitch intervals) is strong evidence for viewing listeners' representations of tonal sequences as embodying the kind of notation given above. Such notations allow the economical coding of real transpositions too. Here, instead of changing the starting note, we change the key. Example 5.21 is a real transposition of Example 5.19, and in our notation would be represented:

Key: F major
Start: 4
Sequence: +1, +1, +1, +1

The foregoing offers a possible explanation for why real and tonal transpositions are often confused. Can it also explain why transpositions to related keys are easier to recognize than transpositions to remote keys? I think it can, if we look more closely at the nature of the experimental tasks which gave rise to this finding. A listener hears one short melodic sequence, and then, without any intervening preparation, hears another transposed sequence. Unless the key of the transposed sequence is close to the initial key in the circle of fifths it is possible that a listener is simply unable to decide a key (or tonic) for the new sequence. If he cannot do this, then he will not be able to assign the correct scale-step intervals to the new sequence. Once a listener has established a key, there is an inherent conservatism which makes him reluctant to shift key (see Chapter 2, section 5.3). Key modulation in much music is effected through movement around the 'circle of fifths', from C to G, G to D, D to A, and so on (or in reverse). A feature of such modulation is that the scales of the two keys share all their notes except one, the leading note, or seventh of the new scale. Thus G major contains all the notes of the C major scale except F which it replaces with F sharp. This has two consequences for transposition. One is that many transposed sequences can be successfully represented in two ways, either as resulting from a change of key, or as resulting from a contour shift within the same key For instance, the sequence CEGAG may be represented as:

Key: C major
Start: 1
Sequence: +2, +2, +1, −1

When the transposed sequence GBDED is heard, it can then either be represented:

Key: G major
Start: 1
Sequence: +2, +2, +1, −1

or

Key: C major
Start: 5
Sequence: +2, +2, +1, −1

This double coding means that a listener has *two* chances of hearing the transposition: crucially, it does not rely on him shifting his key frame.

The second consequence of the close relationship between keys like C and G is that the introduction of the one note *not* shared by the two keys is a strong and unambiguous cue for a key shift to the key which requires the least change of component notes to accommodate the new note. Thus CE DBC, becoming G B A Fsharp G, is strongly suggestive of a modulation from C major to G major. The first three notes of the second sequence (GBA) perform a vital pivotal function. They link the two sequences in a 'tonal space'. Probably most listeners hear these three notes as continuing in the original key of C. Then the F sharp forces a motivated key-shift one step up the circle of fifths. Consider in contrast the impression of CEDBC followed by F sharp A sharp G sharp E sharp F sharp. Here, the first notes of the transposed sequence cannot fulfil a linking function, since none of them are in the scale of the previous sequence. This has the effect of casting the listener adrift from his tonal bearings. He has to forget all about the first scale, and try to construct a plausible scale for the second sequence from scratch. His immediate memory of the first scale may interfere with this attempt, and his efforts to interpret the second sequence may cause him to lose details of the first. It is not surprising that recognition of such transpositions is hard. In much real music, two statements of a theme in distant keys will be separated by the kind of preparatory modulations that allow a listener to keep his tonal bearings and so know in advance what scales are likely to be encountered. In such cases, the transposed theme is recognized with ease.

There is now a small body of research on the mechanisms by which key can most readily be detected by a listener. Some suggestions have already been discussed in Chapter 2, section 5.3. Butler (1983) reports experiments showing that one cue signalling key is the presence of intervallic patterns which are unique to that key, or which can be found in the smallest number of other keys. The interval C-D, for instance, can be found in *five* major scales—C, G, F, B flat, and E flat. On the other hand the tritone F(E sharp)-B is only found in two scales, C major and F sharp major. In Butler's experiments sequences which made this tritone relation most salient were those which gave listeners the strongest sense of a key centre. A third note added to the tritone specifies a unique key. For instance, the sequence FBC can occur only in C major (Brown and Butler 1981).

Once a key is established, each note of the implied scale has a unique configuration of intervallic relationships with the other notes of the scale (because of the uneven distribution of tone–semitone intervals up the scale—see Balzano 1980). Thus, the interval F–C *heard as* in C major has a different tonal quality to F–C *heard as* in F major. In the former case the notes have an implied scalar relationship to a B *natural*, whereas in the latter case they relate to a B *flat*. To hear F–C as in C major is to appreciate the relationship of these notes to an unheard but 'implied' B natural.

These considerations help us to understand why context is of such crucial importance in the recognition of transpositions. In Cuddy, Cohen, and Miller's experiments (1979), the diatonic context helped listeners identify the key of each passage. When the context was non-diatonic it was impossible to assign a key to each passage, and thus impossible to code the sequences in terms of scale steps. Probably the best that could be done would be a rough estimate of interval contour (e.g. 'a large interval up followed by a smaller one down'). Such information would be too crude to be useful in distinguishing exact transpositions from 'false alarms' with similar up–down contours.

Perhaps, however, this 'crude' up–down contour should not be dismissed as playing no role in musical memory. Davies (1978) and Dowling (1978) among others have proposed that such contour information *does* form the basis of our musical memory in some real listening situations, and can be useful even when more exact scalar or intervallic representations are not achieved. Such information could certainly not allow us to *recall* a melody other than very approximately, but it might indeed be sufficient, in some contexts, for a melody to be *recognized* as a repetition or transposition of an original (especially if combined with other information, such as, for example, rhythm).

Edworthy (1983) has attempted to assess the importance of contour memory by means of an experiment where listeners heard two melodies, the second of which was a transposition of the first at the tritone (e.g. C major–F sharp major). The transposition preserved the exact intervals of the original except at one point where a deliberate alteration was introduced. Listeners were required to locate the alteration. There were two types of melody, short (5 notes) and long (15 notes). Example 5.22 gives an example of a typical five-note melody. There were also two listening conditions. In the 'pitch' condition, the altered note was another note chosen from the key of the melody which did not change the original up–down contour (see Example 5.23). Subjects were asked to monitor the pitches of the notes to detect the alteration. In the 'contour' condition, the melody was altered within its key so that the up–down contour was different at one place (see Example 5.25). Subjects were asked to monitor the up–down contour, *not* the precise pitches, so as to locate the contour alteration.

Examples 5.22.–5.25. Examples of stimuli in Edworthy's (1983) study.

Unsurprisingly, the short melodies gave more accurate results than the long ones. The important result, however, is that although the contour condition gave the best results for short melodies, the *pitch* condition gave the best results for long melodies. It seems that as soon as melodies of any length are heard, up–down contour coding becomes inefficient. Subjects must switch to a more difficult form of coding which retains pitch interval information in some form. In the light of the preceding discussion it seems that this processing involves the coding of the melody as a sequence of tonal elements in a particular scale or key.

Dowling and Bartlett (1981) provide similar conclusions to Edworthy in a study where short extracts from Beethoven string quartets were played. Subjects had to classify other extracts from the same work, heard after a delay, as similar or dissimilar on a rating scale. Some of the extracts were 'lures' chosen to resemble the originals in melodic contour but to differ in exact pitch interval, others were dissimilar in both contour and pitch interval. Subjects judged both these types of extract as 'dissimilar' to the original; with the same-contour lures being heard as only marginally more similar than the different contour lures. In further experimentation, Dowling and Bartlett found that shared contour was a better predictor of perceived similarity only when the delay between original and comparison was short. When the delay was longer, an exact pitch-interval match was required for high similarity judgements.

Taken together, these results suggest that contour is a characteristic of music which is most important for listening over short, rather than long spans; and that if a composer wishes to direct a listener's attention to the *contour* similarity of two sequences they must both be rather short (nearer 5 notes than 15) and be close together in the composition. The cases that spring to my mind certainly fulfil this condition. In the first movement of Beethoven's Fifth Symphony, the crucial melodic element is four notes long, and when pitch interval is altered so as to leave only contour identity then the repetitions are often contiguous (e.g. Example 5.26). In Bach's Prelude

Example 5.26. Adapted from Beethoven, Fifth Symphony, first movement.

in C minor (Well-Tempered Clavier, book 2), the repeating motif is eight notes long, and because virtually the whole piece is based on contiguous repetitions of the motif which preserve contour but not precise interval relations, the contour is highly salient (Example 5.27).

Consider, though, how even a small amount of intervening material can camouflage a contour identity. The popular song 'Over the Rainbow' has a three-note motif which is subject to contour repetition (Example 5.28). It was not, however, until I was encouraged to view this very familiar melody

Example 5.27. From J. S. Bach, *Well-Tempered Clavier*, Prelude 2, Book 1.

Example 5.28. Opening melody bars of 'Over the rainbow', Music by Harold Arlen, lyric by E. Y. Harburg. Copyright © 1938, 1939 (renewed 1966, 1967) Metro-Goldwyn-Mayer, Inc. All rights controlled by Leo Feist, Inc., a catalogue of CBS, a division of CBS Inc. All rights reserved. Used by permission.

analytically (by Rosner and Meyer 1982) that I noticed the contour repetition of bar 1 by bar 3. My 'parsing' of the melody had grouped the third note (D) with the other notes in bar 2, undermining its relationship to the previous two notes.

5.4.2. *Sequential pattern*

It seems incontrovertible that musical sequences which can be represented as occurring within a key or scale are easier to remember than those which cannot. However, this generalization needs qualification. Consider the two sequences of Example 5.29. If one spends a few seconds studying each of

Example 5.29.

these with a view to reproduction it will soon become apparent that (*b*) is much easier to remember than (*a*). This is despite the following facts:

1. (*a*) begins with a three-note sequence which uniquely specifies the key as G major, whereas (*b*) does not.

2. (*a*) contains only notes from within the G major scale, whereas (*b*) contains two chromatic notes (C sharp and A sharp).

3. (*b*) is longer than (*a*).

What makes (*b*) easier to remember is that it seems somehow simpler. One hears it as a three-note pattern which repeats four times down a G major arpeggio. Deutsch and Feroe (1981) have provided a detailed formalism which captures some features of music which appear to accompany ease of memorization. They see simple tonal melodies as operating within *alphabets* of notes. An alphabet is a culturally specified pitch-ordered set of intervals which embodies some tonal principle. The primary alphabets of our culture are the diatonic and chromatic scales and arpeggios. Taking any one of these alphabets one can construct an ordered ascending or descending sequence from any note. Applying the alphabet of the G major scale to the note G would give the ascending sequence G A B C D E, etc. Applying the alphabet of the chromatic scale to the same note would give G G sharp A A sharp etc. Applying the alphabet of the G major arpeggio would give G B D G etc. It is proposed that within each of these alphabets, moves of a single step are the simplest and most easily manageable type of change, and that sequences which can be shown to be constructed out of a combination of such moves in the various alphabets are perceived as simple and easily memorable. For instance, Example 5.29 (*b*) can be expressed as a simple hierarchical structure based upon single step movements in the alphabets of the G major arpeggio and the chromatic scale (see Fig. 5.5). At the top of the hierarchy we start

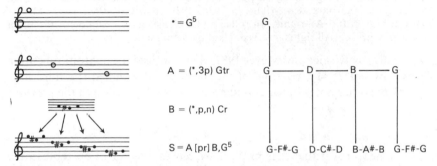

Fig. 5.5. Formal representation of an hierarchically organized tone sequence. Adapted from Deutsch (1981) and Deutsch and Feroe (1980). Key: * = reference note (i.e. the note on which the sequence is constructed); p = downward movement of one step within an alphabet; n — upward movement of one step within an alphabet; Gtr = alphabet of the G major triad; Cr = alphabet of the chromatic scale; A[pr]B = the application of pattern B to each element of pattern A.

with a single note, G4. We than apply the G major arpeggio alphabet to this note, descending in consecutive steps for four notes. We then construct a subsidiary pattern in the chromatic scale which is obtained by taking a note, moving one scale step down, and then returning to the original note.

We now apply this pattern to each note of the arpeggio in turn to produce the final melody. Figure 5.5 shows the consecutive steps in the construction, and also shows the symbolic notation that Deutsch and Feroe have developed to describe such sequences economically.

These theoretical formulations build directly on work by Simon and Sumner (1968) and Restle (1970) concerned with temporal patterning. However, Deutsch and Feroe point out that similar hierarchic structures seem to be implicated in the way we represent other complex inputs such as visual scenes (Palmer 1977) and large-scale environments (Chase and Chi 1981) as well as language (see Chapter 2); and thus represent a general feature of human cognitive functioning.

Deutsch (1980) has provided first-hand evidence for the theory by asking musicians to recall melodies by dictation. Some melodies could be economically described as hierarchic structures [such as Example 5.29 (*b*)]. Others [like Example 5.29 (*a*)] could not. Recall for the former type was 94 per cent correct; that for the latter was only 52 per cent. Furthermore, if the structured melodies were temporally segmented into groups of three (by the introduction of a brief pause after each third note) corresponding to the major hierarchical subdivisions, performance rose to 99 per cent. If, however, the segmenting was in groups of *four*, thus 'breaking up' the melodic groupings by threes, performance dropped to 69 per cent. On the other hand, temporal grouping of *any* sort improved performance on the unstructured sequences by about 10 per cent.

These results introduce an important factor which we have not so far considered in our treatment of music listening; that is the role of timing and rhythm. It is well known that introducing temporal gaps into sequences of any sort increases the tendency for sequences to be perceived as groups or chunks between each gap (Bower and Winzenz 1969; Restle 1972). This is, in part, to be explained by Gestalt grouping principles. The 'law of proximity' states that elements grouped closely together on a particular dimension tend to be perceived as single unit, separate from other, more distant elements. A visual analogy to the auditory phenomenon is provided by the following pattern:

. .   . .

This is seen as five unequally sized groups.

However, as we have already seen (Chapter 2, section 5.4) such simple groupings can be supplemented by a more sophisticated type of grouping based on metre, and displaying much of the same hierarchical structuring as Deutsch and Feroe have proposed for pitch grouping. The operation of both types of grouping is well demonstrated in a study by Smith (1983) who examined memory for rhythmic patterns by asking musicians and non-musicians to listen to rhythmic sequences performed on a synthesized drum, and then attempt to reproduce them. Figure 5.6 gives an example of the type of rhythmic pattern used, together with two alternative ways of grouping the pattern. Above the pattern is a representation of the sound amplitude over

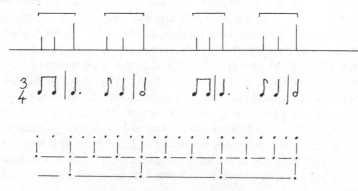

Fig. 5.6. Adapted from Smith (1983).

time. Gestalt grouping by temporal proximity yields the four bracketed groups given. Below the pattern is a representation of its hierarchical metrical structure. This assigns the sequence a 3-beat metre which groups notes *across* the boundaries of temporal groups. Each metrical group begins with a stressed note at the beginning of a bar. When Smith analysed her subjects' errors she found that musicians tended to group by metre, and that their responses tended to maintain the regular metre of the original. The errors of nonmusicians tended not to retain the metre, but their responses preserved the more primitive temporal-proximity grouping. Smith found that

Many subjects reported using a 'counting' strategy, tallying the number of sounds that formed a group, and the number of such groups in the sequence. This meant that although they might tap out the correct number of sounds, the intervals within and between groups of sounds were distorted.

We see, therefore, in Smith's study, not only the importance of relatively abstract underlying patterning in determining memory for rhythm, but also the fact that the use made of such patterning depends upon musical experience. This reminds us of the generally applicable, but sometimes overlooked, fact that many aspects of the ability to deal with music are crucially dependent on musical experience. Such experience allows the learning of the characteristics of common structuring principles in music, and mechanisms for detecting them. We shall return to a more thorough examination of the changes that take place in musical behaviour as a result of experience in the next chapter.

Several other studies confirm the importance of hierarchical organization in the perception of rhythmic patterns (e.g. Handel and Todd 1981; Povel 1981); and Jones, Kidd, and Wetzel (1981) have provided a preliminary demonstration that rhythm can act as a cue to attentional streaming in an analogous way to pitch. In general, rhythm has been 'tonality's poor relation' (Davies 1978) in studies of psychological response to musical structure. We are now beginning to see, however, that not only is rhythm just as important an organizing principle as tonality, but that the two systems are mutually interactive. Thus, in much tonal music, knowledge of the tonal structure can help determine the rhythmic structure, and *vice versa*. We have mentioned before (Chapter 2) how repetition of tonal patterns can act as a cue to metre (Steedman 1977). Thus Example 5.29 (*b*) acquires a 3/4 metre as a result of the repeating three-note pattern. Conversely, rhythmic stress (as communicated through accent or timing variations—see Chapter 3, section 2.3) provides a cue for determining tonal structure. In much music, principal harmonic notes fall on the main beats, with subsidiary or passing notes at other points. Thus, the chromatic sequence of Example 5.30 is most likely to be heard in D minor if the upper accenting scheme is used, but in E minor if the lower scheme is used. In each case the accents specify the primary harmonic notes.

Example 5.30.

5.4.3. *Memory in extended music*

The literature I have reviewed in this chapter shows that we are beginning to build up a detailed, objectively verified, picture of the way listeners represent and memorize short melodic sequences. The question we return to, raised at the beginning of the chapter is, how does this help us to understand what goes on in listening to extended passages of music? One, rather naïve, view would be that listeners form representations in memory of each short sequence in the sort of way outlined here, and then simply retain these sequences in the correct serial order; in much the same way as one might try to remember a list of unrelated sentences. This view raises two problems: firstly, how does a listener segment or 'break up' a continuous musical texture into short sequences of the appropriate sort; secondly, how does he keep what may be many hundreds of such sequences distinct and correctly ordered in memory? We will examine these questions in turn.

To solve the segmentation problem, listeners must be capable of detecting 'closure' at various levels. Sometimes physical characteristics of the music, like a pause, or a change of instrumentation will suggest a suitable segmentation. But there is much music where such cues would not be sufficient. There is some evidence that listeners perceive more abstract types of closure, specified by harmonic or rhythmic considerations. In Chapter 2 we discussed the 'click migration' experiment of Sloboda and Gregory (1980) as providing evidence for perceptual segmentation of melodies into phrases separated by cadences. A study by Tan, Aiello, and Bever (1981) is more particularly relevant to the present discussion because it tested *memory* for parts of a sequence. In this study sequences of equal-duration notes were constructed which contained two melodic phrases, each phrase ending with a melodic cadence. Example 5.31 shows one of the sequences used. When played or sung it will give Western listeners the impression of breaking into two halves, a partial 'close' coming after the tenth note. The sequence leading up to this note (D G E C) is most readily interpreted in this context as a perfect cadence, moving from the harmony of G to that of C. Notes 11–14 form part of a new chord (D minor) leading to a final perfect cadence in C. Tan *et al.* played such melodies to subjects and then asked them to judge whether a particular two-note 'probe' had or had not been present in the melody. Of particular importance were three types of 'true' probe; the pair of notes ending the first phrase (E C in Example 5.31), the pair of notes beginning the second phrase (F A in Example 5.31), and a pair of notes which 'straddled' the phrase boundary (C F in Example 5.31). They found that subjects were less likely

Example 5.31. Example of stimulus used by Tan, Aiello, and Bever (1981).

to recognize the latter type of probe as having occurred than the other two. It appears that they were more likely to form accessible memory representations of intervals *within* phrases defined by cadences than they were for notes equally close in time but coming from two different phrases.

Closure can also be signalled by rhythmic or metrical features of music. For instance, there is a tendency for much melodic music to be constructed in multiples of two-bar units. Thus, a common phrase length is four bars: the 16-bar song contains four four-bar phrases. Meyer (1973) has proposed that a musical form achieves the double ends of articulation or segmentation together with unification and forward-movingness by putting the various cues to closure 'out of phase' with one another. Thus a melody may achieve rhythmic closure at a particular point, but its lack of harmonic closure implies the need for a continuation. On this argument, the end of a well-constructed piece of music is not simply the point where the sounds stop; it is the point where closure is simultaneously achieved at all the various levels. Let us then assume that there are cues which listeners can use to segment music into manageable and 'meaningful' short units.

Our second question relates to the problem of holding a large number of such segments in memory. Estimates of memory capacity for a set of items which are not related in any principled way suggest a limit within single figures (e.g. Miller 1956). As more items are added, memory for other items is lost. The only way to overcome such limitations appears to be to find some way of linking or relating, the items together. In some spheres of memory this is done by 'importing' a structure which can act as a mnemonic to link otherwise unrelated elements together. In music, such relations are, to a large extent, already present in the patterning and structure of a composition. The composer deliberately writes so that the individual segments have a similarity and connectedness that links them together into larger units. It is precisely by discovering such similarities and connections that the limits on memory can be overcome.

First, for instance, economy of coding is achieved if repetitions can be identified and noted. Then, rather than making two representations of the sequence in question, it can be represented once in memory, and 'called up' on its various occurrences through the piece by some sort of 'marker' which locates the repetitions in the longer sequence. Second, inexact similarities could be noticed, and sections coded as *variants* of earlier sections. Maybe on a first hearing, the listener would not have the resources to code all the differences, but would be able to remember it as 'almost like' something that had gone before. Third, the listener could extract some underlying progression or pattern in a sequence of musical statements; such as traversing a familiar tonal path, or moving towards a climax, or conforming to some known form such as theme or variations. This would help him to reconstruct the correct ordering for the sequences, which would no longer be arbitrary, but guided by some rule or pattern. Fourth, the listener may be able to construct an emotional or representational 'plot' or 'drama' from the music, which he can use to help recall and order the various components. For instance, the requirements of the 'plot' at a particular point tells one that the next theme is 'cheeky' or 'resigned'. Delis, Fleer, and Kerr (1978) have provided evidence for this kind of process in an experiment where they found that people remembered musical extracts best when they were labelled with concrete representational titles as opposed to abstract conceptual ones. They argue that the concrete titles allow some kind of story to be constructed, to which the various segments of the music can be associated. In much music, there is, of course, no representational title, and so the listener must construct his own 'story' from the character of the music; but the principle is the same.

The general picture I would like to propose on the basis of such suggestions is that the listener is engaged in building up a multidimensional representation of the music he hears, and that depending upon his knowledge and cognitive style, his early memory for the music will select different dimensions from the many available ones. What is crucially important is that these memories will not necessarily be composed of isolated episodes in the music. It is equally possible that he will have extracted quite global information which specifies some parameters of the overall structure (such as metrical construction or harmonic framework, recurrent melodic types, or emotional 'argument').

How can we demonstrate such processes at work? I can, at present, think of no satisfactory way of tapping what goes on when music of really extended proportions is heard; but one intermediate approach, which David Parker and I have recently begun to explore, is to ask listeners to attempt to reproduce, by singing, moderately extended short musical forms which have a definite melodic phrase structure, but which have too many notes for a perfect first recall to be likely. We can then examine the errors made in reproduction, and also how a representation is built up over repeated hearings, and repeated opportunities to recall the melodies. Our preliminary findings are encouraging. Even people with quite little musical training are capable of providing competent responses; and we find that often the very first recall preserves much high-level information contained in the original whilst losing specific details. For instance, Example 5.33 shows a transcription of a subject's first attempt at recalling Example 5.32. Whilst many of the individual notes do not match the original, it has the correct metrical structure (three two-bar phrases in common time, the correct harmonic sequence (two I–V–I phrases in D minor followed by an implied move to the relative major key of F), and several of the characteristic melodic and rhythmic patterns of the

Example 5.32.

Example 5.33.

original. It seems very much as if this subject was reconstructing some of the details according to constraints laid down by his knowledge of the higher order structure and style of the melody, using general musical knowledge to 'fill in the gaps' in a plausible manner. Further discussion of this study maybe found in Sloboda and Parker (1985).

I hope that the preceding discussion will make it more apparent why I wish to claim that a 'feat of memory' such as Mozart's memorization of Allegri's *Misèrere* (see Chapter 1) does not involve inexplicable processes which set him apart from ordinary musicians. Rather, it distinguishes him as someone whose superior knowledge and skill allows him to accomplish something rapidly and supremely confidently which most of us can do, albeit less efficiently, and on a smaller scale. If we examine the structure of the Allegri *Miserere* we find several features which could assist memory processes of the kind we have been discussing. The work has a simple episodic structure in which a polyphonic 'chorus' is repeated several times, separated by a repeated simple and homophonic chant-like verse passage. Mozart would have had prior access to the words of this choral piece, and possibly to the reports of other listeners, which would have given him a pretty clear idea of the type of structure to expect. The primary problem for him would be to 'fix' the part writing of the 'chorus'. In this, he would be assisted by the several exact repetitions during the course of the performance. Within this section there is a reasonably straightforward harmonic sequence which supports a particularly salient and ornate soprano melody. It was the alleged beauty of this melody, heard in its harmonic and acoustic context, that was responsible for the refusal of the Vatican to publish the music. The fact that this music could only be heard in the Sistine Chapel no doubt added to its fame.

There are several strategies that Mozart could have used to memorize the crucial section. One would be to focus his attention on a different vocal part on each of the hearings (see this chapter, section 2). I suspect, however, that a priority would have been the exact replication of the celebrated soprano line together with the correct harmony. It would not have been so important that the disposition of the harmony notes among the inner voices should be absolutely correct. After all, there was no possibility of the 'illicit' copy being checked against the original score. With the primary melodic line and some of the more salient inner parts fixed, it is quite likely that Mozart could have used his stylistic knowledge to 'fill in' what he did not hear for certain. Furthermore, he would probably have had that 'instant' recognition of chords and intervals which we discussed in the context of 'relative pitch'. Thus he would know that he had heard, say, a dominant seventh chord, without necessarily hearing out the individual notes. Yet his knowledge of the contents of a dominant seventh would allow him to infer the notes 'in the mind's ear'. After a first hearing, he would have identified troublesome sections which needed more attention on a subsequent hearing, because they did not contain instantly recognizable chords or patterns. Finally, for someone with as much musical knowledge as Mozart, there exists the possibility that he recognized sequences as identical to, or similar to, sequences in other pieces already well-known to him. Once recognized, such a sequence can be disposed of as something already available in the memory representation of another work.

These comments, whilst speculative with respect to Mozart, are clearly testable with respect to contemporary musicians who can produce both written evidence of their memorization attempts and verbal protocols of their strategies. Let us hope that such research is undertaken soon. Research on other cognitive tasks (such as copy drawing from memory, e.g. Pratt 1983) offers promising models, as well as confirming the general kinds of explanatory proposal put forward here for music.

6. Musical learning and development

6.1. Introduction

Musical skill is acquired through interaction with a musical environment. It consists in the execution of some culturally specific action with respect to musical sounds. However, musical skill is constructed from a base of innate abilities and tendencies. Every human advance involves building on what is already present. Because all human brains are similar, and because certain aspects of experience are common to all humans (e.g. the experience of the physical world and its properties) it has been possible to isolate certain early aspects of skill acquisition which seem to be shared by all humans. For instance, we all acquire the basic skill of manipulating objects in the first year of life; we acquire competence in our natural language by the age of three or so. Further than this, it has been proposed by some psychologists, notably Piaget (e.g. 1950, 1952) that the *type* of learning we are capable of at any age is determined by the general features of our intellectual equipment at that age. Thus, the reason why children seem not to be able to reliably master mathematical concepts until the age of seven or so is that until that age they do not have the type of cognitive resources that would allow them to grasp necessary notions such as transitivity or conservation.

On this view cognitive development is to be partly explained in terms of the ordered acquisition of new 'general' cognitive abilities and structures ('general' because they are involved in a whole range of specific skills and not just one). Piaget's well-supported view is that there is a universally shared order of passage through various cognitive 'stages' and that each stage is characterized by a fairly rapid advance in skill acquisition as the new capacity is applied to the whole range of specific skills the child is engaged with. These stages should not be seen as mysteriously emerging in the child simply as a result of some biologically determined 'release' of new capacities at various ages. Rather, they are brought about by adjustments or 'accommodations' that occur as the child learns particular skills. When the time is right, these adjustments 'colonize' other areas of endeavour.

If we look at musical development through Piagetian eyes, we should be alert to the possibility of discovering invariant sequences of musical development, possibly linked to general changes in other cognitive domains. These sequences would account not for the precise aspects of musical behaviour found—this would depend upon culture, motivation and opportunity, but for the *types* of musical activities to be found at particular ages in virtue of the general cognitive capacities they require.

There is, however, another powerfully argued view of human cognitive capacity, associated particularly with the work of the linguist Chomsky (see also Chapter 2). This states that the human organism is biologically pre-disposed to excellence in a few *specific* cognitive skills, language being one such, and that there exist special mechanisms for acquiring these skills which do not necessarily form part of a 'general' cognitive capacity, but are confined (at least initially) to the skill in question. Taking this approach we should be alert to the possibility of discovering early aspects of musical development which point to capacities specific to music, and not mirrored in other do-mains.

These two views are not mutually incompatible, and Gardner and Wolf (1983) have pointed out that elements of both may be required to fully explain the course of cognitive development. They argue that human development is characterized by both separate *streams* of specific skill acquisition, possibly supported by special biologically determined mechanisms, and common *waves of symbolization*, where a new achievement in one stream 'spills over' into apparently unrelated streams. The streams are largely linked to, and supported by specific cultural roles—orator, singer, artist, craftsman, etc. Within each stream, explicit instruction or tuition is common. The waves, on the other hand, seem not to be culturally salient. No-one, until very recently, has explored the notion that general cognitive style could be changed through instruction independently of particular skills. Rather, the 'spillage' across skills seems to be a spontaneous human propensity. It might even be a defining characteristic of human thought that there exists some mental medium abstract enough to provided the means of passing general skill between two different specific skills.

It is not my intention to give an exhaustive account of developmental theories as they relate to cognitive psychology. General introductions to the work of Piaget are given by Flavell (1963) and Boden (1979); and a readable critical approach is provided by Donaldson (1978). Reviews of developmental theories in relation to music are provided by Funk and Whiteside (1981) and Shuter-Dyson and Gabriel (1981); the latter also being a comprehensive source reference for research into musical development. What I would like to do here is to use the broad theoretical framework I have outlined above to motivate the division of this chapter into two separate, but complementary, halves.

The first half follows the spontaneous acquisition of musical skill by West-ern children from birth up to the middle years of childhood. The second looks at the later development of specialized musical skills, which typically take place in a self-consciously educational milieu. These two processes may be roughly labelled by the terms enculturation and training respectively.

The main elements of *enculturation* seem to be these. First, we find a shared set of primitive capacities which are present at birth or soon after. Second, there is a shared set of experiences which the culture provides as children grow up. Third, there is the impact of a rapidly changing general cognitive system as the many other skills supported by the culture are learned. These elements combine to yield a roughly similar sequence of achievements for the majority of children in a culture, and a set of roughly similar ages at which the various achievements occur. Enculturation is also typified by a lack of self-conscious effort and a lack of explicit instruction. Young children do not *aspire* to improve their ability to pick up songs, although they do improve. Adults do not *instruct* young children in the art of song memorization, yet children come to be able to memorize songs.

When we turn to *training* we take up a rather different set of concerns. We now concentrate on specific experiences which are not shared by all members of a culture. Rather, they are specific to the sub-culture where aspiration to excellence in a particular skill is encouraged. Such experiences allow a person to build on the general foundation of enculturation to achieve what we may call expertise. Very broadly, we may say that, in our Western culture, musical enculturation is the dominant process up to the age of about 10; thereafter musical training plays an increasingly important part. In general, it appears that training is more likely to contribute to depth of knowledge and accomplishment *within* a particular skill than it is to have broad implications for the whole cognitive system. Gardner's 'waves of symbolization' seem to be particularly potent during the first years of childhood when learning on all fronts is most rapid. At this time the cognitive system seems particularly susceptible to broad upheavals. In contrast the typical adult displays a highly 'skewed' profile of cognitive attainments. Someone may be a master jazz improviser whilst retaining the reasoning powers of a 10-year-old. Someone else may have a profound grasp of mathematics whilst retaining the musical accomplishments of a child. And so on. We see, therefore, a cutting of deeper channels within individual streams rather than general 'waves' of development.

Training also involves self-conscious effort on the part of the person concerned with the specific aim of becoming more accomplished. Typically he seeks, or is given, methods for increasing accomplishment. These methods are conveyed through instruction. As well as seeking to describe and understand the changes that take place during a particular type of training, the psychologist is also interested in evaluating the efficiency of different training methods, and, on the basis of such evaluation, offering prescriptions about the best way to train a particular skill. This evaluative/prescriptive approach is the basis of a branch of psychology known as educational psychology.

Over the past thirty years, relations between educational psychologists and cognitive psychologists have not always been cordial. Cognitive psychologists have viewed educationalists as unconcerned with understanding the psychological mechanisms which account for the success or failure of particular training methods. They have caricatured the typical educational study as randomly allocating children to a number of different types of instructional regime and simply prescribing the instruction which gave the best results. On the other hand educational psychologists have seen cognitive psychologists as unconcerned with solving practical problems, and caricatured the typical cognitive study as dealing with some microscopic portion of a real task and hedging any possible prescription with so many qualifications as to be useless in a real training situation. Both these views have more than an element of truth in them, and it remains as difficult as ever to make instructional prescriptions which are soundly based on real understanding of the psychological processes involved. None the less, I believe that both sides are coming to acknowledge the importance of trying to make links between theory and practice; and writers of cognitive texts now find it almost obligatory to derive some training prescriptions from the results of pure research (e.g. Anderson 1980; Bransford 1979)) Particularly, it has been argued in various places (e.g. Levin and Williams 1970) that an intelligent teacher is more likely to benefit from a greater understanding of the psychological processes underlying a skill than he or she is from being given a particular training prescription. The increased understanding will allow the teacher to devise his or her own methods to suit particular pupils and situations and to modify them in principled ways.

This view has been supported from my own experience with teachers. For instance, I once asked an internationally known performer and teacher to take part in a sight-reading experiment. This was the one described in Chapter 3, section 2.1, where eye–hand span was estimated for 'tonal' and 'atonal' melodies. After the experiment had taken place, I discussed with the teacher my prediction that span would decrease on the atonal melodies. He was sceptical, on the grounds that he specialized in the performance of atonal music. He felt that his immersion in atonal music would counteract the possible effect of my mildly atonal stimuli. Moreover, he had not *experienced* the atonal melodies as any more difficult to read than the others. Later, I analysed the experimental data and found this player to provide results indistinguishable from other musicians whose staple diet was Bach and Beethoven. Like them, his span decreased for the atonal melodies. When I wrote to him with his results he wrote back saying that the results had forced him to change his attitudes to the teaching of sight-reading. How he put his changed attitudes into practice I do not know; but clearly there are any number of educational implications in this result, showing as it does that tonal relationships have an inescapably privileged status in the mental apparatus of a musician (presumably through their early and continued presence in the casual experience of all Westerners). However, I would not be happy to derive a single prescription for teachers from this information. I would expect the competent teacher to be able to make the best use of such information to suit his or her particular circumstances.

Educational psychology has a second major concern besides evaluating training methods, and this is the devising of *assessment* procedures which allow teachers to discover where a particular individual stands with respect to the average achievement for his age on some standardized test. In music such tests have often been labelled 'tests of musical aptitude'. One use of these tests is diagnostic, to isolate particular weaknesses which need extra training. Another use is predictive. High scores on particular tests seem to correlate with later achievement, and so, for instance, music schools use such tests to select candidates for entry to specialist training courses. Such tests are often designed with the explicit or implicit aim of detecting potential excellence in the absence of specific training. We shall examine to what extent they are capable of doing this.

6.2. Musical enculturation

6.2.1. *The first year of life*

The first evidence of musical awareness is some form of differentiation of musical sequences from one another or from non-musical sound sequences. It is not adequate to say, as many writers do, that heightened attention to particular sounds, as such, is evidence of musical awareness. It is well known that infants are particularly responsive to change in the environment (e.g. Kagan and Lewis 1965). It follows that any new or unusual sound will capture a young baby's attention. Parents who are delighted when their babies become quiet and attentive to the sound of a nursery rhyme should be wary of concluding too much about their abilities. It is possible that a child is simply responding to a change in auditory experience from the rapid pitch and amplitude modulations found in speech to the steadier parameters of song, or that he is particularly responsive to definite types of waveform (e.g. Hutt, Hutt, Lenard, Bernuth, and Muntjewerft 1968).

It is, indeed, a necessary precursor of musical awareness that a child should be able to notice differences in crucial dimensions of sound. For instance, he will be unable to notice the defining features of a particular melody if he cannot detect differences in pitch or time. None the less, real musical awareness begins only when the child is able to notice sequential relations between different sounds. How good, then, are young babies at detecting sequence? Studies by Chang and Trehub (1977a, 1977b) suggest that babies as young as five months are already sensitive to sequential structure. In one study (1977a) they repeatedly presented a six-note atonal melody to babies. They measured the perceived novelty of the melody by monitoring heart-rate. It is now well established that changes in heart rate are reliable indicators of perceived novelty, and that as the same stimulus is repeatedly presented, infants 'habituate to' (get used to) the stimulus, with a corresponding stabilization of heart rate (e.g. Bower 1971). When the babies had habituated to the first melody, a second one was played. This could either be a melody with the same starting note as the first but a different up–down contour of pitches, or it could be the same melody transposed up or down to a different pitch level. Chang and Trehub found that heart-rate destabilized to the new melody with a different contour but *not* to the transposition of the old melody. By five months, therefore, it appears that changes in sequential pattern are already salient, whereas simple changes in pitch level are not. In another study (1977b) the same authors showed that five-month-old babies were also sensitive to changes in rhythmic patterns.

It is instructive to compare Chang and Trehub's precise but limited study to a much broader but less controlled study by Moog (1976). Moog carried out a large cross-sectional study of children's responses to a set of prepared tapes. The tape contained six 'tests'. Test 1 consisted of three children's nursery songs, sung by children. Test 2 consisted of words spoken to definite rhythms but without precise pitch. Test 3 consisted of pure rhythms played on various combinations of percussion instruments. Test 4 consisted of instrumental music. Test 5 took one of the tonally consonant items from test 4 and subjected it to various rewritings which introduced a high degree of harmonic dissonance. Test 6 consisted of non-musical sounds such as the sound of a vacuum cleaner and traffic noise. These tests were played to about 500 children at varying ages between three months and five years. Moog observed the nature of response to the various tests, and recorded details of any musical behaviour in response to them.

He reports that six-month-old children typically stop what they are doing and turn towards the source of the sound with facial expressions of astonishment, remaining motionless and attentive at first, then looking at their mothers and smiling. They will even stop feeding to look at the sound source. The response is not equally marked to all the tests. Tests 1, 4, and 5 (songs and instrumental music) attract much more attention than the others. Moog reports that 'if a subject responded to one series only, that one was always either the nursery songs or the instrumental music; if he responded to two series, then they were these same two. If more than two series of tests attracted the baby's attention, then songs and instrumental music were, in every case, among the tests to which he responded.'

It seems that babies are here selecting *quality* of sound as the criterion for attention—smooth treble-register pitched sounds. Test 3 (rhythms) attracted hardly any attention, even though it was much louder than any other test. Valuable as Moog's data are, they do not tell us whether the babies were noticing sequential aspects of the sounds. All the results could be explained on a simple preference for what Moog characterizes as 'sensuously beautiful sound'.

Up to the age of six months, babies show hardly any overt behaviour which could be called musical. It is, of course, necessary to make a distinction between behaviours which can be heard *as* music by adults and those which reveal musical awareness in the child. When Ostwald (1973) talks of the newborn baby's cry as having musical qualities, he is clearly referring to the former interpretation. It is nonsensical to suppose that the baby *intends* anything musical by crying.

The earliest sign of intentional music-like behaviour seems to be the ability of some babies to imitate sung pitches. Kessen, Levine, and Wendrich (1979) investigated this in a study where mothers were taught a technique for training their three- to six-month-old babies to match a pitch sung by them on a pitch pipe. They found that after 40 days of practice, all infants were matching sung pitches more often than failing to match; and this was regardless of the musical ability of the parents. There is, however, no evidence that babies below the age of one can imitate melodic sequences, even as short as two notes. Furthermore, 40 days of intensive training hardly forms a part of the normal enculturation process of most babies.

A much more common behaviour which could possibly be musically relevant is the ability of infants to mimic the intonational contour of speech. This is part of the pre-speech vocal exploration often called 'babbling'. Such intonational babbling is primarily composed of microtonal pitch glides, smooth movements across a range of pitches. Gardner (1981) reports that children do not produce *discrete* pitch intervals until the age of 18 months or so. This conclusion is drawn on the basis of an extensive longitudinal study on symbolic development carried out by Gardner and colleagues (Gardner, Davies, and McKernon 1981). In this study they observed the development of a whole range of abilities, including musical ones, in a group of nine children during the first five years of life. This involved regular visits to the homes of all the children, recording their spontaneous musical behaviour, and also attempting to teach them simple songs. This study provides valuable fine-grained data on musical development, and we shall return to it on several occasions in this chapter.

Overt rhythmic behaviour is not noticeably present in the first year of life; although one must again take care to distinguish that which can be interpreted as rhythmical by an adult from that which is intended to be rhythmical by the child. My eight-month-old daughter repeatedly bangs her spoon on the desk of her chair, or repeats a nonsense syllable over and over in her babbling, but I would not wish to ascribe to either of these approximately regular occurrences a rhythmic intention. Rather, she repeats the action as soon as she can after finishing the previous one, and, because it takes roughly the same time to perform each repetition, a roughly regular pulse is set up. To ascribe rhythmic *intention* I would look for some of the following behaviours:

   (a) subdivision of a beat, so that sometimes there are two or more events within a regular superordinate pulse;

   (b) omission of a beat, with the picking up of the pulse at the correct time after a pause;

(c) imitation of a given rhythmic pattern;

(d) moving or beating in time to music.

None of these behaviours normally occur within the first year of life.

In Moog's (1976) study it was found that nearly all babies made some sort of movement response to his tests. The most common responses were swaying from side to side in a sitting position or bouncing up and down. These responses were most commonly observed to song and instrumental music rather than pure rhythms, and they were not rhythmically co-ordinated with the music. Between the ages of nine months and one year these movements increased in frequency, duration, and intensity. Moog also found that around nine months babies began to make distinctive vocalizations to the music. He calls these vocalizations 'song babbling' in that they tend to be varied in pitch but lacking in phonemic variety, often being 'sung' to an open vowel. Song babbling bears no relation to the pitch or rhythm of the music being played; it seems to be a characteristic response of pleasurable expression to the sounds. This is confirmed by the fact that movements and vocalizations occurred primarily to the song and instrumental tapes, and did not occur so frequently to the rhythm or 'noises' tapes. Indeed, babies over nine months began to make quite clear signs of displeasure at these latter tasks, turning away, pulling 'dissatisfied' faces, even showing signs of fear. The increase in vocalization to music over the first year is quite dramatic. At three months only 5 per cent of children made vocalizations. At six months this proportion had risen to 30 per cent and by nine months 100 per cent of the children tested vocalized during the music. It is not clear, however, from Moog's report whether he checked that vocalizing occurred more during music than at other times, or whether the results simply demonstrate an increasing propensity for babies to vocalize at any time.

Do babies of under one year *recognize* familiar pieces of music? The initial possibility of this occurring rests on the fact that parents very often sing the same nursery tune to their children over and over again. My daughter has 'Baa baa black sheep' from someone in the house at least a dozen times a day. At a later age, signature tunes to familiar TV programmes, often played records, and others, can be added to the list of repeating musical experiences. Moog (1976) reports that children towards the end of the first year are often able to make the appropriate movement when they hear 'action songs' which are associated with particular gestures. However, it is not necessary to have the melody. Children still make the appropriate movement if the words are *spoken* rhythmically. Dowling (1982) reports that 'my daughter at 18 months would run to the TV set when she heard the "Sesame Street" theme come on, but not for other melodies'. Clearly then, young children are capable of recognizing some aspect of familiar music. However, we must not conclude from this that they 'know the tune'. Their recognition may be based on the words, or on some distinctive texture or timbre. It is disappointing for me to discover that I can sing 'Baa baa black sheep' to almost any set of pitches provided I retain the words and rhythm. My daughter will still stop struggling and look pleased.

What, then, can we conclude about musical enculturation in the first year of life? It seems that children come to distinguish musical sounds from non-musical ones, as shown by greater attention, movement and vocalization. The primary qualities that mark the sounds they prefer seem to be those of the singing voice or instrument. It is possible that these responses arise from a biological propensity to respond in a special way to certain classes of sound. We also find that children can imitate individual sung pitches, and can discriminate short sequences with differing pitch or rhythmic contours if heard several times in a row. However, there is little or no evidence that children retain much precise musical information about songs they hear often; and their pitch and rhythm-like productions do not share the or-ganizational features of the melodies that evoke them. It should be said, however, that these broad conclusions urgently require refining through the type of controlled experimental study that other aspects of infancy have now been enjoying for 20 years or more.

6.2.2. *The pre-school child (ages one to five)*

The first striking change in overt behaviour after the first birthday comes at about the age of 18 months when spontaneous singing begins to occur. The main characteristic of spontaneous singing is the use of discrete stable pitches (rather than the microtonal glides of the earlier 'song babbling'). These pitches are joined in sequence to form simple intervallic patterns. Although the child at this age has usually begun to speak, words are not usually used in spontaneous singing. This suggests that musical development at this age is proceeding along a genuinely separate 'stream' to speech. Moog (1976) has observed that 'single words or parts of words may occur, scattered around in a string of nonsense syllables or at the beginning of a babbling song which after beginning with the word continues with the repetition of a single syllable'. At this stage there is no evidence that children are attempting to imitate heard songs; rather it seems as though they are experimenting with melodic interval construction. Gardner *et al.* (1981) noticed that the most frequent intervals initially used approximated to seconds, and major and minor thirds. As the second birthday approaches, children begin to ex-periment with larger intervals such as fourths or fifths. In all cases the intervals are only approximate, and there is little evidence that children are producing the exact intervals of the diatonic scale. Several authors have attempted to transcribe these spontaneous songs using conventional no-tation. Whilst this provides a useful impression of the general characteristics of child song, one must be careful not to ascribe more tonal and rhythmic coherence than is actually present. The temptation for an adult listener is always to assimilate what a child sings to the adult categories.

With this cautionary statement in mind, we may examine some examples of spontaneous song. Moog (1976) provides two typical examples of songs produced in the second year of life (Examples 6.1 and 6.2). A sharp or flat

Babbling song no. 1

Examples 6.1 and 6.2. Spontaneous songs of one-year-old children. From Moog (1976).

sign enclosed by brackets indicates an approximate quarter-tone interval above or below the given note. We may see that the songs are dominated by simple repetitions of the same pitch, or small movements up and down in pitch. They are also rhythmically primitive, being dominated by simple repetition of a single note length. When pauses occur, they seem to be related principally to the need of the child to breathe, rather than any developed notion of rhythmic differentiation. It is, however, of interest that the end of Example 6.1 seems to involve a melodic and rhythmic imitation of a three-note figure. Clearly, though, these songs have little sense of adult tonality or harmony.

Between the ages of two and three, spontaneous songs become longer and begin to display greater signs of internal organization. Example 6.3 gives an

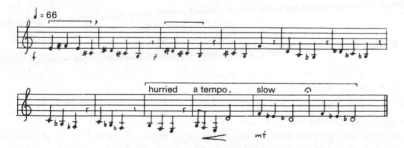

Example 6.3. Spontaneous song of a 32-month-old child. From Dowling (1982).

example of a song provided by a 32-month-old child (from Dowling 1982). Each note was sung to the syllable 'yeah' and brackets indicate regions of relatively accurate intonation. Elsewhere the notated pitch is only approximate. We can now see a quite clear and deliberate use of repetition. A descending major 3–2–1 is repeated nine times at different pitches with the same rhythm. Furthermore, the intervals used often correspond exactly to the diatonic intervals of the scale. Although the pitch of the whole song wanders, and there is no overall sense of a stable tonal centre, each phrase tends to be tonally coherent. By two-and-a-half, the child seems to have assimilated the notions that music is constructed around a small fixed set of pitch intervals, and that repetition of intervallic and rhythmic patterns is a cornerstone of music. What he does not grasp is that there is any hierarchical structure governing groups of patterns which prescribe direction and closure. In general, child song at this age has an 'aimless' quality—it can go on and on without any sense of finishing. The decision when to stop is largely arbitrary.

By the age of two to two-and-a-half a new milestone is reached. Children begin to attempt to *imitate* parts of the songs they hear around them. The first aspects of songs that children imitate are the words—not the complete words, but particularly salient or often repeated sections. Moog reports children often imitating the 'ding ding dong dong' from one of the songs in his test series. Gardner (1981) reports observing 'an oink oink here, an oink oink there' from 'Old MacDonald'. Often these same few words will be repeated over and over. At the beginning there is little attempt to reproduce either the rhythm or the melody of the song concerned. Rather, children seem to couple such word patterns with the type of melodic fragment they have been producing in spontaneous song.

The next stage is the extraction of characteristic rhythmic and pitch patterns from the songs of the culture. In the study by Garner *et al.* (1981) study, this tended to occur towards the age of three. In Moog's (1976) study 50 per cent of the children had reached this stage by two years. This discrepancy is not something that should concern us unduly. Not only were the samples of different nationalities (Gardner—USA; Moog—W. Germany) but the sample sizes were very different. Gardner's generalizations are based primarily on in-depth studies of nine particular children. Moog's generalizations are based on a representative cross-section of 500 children. Both studies agree on the *order* in which the various milestones are reached; and we can see that within Moogs' study there were wide divergences between children at particular ages.

Moog provides an example of the kind of imitation provided by one two-year-old child in interaction with his mother (Example 6.4). We see here an exact imitation of the first four notes of 'Hoppe, Hoppe, Reiter' transposed to a new pitch. Then the child abandons strict imitation and begins spontaneous repetitive song-play on the word 'Hoppe'. In the second example, the mother sings the song 'Little John', and when she has finished, the child repeats the melodic contour of the last five notes (with much diminished intervals).

In general, melodic contour was imitated more often than exact pitch, and in no case did Moog observe *exact* imitation for more than a bar at a time,

Example 6.4. Song interaction between a two-year-old child and his mother. From Moog (1976).

and this only when the child was actually singing simultaneously with the model.

During the third and fourth years of life the child develops imitative capacity to the point where whole songs can be repeated. Generally the rhythm and the pitch contour is mastered before the ability to reproduce precise intervals and maintain the same tonality throughout a song. Most children can accurately reproduce the familiar songs and nursery rhymes of their culture by the age of five.

What happens to spontaneous songs during the child's increasing mastery of imitation? Firstly they get longer. Moog reports that three-year-olds will often produce continuous songs of several minutes' length. They do, however, occur less frequently as the preoccupation with imitation grows. By four years of age, about 30 per cent of Moog's sample were producing what he calls 'pot-pourri' songs. In these songs 'children make up new ones by putting together pieces of several songs which they already know. Words, melodic lines, and rhythms are mixed up, altered, taken apart and put together again in a different way and then fitted in between stretches of 'original ideas''. Usually these 'pot-pourris' were free episodic structures with little sense of overall organization. However, in a few isolated cases figures or phrases from a learned song were altered according to a definite formal principle. One girl of three-and-a-half sang the whole of the Christmas carol 'Ihr Kinderlein kommet' in triple time instead of quadruple time. She did this by altering the dactyl pattern to a triplet wherever it occurred. Such grasp of formal structure at this age is, however, most unusual.

By the age of five, spontaneous song has declined dramatically in frequency of occurrence. The child is now more self-conscious and is concerned with avoiding 'error' and achieving precision of imitation. This concurs with a general trend in children of this age for mastery of detail. Gardner and Wolf (1983) characterize this as a 'wave of symbolization' which moves children from a stage of 'topological mapping' to one of 'digital mapping'. In the earlier stage, children operate mainly with approximate relations of shape and size. In drawing, for instance, they will not be too concerned with getting the right number of fingers on a drawing of a human hand. In the later, digital, stage children become almost obsessed with exact quantification and classification. It is the age at which they will painstakingly put exactly the right number of fingers on each hand even at the expense of stylistic demands of the drawing. For instance, running figures often appear 'frozen' and lifeless because the child is more concerned to try for correct anatomical details rather than convey a sense of motion in which, at a younger age, maybe an extra arm or leg is added.

The same tendency may also account for the love of exact repetition. Moog reports that 'a dozen musically minded parents agreed that small children go on asking to sing the same song for weeks and months on end, just as they go on asking for the same stories over and over again . . . When they look at picture books they look for the same picture, and when they themselves draw they go on drawing the same things for a long time.'

There are a number of possible consequences of this concern with precision and repetition at age four to five. One is that the child is focusing on and using, maybe for the first time, the characteristics of song which are determined by superordinate structures of tonality and rhythm. Although the behaviour of the child may seem externally static, it is very likely that he is using his increasing knowledge of, and memory for, exact pitch and timing relationships to build up knowledge about higher-order structures in music, extracting a new level of knowledge about scales and keys, and about rhythm and metre. We see this knowledge at work in a study by Davidson and McKernon (reported in Gardner 1981) where they taught a new folk song to children aged four and five. They found significant changes between four and five in the imitative products of learning. The five-year-olds were able to maintain a single key throughout, starting on and returning to the tonic, even if some of the individual notes were wrongly remembered. In contrast, the key of the songs produced by four-year-olds tended to 'drift' as the song progressed. Secondly, five-year-olds were able to organize their reproductions in terms of an underlying pulse or beat. Their songs conformed to the beat even if individual rhythms were misremembered. In contrast, four-year-olds tended to organize rhythm 'locally', largely from placements of accents in the words, and they did not maintain a steady pulse.

Another consequence of the concentration on precision is that spontaneous musical experimentation may well cease to play any further real part in a person's life after the age of five unless it is specifically encouraged. Our

Western culture does not provide many opportunities for people to improvise. Much more importance is placed on the shared reproduction of well-known music (e.g. hymn singing, ritual singing among football supporters, the classical concert sub-culture, etc.) In our culture, composers and improvisers do not arise from normal enculturation; their skills are nurtured by specific, and culturally atypical support and training.

We have examined the development of singing between the ages of one and five in some detail. There are, of course, other aspects of musical behaviour and awareness which develop over these years as well; so we should now return and examine some of these.

We first consider the development of movement responses to music. In the second year of life, most children learn to walk. This allows a much increased range of movements, an increase which is represented in movements to music. Moog (1976) found that more than half of his 18-month-old subjects 'danced' in response to music, making circular or turning movements in conjunction with stepping. He also found a large increase in the frequency of 'conducting', that is, a waving of the arms in response to music. These movements are not rhythmically co-ordinated with the music. They seem to reflect a general motor enthusiasm and exuberance which music somehow elicits.

Around two years of age 'about 10 per cent of children begin, for short stretches of time, to match their movements to the rhythm of the music. . . . The few children who are able to do this at all are only able to keep up the co-ordination for a few bars at a time.' Up until the age of five there does not seem to be any marked change in the ability to move in synchrony with music (confirmed by Rainbow and Owen 1979; and Frega 1979). However, two trends are noticeable. First, the variety of movements increases. Second, and perhaps more significant, the number of spontaneous movements decreases very markedly. As children grow older they are more prone to a concentrated, still, attentive listening. By the age of five many children showed no spontaneous movements at all to Moog's tests. This may be part of the same developmental trend to imitation and precision that we noted earlier. Because there is no definite model for specific movements to be made, children prefer to make none.

To elicit movement responses in children of five years it seems necessary to *ask* them to make particular movements, such as clapping or tapping, to see whether they relate to the music. Moog did this, and found that very often the children would make 'any sort of clapping movement, sometimes not even rhythmically regular ones.' Only about two-thirds of the children kept in time with the music for even a short time. On the other hand, when asked to clap whilst singing a song they knew, they could clap in synchrony with the successive notes of the song. It is not clear, however, that children of this age are capable of maintaining a steady clapping *beat* whilst singing a song which variously subdivides the beat and contains silent beats. Rather they are able to use the same mechanisms that time the successive notes of the song to time successive hand-claps.

Here we see a type of dissociation that we shall have cause to consider again. This is the dissociation between implicit knowledge (in this case of metre) that children display in their enactive repertoire (such as in singing the songs they know) and the explicit ability to isolate and use such knowledge in tasks of perception and judgement. In this case, children of five have implicit knowledge of metre but seem not to be able to use this knowledge explicitly.

So much for movement to music. We now consider the development of discrimination. It appears, from Moog's extensive sample, that very few children differentiated between the 'normal' instrumental music and the 'dissonant' manipulations of it. Children attended, made rhythmic and vocal movements just as readily to both tests. 'Not a single child showed the least sign of displeasure' at the dissonances. In contrast *many* children made no response (or a negative one) to the pure rhythms (test 3). At age three, 37 per cent of the children simply ignored the test. Another 24 per cent showed signs of being uneasy; and one little boy asked his mother 'when are we going to have music again?' Another said 'that isn't music, is it, mummy?' We conclude from these observations that harmony is not particularly salient to the pre-school child, but that he has already identified music with some form of melodic content.

In respect of familiar music Moog discovered a gradual increase in true tune recognition up to the age of five. When a familiar nursery tune was played, without words, on an instrument only 40 per cent of four-year-olds recognized it. This proportion rose to 75 per cent of five-year-olds. By this age children are just beginning to reliably catch hold of the notion that melodic identity is carried by a pitch and rhythm pattern, regardless of timbre or words.

Finally, Moog examined the effect of environment on development. He summarizes his findings thus:

Up till the age of about three we could not observe in response to music any significant differences determined by the environment; children from poorer homes reacted no differently to our tests from children in the upper income groups. Children who, according to their parents' reports, were inundated with music from morning till night showed little difference, in either the quantity or quality of their response, from children who were only allowed to hear carefully weighed amounts of carefully chosen musical stimuli. . . . But, between the ages of three and four, differences in home environment begin to show their effect in the field of music. Girls and boys who are taught songs and games by their parents, brothers and sisters, or in nursery schools, have a clear advantage over other children.

Moog also found quite marked differences between children from the *same* kind of background. It is impossible to rule out the possibility of innate differences in musical receptivity, although one should, perhaps, not move to that conclusion as readily as Moog does. What the results do suggest is that after the age of three a child does become receptive to certain types of environmental 'enrichment'. Before that age, immersing one's baby in music may not help him or her become a second Mozart.

How do we sum up the path of musical development between one and five? We see, I think, four main strands. First, the child's increasing propensity to *imitate* words, then melodic fragments, then whole songs. Second, a subordinating of a free improvisatory and unstructured note-play to the forms of the musical culture, by the incorporation of diatonic intervals, then phrases from well-known songs, and finally its disappearance in the service of exact imitation. Third, the increasing ability to organize song behaviour in accordance with tonal and metrical rules. Fourth, a concurrent lack of ability to extract metrical or harmonic information in a situation where some abstracting or evaluative response is sought. Children in this age do not reliably beat time to music, nor do they seem to notice gross dissonance. It seems as if knowledge becomes incorporated in action before it can form the basis of judgement.

This last point can be demonstrated through other aspects of cognitive development. For instance, children find it easier to recall a list of objects when they can be grouped under the headings of two or more common categories (e.g. 'fruits', 'items of clothing'); but at the same age they may be incapable of *judging* a categorized list to be more memorable than an uncategorized one. It is only at a later age that they can accurately judge which lists are likely to be easy and which difficult without actually doing the task of memorization. This reflective grasp of the situation is most generally observed to first occur between the ages of eight and ten (Hunter 1976; Moynahan 1973).

6.2.3. *From age five to 10*

Piaget's investigations of intellectual development led him to propose a profound change in general cognitive ability at around the age of seven or eight. He labels this a change from 'pre-operational' to 'operational' thought. The most celebrated 'symptom' of this change is the child's ability to perform well on tasks involving the notion of conservation of quantity.

Let us take a common example. A child is shown a rolled-up ball of plasticine. Before his eyes, the experimenter then rolls it out into a long thin sausage. The pre-operational child tends to believe that there is now *more* plasticine (because in one crucial respect it *looks* more). The operational child knows that the amount is the same. More than this, he knows it *must* be the same. Other examples of conservation tasks involve pouring liquids from short squat beakers to tall thin ones, or spreading out a line of initially closely bunched counters. In each case the operational child is not fooled. He knows that the amount remains the same.

Several music researchers have attempted to construct musical analogues of these tasks. Pflederer (1964), for instance, played children the same melody at two different speeds and asked them if they were the same. Only 50 per cent of five-year-olds thought the two were the same. By eight years of age this proportion had risen to 94 per cent.

Although this task has a superficial resemblance to Piaget's conservation tasks, it differs in crucial respects. First, children do not observe the melody under continuous transformation between one speed and the other, and so have no independent way of knowing that the two melodies are of the same 'stuff' (Wohlwill 1981). Second, it follows that there is no logical *necessity* that such transformations should conserve musical quantities or qualities. That is to say, one could present two melodies at two different speeds which did *not* have melodic identity. In contrast, there is no way of deforming a piece of plasticine in such a way as to change the quantity. Children become competent at Piagetian conservation tasks precisely when they realize that transformations of configuration are *always* irrelevant to judgements of quantity.

In music the notion of a melody undergoing a continuous observable transformation is problematic, if not incoherent. Each occurrence of music is a separate event in time, totally discrete from the next event. Therefore, there is no necessary relation between one musical event and the next. When Pflederer and others claim to show that children around the age of eight come to conserve musical quantities, it would perhaps be better to say that children of this age are capable of perceiving and remembering invariant aspects of otherwise different patterns. Whilst this ability is of profound psychological interest and importance, it is *not* conservation. Nonetheless, we may suppose that it shares with conservation the increasing awareness by children of the possibility of going behind surface perceptual features in their search for underlying patterns and structures.

If one were to sum up the main developmental trend in music between five and 10 it would seem to be the increasing reflective awareness of the structures and patterns that characterize music and which are already implicit in the child's enactive repertoire. For instance, at age five a child is already capable of singing the same song at different speeds or pitches. In one sense, therefore, this behaviour demonstrates the existence of knowledge that a melody is still the same after transformations. What the child of five lacks is the ability to translate that knowledge into a procedure for making a considered judgement in a perceptual situation where a change, such as in speed or pitch, is highlighted through temporal juxtaposition. The progress from enactive to reflective knowledge does not take place all at once, and we find various aspects of musical awareness undergoing this change in order over the middle years of childhood.

An early aspect of this change is illustrated by the work of Zenatti (1969). She presented children with three-note melodies, each followed by a second melody in which one of the notes had been altered in pitch. Some of the melodies were atonal. The others were tonal. Children were asked to locate the changed note. Zenatti found that five-year-olds performed equally badly on both types of melody, but by six or seven the tonal melodies were producing superior performance. The tonal melodies allowed the extraction of some structural information which could be carried over in memory to aid the comparison with another melody. Although this shows the beginnings of a dissociation of structural knowledge from a purely enactive context, it is still linked to a performance task which does not demand *direct* awareness of structure. We may ask when children are able to form *judgements* about musical sequences when asked to make such judgements in a direct way.

One way of examining this is to ask children to classify musical examples as'good', 'bad', 'complete', incomplete', etc. For instance, Imberty (1969) played excerpts from Bach chorales to children of various ages and asked them to judge whether excerpts were complete or incomplete. Eight-year-old children tended to hear melodies as complete when they ended on the tonic in the context of a perfect cadence; but even at age 10 they tended not to accept as complete perfect cadences with melodic resolution to the mediant.

I have examined the development of judgement in a slightly different context. In my study, children were presented with a pair of musical stimuli and were told that one was played 'correctly' the other one had 'mistakes'. Each member of the pair came from a different sound source, well separated in space and time. Children were asked to indicate (by writing or pointing depending on age) which sound source had produced the 'correct' version. There were four tests. In the first test the 'correct' item resembled a cadential sequence from a typical four-part hymn harmonization; the 'incorrect' item was derived from the correct item by modifying each chord so that it was dissonant. To the adult Western ear such dissonances are extreme (Example 6.5 gives one example of such a pair: all items in this study were played on the piano).

In the second test, the items were single chords, one being highly consonant, the other breaking one or more rule of conventional chord construction (see Example 6.6). In the third test, the items were sequences of

Example 6.5. A stimulus pair from test 1.

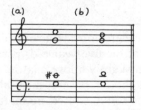

Example 6.6. A stimulus pair from test 2.

consonant chords. In one sequence of each pair the chords were in a 'musical' order that led to a conventional cadence. In the other sequence, the same chords were present but in 'scrambled' order (see Example 6.7). In the fourth and final test, the items were unaccompanied melodic sequences. One item was a diatonic melody which remained in a single key. The other item was a sequence with similar contour but containing notes from several distant keys so that the tonality became obscure (see Example 6.8).

Example 6.7. A stimulus pair from test 3.

Example 6.8. A stimulus pair from test 4.

In each test there were twelve pairs, so that with a score of 1 for the 'correct' item, the maximum score for each test was 12. A subject guessing at random would, on average, score 6 out of 12. I ran the experiment on five different age groups, five-, seven-, nine-, and 11-year-olds, and an adult control group. The average scores of each group on each test are given in Table 6.1. Circled scores are not significantly different from random guessing.

TABLE 6.1

Mean scores (out of twelve) on each test for each age group

	Age	5	7	9	11	Adult
Test 1		7.3	9.1	11.4	11.8	12.0
Test 2		(5.5)	7.7	9.5	9.3	10.6
Test 3		(5.6)	7.3	9.3	10.5	11.6
Test 4		(6.4)	7.3	9.7	9.6	11.6

Scores joined by an underline are not significantly different from one another.

We may first observe that the five-year-olds performed very poorly. Only on Test 1 did they perform slightly above chance. In many cases I observed the children to be making choices on non-musical bases. For instance, one child always chose the same sound source, no matter what music came from it. Another child alternated between sound sources.

By age seven, performance significantly improved on all tests except Test 4 (unaccompanied melodies), although performance was still well below adult levels. At age nine, score on Tests 1 and 2 became indistinguishable from adults. It is pertinent to notice that around this age children began to show strong aesthetic reactions to the 'incorrect' items (dissonant chords)—screwing up their faces in disgust, or laughing and giggling. These tests require least 'work' because the incorrectness arises from simultaneous sounds. Each event is 'wrong' by itself and requires no memory of previous events in the same sequence.

It was not until the age of 11 that scores on Test 3 (chord sequences) approached those of adults. In this test, each chord on its own is acceptable; to detect incorrectness one has to notice the ordering of chords. Performance on Test 4 (unaccompanied melodies) did not improve between ages nine and eleven, and was still significantly below adult performance. Here, the 'work' required is arguably the greatest. Not only do incongruous events not happen simultaneously, but the cues to an underlying key or harmonic framework are much more sparse than in the case of fully harmonized chords.

This study shows, therefore, a progression from age five to adulthood, in which the listener becomes capable of reflective judgement on the musical quality of successively more 'difficult' aspects of music; starting with the ability to reject gross dissonance, and moving on the the ability to detect violations of normal sequential structure.

Two subsidiary findings are of note. Girls performed better than boys on most tests and at most ages. This result has been obtained in quite a lot of musical developmental research (Shuter-Dyson and Gabriel 1981). Secondly, musical training made no difference to the scores. Those children who were receiving regular instrumental tuition fared no better than those who were not. This is a strong indication that the skills we are dealing with here are true products of enculturation, and do not rely on specific training. They arise from the normal child's intellectual encounters with the music of his culture.

The final topic I wish to discuss in this section is the development of the ability to make finer classifications within music which is broadly 'acceptable'. This ability is often given the name 'style sensitivity' and relates to a person's ability to tell whether two extracts of music come from the same composition, composer, or period. Gardner (1973) investigated style sensitivity in an experiment where he played pairs of musical extracts to children, some of which came from the same composition and some of which did not. The children were required to say whether or not they thought the two extracts were from the same piece of music.

There was a significant age improvement in the ability to do this. The youngest children (aged six) had a high tendency to judge extracts 'different' and Gardner suggests that 'pieces had to sound identical or directly continuous in order to be judged as from the same composition'. Six-year-olds had a very limited ability to explain their choices, and those that could offer comments based their discriminations largely on dimensions such as high/low, loud/soft, or fast/slow. Of the 16 pairs presented, six-year-olds judged only 9.7 of them correctly on average (chance score would be 8).

By eight years of age, average scores had risen to 10.5 on 16, and children were able to give 'same' judgements even when the two segments did not sound continuous. Subjects commonly described their perceptions using adjectives or metaphors drawn from outside music: 'peppy', 'dull', 'churchy', 'grown up', 'like a horse race'.

At 11 years of age the average score was 12.4, and subjects began to explicitly refer to aspects of instrumentation, rhythmic character, and texture in making their judgements. Although average scores did not increase above age eleven, subjects aged 14 began to justify their responses in terms of general style, using terms such as 'jazzy' or 'baroque'. Coincident with this was a greater ability to correctly differentiate 'different' pairs when they came from widely different stylistic eras. For instance, they were better at discriminating Boulez from Bach (300 years between them) than Schumann from Brahms (contemporaries). Thus, in this study, we see a progression from judgements based on simple physical features at age six to judgements made on complex multidimensional aspects of style and underlying 'language' by the age of fourteen.

We may summarize the main strands that emerge from our review of musical enculturation as follows. There is some evidence of special propensities which support the early establishment of a 'stream' of specifically musical development. Very young children seem particularly responsive to musically pitched sounds, and are also responsive to changes in pitch and rhythmic sequence. During the second and third years of life we see the emergence of improvisatory song which does not directly mimic the song of the culture (just as children's early speech is not purely imitative). By the age of five children are able to use underlying tonal and metrical structures to guide their song performance, even though they seem to have no reflective awareness of such structures, being almost totally unable, for instance, to identify gross dissonance in simultaneously sounding notes.

We also see the possible influence of wider 'waves' of intellectual development having their effect in the musical sphere. For instance, the increasing concern with precision and imitation around age five mirrors developments in other symbolic domains such as drawing (Gardner and Wolf 1983). This change also corresponds to a change from 'the stage of romance' to 'the stage of precision' suggested many years ago by A. N. Whitehead (1917).

Changes in musical awareness between the ages of five and 10 seem to reflect a general intellectual change from enactive competence, which is displayed only within the bounds of specific and directed activities, to a reflective awareness of the structures and principles which underlie such competence. This change is characterized by Piaget as a change from pre-operational to operational thought. In music it is marked by an increased ability to explicitly classify music as conforming to rule or style, and an increasing advantage in memory and perceptual tasks for those sequences which conform to rule.

6.3. Training and skill acquisition

Musical training is the means to acquisition of specific skills which build on the base of enculturation. We have seen in the previous section that the normally enculturated child already has a set of musical abilities—such as the ability to recall songs and learn new ones; the ability to tell different types of music apart; the ability to make use of underlying features such as metre and tonality in organizing performance. In the 'training' phase, which may overlap with enculturation, and which may extend indefinitely into adult-hood, we see the growth of a variety of skills—performance on instruments and voice, composition, aural analysis, conducting, etc. No single individual necessarily achieves expertise in all these skills, although a culture generally agrees on the skills required by an 'all round musician', and this set of skills becomes institutionalized in the training and examination procedures of music schools and colleges.

Each musical skill poses its own training problems and has related with it a long pedagogic tradition. In a book of this sort it would be impossible to examine all aspects of skill in the detail they deserve. We have already examined some aspects of the acquisition of performance skill (Chapter 3) and improvisatory skill (Chapter 4). What I want to do in this section is draw out some general principles of skill acquisition and training with illustrative examples drawn from some specific skills. My concern with principles is such that I do not pretend to be overly concerned with providing 'advice for teachers and learners'. There are several books of this latter sort, among which Buck's *Psychology for musicians* (1944) is outstanding. Despite its age I would still recommend it as essential reading for any performing musician. Its author has the main prerequisite for writing a book of this sort—a lifetime of high-quality teaching experience at all levels.

Psychology provides many, sometimes apparently conflicting, interpretative frameworks for understanding learning. I would like to organize this section by introducing just one detailed theoretical proposal, and showing, in discursive fashion, how it can be used to support broad generalizations about the business of learning and teaching. The theory is *Production System theory* as applied to skill acquisition by Anderson (1981, 1982). The basic attraction of Production System theory is that it is possible to construct machines (embodied in computer programmes) that operate according to the postulates of the theory. Some typical aspects of human thought and behaviour can be mimicked by such a machine. The basic elements of a Production System are very simple and precise, yet behaviour of some complexity can be obtained when many of these elements are put together with a few simple rules for the way they interact. It is most important to bear in mind that production systems are not in themselves part of the human mind. Rather, they are formal analogies for mental processes. However, to simplify my task, I will talk *as if* production systems are part of the mind. This will save obscuring the argument by repeated qualifications.

Before embarking on detailed exposition, I would like to introduce a few general concepts associated with skill acquisition which I shall be filling out with the aid of theory and example. These are quite fundamental concepts, and turn up, in one form or another, in most writing on learning. First is the concept that skill learning involves acquiring *habits*. The principal feature of a habit is that it is *automatic*, and that it uses up little or no mental capacity to execute. The precursors of habits are conscious, deliberate, and effortful behaviours which commonly involve verbal control. Second is the notion that skill learning involves passing from *factual* knowledge (knowing that) to *procedural* knowledge (knowing how). Knowing what a skill entails is very different to actually executing it, and a theory of learning should be able to refine our understanding of exactly what changes when factual knowledge becomes procedural knowledge. One part of the change seems to be that knowledge comes under direct and more intimate control by *goals*. For most of us, to formulate the goal of performing some familiar task, such as saying a common word, is enough for the task to be accomplished. There seems to be no psychological gap between wanting (or intending) and doing.

Many of our goals are as small and short-lived as saying a particular word. Other goals are larger and more long-term, as, for instance, the goal of being able to play a musical instrument. The ability to form and sustain goals seems to be an essential condition of learning. Such ability is often called *motivation*. Other general conditions essential for most skill learning are *repetition* and *feedback*. People generally become skilled at some task by being presented with repeated opportunities to engage in elements of the task. The sheer amount of time that a person has spent actually doing an activity is one of the best predictors of level of skill. For any complex skill, such as writing a computer program, playing chess, or playing a musical instrument, moderate levels of ability are achieved by those who have devoted hundreds of hours to it. For real expertise, thousands of hours are required. Feedback (or reinforcement as it is called in some contexts) is essential so that only succesful procedures are learned; any procedure which leads to repeated failure is discarded.

We begin our detailed treatment with reference to a proposal by Fitts (1964) that the process of skill acqusition can be broken down into three phases or stages: the *cognitive stage*, the *associative stage*, and the *autonomous stage*. Anderson (1982) succinctly summarizes these stages as follows:

. . . the *cognitive* stage involves an initial encoding of the skill into a form sufficient to permit the learner to generate the desired behaviour to at least some crude approximation. In this stage it is common to observe verbal mediation in which the learner rehearses information required for the execution of the skill. The . . . *associative* stage involves the smoothing out of the skill performance. Errors in the initial understanding of the skill are gradually detected and eliminated. Concomitantly there is a drop out of verbal mediation. The . . . *autonomous* stage is one of the gradual continued improvement in the performance of the skill. The improvements in this stage often continue indefinitely.

Let us now consider what an aspect of the *cognitive* stage might look like for someone who is already competent to read and perform on one instrument beginning to learn a new instrument. I found myself in this situation when, after several years of piano playing, I took up the clarinet. When attempting to play my first simple melodies on the clarinet I had constantly to make recourse to verbal information, sometimes recalled with difficulty from memory, more often retrievable only from my instruction manual. The information was primarily in the form 'the fingering for note X is combination Y.' When the right set of fingers were engaged with the right set of keys, there was still the problem of producing a sound by blowing. This was not straightforward, and to produce any recognizable sound at all required constant adjustment of mouth, tongue, and lips, in accordance with another set of verbal prescriptions. There seemed to be so many different things to attend to at once that fluent performance seemed an impossible dream.

This sense of the crowding in of demands which cannot all be fulfilled is a characteristic of early learning in any endeavour, be it driving a car or learning a new language. There is just too much to think of, too much to remember. Such a sense can be profoundly discouraging, and may cause a learner to give up before any progress is made. The fortunate learner will have available a strategy, possibly imparted by a good teacher or a manual, which may help to circumvent such a block. This is the breaking down of the skill to be learned into a set of components which can be acquired stepwise. In each step the amount of new verbal information is small, and the learner is able to progress beyond the cognitive stage with this small package before proceeding further. In this way the learner is able to shield himself from the ultimate (and daunting oal), setting his sights instead on the very next stage.

On the whole, it seems fair to say that the younger the child, the less able he will be to devise and impose his own schedule. Even adults may find such a task difficult, and will benefit from the advance organization of material to be learned by an experienced teacher. A teacher has oversight which the novice lacks. He knows which aspects of a skill typically cause most difficulty, and which aspects, learned early on, help the course of later learning. On the clarinet, for instance, there is much to be said for acquiring some fluency in the lowest register before attempting music which 'crosses the break'. Each register re-uses the same fingering sequence, uncovering successive holes as the register is ascended. When one arrives at the top of the lowest register, one must depress a register-shift key, re-engage all the fingers, and modify the blow in order to get the next highest note. On a B flat clarinet the top note of the bottom register is the B flat above middle C. A self-directed adult learner might, without guidance, decide to learn the C major scale, one octave up from middle C as his first task. This would involve crossing the break, with all its complications. The experienced teacher (or a good manual) will advise that a better scale to start on would be the F or G major scale that can be totally encompassed within the lower register.

The application of this principle can be extended indefinitely. For instance, in piano learning it makes sense to acquire patterns which do not require shifts in hand position before those that do. In violin learning it makes sense to master open-string positions before learning fingered positions; and so on. Only the experienced practitioner of the particular skill is fully qualified to devise generally useful training schemes by virtue of his oversight of the whole skill. It is, however, worth emphasizing the point that there are very many possible ways of segmenting a learning task which adequately fulfil the requirements of a learner; and it is perhaps more important that the *principle* of segmentation is adopted, than that the learner should have the belief that *one* of the many reputable schemes available is somehow best.

What is happening in a learner as he passes from the cognitive stage to the associative stage with respect to a particular section of skill knowledge? Our overview of concepts in skill acquisition suggested that he is acquiring some *procedural* knowledge in addition to the factual (or declarative) knowledge that was acquired from the printed or spoken word. To continue with the clarinet example, a piece of declarative knowledge might be the following:

D1.   The clarinet fingering for Middle C is the left-hand fingers covering the top three holes.

A simple part of the equivalent procedural knowledge might, in Production System theory, look like Table 6.2.

Each of the statements P1 to P5 is a procedural step called a production rule. Each rule has the form IF condition(s) THEN action(s). It tells one, in simple and unambiguous terms, what to do when a particular state of affairs occurs. Although the language of a production rule is plain, it can often cause perplexity to a first-time reader. One basis for perplexity is that each rule, in itself, seems so trivial and lacking in substance. The reason for this is that by writing out a rule in English for conscious scrutiny one is subjecting it to far more attention than it would ever receive by the individual who possessed such a rule in his procedural repertoire. The whole point about a production rule is that it is so simple that the subconscious mind is capable of executing many dozens of them, without attention and effort, in a few seconds. What appear as single steps in thought to our *conscious* awareness, are actually composed of many subconscious but logically primitive steps which we have run through so many times that they have become completely

TABLE 6.2

Example of Production System

P1.   IF   the goal is to play middle C
and   the fingers are not in the configuration of having the left-hand fingers covering the top three holes (configuration L3)
THEN   the sub-goal is to achieve configuration L3

     P2.   IF   the goal is to achieve configuration L3
     and   no configuration is presently in force
     THEN   place the fingers in configuration L3
     and   the goal is achieved

     P3.   IF   the goal is to achieve configuration L3
     and   a configuration other than L3 is presently in force
     THEN   the sub-goal is to achieve the state of having no configuration in force

         P4.   IF   the goal is to achieve the state of having no configuration presently in force
         and   some configuration is presently in force
         THEN   remove all fingers from the keys
         and   the goal is achieved

P5.   IF   the goal is to play middle C
and   the fingers are in configuration L3
THEN   blow
and   the goal is achieved

---

automated. Thus, a clarinet player using the procedures P1-P5 would actually run through the cognitive steps contained therein in a fraction of a second. This is in contrast to the laborious minutes it took me to write out the productions, or you to comprehend them. I chose a very simple task, that of playing middle C, precisely so that the number of production rules would be few. If I had chosen a more complex and interesting task, it would have taken me many weeks to write out the production rules required, and it would take a reader many hours to comprehend them.

Let us tease out some of the characteristics of production systems, using this example. A crucial feature is the way that the rules embody a hierarchy of goals and sub-goals. In this example, the main goal is to play middle C. The two rules explicitly mentioning this goal as a condition (P1 and P5) are left-aligned to help make the goal structure clear. If the player is lucky enough to find his fingers already in the required position, then all he has to do is blow, and his goal is achieved (P5).) If, however, his fingers are not correctly positioned, then he must get them correctly positioned. So he for the moment sets aside his main goal of playing C and embarks on achieving a subsidiary goal, that of getting his fingers into the right configuration (P1). Rules P2 and P3 (indented one step) relate to this new goal. In this set of rules I have attempted to model the procedures of a fairly raw beginner. One commonly observes beginners completely removing the hand from the keys prior to each note, and then choosing the new configuration 'from cold'. This is, of course, wasteful of effort, and more experienced players learn procedures whereby the existing hand position is used to find the next position. So, for instance, if a sub-set of the required fingers were already in position, they would not be removed.

With our hypothetical performer we assume that if he finds his hands taking up the configuration for playing some other note than middle C, he must set aside the sub-goal of putting the hands in the middle C configuration and pursue a *third* subsidiary goal, that of 'clearing' the keyboard (P3). P4 is the production rule pertaining to this third goal (indented two steps) and its execution allows the goal to be achieved. The system then passes 'control' back to the second goal and now P2 pertains. This allows goal achievment, and finally control is handed back to the original goal, whereupon P5 can come into force and the task is completed. In a 'realistic' system, the goal of playing middle C would itself be a sub-goal of a larger process, and so when it had been achieved, control would pass up to the next higher, and so on. We can represent the goal structure inherent in our little example by reference to a diagram (Fig. 6.1). The goals are enclosed by boxes, and the numbered arrows show how the procedural steps pass control between one goal and another.

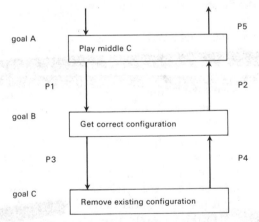

Fig. 6.1. Diagram of goal structure of production system for playing middle C.

It can be seen that a crucial aspect of a Production System is some means of remembering higher goals while sub-goals are being pursued. For instance, it would not be of much use to our clarinet player if he got to the point of executing rule P4 (clearing the keys) only to discover that he had forgotten what he had cleared the keys in order to do. What efficient performance requires is some form of *goal stack*. The idea of a goal stack is very simple, and based on the mechanical analogy of the spring-loaded plate holders that one finds in canteens and restaurants. The design is such that as more plates are put into the holder the base drops so that the top plate is always just flush with the lip of the holder. When a plate is removed, the next highest plate 'pops' back into view. In this analogy the primary goal corresponds to the first plate put into the holder. The next plate is the first sub-goal, which 'pushes' down the original goal. The second sub-goal pushes down the previous ones and so on. When a particular goal is achieved it is jettisoned from the stack and forgotten, and the preceding goal 'pops' back into control.

When executing a complex skill it should be apparent that the goal stack can easily become very large. Capacity for holding goals in memory is not unlimited, and it often occurs, especially in early learning that the goal stack becomes overloaded, and some higher goals are lost. Some varieties of 'absent-minded error' can be attributed to goal forgetting (Reason 1977), such as going into a shop and then not knowing why one went in. In music performance, goal-forgetting can help explain why learners sometimes find it difficult to 'manage' large-scale form by appropriate long-term changes in dynamic and other performance qualities. They have so many subsidiary goals to fulfil in the execution of individual notes that the goal stack overloads, and the overall 'direction' of the performance is lost. We shall return later to the issue of how increased experience allows such difficulties to be overcome.

Another crucial aspect of a production system is that each rule operates entirely automatically (with certain restrictions which need not concern us here) if it finds evidence that its *conditions* pertain. When it does find such evidence, then the actions that it prescribes automatically take place. It does not seem to matter how many *other* production rules the system contains; as soon as the conditions for a particular rule pertain, then its actions are immediately and automatically carried out. The capacity of the human organism for skill learning is apparently unlimited.

The place where production rules 'look' to see if their conditions pertain is called *working memory* by Production System theorists. A close lay approximation to this term would be 'consciousness'. Working memory contains details of aspects of the external environment that one is currently observing. It contains items of declarative (factual) information that have recently been received or retrieved from memory; the current goal stack; details of one's own internal or bodily state; and like things. It specifically does *not* contain all the facts and memories that are stored in the mind and retrievable *somehow*. For instance, most readers will know the name of the city that is the capital of France. It is, of course, Paris. However, until the moment that the topic was raised, the fact that 'Paris is the capital of France' was not part of working memory—it was not in conscious awareness. Rather it had to be retrieved from 'long-term' memory, and the retrieval process took time. In the case of this example, the time taken was probably not very long; but for less well-known facts, the time could be considerable, and indeed the search could fail on a particular instance.

The conditions of production rules are, therefore, contents of working memory. They can be facts about the observable world. They can be items of factual knowledge retrieved from long-term memory. They can be current goals (i.e. goals that are at the top of the goal stack). The actions of production rules can involve overt behaviours; but they need not do so. What they must do is alter the contents of working memory in some way. An overt behaviour will normally do this because it will result in an observable change in the environment or bodily state. However, other kinds of action are just as common. Sometimes some mental operation is demanded. For instance, in a production system for mental arithmetic, a rule might specify that two digits, both in working memory be added together, and their sum recorded in working memory. A third type of action involves either adding a new goal to the goal stack, or noting that a goal is achieved and jettisoning it from the stack. In our simple example, the rule P1 involves no overt behaviour. Its only action is to set a new goal.

Thus, although production rules have several similarities to the 'stimulus-response' link beloved of learning theorists in the behaviourist tradition, they are more sophisticated and versatile in many ways. They directly incorporate inner mental states and goals rather than trying to explain them away.

The production rules possessed by our hypothetical clarinet player incorporated specific knowledge about several things, including the finger configuration needed to play middle C. At one time he did not have such specific knowledge. It follows that these rules must somehow have been *constructed* as a result of his ongoing experience with clarinet playing. How were these rules added to his knowledge?

A primary postulate of Production System theory is that knowledge can only affect behaviour if there is a production rule that can act on it. Another way of putting this is to say that all behaviour is procedural, and that a fact cannot influence the course of behaviour unless there is a procedure that can use it. By analogy, although a book contains many ideas, those ideas can have no influence on the course of history unless someone reads those ideas and acts on them. Earlier on, we said that the passage from the cognitive to the associative stage involved acquiring procedural knowledge from declarative knowledge. At the outset of learning, there were no production rules which *directly* incorporated knowledge about the fingering for middle C. It would be wrong, therefore, to imagine that the fact 'the fingering for middle C is . . . etc.' could directly evoke the required behaviour. Rather, there must have been some more general procedures *already available* which could pick up and use the new knowledge. In Production System terms, there must have existed a set of production rules with 'empty slots' into which specific pieces of information could be fitted.

Perhaps the easiest way to get a grasp on this notion is to write out part of the set of production rules which, hypothetically, could have been present at the initial cognitive stage of performance. The terms (VA) and (VB) represent the empty slots which can be filled by a variety of specific values. In formal language, VA and VB are *variables*.

P6.   IF   the goal is to play a note (VA)
        and   information of the form 'the fingering for note (VA) is configuration (VB)' is not in working memory
        THEN the goal is to place information of the form 'the fingering for note (VA) is configuration (VB)' in working memory

P7.   IF   the goal is to play a note (VA)
        and   information of the form 'the fingering for note (VA) is configuration (VB)' is in working memory
        and   the fingers are not in configuration (VB)
        THEN the sub-goal is to achieve configuration (VB).

P8.   IF   the goal is to play a note (VA)
        and   information of the form 'the fingering for note (VA) is configuration (VB)' is in working memory
        and   the fingers are in configuration (VB)
        THEN blow
        and   the goal is achieved.

P6 is an expression of the knowledge that if one wants to play any particular note and one does not know the fingering for that note, one must discover the fingering before one can proceed. The complete sete of production rules would thus incorporate a set of procedures for getting the required knowledge into working memory (by scanning long-term memory, consulting the manual, attempting to work it out from first principles, etc.). Only when this is done can P7 come into force. It is worth pointing out that P6 is a general rule which would help *any* instrumental learning to get off the ground. It is not specific to clarinet. It is, however, specific to music in its application, but is related to an even more general class of rules which can be obtained by turning *all* the specific values in the rule ('play', 'note', 'fingering', etc.) into variables. Roughly, such a rule would state that if you want to achieve a goal and you do not know what state of affairs would bring about that goal, then you must undertake to discover what that state of affairs is. Such a sentiment may seem trivial, but it remains true that without a procedure that embodied it, people would never be motivated to search for solutions that were not immediately obvious. In such a situation the problem would simply be abandoned.

We see, therefore, in most specific examples of learning behaviour the application (through specification of variables) of a set of very general procedures or strategies for setting about learning. With these strategies, it is possible to make some kind of coherent attempt to master any task. Newell and Simon (1972) have constructed a computer system embodying these principles which they call 'General Problem Solver'. We cannot pursue the characteristics and capabilities of the General Problem Solver in any depth here. Suffice to say that it incorporates the general feature of goal structuring; breaking down a larger goal into a set of sub-goals to be achieved on the way.

It is pertinent to ask where these general strategies come from. Are we born with them, or do we have to acquire them? Although no-one has constructed a detailed answer to this question, it appears that we are born with a set of very specific production rules which allow us to respond instinctively to certain states of affairs. A young baby does not, for instance, realize what is trivially obvious to you or me, that if you lose sight of something and want to find it again, you increase your changes of doing so by searching for it. Rules of this generality are acquired gradually through childhood by some kind of process of abstraction from specific successes. The mechanisms for this abstraction process are little understood, although it is clear that humans have a particular gift for doing this, and that language is an important mediator of the process. What we can say with certainty is that when a child of 10 or so tackles a new learning problem, he or she has already acquired a large set of general abstract procedures which can be brought into play.

If we return to our specific production rules, it will be easily seen that P7 is a general version of P1, and that P8 is a general version of P5. By a similar process of replacing specific notes and fingerings with variables the corresponding general versions of P2, P3 and P4 may be constructed. This *general* set would, in some ways, seem much more economical that a set *specific* to middle C. This is because, for clarinet playing to be possible, one would need a different specific set for *every* note on the clarinet. In contrast the one *general* set will do for the whole instrument. This economy is, however, a false one precisely because the general rules will not work until specific fingering information has been found. If such information is not available, then the set of procedures which a rule like P6 would initiate might be very complicated, and uneconomical of time or effort. Under the right conditions, therefore, which we shall specify in more detail shortly, there is every reason for a learner to construct the large number of specific production rules which will absolve him from the need to search for particular information in the service of more general productions.

What, then, are the conditions under which a learner adds production rules like P1–P5 to his repertoire, where before only general rules like P6–P8 existed? Production System theorists are only just beginning to formulate a detailed answer to this question (Anderson 1982) but we can already see the general outlines of an answer. Such additions to knowledge occur when a general production rule is repeatedly and successfully used in conjunction with specific factual information. The cornerstones of any procedural learning are thus *repetition* and *feedback*.

A naïve view of the role of repetition is that it somehow 'stamps in' new learning, as repeated swings of the axe gradually bite further into a piece of wood. The cognitive view espoused here is a little more sophisticated. We suppose that an adaptive system is necessarily conservative, and will not add a new *specific* production rule to its repertoire unless there is some evidence that it is going to be generally useful. This is because, once inserted into the system, a production rule is immensely powerful. When its conditions are fulfilled it automatically 'takes control'. The system has to be quite sure that it wants to give so much control to a single rule before incorporating it. The best evidence a system can have that a rule is going to be useful is that the situation which demands its application has occurred very often. In many 'natural' learning situations the repetitions which suggest the usefulness of a new procedure to the organism are supplied by the natural environment as the organism interacts with it in the pursuance of its fundamental goals. On the other hand, it is possible to self-consciously construct an environment in which one's cognitive system is presented with many more repetitions of the same circumstances than would otherwise occur. In this way one can 'force feed' the learning system. This is not to entirely distort the normal patterns of human learning. Children are often spontaneously repetitive in many aspects of behaviour, and the urge for repetition may well be part of a natural tendency which has survived in part because it is so beneficial to learning.

Pedagogic techniques of rehearsal, exercise, etc. are extensions of the natural repetitive urge rather than totally alien impositions. None the less, many experts will testify that rapid progress is often achieved only by degrees of repetitive practise far in excess of what is pleasant or intrinsically rewarding. To achieve culturally valued goals a learner must often find ways of making intrinsically disagreeable effort enjoyable, or at least bearable. Much of teaching and learning technique is concerned with this problem.

Feedback is also essential to an adaptive sytem in order to prevent unsuccessful or potentially damaging productions being formed. The learner must have a way of discovering the success of the application of a specific piece of declarative knowledge in a general production system. If it is repeatedly successful, only then will it become proceduralized. As Anderson (1982) puts it:

if a new piece of declarative knowledge proves to be faulty it can be tagged as such and so disregarded. It is much more difficult to correct a faulty procedure. As a gross example, suppose I told a gullible child If you want something, then you can assume it has happened. Translated into a production it would take on the following form:

> IF   the goal is to achieve X
> THEN   the goal X is achieved

This would lead to a perhaps blissful but deluded child who never bothered to try and achieve anything because he or she believed it was already achieved. As a useful cognitive system he or she would come to an immediate halt. However, even if the child were gullible enough to encode this in declarative form at face value and perhaps even act upon it, he or she would quickly identify it as a lie (by contradiction procedures he or she has), tag it as such, and so prevent it from having further impact on behaviour and continue on a normal life of goal achievement.

Feedback comes in several ways. In some instances failure is indicated rather directly by a complete breakdown of behaviour or a manifest failure to achieve a goal. In our clarinet example, if a particular configuration is physically impossible to take up then this is dramatic evidence of something very wrong with the 'knowledge' with which one is operating. At the other extreme, a learner has no way of knowing whether he has succeeded other than by being told so. A good example of this would be the early stages of 'ear training' when a particular chord or interval is to be identified. The learner hears the chord, makes an attempt to identify it, and then receives the 'correct' answer from a teacher or manual. Most situations are intermediate between these two extremes, in that there *is* 'internal' feedback available to the learner, if he can notice it. A teacher can help by directing a learner's attention to such feedback.

When a production rule of a general sort repeatedly calls up a piece of specific knowledge and is repeatedly successful such specific declarative knowledge becomes incorporated into a specific version of the production rule. There is some evidence, however, that the cognitive system has a tendency to incorporate into a production rule *any* part of the contents of working memory that has appeared there on every occasion of the rule's operation, even if it is, in fact, irrelevant to the rule's success. This can be offered as an explanation of why it is often claimed that *distributed* practice is better than *massed* practice. To distribute practice is to spread it over several separate periods rather than massing it all together in a single session. Thus, if one has seven hours to devote to practice in a particular week, it may be better to do one hour on each of seven days rather than seven hours on one day.

In Production System terms, massed practice encourages the formation of production rules containing spurious conditions associated with the particular practice period in question. These conditions have to be fulfilled before the production operates. To take a ludicrously exaggerated example, we might imagine someone who only ever practised at night forming the production rule:

> IF　　the goal is to play C
> and　　it is night-time
> and　　the fingers are not in the configuration Z
> THEN　the sub-goal is to achieve Z

This rule would work only at night! We call learning of this sort 'context' or 'state' dependent. Music teachers and others often observe the effects of such learning. A pupil who is shown a fingering pattern or phrasing suggestion for one passage may fail to transfer it to an exactly similar sequence elsewhere.

What distributed practice seems to do is to allow more opportunity for context to be varied so that only essential and not spurious conditions get incorporated into a new production. In fact, one of the important consequences of persistently practising a skill for a very long time is that it becomes more and more 'decoupled' from particular contexts.

After relevant production rules have been added in the associative stage of learning, there follows a period of gradual improvement of the skill which Fitts calls the 'autonomous stage' in which performance gradually becomes faster and more fluent. There are several reasons why this might be. One is that several simple productions become merged into a single production sharing a common goal. Therefore, instead of a sequence of productions applying in turn, each taking some finite time to be found and used, only one production is needed.

For instance, if the goal is to play an arpeggio pattern (say C E G C in C major) then one could imagine an early stage of learning where there were four separate rules, one for each note of the arpeggio. Thus the first rule would apply if and only if the first note had not yet been played, and so on. If such rules were constantly and successfully applied in sequence, the cognitive system would eventually 'couple' them together so that the condition of having the goal of playing the arpeggio would, within one rule, entail the action 'play note 1 *then* note 2 *then* note 3 *then* note 4'. In traditional terms, the arpeggio would have become an integrated and automated performance pattern.

Such a 'compilation' could not take place, of course, until the performer were capable of *having* a goal such as 'perform a C major arpeggio'. This would in its turn depend upon having already understood what a C major arpeggio is, either by demonstration or by inference from its repeated occurrence in music. In performance from a score, a performance production rule such as the above would need a corresponding *perceptual* production rule which could *recognize* a C major arpeggio as being present on the page. Early instrumental learning is often hard because one is learning the perceptual and motor 'halves' of the skill at the same time.

It should be emphasized that the forming of a production rule for a performance pattern such as a C major arpeggio is not to specify every performance parameter. The performance will *not* be a rigid 'fixed action pattern' which comes out with the same timing and dynamic parameters each time. Rather, the rule specifies a series of sub-goals (of playing the various notes in turn) each of which may call up new procedures which determine the precise parameters for the notes according to transient information in working memory.

Another aspect of the 'autonomous' stage is the acquisition of further specific production rules which relieve the load on the goal stack. Consider once again the little production system for playing middle C (P1–P5). We observed that it had three levels of goal stacking. The third goal (removing all the fingers) was set by P3. We could eliminate the need for P3 (and thus P4) if we were able to incorporate a rule for going from each specific other finger position to the desired one. One such rule might be:

P9.   IF   the goal is to achieve the configuration of having the left-hand fingers covering the top three holes and the left-hand fingers are presently covering the top two holes
        THEN   cover the third hole and the goal is achieved.

To get to middle C from any other note would require about 30 such rules. To get from any note to any other note would require about 900. It is not unreasonable to suppose that the expert clarinet player has all 900 of these rules in his production system. The time and effort required to get them all there is great, but it is worth it for the elimination of one goal from the stack, and the consequent lightening of the load on working memory. Typically, such new productions will be acquired piecemeal, so that common transitions, such as moving from one note to the next member of a scale or arpeggio, are acquired early on, at a stage where the learner still reverts to P3 and P4 for more unusual transitions.

The task of writing a production system for a non-trivial aspect of musical skill has not yet been undertaken; nor yet has the even more crucial task of modelling some aspect of musical learning in detail. It is not clear, at this stage, whether the theoretical notions available are fully up to the job of music learning, and I do not wish to pretend otherwise. It does, however, seem to me that there is no other theoretical framework currently available which allows such detailed formalization of cognitive processes but at the same time supports many general but more vague conceptualizations and observations about learning. We thus move away from detailed analysis of production systems to some more general remarks which such an approach pulls into focus.

It has long been clear to insightful teachers that one does not create learning simply by offering people facts or prescriptions. Such offerings are of no use to people unless they can incorporate them in procedures they already have. Otherwise the facts remain insulated from any real influence on skill. Teachers in all spheres of activity, including music, often experience the sense that they are not 'getting through' to a learner. Facts are acquired and reproduced, yet there is some sense that the learner has not really grasped the essence of what is being said. For instance, I have had piano pupils whose playing has somehow been wooden and lifeless. I have talked to them about tonal variety, planning *crescendos* to points of accent or climax, rubato, etc., and at a 'declarative' level it has all been understood, in that they can provide definitions of what terms like *rubato* and *accent* mean. Furthermore, they have been able, under instruction, to obey the letter of these prescriptions in particular contexts. A pupil took my advice that a particular cadential chord should be accompanied by a holding back of the tempo; but the application of the advice achieved a grotesque result, an arbitrary 'hiccup' in the music, rather than a measured pause which emphasized the importance of the chord, but allowed the music to continue. It was clear that my pupil had no sense of the 'rightness' of my advice in virtue of which it would be possible to tailor it to the demands of the specific context. I do not know whether or how, such sensitivity can be taught. All a teacher can do is watch diligently for signs of it, and when it appears, encourage it and build on it. With all learners and at all levels there comes a point when a tactful teacher must just pass over a failing, knowing that, at this juncture, further comment will not improve it.

The greatest determiner of the progress of any piece of learning is the learner himself, the procedures he has available, and the motivations he has. To use an agricultural analogy, a teacher is like a gardener; tending, watering, pruning, and 'training' his plant. Without his attentions the plant would still grow, possibly not so straight and tall; but it remains true that the gardener cannot alter the essential form and nature of the growth. This is also, to a certain extent, true of the learner himself. Even in a self-consciously 'engineered' learning environment the learner cannot totally control his progress. He finds some things easier to grasp than others, he finds he has just not got the motivation or concentration to cross a particular hurdle, his recalcitrant fingers will just not take up the patterning he wants. And so, in many respects, the learner *observes* his own progress, sometimes with delight and sometimes with despair, rather as an outsider would.

In Production System terms we may say that a learner's conscious efforts tend to alter the contents of the 'declarative' part of his knowledge, but cannot actually get 'down among the production rules' where it really counts. He must patiently wait for the production system, operating according to its own laws and pace, to pull down from declarative knowledge that which it can make its own.

The engineering of learning is, thus, a hit-and-miss affair. No-one not even the learner himself, can be fully aware of the automatic thought procedures which form the basis of his competence. It is impossible, therefore, for anyone to plan the 'ideal' training diet in a way which is exactly tailored to the competences of the individual concerned. Rather, teachers and learners evolve broad strategies which, on the whole, seem to produce results. This helps to explain the huge gap between cognitive theory and learning/teaching practice. It is impossible to derive foolproof prescriptions for a situation in which, almost by definition, the crucial determining factors (the existing set of production rules within an individual) cannot be easily known. What good teachers (and good learners) seem to do is build up a stock of commonly observed facts about learning environments and schedules which, on the whole, work for them. As a learner becomes more expert, the more likely are such conditions to be specific to that individual, because the shape of his knowledge is different from anyone else's. Our best hope of deriving generalizations would seem to be at the beginning of training, when one may hope that learners share a reasonably common heritage of procedures and motivations supplied by the interaction of biological propensities with the experiences of enculturation.

Thus, for instance, it seems true for our culture that most well-motivated children learn to read if they are supplied with some means of acquiring information about the sounds of letters and words together with a stock of suitably attractive books. The motivation to be able to read their *own* stories, when they want, seems strong enough for children to effectively teach themselves. Teachers assist the process by providing information and feedback when it is needed, and by some elementary structuring of sequence, so that, for instance, the words that a child first meets relate to well-known objects and ideas in his experience. The main conclusion to be drawn from a massive amount of research into teaching methods seems to be that, for the majority of children, it does not much matter what official 'method' is adopted, they learn to read just as well. The main factor determining success seems to be the individual teacher (Williams 1970). It has been observed that two teachers from the same school, with the same type of children, can produce consistently different results, although using the same 'method'. It is not unreasonable to conclude that good teachers are those who provide, reliably and efficiently, the information, feedback and encouragement that children seek as they go about the business of becoming skilled at reading. This can often boil down to such basic things as providing the kind of environment in which a child who wishes to pursue some learning is not likely to be interrupted by other children.

In music an early motivation is often the wish to be able to reproduce the musical sounds of the culture. In more cases than one might expect, the mere presence of a musical instrument in a home can allow a child the opportunity to learn some idiosyncratic music making—picking out combinations and sequences which sound familiar or interesting. In some cultures, where improvisation dominates, such idiosyncratic beginnings can, under their own momentum, produce an expert performer of some distinction, whose technique and style may be unusual, but effective for the music he chooses to play. In our own culture, where the emphasis is on reproductive performance of significant 'art' compositions, teachers feel a duty to steer their pupils towards the kind of technical and formal grasp which will eventually, enable a culturally acceptable performance of, say, a Mozart sonata, or a Chopin Etude. In this case, it is necessary to introduce learners to ways of holding their hands and moving their fingers which will at first, seem very unnatural, but which are necessary if they are to execute fast passagework with the kind of fluency and control that the reproductive goal requires.

This contrast is exemplified by the difference between a largely self-taught jazz pianist and a graduate from a music conservatoire where a 'rigorous' technical approach is taken, and where learners are coached on the same relatively small concert repertoire that will enable them to participate in international competitions. The former will often have a technique which would be perceived as 'hopelessly awkward' by a trained concert pianist, yet it serves its purposes well. The latter will usually have a technique which is very similar to other pianists trained at the same school, often to the point where individuality becomes submerged. A 'balanced' relationship between teacher and learner will probably steer a middle course between these two extremes. The teacher will try to shape and mould what is already present without 'going back to square one', and the learner will incorporate, and make his own, what the teacher is offering.

If one accepts the way of looking at learning that I have attempted to outline in this section then it seems to me necessary to accept that the training (of oneself or others) is more an art than a science. However much information scientific research and theory can supply it will never allow a total knowledge of the learner's cognitive system, because each learner is unique. No matter how much scientific information is available, teachers and learners must still make decisions on a largely intuitive basis. I confess to experiencing some relief that this conclusion may be drawn on theoretical grounds, because if one *had* to rely on research in music education it would be hard to find a consistent and universally applicable set of findings.

Consider, for instance, the question of how to correct habitual errors in performance (such as the execution of a wrong note or a wrong fingering in a passage of music). Buck (1944) has characteristically forthright advice on this point:

> If you work at a passage where the difficulty is the fingering, your only chance is to decide on how you will finger it, and work on it with concentrated thought until it is automatic. It may mean a thousand repetitions. But if, after fifty of them you are careless and and stumble, you have not merely done it wrong for once; you have wiped out all the benefit derived from probably twenty-five of your trials (p. 20).

On this view, the only way to correct error is to play the correct fingering a very large number of times. This is intuitively plausible. However, an extraordinary study by Reitmeyer casts serious doubt on this conclusion (Reitmeyer 1972). In this study, some subjects were asked to indulge in *negative* practice. This involved deliberately practising the error, being aware all the while of the correct fingering. Other subjects practised in the 'conventional' way, playing the correct fingering. The two groups of subjects were then asked to provide repeated correct performances as a measure of the extent to which the error had been corrected and eliminated. Reitmeyer found that there was no significant difference between the effectiveness of the two techniques.

Without a theoretical framework, such a result is practically un-interpretable, and leads to such weak conclusions as those given by the author, e.g. 'instrumental students and teachers might consider negative practice as an occasional alternative to positive practice'. On the face of it, the result renders Buck's statements false. Yet I would be loath to alter Buck's advice. It is clear that positive practice is *a* road to success, and one which is supported by teaching tradition and intuition. Even if negative practice had turned out to be *better* than positive practice in Reitmeyer's study, I would still be loath to recommend it, since I would imagine that learners would find it very hard to live with, and believe in, such a counterintuitive strategy.

As a cognitive psychologist, I am, of course, fascinated to know how it is possible for negative practice to work. It is possible that repeated attentive *thinking* about the right fingering is more important than actually *playing* the right fingering. This is supported by Neisser's (1983) studies of dart playing. He found that his subjects improved if asked simply to *imagine* themselves throwing darts. In Production System theory, it is what is going on in working memory (or consciousness) that determines the course of learning. Because Reitmeyer's subjects were actively labelling what they played as 'wrong' and another, unplayed, fingering as 'right', we may conclude that production systems picked up only that information labelled as 'right'. We may contrast this case with another outwardly similar case where someone plays the wrong note, but does *not* simultaneously think of the right note in a focused manner. In such a case, it would be *really* extraordinary if there were any improvement. Unfortunately, a teacher cannot easily know whether a learner is or is not thinking of the correct note whilst practising the wrong note. Negative practice is, therefore, an educationally disastrous technique, precisely because an observer cannot check whether it is being carried out effectively. Positive practice has the advantage that the learner *must* be thinking of the correct note in order to play it (unless, of course, he already knows the passage so well that it is automated; in which case there is no learning problem).

The problems that arise when one makes any attempt to derive specific training prescriptions from educational research have been illustrated through this (not atypical) example. This is not to suggest that such research is without value. However, it seems to me that the most useful research is that which offers the musician a general resource which he can use to suit his own purposes rather than a detailed method. One area in which this condition is fulfilled is the development of new technology which offers a musician the opportunity of enhancing the feedback available to him.

For instance, Tucker, Bates, Frykberg, Howarth, Kennedy, Lamb, and Vaughan (1977) describe a computer-based interactive aid for musicians that allows a passage played on the keyboard of an electronic organ to be displayed visually in a modified notation that reflects the exact duration of the notes played. With the aid of this feedback, a pianist of concert standard improved his performance of a triple trill quite dramatically within minutes. Similarly, Basmajian and Newton (1974) showed that with visual electromyographic feedback, wind players learned within minutes to suppress or activate specific parts of the buccinator muscle in the cheek. Singers can also be helped in a similar way (Fourcin and Abberton, 1971).

6.4. Assessing musical ability

We finish this chapter by briefly considering 'tests of musical ability'. Within musical cultures where there is an organized pedagogic tradition, achievement in specific musical skills such as performance and theory are measured directly through examination. Apart from the problems caused by 'nerves' and 'stage fright' such examinations seem to fulfil their purpose in a direct and unexceptionable manner. We shall not consider them further here. The purpose of 'tests of musical ability' are rather different. Whilst examinations presuppose intensive preparation of specific materials, tests of ability involve no foreknowledge of test content. Indeed, such tests are invalidated by extensive practice on the particular tasks they contain. This is because of the rationale which underlies their construction.

The argument is that all children within a culture experience a relatively common exposure to, and involvement in, music, at least to begin with. However, because of differences in innate potential, motivation, or experiences at certain critical periods, the 'take-up' of musical knowledge varies from child to child. Thus, even before some children are selected for specialist training, they have come to differ from one another quite widely in the stock of underlying skills and sensitivities they possess. Sometimes these differences are not immediately apparent in the overt musical behaviour of the children. For instance, there may be differences in the ability to listen to and appreciate music. Or again, a child with relatively few musical skills could have received instrumental coaching which provided him with an overt accomplishment not displayed by a child without such coaching who, nevertheless, had many more 'unnoticed' skills rather than the ones which are on the official training agenda. A child who possesses these skills in a measure above those of his age-mates is more likely to make rapid progress under formal training and is more likely to achieve excellence. A child who lacks these skills is unlikely to make such rapid progress, will require more training effort to achieve excellence, and possibly has passed some critical period of development after which it is unlikely that excellence can be achieved.

Without questioning this line of argument, let us look at a few typical situations where such tests might be of use. One example might be the case of a school with a very good choir that gives frequent public performances and broadcasts (such as many English choir schools). Members of the choir spend many hours a week rehearsing at the expense of other school activities, and the majority of the children selected for training must reach the required level within a relatively short time if the numbers in the choir are to be maintained to take account of the older children who leave the choir every year. Very few potential entrants have had intensive singing experience. After ensuring that candidates can sing simple melodies pleasingly and with good intonation, the choirmaster makes the final selection on the basis of a test of musical ability.

A second example might be the case of an older child, in early or mid-teens, who becomes seriously interested in music after years of relative neglect. He wonders whether he would have a chance of succeeding in a musical career. He attends vocational counselling and is given a test of musical ability. His score is well below the average for his age, and he is advised that he will be unlikely to cross the selective and competitive hurdles that would gain him a place at a music college.

These two examples have in common that they are being used to assist some kind of educational selection. Although the principle of selection can have unfortunate and undesirable consequences, there are benign aspects too. It does a child no good to allow him to embark on a course of training for which he is temperamentally or intellectually unsuited, whatever his current 'wants' might be. Given that some selection is inevitable and possibly helpful, we may ask if and how 'tests' can be used to make such selection as fair and accurate as possible.

First, a test should only be used when there are no more direct signs of achievement to examine. Instrumental or vocal performance which shows technical and expressive mastery provides better evidence of musical ability than any test can do. In both our examples, the sensible teacher or counsellor would have ensured that there was no direct clinching evidence of accomplishment before embarking on testing.

Second, test results should be taken in conjunction with other evidence, formal and informal, where possible. For instance, a child who performs well on a test but does not seem particularly interested in, or excited by, music may still be unsuited to an intensive musical education. It is always possible, for instance, that over-keen parents have discovered the general nature of the tests used, and obtained special coaching for their child on the types of task to be tested.

Third, testing should only be carried out with respect to a particular educational question to be answered at a particular time, not to provide a once-for-all statement about capacity or potential for achievement. In the choir example, the tests used to select those children who, within a few months of testing, would be likely to be able to 'hold their own' in a fast-moving training programme. For the teenager the question was whether he would be able to raise his achievement level to competitive examination standard within a few years. In neither case should relatively poor results lead to the conclusion that a person is 'unmusical' or 'incapable of musical achievement'. The person concerned is simply judged unlikely to meet *particular* achievement targets within *particular* limited time-spans.

Fourth, the test should be a *valid* measure of musical ability. Validity may be assessed in two ways. A test has 'face' or 'content' validity if it manifestly demands use of the ability it is purporting to test. A test which involves a subject hearing, and then singing back, a short melody has high content validity as a test of musical ability. A test which requires a subject to remember a list of numbers has low content validity. A test may be valid in a second way, however, even when content validity is low. This second type of validity is called 'associative validity' and arises when there are good correlations between a test and some other measure of achievement. One way of assessing associative validity is to see how well one test result correlates with some *other* test of ability. This is often a little circular, because this still leaves one with the problem of assessing the validity of the other test. A better method is to see how test performance correlates with future achievement. If there is a high positive correlation, the test is said to have good 'predictive validity'. Thus, if ability to remember numbers correlated highly with later musical achievement, it would be a valid test of musical ability. The problem with tests that have only predictive validity is that one has to place one's whole faith in the adequacy of the studies which purported to establish the validity. There may be any number of reasons why the conditions which pertained in the validation study do not pertain in a particular testing situation. For this reason, it would seem advisable to use tests which, where possible, have high content validity. If evidence exists of high associative validity, so much the better. However, it is worth saying that it is often quite difficult to obtain really convincing estimates of predictive validity. To obtain such estimates requires a non-selective use of the test with a large population, and a subsequent follow-up study to assess achievement. Ideally the validation study should be carried out in an educational context similar to the one in which the test is being proposed for use. Thus, in our choir school example, the 'ideal' validation would involve the school selecting children for entry to the choir on some basis other than a musical test. Meanwhile, the specific test of musical ability in question would be administered to all the children by a third party, and the results kept secret. All the children would then undergo normal training, and at the end of the training period their achievement assessed by conventional means. Then the test results would be unlocked and their predictive power assessed. In reality, few schools could afford this sort of experiment.

Fifth, the test should be reasonably *reliable*. A test is reliable if the same subject achieves the same score when tested more than once. In practice no test is 100 per cent reliable, and the scores of an individual will fluctuate from testing to testing. Much of this has to do with concentration and other personal factors. A test will tend to be unreliable for a given individual if a lot of the items are just at the limits of his ability. On a 'good day' he will just succeed at all these items. On a 'bad day' he will just fail. Good test preparation can reduce this problem. A standard technique is to have a series of items of graded difficulty, starting with very easy ones, and moving through to very difficult ones, so that all subjects will find several items that they can always get right, and several that they always get wrong, good day or bad day alike. What will vary from test to test are the scores on the few items which lie around his 'cut-off' point. Because no test is completely reliable, an experienced tester will resist the temptation to make distinctions between people on the basis of small differences in test result. Tests should only be used to place people in broad categories (such as 'top quarter' or 'bottom third'). Even this does not make a test completely fair. Suppose, for instance, one can only take 25 per cent of a given population, and one uses a test as the sole criterion for selection. There is no coherent alternative to simply selecting the highest scoring quarter. This may well mean accepting someone with a score of, say, 62, and rejecting someone who scores 61, even though it is entirely possible that, on another testing, their positions would have been reversed. There is no entirely satisfactory solution to this vexing problem. One flexible and humane response is to abandon rigid quotas and examine the distribution of test scores. Quite often one can find that the scores 'cluster' around certain values, with definite gaps between the scores of different groups. In such a case it would considerably increase the fairness and re-liability of the selection to place the 'cut-off' point in the largest convenient gap, even if this meant taking rather more, or rather less, than quota. Another response would involve using test scores as one among several selection criteria, so that 'borderline' cases could be distinguished on some more discriminating criterion.

There are some 24 tests of musical ability documented in the recent litera-ture. Shuter-Dyson and Gabriel (1981) provide a comprehensive description and discussion of all these tests. All of the tests have basic content validity. That is, they all require children to listen to, and make judgements about, short extracts of music. None of the tests require overt musical performance such as singing or beating time. The most common type of test item is a pair of notes, chords, or sequences, which may or may not differ in some respect. The subject is required to say whether the members of a pair are the same or different, or to make a simple judgement about the difference ('which is louder?', 'which is better?', etc.). All of the tests comprise two or more sub-tests, examining different aspects of music. The same types of sub-test occur in many of the tests. One of the most common sub-tests, for example, involves the subject hearing two short melodies of identical length. In the second melody, one note may be changed in pitch from the first melody. The subject has to judge whether the melodies are the same or different, and if different, where the different note lies in the sequence.

Differences between the tests lie in the selection of sub-tests used, the age-group for which the test has been designed, and the efficiency of the standardization procedures and reliability and validity studies. Several of the tests are not commercially published, and others have gone out of print. The two tests most readily available and most widely used (at least in Britain) seem to be the Seashore Measures of Musical Talents (Seashore, Lewis, and Saetvit 1960) and the Wing Standardized Tests of Musical Intelligence (Wing 1962). For a detailed evaluation of these tests see Sloboda (1984).

Both the Wing and Seashore tests have been designed for use with children of age eight and upwards. As we saw earlier in the chapter most eight-year-olds have an enactive repertoire of songs they have learned from the culture, and which they are capable of reproducing with rhythmic and tonal accuracy. They are beginning to enhance their reflective awareness of the structures and styles that the music of their culture contains. They are beginning to differentiate consonance from dissonance, and to gain a sense of harmonic direction and closure. They also have started to detect high-level 'style' similarities. The period up to the age of 12 or so is, in general, one of rapid and significant changes in musical awareness; and most of the observational and experimental studies reported in the first part of this chapter found wide variation in ability at each age. Unfortunately, both the Wing and Seashore tests were designed long before much of this research was published (Wing 1948; Seashore 1919). If one were designing a new test today it would be only rational to test the very abilities that recent investigators have shown to be developing in middle childhood. Thus the test might include versions of Gardner's (1973) style-sensitivity test, Zenatti's (1969) tonal memory tests, Imberty's (1969) harmonic closure tests, and so on.

Some of the Wing and Seashore sub-tests approximate quite well to these research tests. Both, for instance contain a test of melodic memory. The Wing tests contain a test for discriminating conventional from unconventional harmonizations, and metrical from unmetrical accenting. Other tests seem more hard to justify. The Seashore tests, for instance, contain a test of pitch discrimination with pitch differences going down to as little as 2 Hz (about one-tenth of a semitone in the pitch range tested). Research we have discussed in Chapter 5.4 shows that many experienced adult musicians are incapable of such fine discrimination, and that assimilation to pitch/scale categories is a more characteristic (and useful) feature of the musical mind. Manor (1950) found a zero correlation between scores on the Seashore pitch test and success at clarinet or trombone playing. A small positive correlation *was* obtained for success at violin playing; a skill where accurate pitch perception is arguably more important than most.

Similarly, the Seashore tests include a loudness discrimination test which requires finer discriminations than many professional bassoonists seem capable of (Patterson 1974).

It is certainly true that a total failure to make discriminations along sound dimensions such as a pitch and loudness would render musical achievement impossible. However, we are entitled to question the value of extremely fine discriminations below a generous minimum. The thrust of most of the evidence presented in this book is that musical expertise consists in grasping the various levels of structure that exist in musical sequencing. A test of musical ability or aptitude should be demonstrably concerned with such structural skills. On these grounds the Wing test is to be preferred to the Seashore, and seems to produce better validity estimates than the Seashore (Shuter-Dyson and Gabriel 1981). Even so, there are serious technical deficiencies in the presentation of the Wing tests which makes them hard to recommend wholeheartedly (Sloboda 1984). Both tests are somewhat dated, and need re-standardizing for contemporary populations.

Tests of musical ability have never made the same kind of impact on the music teaching profession as have tests in 'core curriculum' areas such as reading or mathematics. It would be interesting to pursue the reasons for this, but here is not the place. It does seem likely, however, that lack of strong and consistent teacher demand is a major factor behind the relative unsatisfactoriness of the music test market. Without such demand it is unlikely that the funds and research impetus will be found to devise a test which serves the musical community really well. This is not to say that an individual teacher or institution will not find a test of musical ability useful in a particular context. However, it would be wise to treat test results with considerable caution. In particular, it would be foolish, and possibly unfair, to make major educational decisions on test scores alone.

7. The musical mind in context: culture and biology

7.1. Introduction

The discipline of psychology occupies a curious and rather precarious position in the world of science. It stands mid-way between the 'physical' sciences such as biology and physiology, and the 'social' sciences such as sociology and anthropology. Within its own boundaries it experiences the tension created by the opposite pulls which the 'physical' and 'social' sciences exert. Thus, there exists a sub-discipline of physiological psychology and one of social psychology. Cognitive psychology occupies a middle position between these sub-disciplines rather as psychology is between the biological and social sciences.

The biological approach to psychology attempts to account for human behaviour in terms of the operation of the brain and nervous system, which is, in its turn, influenced by the genetic constitution of the human organism. It is often 'reductionist' in that it seeks to replace psychological entities such as 'consciousness', 'intentions', 'memories' with combinations of physiological entities and events such as activities in certain brain areas. This approach tends to stress the innate basis of much human mental equipment, the universality of human psychological makeup as a result of shared genetic material, and proposes that many of our basic social conventions and institutions have arisen because they further the survival of individuals within the species, and so have been selected through Darwinian evolution. Critics of this approach point out that cultural and historical variation in human behaviour are very wide; and philosphers have argued with some cogency that the attempt to reduce mental events to brain events fails on conceptual grounds.

The social approach to psychology attempts to account for human behaviour in terms of the social institutions and conventions within which a person develops. On this account, significant behaviour thought patterns are learned through interaction with the culture, and they are specific to the particular culture. This approach stresses the *relative* nature of most human abilities, and their dependence on particular social contexts for their execution. Critics of this approach point out that all humans share a genetic heritage, a common physical environment, and certain cultural constants such as upbringing by adults, language learning, and so on. These factors converge to give rise to psychological universals.

As with most crude dichotomies, each approach states something important about man, but fails to encompass the whole truth. Cognitive psychology occupies a vital pivotal position between the extremes because both 'biologists' and 'sociologists' identify individual human thought and action as the 'given' which requires explanation. The 'neutral' cognitive psychologist attempts to articulate the structure of human thought and action in a way that leaves aside the question of cause—biological or social. For this reason, the typical cognitive psychologist is not concerned to examine a wide range of developmental and cultural contexts. Instead he takes a *particular* stage of behavioural development of an activity within a *particular* culture, and asks the question: how can we best characterize the system that is operating at that time and place? On the whole, I have tried to take a relatively 'neutral' line in this book; although authors such as Sampson (1981) argue that such a stance cannot help but offer implicit support for strong assumptions about the nature of man and society.

Whether or not one accepts such criticism, it is clear that neutrality can be, at best, a temporary strategy which leaves vitally important questions untouched. Biological and social influences must be included in a full explanation of human conduct. Accordingly, this chapter explores a few of the social and biological considerations relevant to musical thought and behaviour.

On the social/cultural side we look at some of the factors which may be responsible for cultural differences in music, and ask whether, none the less, there is any evidence of underlying universal features of music. On the biological side we examine some studies which shed a little light on the neural organization of musical function. We also ask whether there is a biological base for the origins of music in our species. Does music fulfil a biological function, and has it got evolutionary precursors in our immediate ancestors?

7.2. Culture and musical thinking

The musics of the world contain enormous variety. Just what variety has not, perhaps, been fully appreciated until the present century when Western scholars have begun systematically to study and record music of other cultures than their own.

One important approach to the study of the world's music is essentially taxonomic or classificatory. It is a first step in understanding the relation of music to culture. In this approach the musical sounds of a culture are classified in terms of, for instance, the instruments they use, the typical forms found, the scales and tuning systems used, the social contexts in which the music occurs, and so on. Using such information it is possible to build up a comparative 'world map' of music, grouping together those cultures whose musics seem most similar.

To take one example, it seems possible to divide the continent of Africa into two main musical sub-continents, with the Southern boundary of the Sahara Desert as the approximate dividing line between the two. In Northern Africa, where Muslim influence has been particularly strong, one can discern features of the indigenous music which links it to the music of the Near East. Here the voice is paramount. There is relatively little instrumental music, and instruments are more often used to provide an accompanying drone or rhythm for a vocal line. The music is mainly monophonic and soloistic, and the solo singer uses a particular type of voice production which gives it (to Western ears) a forced nasal quality. Melodies are based on pentatonic (five-note) or heptatonic (seven-note) scales, but are decorated with micro-tonal shakes. Social contexts for music making include religious ceremonies and festivals, and the recounting of epic poems. The music of Northern Africa is generally seen as part of a larger 'Pan Islamic' tradition which extends as far up as Turkey and Eastern Europe. The Yugoslavian epic songs discussed in Chapter 4 fall into this Pan-Islamic tradition.

The music of Southern Africa has distinctly different charcteristics from Pan-Islamic music. Here music is rarely soloistic but involves groups of people. A fundamental form is the call–response, in which a solo leader sings some short phrase, followed by an answering phrase from a chorus. The music is usually polyphonic, which is to say that there are often at least two independent, but equally important and co-ordinated, things going on at once. Instruments, particularly drums, are very important, and much music has a rhythmic strength and vitality brought about by the repetition of short, highly complex, multi-layered rhythmic patterns, produced by different drummers simultaneously executing their own rhythmic devices. The tonal content of the music seems more accessible to Western ears than that of Pan-Islamic music. Singing is full throated and less prone to microtonal variation. Harmony is common, and typical chords are built from intervals of major and minor thirds, perfect fourths, and perfect fifths. The social contexts for music are many and varied. Practically any social gathering, whether for work, celebration, or religion, is the occasion for group music making. Nearly all music is text-based, with poetic or song structures lying at the core of musical forms. Even purely instrumental music usually derives from a vocal model.

This much simplified contrast between the music of Northern and Southern Africa gives a flavour of the kind of descriptions that ethnomusicologists have been able to give of the world's musics. Of course, there are many more fine distinctions within small regions than this sketch suggests, and Africa contains no less diversity than any comparable area of the world. I have neither the competence nor the space to offer a survey of the world's musics, even at the most general level. There is a large and detailed literature on all aspects of world music. Much of the fundamental research is published in the journal *Ethnomusicology*, but helpful summaries are provided by Kunst (1959), Malm (1977), and Nettl (1964, 1973). Up to date summaries and bibliographies are provided in *The new Grove's dictionary of music and-musicians* (ed. Sadie 1980).

What I wish to do here is go beyond taxonomy to questions of cause. What factors, cultural or social, can help account for the wide differences between musical cultures in the world? I shall focus on a single factor which, although not the only significant one, seem to me to have far-reaching consequences. It is particularly important because it seems to relate particularly strongly to differences between Western Art music (about which this book has mainly been) and other forms. I shall be suggesting that the form of Western music, and the nature of the cognitive skills it supports, are closely linked to the existence of a developed system for notating music. In doing this I draw particularly strongly on the ideas of Blacking (1976) and Shepherd, Virden, Vulliamy, and Wishart (1977). After this I shall turn to the question of the evidence for 'universals' underlying the surface diversity of music.

My aim is to raise a few of the issues which seem to be important for a broader understanding of musical cognition than can be gained from examining only one type of music. Psychologists have not been noticeably interested in music outside their own culture, and there has been little empirical work carried out within the framework of modern psychological thought. In this section I shall be offering some broad, even provocative, general hypotheses, which clearly need refinement in the light of psychologically oriented research. A psychologically informed evaluation of the vast ethnomusicological literature is also needed. It is only the absence of such major achievments that justifies my rashness in dealing with this vast and complex issue at all.

7.2.1. *Music notation as a cultural force*

Many world cultures are, or have recently been, essentially non-literate (or *oral*). That is, they have not used visual notational means of recording details of human transactions. There are many contrasts to be made between literate and oral cultures. I wish to concentrate on four broad proposals about the effects of the availability of notation:

1. The existence of written notation allows lengthy verbatim recall of complex meaningful material.

2. Notation allows proliferation and migration of material so that it exceeds the capacity of any one individual to know it all.

3. Notation encourages the separation of the content of an utterance from its context, and makes it easier for an utterance to be treated as a 'thing in itself'.

4. Notation selects certain aspects of sound for preservation, and, in doing so, both embodies current theory and also tends to restrict the future development of music in certain ways.

First, I will enlarge on these points with reference to language, and then suggest how they may also apply to music. Before doing these things, it is necessary to make some qualifying remarks. Contemporary cultures can be ranged on a continuum from those where literacy is non-existent to those where literacy pervades all aspects of social activity. There are many 'semi-literate' cultures, where literacy exists within restricted classes or situations, and where this has effects which permeate to the oral members of the culture. Even in a predominantly literate culture such as ours there may be individuals who are not literate, but indulge in activity which is supported, directly or indirectly, by the literacy of others. Conversely, individuals who are fully literate can, at the same time, possess significant areas of activity which are essentially oral. Many Westerners are linguistically literate and musically oral. Some musically literate people maintain areas of musical activity, such as jazz or folk music, which are essentially oral. So the literate/oral distinction is not as culturally clear-cut as I sometimes assume for argument's sake.

There is also another complicating factor in the form of new modes of preserving the past, particularly electrophonic and photographic recording. These fulfil many of the functions of notation, but have new properties too. Because these modes of recording are not symbolic, people can use them without acquiring literacy. This tends to increasingly blur some of the distinctions I make, at least when applied to the contemporary scene. With these reservations in mind, we may proceed.

For many people, notation is so important that reality becomes, in many ways, mediated *by* their notations. What can be written down and preserved is *correct* and definitive: man's performance or memory is judged against the written record. In oral culture, present knowledge and memory are the only guides. Disagreements are settled by negotiation, or by recourse to the judgement of respected individuals (D'Azevedo 1962). When members of a literate and an oral culture interact these differing 'world views' can cause mutual incomprehension. Goody and Watt (1963) give a clear example of this (cited in Shepherd 1977):

Early British adminstrators among the Tiv of Nigeria were aware of the great importance attached to . . . genealogies which were continually discussed in court cases where the rights and duties of one man towards another were in dispute. Consequently they took the trouble to write down the long list of names and preserve them for posterity, so that future administrators might refer to them in giving judgement. Forty years later . . . their successors were still using the same genealogies. . . . However, these written pedigrees now gave rise to many disagreements, the Tiv maintained that they were incorrect, while the officials regarded them as statements of fact, a record of what had actually happened, and could not agree that the unlettered indigenes could be better informed about the past than their literate predecessors. What neither party recognized was that in any society of this kind changes take place which require a constant readjustment in the genealogies if they are to continue to carry out their functions as mnemonics of social relationships.

It is common for many literate people to assume that the life and knowledge of a literate culture is somehow *superior* to that of a oral culture; that literacy adds to man's resources and takes nothing away. It would be more correct to say that literate and oral cultures are *different*, and that there are both gains and losses involved in becoming literate. The advantages are so clear to us that they hardly need spelling out: the increased availability and durability of knowledge, allowing complex and geographically widespread social and knowledge structures to develop. The disadvantages sometimes escape us and need more emphasis. In a completely oral society, gaining knowledge cannot be divorced from the fundamental human interactions of that society. Knowledge is preserved in the very customs and rituals which bind the society together. In so far as the social group is stable, the knowledge it transmits tends to be stabilizing, dependable, and sufficient for life. There is little possibility of a person falling foul of society through failure to know something of importance. The limitation of knowledge to that which is important enough to become enshrined within oral traditions guarantees that each individual knows what he needs.

Literacy, in contrast, involves the possibility that knowledge becomes esoteric and unmanageable. There is so much stored knowledge in a literate culture that it is impossible for any individual to interact with anything other than a small fraction of it. Thus man becomes dependent on other 'experts' to mediate and use knowledge for him. Because written knowledge can be disseminated far from the social context that generated it, the amount of 'useless' knowledge (with respect to a particular individual or group) becomes very large. At best this can mean that a person will waste a lot of time and energy before discovering useful knowledge. At worst it can seriously mislead by supplying knowledge which is simply inappropriate to a person's own situation.

Written notation also encourages us to *distance* ourselves from our words and those of others. When they are captured in permanent form on paper it is easier to analyse, dissect, and treat them as lifeless *objects* distinct from us and our thoughts. In this way, they lose some of their power and immediacy. This has some good consequences. It allows us, for instance, to resist the power of words used for persuasion, seduction, or demagoguery, at least to some extent. But it also encourages the formation of an image of ourselves as *separate* from our words and actions. We see ourselves as observing and acting on the world rather than being part of it.

Finally, by *selecting* the aspects of an utterance which are preserved, notation can lead to impoverished communication. Our own alphabetic notation fails to preserve significant information about timing, intonation, voice, gesture—and selects phonetic information for preservation. This can have a profound influence on some forms of spoken language, legitimizing speech where the phonetic element carries more and more of the burden of the communication. In some contexts it may be implied that educated, literate, speech is grammatically correct, phonetically well-articulated, de-contextualized, unsupported by gesture, and smooth in pace and tone, compared to the speech of the oral or the child. The temptation is to make spoken language more and more like its written counterpart, so that the un-notated currency of speech, in all its richness of expression, becomes debased and devalued. The epitome of this trend is to be found, perhaps, in the radio newscaster of whom (at least in Britain) it can truly be said that he supplies no more than what a listener would have learned from reading the text himself. War atrocities and Stock-Exchange fluctuations are reported in the same measured tones.

Having outlined some general aspects of the effects of literacy, let us now see how these arguments might be applied to music. In oral cultures, music is handed on from person to person without notation and so it is, like verbal knowledge, subject to mutation over time. Only the scribe or the tape-recorder can record that change, however. Within the oral culture there is no way of checking that a particular performance is 'the same music' as before, other than through consensus. There is no evidence that oral cultures support any lengthy musical recall that is exact (i.e. *note-for-note* the same as a model). The music is 'recreated' anew at each performance. What we observed to be true of Yugoslav song characterizes most of the lengthy musical products of oral cultures. Although a basic pattern or kernel may be retained, successive performances demonstrate significant differences of detail and elaboration. This is not to say that the members of the culture view the music as fluid or unfixed. There is real and detailed learning of particular pieces of music; but what is learned is inevitably a relatively high-level abstraction from a succession of performances which *are* different in notatable detail. The kind of exact knowledge which we can gain of particular pieces of music through repeated examination of scores or through repeated hearings of the same record is literally impossible in an oral culture.

There are several things to be borne in mind when evaluating this assertion. First, it is not denying the possibility of *all* verbatim recall. Short melodies *can* be easily memorized, and we have some reason to believe that the orally transmitted nursery rhymes and folk songs of our own and many other cultures have changed remarkably little over the years. These usually have a repeating verse structure, and the musical material is rarely longer than 50 or 60 notes. Second, the assertion does not deny the existence of 'prodigious' feats of memory. In oral settings, people do remember very long pieces of music. My point is that it is unlikely that the memory will be a note-for-note replica of a previous performance. In literate cultures we find many accounts of lengthy verbatim recall in cases where the memorizer is not necessarily making use of notation. This does not contradict the general assertion because it seems fairly clear that such achievements rest indirectly on the existence of notation. We may argue that lengthy verbatim recall depends upon the culture being able to provide several exact repetitions of the same piece of music. Before the advent of modern recording techniques notation would be the only means of providing performers with the opportunity to produce note-for-note repetitions of lengthy works. When such repetitons are available to a listener, then he may begin to develop the representational skills required to achieve verbatim recall. Eventually an individual may get to the point where he can memorize a long work after one or two hearings (cf. Mozart and Allegri's *Miserere*, discussed in Chapters 1 and 5). There is, however, no psychologically plausible account of lengthy verbatim recall which does not rest on a prior history of 'training up' recall ability on shorter pieces which are repeatedly heard.

Third, the assertion is not to claim totally different memory mechanisms for people in oral and literate contexts. The fundamental basis for musical memory, as has been argued throughout this book, is the ability to extract higher-order structure from sequences of notes. In an oral context, the musician uses a stored structure to generate different, but structurally linked, note sequences on different occasions. This ability becomes labelled as 'improvisation' in a literate context. When notation (or recording technology) allows for several hearings of the identical note sequence, then a musician can elaborate his structural memory to provide for exact note-for-note recall. The memory is still *structural* as the experimental evidence reviewed in Chapter 5 shows.

A different, but related, effect of the existence of notation is on the *forms* of music that exist within a culture. One may argue that notation enables the construction of complex and lengthy forms where relationships spanning many hundreds of notes are planned in detail. It also enables the use of devices such as inversion or retrogression, and strict counterpoint. This is because a composer can make detailed records of early events and construct later events by repeated reference to them. In a purely oral context, thematic relations are unlikely to have the almost mathematical exactitude of some notated forms, but to have a looser, although still musically effective, association.

In general the forms of oral music do not match those of literate music in 'architectural' complexity, where multiple hierarchical embeddings can produce long, varied, yet integrated compositions. Rather, we find a preponderance of 'chain' structures where the same kind of short element is repeated, with variations, over and over again. The 'theme and variation' structure that we discussed in Chapter 4 with respect to Western improvisatory performance seems to incorporate fundamental characteristics of oral music, of whatever culture.

It is worth noting that even if notation is necessary for the development of such forms as sonata form, fugue, etc., it certainly cannot be a sufficient condition. There are several cultures with develped notational systems which use very different musical forms to those of the Western classical tradition. We must see notation as only one of a range of interacting influences on the development of form.

In addition, to say that oral music lacks the formal complexity of some Western forms is not to say that it lacks all complexity. Oral music provides all sorts of opportunity for elaboration and detailed craftsmanship. However such complexity tends to be due to elaborations *within* sections rather than relations *between* sections. Consider, for instance, the Venda song (South Africa) given by Blacking (1976) in Example 7.1. It repeats the same short

Example 7.1. South African Venda song. From Blacking (1976) Used by permission of Faber and Faber Publishers, London.

phrase over and over again, yet the rhythmic asymmetries would defeat many a Western performer. The time signature is, in effect, a very fast 5/8 + 7/8 + 5/8 + 7/8, a rhythm which the drummers sustain through a number of possible polyphonic permutations, two of which are given.

There are at least two different, but complementary, ways of understanding a piece of music. One is through its context, the other is through its content. Both ways of looking at music are available in all situations, but it is possible to argue that notation tips the balance in favour of the content approach, and tends to devalue the context. This is precisely because notation (and sound recording) allow us to examine musical content detached from particular performing contexts. Oral music cannot be detached from its context in this way, and a degree of its 'meaning' is supplied by the context. Without such context we are encouraged to view the music as a 'thing in itself', and to search for what Goodman (1976) has described as 'repleteness', where every noticeable aspect of content is taken to be significant, and *designed* to be significant. We must be careful, however, to make sure that the originator of the music intends it to be replete in this sense. We can 'read too much' into a notated composition, but the danger is exacerbated when we approach oral music with this set, for the oral musician is less likely to have turned every element over in his mind, searching for the *exact* notes to capture his *exact* meaning. There is, of course, nothing inherently wrong in listening to any music in an analytic way. Intellectual disciplines such as musicology would be impossible without it. There is, however, the danger that such analysis will take one further away from, rather than nearer to, the mind of a musician engaged in oral music, for whom such an analysis would seem inappropriate, even meaningless.

A final important aspect of music notation to observe is that, like language, it *selects* some aspects of sound for preservation and discards others. This has important influences on theoretic conceptions of music and, over the long term, on the nature of music itself. To illustrate this we may briefly survey the development of standard Western notation over the past 1000 years or so. The serious scholar should consult Apel (1953), Cole (1974), Karkoschka (1972), and Read (1974) for full details on this topic. I have written elsewhere at more length on psychological aspects of music notation (Sloboda 1981).

Modern Western notation arises, through a complex chain of developments, from *neumes*, which are first found with frequency in religious manuscripts of the eighth century AD. These were used to notate chants to which fixed prayers were sung in religious communities. Example 7.2 shows

Example 7.2. Ninth century neumatic notation. Photograph from Bibliotheque Nationale, Paris.

one of the earliest examples of neumes from a French manuscript *c.*871. The neumes are written above the Greek text and indicate the approximate shape of the melodic contour (the rises and falls in pitch). Thus, ∕ denoted a rise, ＼ a fall and ∨ a fall and a rise. Wishart (1977) comments on neumes as follows:

The neume did not attempt to mark out what we now have come to regard as individual pitches and units of rhythm, but only shapes and contours of melodic lines customary in current practice, and hence also requiring a complete familiarity with current melodic practice, and an adherence to it before becoming usable.

Neumes were designed without any intention of recording music for posterity or dissemination to other places. Rather they served as mnemonics for recall to people already familiar with local performing conventions. A person faced with neumatic notation alone could not possibly reconstruct the melody notated, even to a first approximation.

By the twelfth and thirteenth centuries, music notation had undergone a series of changes which significantly widened and decontextualized its use. First, symbols became linked to conceptually static entities, 'notes' rather than mobile 'contours'. A note is a sound which remains notionally at the same pitch for the whole of its duration. Second, a means of calibrating the pitch distance between notes was devised by the introduction of stave lines. In the earliest examples, only one line was supplied, identifying a single fixed pitch. In Example 7.3 from the tenth century, the fixed pitch is F below

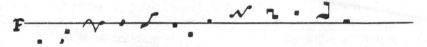

Example 7.3. Tenth century neumatic notation. From Read (1974).

middle C. It requires some guesswork to decide what the other notes might be. Eventually, however, multiple lines became the rule, as we know them today, with lines and spaces indicating principal melodic pitch levels. Third, aspects of timing began to be notated through the shape of the note symbols. At first, such timing distinctions were fairly crude (e.g. long, short, very short) but gradually the binary subdivision of time units into halves, quarters, eighths, etc., became codified. Whilst notation was linked to chanted texts, timing information was arguably not so important, since the performers were all singing the same text, whose words regulated the timing. The accurate notation of time was, however, crucial to the development of polyphony and instrumental music. An accomplishment such as the performance of a string quartet would be totally impossible were there not accurate means of ensuring synchrony and coordination among the instruments (see Sloboda 1981). Although notation is not the only possible means of promoting synchrony, it has undoubtedly contributed to the rapid development of complex polyphony in Western culture.

For any notational system to work beyond the immediate realm of particular social groups it must become systematic and reliable. This is accomplished mainly by the existence of a small number of finite and discrete constituents out of which all music can be constructed by combining the constituents. But natural music, particularly that of the voice, is not necessarily made up of discrete elements. Pitch, timing, timbre, loudness can all vary continuously along the various dimensions of sound. Fitting vocal music into the procrustean bed of discrete notation can thus be very unreliable, it would seem. Unreliable, that is, unless the voice actually conforms to the requirements of the notational system by tending towards discrete 'jumps' along the dimensions under its control, particularly the pitch dimension. Within contemporary Western culture it is certainly true that much vocal music aspires to the discreteness that our notational system embodies. Early school training involves emphasis on singing 'in tune' and 'in time', avoiding pitch glides and gross deviations from small whole-number subdivisions in timing. Performed music is thus 'like' notated music in crucial respects. Explications of pitch and time within conventional music theory embody this discreteness through elaborations of concepts of scale, metre, etc. (see Chapter 2). Thus theory, notation, and performing practice form a mutually supporting closed system within which music can be described, notated, transmitted, and understood.

Although notation helped cement theory and practice over the ages, it would, I believe be wrong to assume that pre-notated vocal music had no qualities of discreteness in the pitch and other dimensions. At any stage of history, a notational system used in performance would have to be perceived as providing a relatively good fit to current practice before it would be accepted by performers. We know that discreteness exists in contemporary oral cultures, although it is often blurred through a greater freedom in the use of microtonal and microrhythmic embellishment. Above all, we know that, since prehistory, musical *instruments* have possessed the precise qualities of discreteness that conventional notation codifies, at least in the pitch domain. A plucked string issues a single unchanging pitch. A set of pipes or strings offers a set of relatively fixed pitches, and music played on such instruments must, of necessity, be confined to this set. To notate instrumental music with discrete pitch symbols is not a procrustean operation. It very closely mirrors the sonic state of affairs. In so far as we can assume that the sounds of fixed pitch instruments would influence the vocal practice of oral musicians, we have good reason to suppose that instruments have provided a continuous force towards discreteness in vocal practice.

We may also note that early theories of harmony were based on discrete pitch intervals, and that theoretical notations employing alphabetic conventions were used by Ancient Greek and Chinese writers. However, we should not, perhaps, make too much of this, because until the late Middle-Ages music theory based on the properties of vibrating strings and air columns, as codified in the writings and notations of philosophers, had almost nothing to do with the actual practice of making music. It would not have occurred to philosophers to use their notations and theories to record contemporary musical *practice*. We know almost nothing about what Ancient Greek singers and instrumentalists actually did from the writings of these theorists. This is also true of early medieval writers such as Boethius (*c*.480–524) who taught that performers and composers were 'separated from the intellect of musical science'.

What makes the later development of notation in medieval Europe so different is that it was rooted in *practice*, drawing theory, so to speak, in its wake. Furthermore, it arose in a religious context where instruments were frowned upon (although such instruments as the organ became gradually acceptable from the eighth century on: Caldwell 1978). Instrumental music was almost entirely secular—the province of the essentially oral laity—and it did not begin to be notated until long after stave notation was widely accepted.

The acceptance of stave notation seems to rest largely upon the work of Guido of Arrezzo (*c*.1000–50). It is he who is generally credited with the completion and systematization of the four-line stave still used for plainchant notation today (Hoppin 1978). Guido was fully aware of the importance of the need that his own system filled. He was able to 'produce a perfect singer in the space of one year, or at the most in two' whereas previously 10 years of study had yielded 'only an imperfect knowledge'. With his system, singers could now read and perform a melody they had never heard before. As well as perfecting the four-line stave system, Guido was also responsible for devising the 'sol-fa' mnemonic for singers. This is a way of remembering the pitch relations between notes on the stave by referring back to notes in a well-known melody The melody he chose was the hymn to St John the Baptist, '*Ut queant laxis*' (Example 7.4). This hymn 'spells out' a six-note

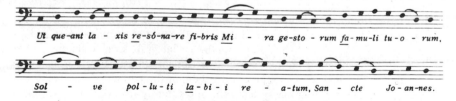

Ut que-ant la - xis *re*-só-na-re fi-bris *Mi* - ra ge-sto - rum fa-mu-li tu-o - rum,

Sol - ve pol - lu - ti *la* - bi - i re - a-tum, San - cte Jo - an-nes.

Example 7.4. Plainsong hymn to St. John the Baptist. From Hoppin (1978).

scale, *ut-re-mi-fa-so-la*. The system, with minor modifications is still in use today, although the archaic '*Ut queant laxis*' has been replaced with more appropriate contemporary songs (as immortalized in Rogers and Hammerstein's *Sound of Music*).

Guido's system rapidly spread through Europe, and soon, all chants of the Roman liturgy had to be notated within his system. That not every existing chant fitted into this system easily is suggested by the fact that some chants underwent significant rewritings and transpositions over the years which can be seen as attempts to 'bring them into line' (Hoppin 1978).

The notational system perfected by Guido paved the way for the emergence of a new breed of musician, the sight-reader (see Chapter 3, section 2). This is the performer who uses notation to give a reasonably polished performance of music without prior rehearsal. He does this through his intense familiarity with the notational system. With advances in printing techniques and resultant increases in legibility, sight-reading reached its apotheosis in the present century.

One should emphasize that the selectivity of music notation does not *force* performance practice to be restricted to what is notated. Even with standard Western notation, performers still have considerable interpretational latitude (see Chapter 3), and one requires much more than the ability to read music to give a culturally acceptable peformance of a Beethoven sonata. What our notation does is to fix a level of detail at which we are prepared to say that anyone providing a performance in accord with the notation has provided a performance of *that* piece, and no other. Thus, the most idiosyncratic and ill-informed performance of a Beethoven sonata is still *that* sonata. This would not be true of someone attempting to provide a performance of Gregorian chant from early neumatic notation. The notation is just not specific enough. Modern notation is normative in a way that early neumatic notation could not be. This does not, however, prevent modern notation being used for purposes where it is *not* normative, and where it significantly underdetermines performance (e.g. the baroque ground bass).

Although notation has supported positive developments, it has its negative aspects too. Wishart (1977) argues that the sterile 'dead end' of twelve-tone music was due to a constriction of the musical imagination by the categories implicit in the notational system:

In its constant search for new modes of expression, the Western classical music tradition was . . . constrained by its very concentration upon relationships of a limited set of thus notatable 'pitches', to extend the notatable field of harmonic relationships to the limit. The final step into a 12-tone and thence 'integral', serial technique, rather than being a 'liberation' from this restricted set tonality, must be seen in historical perspective as the final total capitulation to the finitistic permutational dictates of a rationalized analytic notation system, and the gateway to much sterile rational formalism . . . More subtle uses of pitch, such as sliding inflections, which can vary over an infinitude of possible speed, interval of sliding and curvature of the slide . . . were not amenable to this finitistic approach.

The freedom from sterile and formal music has been made possible, not so much through new notational systems, as through the opportunity now afforded to composers to bypass notation entirely and compose directly into sound with the assistance of electronic machines. This is partly because it is difficult to see how *any* notational system could cope with things like sliding inflections reliably; and partly because the fixed 12-tone system has become enshrined in conventional instrument technology. One cannot do pitch glides on a piano.

I have suggested that the selectivity of music notation reinforces the tendency to view musical elements as falling into discrete categories, a tendency which is, in any case, encouraged by the existence of discrete pitch instruments. We may still be entitled to ask, however, *why* it is that man has favoured fixed pitch instruments for his music. It has recently been argued (e.g. Balzano 1980; Pressing 1983) that discreteness in both the pitch and time dimensions are essential if music is to serve certain communicative functions. We shall see, in the following discussion, that much music in both oral and literate traditions shares basic characteristics, in view of which we must conclude that even such potent cultural forces as notation are not all-important in determining the nature of music.

7.2.2. *Musical universals*

We have examined one factor which can contribute towards cultural variation in music. There are, of course, many other such factors. For instance, not all cultures support the existence of musician 'specialists' such as composers, instrumentalists, etc. This can have a profound influence on the type of musical activity that takes place. Is it possible that, despite all such factors, there are some underlying features which typify most music? If there are, then these might be related to some universal cognitive basis for music which transcended individual cultures. We have already suggested the possibility of primitive auditory grouping strategies playing a part in the way that music is heard (Chapter 5.2). Another possible set of universals arises in connection with the use of the pitch dimension in different cultures.

A very large number of cultures contain, both in theory and practice, the notion that music takes place with respect to fixed *reference* pitches. These pitches need not be fixed for all time, but are usually fixed for the duration of a single piece of music. In many cultures, the principal reference pitch (or pitches) are maintained throughout the music in the form of a (usually instrumental) 'drone'. Even where drones are absent, we can usually see that certain pitches are 'privileged', in that the music often returns to them, and circles round them. Ethnomusicologists sometimes represent this feature by deriving a *weighted scale* for a given piece of music. This orders the principal pitches in ascending sequence, and associates with each pitch a notated duration which roughly reflects the number of occurrences of that note in the piece. Example 7.5 for instance, gives the weighted scale associated with a particular Aboriginal song (Malm 1977). It shows that there are five principal

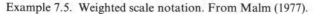

Example 7.5. Weighted scale notation. From Malm (1977).

notes, with F occurring most frequently, and A flat occurring least frequently.

Thus, although tonality, as we know it, is by no means universal, the notions of scale and tonic have formal analogies in most cultures. One of the influences on the development of fixed discrete points along the continuum is, as we have argued earlier, the existence of instruments which are either of permanently fixed pitch (e.g. the *metallophones* such as gongs, bells, and xylophones) or else which can be tuned, but which offer a fixed set for the duration of a single performance (e.g. the stringed instruments such as harp, sitar, or guitar). Moreover, within most of these scales the *octave* appears to be a particularly privileged interval. The disposition of pitches repeats within each octave, and the octave frequently appears as an interval in polyphonic music. It is particularly common to find the principal reference pitch being reinforced by voice or instruments at several different octaves. In addition, intervals close to our perfect fifth and perfect fourth appear in the polyphony of most cultures.

The similarities do not end here, however, because it seems that the subdivisions of the octave into scale steps follow common principles in most cultures. First, the number of subdivisions is always moderately small. Miller's (1956) 'magic number seven plus or minus two' would encompass most of the world's scales. Particularly common are five- and seven-note scales. In fact, the term *octave* derives from the fact that, in a seven-note scale, the eighth note marks the start of the repetition of the scale pattern at a pitch with a frequency of approximately double that of the first note. A second similarity is that practically no scale divides the octave up into equal ratio steps. In other words, scales are almost never found where the pitch intervals between adjacent notes are the same for each and every pair. Rather, scales are composed by selecting from a number of smaller (often notionally equal) steps, but in such a way that there are different numbers of steps between some of the adjacent scale members. Thus, our own diatonic major scale selects seven notes from a nominal equal-interval 12-note chromatic scale (Fig. 7.1). The Indian *Sa-grama* scale is derived from a theoretical 22-interval *sruti* scale (Fig. 7.2).

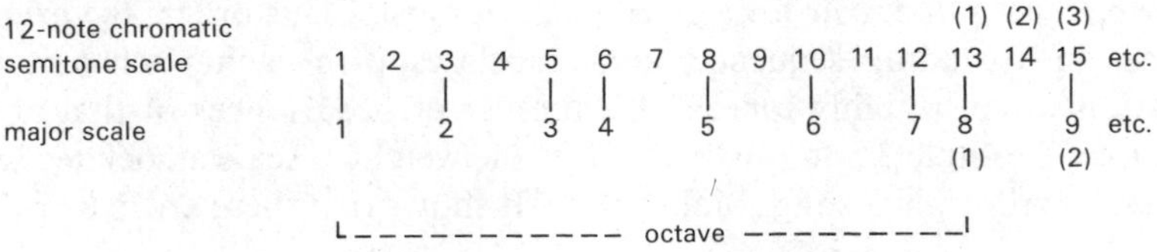

Fig. 7.1. Octave subdivision of the diatonic major scale.

The ubiquity of this unequal interval principle leads one to ask whether it serves some fundamental psychological purpose. It has been suggested earlier (Chapters 2 and 5) that one consequence of this unequal distribution is to allow a listener to 'get tonal bearings' on hearing a subset of the notes of a

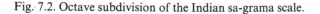

Fig. 7.2. Octave subdivision of the Indian sa-grama scale.

scale, without any necessary explicit marking of the tonic by repetition or priveleged performance treatment. For instance, in the case of a major scale, the interval separating notes four and seven (six semitones) is unique. No other pair of notes is separated by this interval (the *tritone*); and so a listener hearing a melodic sequence such as 4–7–8 in a major scale can identify the last note played as the tonic. In the Indian *Sa-grama* scale, the interval between notes three and five is similarly unique (eight *sruti*), at least in theory.

Shepard (1982) argues that it is this property of uneven spacing which

enables the listener to have, at every moment, a clear sense of where the music is with respect to such a framework. Only with respect to such a framework can there be things such as motion or rest, tension and resolution, or, in short, the underlying dynamisms of tonal music. By contrast, the complete symmetry and regularity of the chromatic and whole-tone scales means that every tone has the same status as every other. The fact that for such scales there can be no clear sense of location, and hence of motion is, I believe, the reason that such scales have never enjoyed wide or sustained popularity as a basis for music.

It has been further argued (e.g. Balzano 1980) that the burden of the musical significance of a scale rests, not in its precise tuning, or in the degree to which perfect whole number frequency ratios are represented between its members (e.g. 3:2, 4:3, etc.), but in the configuration that the scale takes up by virtue of selecting its members from a larger set of notionally equal steps. Although 'perfect' intervals have been *historically* important in the development of scale systems, scales achieve much of their psychological significance through configurational properties which Balzano has captured in terms of group-theoretic notions borrowed from mathematics. As he points out,

When we look at the Just, Pythagorean, and Equal Temperament tunings of our familiar major scales, it is evident that there is an important sense in which they all work in substantially the same way: we don't have to learn to compose or hear separately for each one. The ratios, which are different in all three tuning schemes, do not really address this fundamental commonality.

The evidence we have already reviewed on categorical perception (Chapters 2 and 5) shows that precise tuning of intervals is without psychological consequence in many situations. What Balzano has done is to formalize the level of description at which we can see that all the various tunings of the major scale are doing the same (group theoretic) job. It is only possible for a very limited number of other scales to perform the same functions.

Oue function of a scale, as we have argued, is to give a listener a sense of *location* by virtue of the different intervallic relations that hold between the various members. If this was the only function of a scale, then the 'best' kind of scale would be of the type illustrated in Fig. 7.3 where intervals between

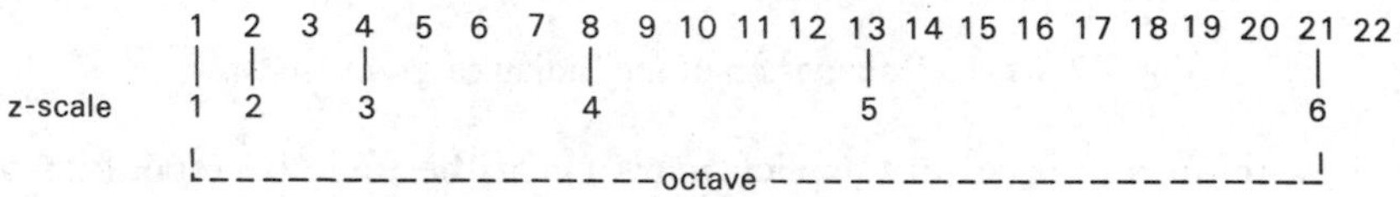

```
        1  2  3  4  5  6  7  8  9 10 11 12 13 14 15 16 17 18 19 20 21 22
        |  |     |           |              |                       |
z-scale 1  2     3           4              5                       6
        |                                                            |
        |_____ octave _____|
```

Fig. 7.3. Octave subdivision of the 'Z' scale.

adjacent notes are all different, and most non-adjacent intervals are different too. We can arbitrarily name this scale, based on a 20-fold division of the octave, the Z-scale. There are other properties of scales like the major scale, however, which the Z-scale does not share. Perhaps the most important of these is the special relationship that holds between the twelve major scales generated by starting on each note of the chromatic scale in turn. Each scale shares all but one of its notes with the scale that starts on its fifth degree. The fourth note of the old scale is sharpened to form the seventh note of the new scale; and by recursively performing this operation round the 'circle of fifths' one can generate all the major scales. This allows concepts of scale- or key-relatedness to enter music. G major is *close* to C major because it shares all but one note. F sharp major is *remote* from C major because it shares *only* one note. The Z-scale does not have this property. There is nowhere that one can start a Z-scale which causes an overlap of all notes but one with another Z-scale. One can see, intuitively, that the large number of different intervals makes that impossible. The major scale contains only two types of interval between adjacent notes, tone and semitone; and it seems that this property is crucial.

Balzano (1980) has demonstrated that there is a restricted set of artificial scales which share crucial group-theoretic properties with the diatonic major scale. These scales require the octave to be subdivided into 12, 20, 30, or 42 equal intervals, or any larger number given by the formula $n(n-1)$. Each of these subdivisions yields one, and only one, scale type with the desired properties. For the 12-fold division, that scale is the diatonic major scale. For the 20-fold division, that scale is the nine-note scale given in Figure 7.4. Its closest relation is generated by starting on the fifth degree and sharpening

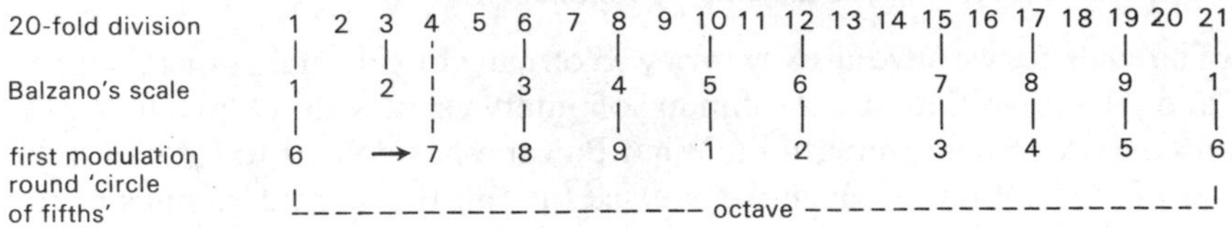

```
20-fold division    1  2  3  4  5  6  7  8  9 10 11 12 13 14 15 16 17 18 19 20 21
                    |     |     |     |     |     |        |     |     |     |
Balzano's scale     1     2     3     4     5     6        7     8     9     1
                    |     |     |     |     |     |        |     |     |     |
first modulation    6  →  7     8     9     1     2        3     4     5     6
round 'circle
of fifths'          |_____ octave _____|
```

Fig. 7.4. Octave subdivision of Balzano's (1980) nine-note scale.

just one note (the second note of the old scale). Applying this operation recursively yields all 20 possible scales of this mode. Note that there are only two different intervals between adjacent notes, 2/20 or 3/20 of an octave. It is a general feature of Balzano's scale set that the two intervals which are found between adjacent notes are separated in size by just one subdivision of the octave. So, the eleven-note scale derived from a 30-fold subdivision of the octave has adjacent intervals of either 2/30 or 3/30 of an octave. The 13-note scale derived from a 42-fold subdivision of the octave has adjacent intervals of either 3/42 or 4/42 of an octave. As the size of the subdivisions becomes smaller, the absolute and relative difference between these intervals becomes smaller. It is much easier to discriminate between a tone and a semitone than between the analogous intervals in the other scales of the set. It can be argued, therefore, that the 12-fold division is psychologically optimal; and although Balzano advocates the experimental use of the other microtonal scales in computer music, it is perhaps not surprising that there is little evidence of these other scales having been developed in the world's cultures.

The considerations on which Balzano bases his formulations are essentially algebraic. Traditional formulations of scale structure have been essentially acoustic, pointing to the natural occurrence of some scale intervals in the harmonic series. The 12-note chromatic scale can be seen as the single system which satisfies both algebraic and acoustic constraints, and to which music therefore, in some sense, tends. Three observations support the centrality of the diatonic scale:

1. Many pentatonic scales are based on a subset of the full diatonic scale, and so can be converted to a diatonic scale by the addition of two further notes.

2. Far from being a recent Western invention, the diatonic scale can be traced back to the most ancient tuning systems so far deciphered from archaeological records (Kilmer, Crocker, and Brown 1976; cited in Shepard 1982).

3. Even in cultures where the octave is *theoretically* divided into other than 12 parts, practice often diverges from theory in the direction of a 12-fold system. Thus, for instance, although we have seen that Indian music theory postulates a 22-fold division of the octave in its *sruti* scale, contemporary music practice seems to be based on a 12-fold subdivision of the octave though each has a fairly wide range of tolerance as to the actual pitch (Jairazbhoy 1971). It is important to remember that many excellent Indian performers have no overt knowledge of, or interest in, music theory (Malm 1977).

We now move from the pitch domain to a consideration of possible musical universals in the temporal domain. Just as reference pitches seem universally important, so do reference *times*, important moments in relation to which other sounds are organized; and, just as many cultures maintain the reference pitch in awareness through the use of a drone, so many cultures maintain reference times in awareness through the use of instruments marking out a regular pulse or metre. The simplest pulse involves a series of equally spaced sounds, such as is provided by a clock ticking, but in nearly every culture, such a basic pulse becomes elaborated through intermediate detail. Example 7.6 shows the first two 'bars' of an Australian Aboriginal song given by

Example 7.6. Opening of Aboriginal song. From Malm (1977).

Malm (1977). Here we see that the rhythm sticks provide a basic unadorned pulse. The didjeridu is, however, doing something more complex. It synchronizes with each beat of the rhythm sticks, but adds a second 'pulsing' sound after each beat, which has the effect of subdividing the beat, marking its passage by an asymmetric disposition of sounds (the long 'pulsing' sound marks the end of the beat, the shorter sound the beginning). Through such asymmetry, a sense of *location* within the beat is created. Such ascribing of location is given the general name of *accenting*, and it is crucial to the music of nearly all cultures. Differentiation through accenting can be achieved in a variety of ways. For instance, the time subdivision can be symetrical, with asymmetry in terms of pitch or dynamic pattern. This can also be seen in the didjeridu part of Example 7.6. Every fourth pulse of the rhythm sticks is marked by a pitch change in the didjeridu, thus creating a superordinate pulse, which justifies the positioning of the bar-lines in the transcription.

Thus, a hierarchy of reference times can be created, since a superordinate pulse can itself form the basis of a yet higher grouping. In Javanese Gamelan music, for instance, the fundamental time unit is the *gongan*. Each *gongan* is marked by the sounding of the largest gong in the ensemble. The *gongan* is divided into two equal halves by the sounding of the *kenong*. Each *kenong* is divided into two equal halves by the sounding of the *kempul*. Each *kempul* is divided into two equal halves by the sounding of the *kethuk*. Each *kethuk* may then be further subdivided (a *kethuk* corresponds very roughly to a bar in Western music, so a *gongan* is an eight-bar unit).

When a pulse unit at some level is subdivided asymmetrically in time, we usually talk of the subdivisions as forming a rhythm, or rhythmic pattern. Just as scales are usually made up by selecting pitch intervals asymmetrically from a larger set of small equal intervals, so rhythmic patterns are made up by selecting time intervals asymmetrically from a larger set of small equal time intervals; and in the same way that scales tend to repeat at the octave, so rhythmic patterns tend to repeat in such a way as to mark off time into equal segments.

One of the simplest rhythms of many musical cultures is the *dactyl* (a long interval followed by two short ones). In Western music, this is notated as a minim followed by two crotchets, and signifies the selection of the first, third, and fourth of four equal underlying beats for marking. When this figure is repeated over and over in an *ostinato*, most listeners hear the long note as strongly marking (*accenting*) the beginning of the next four-beat grouping. On the whole, in Western music, the underlying and repeating sequence of equal time units (metre) from which rhythmic patterns are derived tends to contain small even numbers of units. The dactyl requires a four-unit metre, but six and eight are also very common. Furthermore, rhythmic asymmetries are often constructed on a principle of binary subdivision of the metrical unit. Thus, we can conceive of the dactyl as being constructed by subdividing the four-unit metre into two equal halves containing two beats each. The first half is then 'filled' by a single note, whilst the second half is further subdivided into two equal 'quarter notes'.

In some other cultures (e.g. Southern Africa and India) we find more complex rhythms. First, the number of beats contained within the metrical unit can be large and uneven. In Indian music, *tala* of between seven and sixteen beats are common. Second, subdivisions are frequently not made on a principle of binary subdivision. When the number of beats is odd, binary subdivision is impossible; but even when there are an even number of beats we often find non-binary subdivisions. Consider, for instance, the rhythmic pattern of the drum parts in Example 7.1 (South African Venda song). The pattern repeats every twelve beats, but the effect of the two long notes (crotchets on the lowest stave) is to create an unequal subdivision of five plus seven.

The ability of rhythm to give a listener a fine-grained sense of temporal location within the metrical unit through asymmetric subdivision of time units suggests that, in some sense, complex rhythmic structures perform the same kind of cognitive functions that are supported by diatonic tonality in our culture (Pressing 1983). Regardless of how far this analogy can be pursued, it is certainly true that scale and rhythm perform the same essential function, that of dividing up the pitch and time continua into discrete and re-identifiable locations, on which backdrop all the essential dialectical activities (tension–resolution, motion–rest) can flourish.

Finally, these fixed points provide cues for synchrony, so that musicians can organize their behaviour with respect to what others are doing. A universal feature of polyphonic music is the temporal and pitch co-ordination of the parts. Without reference points, it would be impossible for people to make the necessary anticipatory and planned adjustments to bring their behaviour into co-ordination with others, and thus make musical behaviour the structured *social* phenomenon that it is the world over.

7.3. Biology and musical thinking

7.3.1. *The neural organization of musical function*

On 9 October 1959 the distinguished Russian composer V. G. Shebalin (1902–63) suffered a severe stroke. When he recovered consciousness he was suffering from a partial paralysis which affected the right side of his body. He also suffered severe disturbance in speech function, which remained with him to the end of his life. He found it hard to understand, produce, or reproduce speech. About a year after his stroke, for instance, when asked to repeat three short sentences: 'The moon is shining. The house is burning. The dog is barking', he replied: 'The moon is shining . . . and the house . . . no . . . I really don't understand.' In trying to describe his compositional history he offered:

An oratorio is descended . . it was a long time ago . . . that is a kind of spiritual . . . oh . . . gradually it became . . . it was extended . . . and then . . . and now . . . gradually . . . ah . . . it became very different . . . how may I say . . . I have to recall . . . oh . . . nothing . . . I have thoughts . . . no . . . it is too difficult . . .

Reading and writing were also disturbed, although not so badly.

Despite these severe difficulties (as Luria, Tsvetkova, and Futer 1965, report) he continued to work as a composer.

He worked hard with his pupils, listening to their compositions, analyzing and correcting them. He spent a considerable time over his own creative work. While aphasic, he finished compositions which he had started to write before he was taken ill, and he created a series of new compositions which other musicians considered to be up to standard, and which did not significantly differ from the compositions of his earlier years.

Of his Fifth Symphony, composed in 1962, Dimitri Shostakovitch said, 'it is a brilliant creative work, filled with highest emotions, optimistic and full of life. This symphony composed during his illness is a creation of a great master.'

How is it possible that a man's verbal ability could disintegrate, leaving his musical intellect unchanged? A large body of evidence has now been amassed to support the view that intellectual functions are localized in different areas of the brain, so that damage to one area may only disrupt a proportion of normal intellectual functions. Post-mortem examination of Professor Shebalin revealed massive damage in the left temporal and parietal regions of the brain, but not elsewhere. Such damage is often associated with language disorder, and sensorimotor defects on the right side of the body.

In order to discuss this issue in more detail, it is necessary to outline a few basic neuroanatomical facts. The human brain (and body) is divided into two roughly symmetrical halves. Each half of the brain receives nervous input from, and issues nervous commands to, one side of the body. However, for reasons which are not well understood, there is a 'crossover' of nerves going in and out of the brain, such that nerves belonging to the right side of the body connect with the left brain, and nerves belonging to the left side of the body connect with the right brain. We say that nervous organization is essentially *contralateral* (literally 'opposite sided').

The part of the brain which seems most deeply implicated in learned cognitive skills is the cerebral cortex which, in man, is the largest part of the brain. The cortex surrounds the rest of the brain like a thick cap, but it is divided down the midline into two cerebral *hemispheres*. Although the two hemispheres are to a certain extent capable of independent operation, they are connected by a fat bundle of nerve fibres called the *corpus callosum*. When this is intact, information can be transferred from one side of the cortex to the other. In most animals, each cerebral hemisphere seems to do roughly the same job. In some higher mammals, however, especially man, there is now incontrovertible evidence that each hemisphere is, or becomes, specialized to some degree. For most people (the 90 per cent or so who are unambiguously right-handed) the mechanisms controlling language behaviour seem to be primarily concentrated in the *left* hemisphere, and those controlling spatial orientation and other non-verbal skills seem to be concentrated in the *right* hemisphere.

There are several converging sources of evidence which support this conclusion:

1. Studies of people with brain damage show that left-hemisphere damage is often associated with language disorder (as in the case of Professor Shebalin), whereas right-hemisphere damage rarely causes significant language disruption.

2. By temporarily anaesthetizing one or other hemisphere, one can selectively disrupt different intellectual functions. For instance, Gordon and Bogen (1974) found that left-hemisphere intervention caused speech disturbance whilst right-hemisphere disturbances caused disruption of singing.

3. One can observe asymmetries of various sorts in the gross electrical activity of the brain which alter according to the task being carried out. For instance, McKee, Humphrey, and McAdam (1973) took electro-encephalograph (EEG) recordings from points on the scalp above the temporo-parietal regions of both hemispheres. They took recordings whilst subjects carried out various musical and linguistic tasks. The left hemisphere was more active during the linguistic tasks than during the musical ones.

4. When linguistic or non-linguistic input is restricted to one ear, then linguistic material is better processed if it is presented to the right ear (left hemisphere), and non-linguistic material such as music is better processed if presented to the left ear (right hemisphere). A well-used technique is that of 'dichotic presentation' in which two different stimulus sequences are simultaneously presented to the two ears (e.g. Kimura 1964, 1967). When the two messages are speech sequences then the message reaching the right ear

tends to be better perceived. When the two messages are musical sequences then the pattern tends to be reversed, with the left ear doing better.

The literature on hemispheric specialization is very large, and is growing all the time. Recent general introductions to the area are provided by Springer and Deutsch (1981), and Kinsbourne and Smith (1974). Reviews of the literature with particular respect to music have been provided by Benton (1977), Damasio and Damasio (1977), Gates and Bradshaw (1977), Marin (1982), Shuter-Dyson and Gabriel (1981), and Wyke (1977). Rather than attempt to review this large, and not altogether homogenous, body of research, I will confine myself to a critical examination of a few of the most noteworthy findings in the area, those that seem to have particular relevance for the arguments that we have been pursuing in the rest of the book.

The first point to make is that music is not a single, monolithic, capacity which either exists in an individual or does not. Musical skill has many, logically independent, sub-skills which may, therefore, be anatomically independent as well. A region of a cerebral hemisphere is a very big place in neural terms, and even if it were possible to assert that music was 'in' a part of the right hemisphere, it would still be pertinent to ask whether different components of the skill were in different anatomical locations *within* that region. Psychologists have been particularly alerted to the possibility that very specific sub-skills can be considered as functionally and anatomically distinct by finely analytic work carried out over the last decade or so on people with language disorders caused by brain damage (see Coltheart, Patterson, and Marshall 1980). It has been known for many years that a person may suffer receptive disorders of language without production being affected, and *vice versa*. The recent research goes beyond this in demonstrating that disruption may be confined to a specific *part* of a single skill like reading. Thus, for instance, a person may be able to read familiar concrete nouns, but have the greatest difficulty with connectives and other function words (e.g. 'and', 'which', 'that', etc.). This is important psychologically, because it shows that the mechanisms by which content and function words are understood must be, to some extent, functionally distinct.

Using such an analytic approach it has been discovered that language function is not entirely confined to the left hemisphere, even in fully right-handed people. For instance, it seems that the right hemisphere can understand words and simple sentences provided that such understanding can be signalled by non-verbal actions, such as obeying a command, pointing to, or picking up a named object.

One of the major problems in studying the effect of brain damage on musical skill is that the level of skill prior to damage can be very varied, and is often unknown; whereas most people have a high, and verifiable, level of linguistic skill prior to damage. The most informative musical cases are those where the patient was a professional musician before receiving brain damage. Here we can be fairly sure what skills were present prior to damage. Thus, a case like that reported by Wertheim and Botez (1961) is of particular interest. The patient they studied was a professional violinist known to have perfect pitch before brain damage. He developed right sensorimotor disturbances consistent with left hemisphere damage, and experienced difficulties in receptive aspects of language functioning. Some aspects of music function remained undisturbed. These included:

1. Reproduction by singing or violin playing of single pitched notes.
2. Pitch discrimination down to intervals smaller than a semitone.
3. Noticing differences between pairs of melodies or chords.
4. Detection of tonal violations in melodies.
5. Naming of single written notes.
6. Identification of major and minor scales.

Other aspects were disturbed. These included:

1. Loss of perfect pitch (i.e. the ability to name pitches).
2. Inability to recognize familiar pieces of music, or to identify composer and/or style.
3. Inability to identify melodic intervals.
4. Inability to reproduce rhythmic patterns.
5. Inability to read note sequences.
6. Errors in singing familiar melodies.
7. Errors in copying and transcribing music.

The pattern of disorders does not admit of easy explanation, but Marin (1982) suggests that the pattern is compatible with preservation of simple perceptual abilities (pitch discrimination, pitch reproduction) along with some highly overlearned and automated knowledge structures (the major and minor scales, basic tonal progressions) together with the loss of recognition and identification of musical sequences, particularly where some lexical operation (such as naming) is required.

This patient shows a very different profile of disorders to Professor Shebalin, who seems to have suffered no musical loss at all. It turns out that Shebalin is rather unusual in the clinical literature. There exist only about twelve reported cases of language disorder in musicians which is unaccompanied by musical disorder. More commonly, both language and music are affected, especially when damage occurs to the left hemisphere. There is also a small group of documented cases where musical disorder (primarily of a receptive nature) is unaccompanied by noticeable language disruption. In these cases, brain damage is usually in the right hemisphere.

We see, therefore, that although right hemisphere damage nearly always disrupts musical functioning in musicians, left hemisphere damage often disrupts it too. It is, therefore, oversimplistic to say that music is 'in' the right hemisphere. What the complex, and somewhat unsatisfactory literature on brain damage does at least show is that musical skills are just as dissociable and separately disruptable as are language skills.

For further insight into the neural organization of musical skill we turn from studies on brain-damaged patients to a series of studies on normal intact subjects. The line of enquiry I wish to focus on was initiated by Bever and Chiarello (1974). In their experiment they used two groups of subjects. 'Musicians' were those who had been attending music lessons for at least five years, and were currently playing or singing. 'Non-musicians' were those who had received less than three years of music lessons and had not been musically active in the last five years. The subjects were all right-handed. They listened to a tape of specially prepared melodies, and were asked to say whether each melody had occurred before in the sequence. Half the subjects had the melodies presented to the right ear (left hemisphere) and the other half had them presented to the left ear (right hemisphere). Bever and Chiarello found that non-musicians performed best when the melodies went to the left ear. This confirmed the 'traditional' view that music is processed in the right hemisphere. The musicians, however, showed exactly the reverse pattern of results; they performed best when the melodies went to the *right* ear.

Bever and Chiarello attempted to account for these results by recourse to the widely held view (first proposed by Hughlings-Jackson, see Taylor 1932) that the left hemisphere is specialized for 'analytic' and 'sequential' processing, whilst the right hemisphere is specialized for 'holistic' or 'global' processing. On this view, the 'crossover' of laterality in music recognition occurs because the musicians adopt a analytic strategy whereas the non-musicians adopt a holistic strategy. The terms 'analytic' and 'holistic' are rather broad in their connotation, but their application to music has been taken to relate to such distinctions as that between processing the contour of a melody and processing the precise pitch intervals of which the melody is composed (see Chapter 5.3), the former being a holistic process, the latter being analytic.

The work of Bever and Chiarello has stimulated a spate of experimental studies looking at the way in which musical ability and experience, processing strategy, and stimulus material, interact to give different patterns of hemispheric differences. It seems that the left hemisphere advantage is not confined to musicians. People who score highly on a test of musical aptitude tend to show left hemisphere advantage, regardless of training (Gaede, Parsons, and Bertera 1978), as do non-musicians who consciously adopt an 'analytic' strategy in a music perception task (Peretz and Morais 1980). It would be fair to say that the literature does not yet provide a fully coherent picture of hemispheric asymmetry in musical function. The differences between left and right ear scores, although statistically significant, are often very small, and they are highly sensitive to the nature of the task, the stimulus material, and subject strategy. In addition, experimenters have by no means tapped the whole range of musical activities, concentrating on the recognition of small changes in chords or brief melodic sequences. For all these reasons, although the analytic–holistic distinction seems a current 'best bet' as an explanation of left–right differences in normal subjects, the picture is by no means complete.

Marin (1982) argues cogently that the study of the neurological bases for music will not advance substantially until the categories and distinctions between musical activities made on psychological and music-theoretic grounds are taken seriously by researchers. Too often tests are devised on the basis of methodological convenience rather than with precise and well-grounded musical considerations in mind. Traditional distinctions between, for example, receptive and productive skills, are just not fine-grained enough to tell us, for instance, whether the phenomenon under study operates at the phonological, syntactic, or semantic level (Chapter 2).

What we can see clearly, even in this rather incomplete picture, is that various sub-skills of music have a certain degree of neural independence. There is little evidence for a single 'music centre' in the brain. Furthermore, the brain areas responsible for music seem to have a partial, but incomplete, overlap with those responsible for language. We should, therefore, not be surprised if the behavioural and cognitive analogy between music and language (Chapter 2) is, whilst compelling, not complete. Music, if not a totally distinctive neural function, almost certainly employs a distinctive configuration of neural resources.

7.3.2. *The origins and functions of music*

The principles of evolution and natural selection propounded by Darwin continue to play a central role in theories of biological development (Dawkins 1976). Darwin proposed that man's music evolved from the vocalizations of sub-human primates like the apes (Darwin 1874, Chapter XIX) which served as 'emotional' signals. Correct though Darwin's general theory may be, his explanation of musical evolution is far from satisfactory. For one thing, the vocalizations of apes seem to be involuntary patterns, having more in common with human behaviours like laughing, crying, and screaming, which survive very distinctively in humans as something quite different from music. For another, ape vocalizations do not share any of the organizational qualities of human music. They are not based on scales or rhythmic patterns, as are all human forms, and they do not show any of the the planning or purposiveness that characterize other areas of ape behaviour such as locomotion and manipulation of objects. If apes have an intellect, there is little evidence that their vocalizations are at its service. It is for this reason that attempts to teach chimpanzees a vocal language have been such a dismal failure. Only when chimps were taught a manual sign-language was any modest progress made (e.g. Gardner and Gardner 1969).

Darwin's notion was that the most musical (i.e. pitched) sounds of apes were produced by the male during courtship, and that correspondingly man's earliest music was in the form of love songs. Modern ethnological studies force us to reject both parts of this notion. The call cries of most primates are signal calls expressing 'all is well', 'I am here', 'danger', and variants of these (Marler 1965; Petter and Charles-Dominique 1979; Williams 1980). Williams reports that 'monkeys and apes in fact have no specific sex-calls, and there is no reason for assuming that the ancestors of primitive man serenaded their prospective mates.' Secondly, the most primitive songs about which we know are not concerned with personal love or sexual relations. The poetic songs of the Aborigines, for instance, express the feelings of men and women as members of the community rather than as individuals. Even when fertility is celebrated, it is seen in its wider role of sustaining the natural and social order.

A major function of primate calls seems to be 'group cohesive' (Petter and Charles-Dominique 1979). Calls are used so that members of a social group can locate one another, and indicate their motivational state. It is possible to argue that primitive human music has analogous group cohesive functions. For instance, Blacking (1976) reports that a Venda person can often know exactly what a distant group is doing by the song they are singing. Songs and dance rituals serve to unite and define social groupings. This analogy between apes and men is, however, by no means exact, and fails by itself to account for the temporally organized nature of human music. It seems as if some specifically human tendency to create and notice organized patterns, hierarchies, and sequences, has overrun and overhauled almost every type of behaviour 'inherited' from non-human primates.

Comparing man to his nearest biological neighbours, it has seemed to many that, despite observable similarities, there is an unbridged 'quantum leap' between the highest achievements of apes and what every normal human being can achieve as a matter of routine. Of course, in standard theory, evolution does proceed by discrete leaps, each leap being occasioned by a genetic mutation in an individual. However, simply to state this theory does not provide a satisfactory explanation of any given case. We have no idea if it is possible that a single mutation (or a manageably small number of them) could turn an ape-like creature into something resembling a man. Furthermore, in the case of music, it is not at once clear how musical behaviour makes for better adapted individuals that are more likely to survive; and this, of course, is a precondition for any mutation to be selected for transmission to future generations. This puts music in a special case apart from language and other 'practical' skills whose survival values are numerous and obvious.

Does man *need* music? If he does, then deprivation should be harmful in some way. We know, for instance, that sleep is necessary to humans, since continued deprivation of sleep causes physical and psychological ill effects. On this count music is very unlike sleep. People can go without music for very long periods without suffering noticeable ill effects. Perhaps, however, this is to take a too naïve approach. There are several activities (such as sex) which are vital for the continuance of the species, but which can be refrained from by individuals without any apparent personal harm. Music may be like this, necessary to the species, but not to any particular individual.

If this is an appropriate line of argument, then the 'unit' for a deprivation experiment might need to be a whole culture. Cultures without music do not, in fact exist, but it seems hard to imagine why lack of music should be harmful to a civilization like our own. We may argue, however, that modern cultures have outgrown the *need* for music, and it is in primitive non-literate cultures that music is of major survival value. Society requires organization for its survival. In our own society we have many complex artefacts which help us to externalize and objectify the organizations we need and value. Primitive cultures have few artefacts, and the organization of the society must be expressed to a greater extent through transient actions and the way people interact with each other. Music, perhaps, provides a unique mnemonic framework within which humans can express, by the temporal organization of sound and gesture, the structure of their knowledge and of social relations. Songs and rhythmically organized poems and sayings form the major repository of human knowledge in non-literate cultures. This seems to be because such organized sequences are much easier to remember than the type of prose which literate societies use in books. It would, perhaps, be an exaggeration to say that there was no logical alternative to music as a mnemonic device. It does seem to me, however, that there are very few things which 'natural' peoples could congenially do with their speech that did not tend towards what we understand as music. They can move their bodies and modulate the timing of their speech. When this is done in an organized way, *rhythm* is created. They may modulate the pitch of the voice. When this is done in a organized way, *melody* and some form of *tonal structure* is created.

We began this book with the observation that music is emotionally appealing to almost all people, and ventured the view that its appeal came *through* its structure, so that there was an inescapable cognitive component to the act of musical appreciation. We have explored the nature of these cognitive structures and processes in some detail through the seven chapters of the book. I have tried to present as complete as possible a picture of what is known about human musical cognition, without too much speculation, but with an eye to the considerable gaps in our knowledge. Perhaps I may be allowed to end on a note of pure speculation with respect to the fundamental question which, in many ways, must motivate all scientific enquiry into music. This question is, of course, *why* does music pervade human culture?

Even though humans have an intellect which, in some respects is very powerful, they do not find it easy to evaluate the long-term effects of their actions, or to predict which course of actions will lead to the most desired result in a complex situation. This is why the development of scientific thinking has been one of the most important steps in human development. It allows a method for arriving at such evalutions by the application of logical thinking and controlled observations of the world. However, long before the development of scientific method, people were notably successful at mastering their environment. They achieved success precisely through the kinds of mental processes which we can now formally defend as being effective ways of modelling and conceptualizing events in the world. They used these processes, not primarily because they had emerged through a rational process of calculation, or through trial and error, but because it was appealing to behave in that way. Evolution had supplied a natural propensity to behave in adaptive ways. This included a propensity to use language and music. Music is indeed of immense benefit as a mnemonic aid, but evolution did not implant a rational awareness of this fact in the human mind. Rather, it supplied a *motivation* for music, so that it became enjoyable and 'natural' for people to indulge in it.

Society has now changed, so that we have many more powerful mnemonics than music available to us. Our instincts and motivations, however, change more slowly. We still enjoy music, and thank goodness we do. Detached from its mundane origins, it can now serve as a vehicle for a whole range of aesthetic and transcendent experiences. Two words of caution are necessary, however. Because our instincts for music are rooted in the conditions that prevailed in the infancy of humanity, the *forms* that were available to early people have a primal and inescapable influence. In particular, it is the *voice* and the human body in rhythmic movement which form the motivational mainspring of music. If music departs too far from this mainspring, it will cease to have deep meaning and power for us. Contemporary musicians have, I believe, already come to realize that the unfettered development of electronic music leads to sterility and lifelessness. Electronic instruments must always be constrained by the parameters of 'human' music-making, enhancing and enriching these parameters rather than striking off in arbitrary directions.

The second, final, point is more sombre. For all its achievements, our Western society has a degree of precariousness about it. It is all too easy to construct scenarios which would entail the destruction of the delicate balances which preserve our complex social arrangements. In such a situation, those of us who survived would find ourselves in a world where the artefacts of our present society would, by and large, have disappeared. The resources that we carried around in our heads would, once again, form the mainstay of our attempts to survive. Songs and poems would become vital mnemonic and cohesive tools for the construction of a new society, and musical skill would, indeed be a skill for survival. It is not, therefore, simply a task of disinterested scientific curiosity to come to a better understanding of musical skill. Music is a fundamental human resource which has played, and may well play again, a vital role in the survival and development of humanity.

References

Allport, D. A., Antonis, B., and Reynolds, P. (1972).On the division of attention: a disproof of the single channel hypothesis. *Quart. Jl. Exp. Psychol.* **24,** 225–35.

Alvin, J. (1975). *Music therapy.* Hutchinson, London.

Anderson, E.,(ed) (1966). *The letters of Mozart and his family.* Macmillan London.

Anderson, J. R. (1980). *Cognitive psychology and its implications.*Freeman, San Francisco.

Anderson, J. R. (1981). *Cognitive skills and their acquisition.* Erlbaum, Hillsdale, New Jersey.

Anderson, J. R. (1982). Acquisition of cognitive skill. *Psychol. Rev.* **89,** 369–406.

Apel, W. (1953). *The notation of polyphonic music 900–1600* (4th edn.). The Mediaeval Academy of America, Cambridge, Massachusets.

Attneave, F. and Olson, R. K. (1971). Pitch as a medium: a new approach to psychophysical scaling. *Am. J. Psychol.* **84,** 147–66.

Balzano, G. J. (1980). The group-theoretic description of twelvefold and microtonal pitch systems. *Comput. Mus. J.* **4,** 66–84.

Barbour, J. M. (1951). *Tuning and temperament.* Michigan State College Press, East Lansing.

Bartlett, J. C. and Dowling, W. J. (1980). The recognition of transposed melodies: a key-distance effect in developmental perspective. *J. Exp. Psychol. Hum. Percept Perform.* **6,** 501–15.

Bartók, B. and Lord, A. B. (1951). *Serbo-Croatian folk songs.* Columbia University Press, New York.

Basmajian, J. V. and Newton, W. J. (1974). Feedback training of parts of buccinator muscle in man. *Psychophysiol.* **11,** 92.

Bent, I. (1980). Analysis. In *The new Grove's dictionary of music and musicians* (ed. S. Sadie). Macmillan, London.

Benton, A. L. (1977). The amusias. In *Music and the brain* (eds. M. Critchley and R. A. Henson). Heinemann, London.

Bernstein, L. (1976). *The unanswered question.* Harvard University Press, Cambridge, Massachusetts.

Bever, T. G. and Chiarello, R. J. (1974). Cerebral dominance in musicians and non-musicians. *Science* **185,** 537–9.

Blacking, J. (1976). *How musical is man?* Faber, London.

Blechner, M. J., Day, R. S., and Cutting, J. E. (1976). The processing of two dimensions in nonspeech stimuli: the auditory–phonetic distinction reconsidered. *J. Exp. Psychol. Hum. Percept. Perform.* **2,** 257–66.

Boden, M. A. (1979). *Piaget.* Fontana, London.

Bond, Z. S. (1971). Units in speech perception. *Working papers in linguistics.* No. 9. Computer and Information Science Research Center, Ohio State University.

Bower, G. H. (1976). Experiments in story under standing and recall. *Quart. Jl. Exp. Psychol.* **28,** 511–34.

Bower, G. H. and Winzenz, D. (1969). Group structure, coding, and memory for digit series. *J. Exp. Psychol. Monog.* 80, 1–17.

Bower, T. G. R. (1971). The object in the world of the infant. *Scient. Am.* **225**, 30–8.

Brady, P. T. (1970). Fixed-scale mechanism of absolute pitch. *J. Acoust. Soc. Am.* **48**, 883–7.

Bransford, J. D. (1979). *Human cognition.*Wadsworth, Belmont.

Bregman, A. S. (1981). Asking the 'what for' question in auditory perception. In *Perceptual organization* (eds. M. Kubovy and J. R. Pomerantz). Erlbaum, Hillsdale, New Jersey.

Bregman, A. S. and Campbell, J. (1971). Primary auditory stream segregation and perceptual order in rapid sequences of tones. *J. Exp.Psychol.* **89**, 244–9.

Broadbent, D. E. (1958). *Perception and communication.* Pergamon, London.

Brown, R. and Butler, D. (1981). Diatonic trichords as minimal tonal cue-cells. *In Theory Only* **5**, 39.

Buck, P. C. (1944). *Psychology for musicians.* Oxford University Press, London.

Bulbrook, M. E. (1932). An experimental inquiry into the existence and nature of 'insight'. *Am. J. Psychol.* **44**, 409–53.

Bullivant, R. (1971). *Fugue.* Hutchinson, London.

Butler, D. (1979). A further study of melodic channelling. *Perc. and Psychophys* **25**, 264–8.

Butler, D. (1983). The initial identification of tonal centres in music. In *Acquisition of symbolic skills* (eds. D. Rogers and J. A. Sloboda). Plenum, New York.

Caldwell, J. (1978). *Medieval music.* Hutchinson, London.

Carlsen, J. C. (1981). Some factors which influence melodic expectancy. *Psychomusicology.* **1,**12–29.

Chang, H. and Trehub, S. E. (1977a). Auditory processing of relational information by young infants. *J. Exp. Child Psychol.* **24**, 324–31.

Chang, H. and Trehub, S. E. (1977b). Infant's perception of temporal grouping in auditory patterns. *Child Dev.* **48**, 1666–70.

Chase, W. G. and Chi, M. T. H. (1981). Cognitive skill: implications for spatial skill in large-scale environments. In *Cognition, social behaviour and the environment* (ed. J. Harvey). Erlbaum, Potomac, Maryland.

Chase, W. G. and Simon, H. A. (1973). The mind's eye in chess. In *Visual information processing* (ed. W. G. Chase). Academic Press, New York.

Cherry, E. C., (1953). Some experiments on the recognition of speech, with one and two ears. *J. Acoust. Soc. Am.* **25,**975–9.

Chomsky, N. (1957). *Syntactic structures.* Mouton, The Hague.

Chomsky, N. (1965). *Aspects of the theory of syntax.* MIT Press, Cambridge, Massachusetts.

Chomsky, N. (1968). *Language and mind.* Harcourt Brace Jovanovitch, New York.

Chomsky, N. and Halle, M. (1968). *The sound pattern of English.* Harper and Row, New York.

Clark, H. H. and Clark, E. V. (1977). *Psychology and language.* Harcourt Brace Jovanovitch, New York.

Clarkson, J. K. and Deutsch, J. A. (1978). Pitch control in the human voice: a reply to Rostron. *Quart. J. Exp. Psychol.* **30**, 167–9.

Claxton, G. (Ed). (1980). *Cognitive psychology: new directions.* Routledge and Kegan Paul, London.

Clynes, M., (ed) (1982). *Music, mind and brain: the neuropsychology of music.* Plenum, New York.

Cohen, A. and Cohen, N. (1973). Tune evolution as an indicator of traditional musical norms. *J. Am. Folklore.* **86** 37–47.

Cole, H. (1974). *Sounds and signs: aspects of musical notation.* Oxford University Press, London.

Cole, R. A. and Scott, B. (1974). Towards a theory of speech perception. *Psychol Rev.*. **15**, 348–74.

Coltheart, M., Patterson, K., and Marshall, J. C.,(eds) (1980). *Deep dyslexia.* Routledge and Kegan Paul, London.

Cooke, D. (1959). *The language of music.* Oxford University Press, London.

Critchley, M. and Henson, R. A.,(eds) (1977). *Music and the brain.* Heinemann, London.

Cuddy, L. L. (1970). Training the absolute identification of pitch.*Percept. Psychophys.* **8**, 265–9.

Cuddy, L. L. (1977). Perception of structured melodic sequences. Paper given at conference on musical perception, Paris, France, July 10–13.

Cuddy, L. L. and Cohen, A. J. (1976). Recognition of transposed melodic sequences. *Q. Jl. Exp. Psychol.* **28**, 255–70.

Cuddy, L. L., Cohen, A. J., and Miller, J. (1979). Melody recognition: the experimental application of musical rules. *Can. J. Psychol.* **33**, 148–57.

Cutting, J. E. and Rosner, B. S. (1974). Categories and boundaries in speech and music. *Percept. Psychophys.* **16**, 564–70.

Cutting, J. E., Rosner, B. S., and Foard, C.F. (1976). Perceptual categories for musiclike sounds: implications for theories of speech perception. *Quart. Jl. Exp. Psychol.* **28**, 361–78.

D'Azevedo, W. L. (1962). Uses of the past in Gola discourse. *J. Afr. Hist.*3, 11–34.

Damasio, A. R., and Damasio, H. (1977). Musical faculty and cerebral dominance. In *Music and the brain* (eds M. Critchley and R. A. Henson). Heinemann, London.

Darwin, C. (1874). *The descent of man* (2nd edn.). John Murray, London.

Davies, J. B. (1978). *The psychology of music.* Hutchinson, London.

Davies, J. B. (1979). Memory for melodies and tonal sequences: a theoretical note. *Brit. J. Psychol.* **70**, 205–210.

Dawkins, R. (1976). *The selfish gene.* Oxford University Press, Oxford.

Delis, D., Fleer, J., and Kerr, P. (1978). Memory for music. *Percept. and Psychophys.* **23**, 215–8.

Deutsch, D. (1970). Tones and numbers: specificity of interference in short-term memory. *Science* **168**, 1604–5.

Deutsch, D. (1972). Mapping of interactions in the pitch memory store. *Science* **175**, 1020–2.

Deutsch, D. (1973) Interference in memory between tones adjacent in the musical scale. *J. Exp. Psychol.* **100**, 228–31.

Deutsch, D. (1975). Two-channel listening to musical scales. *J. Acoust. Soc. Am.* **57**, 1156–60.

Deutsch, D. (1980) The processing of structured and unstructured tonal sequences. *Percept. and Psychophys.* **28**, 381–9.

Deutsch, D. (ed). (1982a). *The psychology of music.* Academic Press, New York.

Deutsch, D. (1982b). Grouping mechanisms in music. In *The psychology of music* (ed. D. Deutsch). Academic Press, New York.

Deutsch, D. (1982c). The processing of pitch combinations. In *The psychology of music* (ed. D. Deutsch). Academic Press, New York.

Deutsch, D. and Feroe, J. (1975). Disinhibition in pitch memory. *Percept Psychophys.* **17**, 320-4.

Deutsch, D. and Feroe, J. (1981). The internal representation of pitch sequences in tonal music. *Psychol. Rev.* **86**, 503-22.

Deutsch, J. A. and Clarkson, J. K. (1959). Nature of the vibrato and the control loop in singing. *Nature (Lond.).* **183**, 167-8.

Deutsch, J. A., and Deutsch, D. (1963). Attention; some theoretical considerations. *Psychol. Rev.* **70**, 80-90.

Donaldson, M. (1978). *Children's minds.* Fontana, London.

Dowling, W. J. (1973). The perception of interleaved melodies. *Cog. Psychol.* **5**, 322-37.

Dowling, W. J. (1978). Scale and contour: two components of a theory of memory for melodies. *Psychol. Rev.* **85**, 341-54.

Dowling, W. J. (1982). Melodic information processing and its development. In *The psychology of music* (ed. D. Deutsch). Academic Press, New York.

Dowling, W. J., and Bartlett, J. C. (1981). The importance of interval information in long-term memory for melodies. *Psychomusicology* **1**, 30-49.

Durkin, H. E. (1937). Trial-and-error, gradual analysis and sudden reorganization: an experimental study of problem solving. *Arch. Psychol.* **210**.

Edworthy, J. (1983). Towards a pitch-contour continuum theory of memory for melodies. In *Acquisition of symbolic skills* (eds D. Rogers and J. A. Sloboda). Plenum, New York.

Eimas, P. D. (1975). Speech perception in early infancy.In *Infant perception: from sensation to cognition* (ed. L. B. Cohen and P. Salapatek) Vol.2. Academic Press, New York.

Eimas, P. D. and Corbit, J. D. (1973). Selective adaptation of linguistic feature detectors. *Cog. Psychol.* **4**, 99-109.

Eimas, P. D., Siqueland, E. R., Jusczyk, P. and Vigorito, J.M. (1971). Speech perception in infants. *Science* **171**, 303-6.

Ericsson, K. A. and Simon, H. A. (1980). Verbal reports as data. *Psychol. Rev.* **87**, 215-51.

Farnsworth, P. R. (1968) *The social psychology of music* (2nd edn). Iowa State University Press, Iowa.

Fitts, P. M. (1964). Perceptual-motor skill learning. In *Categories of human learning* (ed. A. W. Melton). Academic Press, New York.

Fitzgibbons, J., Pollatsek, A., and Thomas, I. B., (1974). Detection of temporal gaps within and between perceptual tonal groups. *Percept. and Psychophys.* **16**, 522-8.

Flavell, J. (1963). *The developmental psychology of Jean Piaget.* Van Nostrand, Princeton, New Jersey.

Fodor, J. A. and Bever, T. G. (1965). The psychological reality of linguistic segments. *J. Verb. Learn. Verb. Behav.* **4**, 414-21.

Fodor, J. A., Bever, T. G., and Garrett, M. F. (1974). *The psychology of language.* McGraw Hill, New York.

Forte, A. (1961). *The compositional matrix.* Baldwin, New York.

Forte, A. (1962). *Tonal harmony in concept and practice.* Holt Rinehart and Winston, New York.

Forte, A. (1978). *The harmonic organization of the Rite of Spring.* Yale Univerity Press, New Haven.

Fourcin, A. J. and Abberton, E. (1971). First applications of a new laryngograph. *Med. Biol. Illust.* **21,** 172.

Frega, A. L. (1979). Rhythmic tasks with 3-, 4-, and 5-year old children. A study made in the Argentine Republic. *Bull. Council Res. Mus. Educ.* **59,** 32-4.

Funk, J. and Whiteside, J. (1981). Developmental theory and the psychology of music. *Psychol. Mus.* **9.2,** 44-53.

Gabriel, C. (1978). An experimental study of Deryck Cooke's theory of music and meaning. *Psychol. Mus.* **6,** 13-20.

Gabrielsson, A. (1974). Performance of rhythm patterns. *Scand. J. Psychol.* **15,** 63-72.

Gaede, S. E., Parsons, O. A., and Bertera, J. H. (1978). Hemispheric differences in music perception: aptitude *versus* experience. *Neuropsychologia* **16,** 369-73.

Gardner, H. (1973). Children's sensitivity to musical styles. *Merrill-Palmer Q. Behav. Dev.* . **19,** 67-77.

Gardner, H. (1980). Composing symphonies and dinner parties. *Psychol. Today.* **14.** 4, 18-27.

Gardner, H. (1981). Do babies sing a universal song? *Psychol. Today.* **15.** 12, 70-6.

Gardner, H. and Wolf, D. (1983). The waves and streams of symbolization. In *Acquisition of symbolic skills* (eds D. Rogers and J. A. Sloboda). Plenum, New York.

Gardner, H., Davidson, L., and McKernon, P. (1981). The acquisition of song: a developmental approach. In *Documentary report of the Ann Arbor Symposium.* Music Educators' National Conference, Reston, Virginia.

Gardner, R. A. and Gardner, B. T. (1969). Teaching sign language to a chimpanzee. *Science* **165,** 664-72.

Gates, A. and Bradshaw, J. L. (1977). The role of the cerebral hemispheres in music. *Brain Language.* **4,** 403-31.

Ghiselin, B. (1952). *The creative process.* Mentor, New York.

Gibson, E. J. (1969). *Principles of perceptual learning and development.* Appleton-Century-Crofts, New York.

Goodman, N. (1976). *Languages of art.* Hackett, Indianapolis.

Goody, J. and Watt, I. (1963). The consequences of literacy. *Comp. Stud. Soc. Hist.* **5,** 27-68.

Gordon, H. W. and Bogen, J. E. (1974). Hemispheric lateralization of singing after intracarotid sodium amylobarbitone. *J. Neurol. Neurosurg. and Psychiat.* **37,** 727-38.

Green, D. W. and Mitchell, D. C. (1978). The effects of context and content on immediate processing in reading. *Q. Jl. Exp. Psychol.* **30,** 608-36.

Greene, J. (1972). *Psycholinguistics.* Penguin, Harmondsworth.

Gregory, A. H. (1978). Perception of clicks in music. *Percept. Psychophys.* **24,** 171-4.

Gruneberg, M. M., Morris, P. E., and Sykes, R., (eds) (1978). *Practical aspects of memory.* Academic Press, London.

Gruson, L. M. (1981). Investigating competence: a study of piano practising. Paper presented at the 89th Annual convention of the American Psychological Association, Los Angeles.

Haber, R. N. and Schindler, R. M. (1981). Error in proofreading: evidence of syntactic control of letter processing? *J. Exp. Psychol. Hum. Percept. and Perform.* **7**, 573–579.

Halpern, A. R. and Bower, G. H. (1982). Musical expertise and melodic structure in memory for musical notation. *Am. J. Psychol.* **95**, 31–50.

Hamburger, M. (1952). *Beethoven: letters, journals and conversations.* Pantheon Books, New York.

Handel, S. and Todd, P. (1981). Segmentation of sequential patterns. *J. Exp. Psychol. Hum. Percept. and Perform.* **7**, 41–55.

Healy, A. F. (1980). Proofreading errors on the word *the*; new evidence on reading units. *J. Exp. Psychol. Hum. Percept. Perform.* **6**, 45–57.

Henry, L. K. (1934). The role of insight in the analytic thinking of adolescents. *Stud. Educ. Univ. Iowa Stud.* **9**, 65–102.

Hevner, K. (1936). Experimental studies of the elements of expression in music. *Am. J. Psychol.* **48**, 246–68.

Hindemith, P. (1952). *A composer's world: horizons and limitations.* Harvard University Press, Cambridge, Massachusetts.

Hirsh, I. J. (1959). Auditory perception of temporal order. *J. Acoust. Soc. Am.* **31**, 759–67.

Hochberg, J. (1974). Organization and the Gestalt tradition. In *Handbook of perception* (eds E. C. Carterette and M. P. Friedman) Vol. 1. Academic Press, New York.

Hodeir, A. (1956). *Jazz: its evolution and essence.* Secker and Warburg, London.

Hoppin, R. H. (1978). *Medieval music.* W. W. Norton, New York.

Hughes, E. (1915). Musical memory in piano playing and piano study. *Mus. Q.* **1**, 592–603.

Hunter, I. M. L. (1976). Memory: theory and application. In *Piaget, psychology and education* (eds V. P. Varma and P. Williams). Hodder and Stoghton, London.

Hutt, S. J., Hutt, C., Lenard, H. G., Bernuth, H. V., and Muntjewerff, W. J. (1968). Auditory responsivity in the human neonate. *Nature* **218**, 888–90.

Ibbotson, N. R. and Morton, J. (1981). Rhythm and dominance. *Cognition.* **9**, 125–38.

Idson, W. L. and Massaro, D. W. (1976). Cross-octave masking of single tones and musical sequences: the effects of structure of auditory recognition. *Percept. Psychophys.* **19**, 155–75.

Imberty, M. (1969). *L'acquisition des structures tonales chez l'enfant.* Klinksieck, Paris.

Jackendoff, R., and Lerdahl, F. (1982). A grammatical parallel between music and language. In *Music, mind, and brain: the neuropsychology of music* (ed. M. Clynes). Plenum Press, New York.

Jairazbhoy, N. (1971). *The ragas of North Indian music.* Wesleyan University Press, Middletown.

Jeans, J. (1937). *Science and music.* Cambridge University Press, London.

Johansson, G. (1976). Visual motion perception. In *Recent progress in perception: readings from Scientific American* (eds R. Held and W. Richards). Freeman, San Francisco.

Johnson, D. P. (1980). *Beethoven's early sketches in the 'Fischof Miscellany' Berlin Autograph 28.* Vols 1 and 2. UMI Research Press, Ann Arbor, Michigan.

Jones, M R., Kidd, G., and Wetzel, R. (1981). Evidence for rhythmic attention. *J. Exp. Psychol.: Hum. Percept. Perf.* **7**, 1059–73.

Joseph, L. G. (1978). An observational study on the acquisition of musical skills. Unpublished M. A. thesis, University of Waterloo, Canada.

Jusczyk, P. W., Rosner, B. S., Cutting, J. E. Foard, C. F., and Smith L. B. (1977). Categorical perception of non-speech sound by 2-month-old infants. *Percept. Psychophys.* **21**, 50–4.

Kagan, J. and Lewis, M. (1965). Studies of attention in the human infant. *Merrill-Palmer Q. Behav. Dev.* **11**, 95–127.

Karkoschka, E. (1972). *Notation in new music*. Universal Edition, London.

Kessen, W., Levine, J., and Wendrick, K. A. (1979). The imitation of pitch in infants. *Infant Behav. Dev.* **2**, 93–9.

Kilmer, A. D., Crocker, R. L., and Brown, R. R. (1976). *Sounds from silence: recent discoveries in ancient Near East music*. Bit Enki Publications, Berkeley.

Kimura, D. (1964). Left-right differences in the perception of melodies. *Q. Jl. Exp. Psychol.* **16**, 355–8.

Kimura, D. (1967). Functional asymmetry of the brain in dichotic listening. *Cortex*. **3**, 167–78.

Kinsbourne, M. and Smith, W. L., (eds) (1974). *Hemispheric disconnection and cerebral function*. Charles C. Thomas, Springfield, Illinois.

Klinger, E. (1971). *Structure and functions of fantasy*. Wiley, New York.

Kosslyn S. M. and Pomerantz, J. R. (1977). Imagery, propositions, and the form of internal representations. *Cog. Psychol.* **9**, 52–76.

Kramer, R. (1973). *The sketches for Beethoven's violin sonatas opus 30; history, transcription, analysis.* Princeton University, Unpublished Ph.D. dissertation.

Kubovy, M. (1981). Concurrent-pitch segregation and the theory of indispensable attributes. In *Perceptual organization* (eds M. Kubovy and J. R. Pomerantz). Erlbaum, Hillsdale, New Jersey.

Kuhn, T. S. (1962). *The structure of scientific revolutions*. University of Chicago Press, Chicago.

Kunst, J. (1959). *Ethnomusicology*. Nijhoff, The Hague.

Ladefoged, P. and Broadbent, D. E. (1960). Perception of sequence in auditory events. *Q. Jl. Exp. Psychol.* **12**, 162–70.

Lashley, K. (1951). The problem of serial order in behaviour. In *Cerebral mechanisms in behaviour* (ed. L. A. Jeffries). Wiley, New York.

Laske, O. E. (1975). On psychomusicology. *Int. Rev. Aesth. Sociol. Mus.* **6**, 269–81.

Lehiste, I. (1972). The units of speech perception. *Working papers in linguistics* No. 12. Computer and information science research center, Ohio State University.

Lerdahl, F. and Jackendoff, R. (1983). *A generative theory of tonal music*. MIT Press, Cambridge, Massachusetts.

Levin, H. and Addis, A. B. (1980). *The eye-voice span*. MIT Press, Cambridge, Massachusetts.

Levin, H. and Kaplan, E. A. (1970). Grammatical structure and reading. In *Basic studies on reading* (eds H. Levin and J. P. Williams). Basic Books, New York.

Levin, H. and Williams, J. P. (eds) (1970). *Basic studies in reading*. Basic Books, New York.

Liberman, A. M., Cooper, F. S., Shankweiler, D. P., and Studdert-Kennedy, M. (1967). Peception of the speech code. *Psychol. Rev.* **74**, 431–61.

Liberman, A. M., Harris, K. S., Kinney, J. A., and Lane, H. (1961). The discrimination of the relative onset time of the components of certain speech and non-speech patterns. *J. Exp. Psychol.* **61,** 379-88.

Locke, S. and Kellar, L. (1973). Categorical perception in a non-linguistic mode. *Cortex.* **9,** 355-69.

Longuet-Higgins, H. C. (1972). Making sense of music. *Proc. R. Inst. G. Br.* **45,** 87-105.

Longuet-Higgins, H. C. (1976). Perception of melodies. *Nature* **263,** 646-53.

Longuet-Higgins, H. C. (1978). The perception of music. *Interdisc. Sci. Rev.* **3,** 148-56.

Longuet-Higgins, H. C. and Lee, C. S. (1982). The perception of musical rhythms. *Perception* **11,** 115-28.

Lord, A. B. (1960). *The singer of tales.* Harvard University Press, Cambridge, Massachusetts.

Luria, A. R., Tsvetkova, L. S., and Futer, D. S. (1965). Aphasia in a composer. *J. Neurol. Sci.* **2,** 288-92.

Lyons, J. (1970). *Chomsky.* Fontana, London.

McKee, G., Humphrey, B., and McAdam, D. W. (1973). Scaled lateralization of alpha activity during linguistic and musical tasks. *Psychophysiology.* **10** 441-3.

Makeig, S. (1982). Affective versus analytic perception of musical intervals. In *Music, mind and brain: the neuropsychology of music* (ed. M. Clynes). Plenum Press, New York.

Malm, W. P. (1977). *Music cultures of the Pacific, the Near East and Asia* (2nd edn). Prentice Hall, Englewood Cliffs, New Jersey.

Manor, H. C. (1950). A study of prognosis. *J. Educ. Psychol.* **41,** 31-50.

Marin, O. S. M. (1982). Neurological aspects of music perception and performance. In *The psychology of music.* Academic Press, New York.

Marler, P. (1965). Communication in monkeys and apes. In *Primate behaviour* (ed. I. DeVore). Holt Rinehart and Winston, New York.

Marr, D. (1982). *Vision.* Freeman, San Francisco.

Martin, J. G. (1972). Rhythmic (hierarchical) versus serial structure in speech and other behaviour. *Psychol. Rev.* **79,** 487-509.

Massaro, D. W. and Klitzke, D. (1977). Letters are functional in word identification. *Memory and Cognition* **5,** 292-8.

Mattingley, I. G., Liberman, A. M., Syrdal, A. K., and Halwes, T. (1971). Discrimination in speech and non-speech modes. *Cog. Psychol.* **2,** 131-57.

Meyer, L. B. (1956). *Emotion and meaning in music.* University of Chicago Press, Chicago.

Meyer, L. B. (1973). *Explaining music.* University of California Press, Berkeley.

Michon, J. A. (1974). Programs and 'programs' for sequential patterns in motor behaviour. *Brain Res.* **71,** 413-24.

Miller, G. A. (1956). The magical number seven plus or minues two: some limitations on our capacity for prcessing information. *Psychol. Rev.* **63,** 81-97.

Miller, G. A. and Heise, G. A. (1950). The trill threshold. *J. Acoust. Soc. Am.* **22,** 167-73.

Minsky, M. (1977). Frame-system theory. In *Thinking: readings in cognitive science* (eds. P. N Johnson-Laird and P. C. Wason). Cambridge University Press, London.

Moog, H. (1976). *The musical experience of the pre-school child* (translated C. Clarke). Schott, London.

Moore, B. C. J. (1982). *An introduction to the psychology of hearing* (2nd edn). Academic Press, London.

Morgenstern, S. (1956). *Composers on music: an anthology of composers' writings from Palestrina to Copland.* Pantheon Books, New York.

Moynahan, E. D. (1973). The development of knowledge concerning the effect of categorization upon free recall. *Child Dev.* **44**, 238–46.

Mozart, W. A. (1979). *Die Zauberflote.* Documenta Musicologica. Zweite Reihe: Handschriften-Faksimiles. Barenreiter, Kassel.

Narmour, E. (1977). *Beyond Schenkerism: the need for alternatives in music analysis.* University of Chicago Press, Chicago.

Navon, D. (1977). Forest before trees: the precedence of global features in word identification. *Cog. Psychol.* **9**, 353–83.

Neisser, U. (1967). *Cognitive psychology.* Appleton Century Crofts, New York.

Neisser, U. (1976). *Cognition and reality: principles and implications of cognitive psychology.* Freeman, San Francisco.

Neisser, U. (1981). John Dean's memory: a case study. *Cognition.* **9**, 1–22.

Neisser, U. (1982). *Memory observed: remembering in natural contexts.* Freeman, San Francisco.

Neisser, U. (1983). Toward a skilful psychology. In *The acquistion of symbolic skills* (ed. D. R. Rogers and J. A. Sloboda). Plenum, New York.

Nettl, B. (1964). *Theory and method of ethnomusicology.* Free Press of Glencoe, New York.

Nettl, B. (1973). *Folk and traditional music of the Western continents* (2nd edn). Prentice Hall, Englewood Cliffs, New Jersey.

Newell, A. and Simon, H. A. (1972). *Human problem solving.* Prentice Hall, Englewood Cliffs, New Jersey.

Newell, A., Shaw, J. C., and Simon, H. A. (1962). The process of creative thinking. In *Contemporary approaches to creative thinking* (eds H. Gruber, G. Terrell, and M. Wertheimer). Prentice Hall, New York.

Newmarch, R. (1906). *Life and letters of Peter Ilich Tchaikovsky.* John Lane, London.

Nisbet, R. E. and Wilson, J. D. (1977). Telling more than we can know: verbal reports on mental processes. *Psychol. Rev.* **84**, 231–59.

Nottebohm, G. (1887). *Zweite Beethoveniana* (ed. E. Mandyczewski). J. Reiter-Biedermann, Leipzig.

O'Regan, K. (1979). Moment to moment control of eye saccades as a function of textual parameters in reading. In *Processing of Visible Language* (ed. P. A. Kolers, M. E. Wrolstad, and H. Bouma) Vol. 1. Plenum Press, New York.

Olson, G. M. and Clark, H. H. (1976). Research methods in psycholinguistics. In *Handbook of perception* (eds E. C. Carterette and M. P. Friedman) Vol. 7, *Language and speech.* Academic Press, New York.

Ostwald, P. F. (1973). Musical behaviour in early childhood. *Dev Med. Child Neurol.* **15**, 367–75.

Palmer, S. E. (1977). Hierarchical structure in perceptual representation. *Cog. Psychol.* **9**, 441–474.

Parrott, I. (1978). *The music of Rosemary Brown.* Regency Press, London.

Parry, M. (1971). *The making of Homeric verse.* Oxford University Press, London.

Patterson, B. (1974). Musical dynamics. *Sci. Am.* **233**, 78–95.

Peretz, I. and Morais, J. (1980). Modes of processing melodies and ear asymmetry in non-musicians. *Neuropsychologia.* **18,** 477-89.

Petter, J. J. and Charles-Dominique, P. (1979). Vocal communication in prosimians. In *The study of prosimian behaviour* (eds G. A. Doyle and R. D. Martin). Academic Press, New York.

Pflederer, M. (1964). The responses of children to musical tasks embodying Piaget's principles of conservation. *J. Res. Mus. Educ.* **12,** 251-68.

Piaget, J. (1950). *The psychology of intelligence.* Harcourt Brace Jovanovitch, New York.

Piaget, J. (1952). *The origins of intelligence in the child.* Routledge and Kegan Paul, London.

Pick, A. D. (1979). Listening to melodies: perceiving events. In *Perception and its development* (ed. A. D. Pick). Erlbaum, Hillsdale, New Jersey.

Pillsbury, W. B. (1897). A study in apperception. *Am. J. Psychol.* **8,** 315-93.

Plomp, R. (1977). *Aspects of tone sensation.* Academic Press, New York.

Poincaré, H. (1924). Mathematical creation. From *The foundations of science* (translated G. B. Halstead). Science Press, New York.

Pollard-Gott, L. (1983). Emergence of thematic concepts in repeated listening to music. *Cog. Psychol.* **15,** 66-94.

Povel, D. J. (1981). Internal representation of simple temporal patterns. *J. Exp. Psychol Hum. Percept. Perform.* **7,** 3-18.

Pratt, F. (1983). Intellectual realism in adults' and children's drawings of cubes and straight lines. In *Acquisition of symbolic skills* (ed. D. R. Rogers and J. A. Sloboda). Plenum, New York.

Pressing, J. (1983). Cognitive isomorphisms in pitch and rhythm in world musics: West Africa, the Balkans, Thailand and Western Tonality. *Studies in Mus.* **17.**

Priestley, M. (1975) *Music therapy in action.* Constable, London.

Pylyshyn, Z. (1973). What the mind's eye tells the mind's brain: a critique of mental imagery. *Psychol. Bull.* **80,** 1-24.

Rainbow, E. L. and Owen, D. (1979). A progress report on a three year investigation of the rhythmic ability of pre-school aged children. *Bull. Council Res. Mus. Educ.* **59,** 32-4.

Rasch, R. A. (1979). Synchronization in performed ensemble music.*Acustica.* **43,** 121-31.

Rayner, K. (1978). Foveal and parafoveal cues in reading. In *Attention and Performance VII* (ed. J. Requin). Erlbaum, Hillsdale, New Jersey.

Read, G. (1974). *Music notation.* Gollancz, London.

Reason, J. (1977). Skill and error in everyday life. In *Adult learning* (ed. M. Howe). Wiley, London.

Reber, A. S. and Anderson, J. R. (1970). The perception of clicks in linguistic and nonlinguistic messages. *Percept. Psychophys.* **8,** 81-9.

Reitman, W. R. (1965). *Cognition and thought.* Wiley, New York.

Reitmeyer, J. W. (1972). The application of negative practice to the correction of habitual fingering errors in clarinet performance. Unpublished thesis, The Pennsylvania State University (Abstract in *Diss. Abstr. Int.* 1973, **33,** 3403).

Restle, F. (1970). Theory of serial pattern learning: structural trees. *Pschol.Rev* **79,** 487-509.

Restle, F. (1972). Serial patterns: the role of phrasing. *J. Exp. Psychol.* **92,** 385-90.

Robinson, I. (1975). *The new grammarians' funeral*. Cambridge University Press, London.

Rosner, B. S. and Meyer, L. B. (1982). Melodic processes and the perception of music. In *The psychology of music* (ed. D. Deutsch). Academic Press, New York.

Sadie, S. (ed.) (1980). *The new Grove's dictionary of music and musicians*. MacMillan, London.

Salzer, F. (1952). *Structural hearing*. Charles Boni, New York.

Sampson, E. E. (1981). Cognitive psychology as ideology. *Am. Psychologist*. **36**, 730–43.

Sanchez, M. and Reitman, W. R. (1960). The composition of a fugue: protocol and comments. Unpublished report. Carnegie Institute of Technology, Pittsburgh.

Sandford, A. J. and Garrod, S. C. (1980). *Understanding written language: explorations in comprehension beyond the sentence*. Wiley, London.

Scharf, B. (1970). Critical bands. In *Foundations of modern auditory theory* (ed. J. V. Tobias) Vol. 1. Academic Press, New York.

Schenker, H. (1935). *Der Freie Satz* (translated E. Oster, 1979). Longman, New York.

Seashore, C. E. (1938). *The psychology of music*. McGraw Hill, New York.

Seashore, C. E., Lewis, D., and Saetvit, J. G. (1960). *Seashore measures of musical talents* (2nd revision of 1939 revision). The Psychological Corporation of New York, New York.

Sergeant, D. (1969) Experimental investigation of absolute pitch. *J. Res. Mus. Educ.* **17**, 135–43.

Sessions, R. (1941). The composer and his message. In *The intent of the artist* (ed. A. Centeno). Princeton University Press, Princeton.

Shaffer, L. H. (1976). Intention and performance. *Psychol. Rev.* **83**, 375–93.

Shaffer, L. H. (1980). Analysing piano performance: a study of concert pianists. In *Tutorials in motor behaviour* (eds G. E. Stelmach and J. Requin). North Holland, Amsterdam.

Shaffer, L. H. (1981a). Creativity in skilled performance. Paper presented at NATO conference on adaptive control of ill-defined systems.

Shaffer, L. H. (1981b). Performance of Chopin, Bach, and Bartok: studies in motor programming. *Cog. Psychol.* **13**, 326–76.

Shepherd, J. (1977). Media, social process and music. In *Whose music? sociology of musical language* (by J. Shepherd, P. Virden, G. Vulliamy, and T. Wishart). Latimer, London.

Shepherd, J., Virden, P., Vulliamy, G., and Wishart, T. (1977). *Whose music? A sociology of musical language*. Latimer, London.

Shepherd, R. N. (1982). Structural representation of musical pitch. In *The psychology of music* (ed. D. Deutsch). Academic Press, New York.

Shiffrin, R. M. and Schneider, W. (1977). Towards a unitary model for selective attention, memory scanning and visual search. In *Attention and performance 6* (ed. S. Dornic). Erlbaum, Hillsdale, New Jersey.

Shuter-Dyson, R. and Gabriel, C. (1981). *The psychology of musical ability* (2nd edn). Methuen, London.

Siegel, J. A. (1974). Sensory and verbal coding strategies in subjects with absolute pitch. *J. Exp. Psychol.* **103**, 37–44.

Siegel, J. A. and Siegel, W. (1977a). Absolute identification of notes and intervals by musicians. *Perc. and Psychophys.* **21**, 143–52.

Simon, H. A. (1979). *Models of thought*. Yale University Press, New Haven.

Simon, H. A. and Sumner, R. K. (1968). Pattern in music. In *Formal representation of human judgement* (ed. B. Kleinmuntz). Wiley, New York.

Skinner, B. F. (1957). *Verbal behaviour*. Appleton Century Crofts, New York.

Sloboda, J. A. (1974). The eye-hand span: an approach to the study of sight-reading. *Psychol. Mus.* **2**, 4-10.

Sloboda, J. A. (1976a). Visual perception of musical notation: registering pitch symbols in memory. *Q. J. Exp. Psychol.* **28**, 1-16.

Sloboda, J. A. (1976b). The effect of item position on the likelihood of identification by inference in prose reading and music reading. *Can. J. Psychol.* **30**, 228-36.

Sloboda, J. A. (1976c). Decision times for word and letter search: a wholistic word identification model examined. *J. Verb. Learn. Verb. Behav.* **15**, 93-101.

Sloboda, J. A. (1977a). Phrase units as determinants of visual processing in music reading. *Br. J. Psychol.* **68**, 117-24.

Sloboda, J. A. (1977b). The locus of the word-priority effect in a target detection task. *Memory Cognition.* **5**, 371-6.

Sloboda, J. A. (1978). Perception of contour in music reading. *Perception* **6**, 323-31.

Sloboda, J. A. (1981). The uses of space in music notation. *Visible Lang.* **25**, 86-110.

Sloboda, J. A. (1982). Music performance. In *The psychology of music* (ed. D. Deutsch). Academic Press, New York.

Sloboda, J. A. (1983). The communication of musical metre in piano performance. *Q. Jl. Exp. Psychol.* **35**, 377-396.

Sloboda, J. A. (1984). Review of Wing and Seashore tests. In *Tests in education: a book of critical reviews* (eds H. Goldstein and P. Levy). Academic Press, London.

Sloboda, J. A. and Edworthy, J. (1981). Attending to two melodies at once: the effect of key relatedness. *Psychol. Mus.* **9**, 39-43.

Sloboda, J. A. and Gregory, A. H. (1980). The psychological reality of musical segments. *Can. J. Psychol.* **34**, 274-80.

Sloboda, J. A. and Parker, D. H. H. (1985). Immediate recall of melodies. In *Musical structure and cognition* (eds. P. Howell, I. Cross, and R. West). Academic Press, London.

Smith, J. (1983). Reproduction and representation of musical rhythms: the effects of musical skill. In *Acquisition of symbolic skills* (eds D. Rogers and J. A. Sloboda). Plenum, New York.

Smith, J., Hausfield, S., Power, R. P., and Gorta, A. (1982). Ambiguous musical figures and auditory streaming. *Percept. Psychophys.* **32**, 454-64.

Solso, R. L. (1980). *Cognitive psychology*. Harcourt Brace Jovanovitch, New York.

Spender, N. (1980). Psychology of music. In *The new Grove's dictionary of music and musicians* (ed. S. Sadie). MacMillan, London.

Spender, S. (1946). The making of a poem. *Partisan Rev.* Summer issue.

Springer, S. P. and Deutsch, G. (1981). *Left brain, right brain*. Freeman, San Francisco.

Steedman, M. J. (1977). The perception of musical rhythm and metre. *Perception* . **6**, 555-70.

Sternberg, S., Knoll, R. L., and Zukofsky, P. (1982). Timing by skilled musicians. In *The psychology of music* (ed. D. Deutsch). Academic Press, New York.

Strauss, R. (1949) *Betrachtungen und Erinenrungen*. Atlantis, Zurich.

Stravinsky, I. (1936). *Chronicle of my life*. Gollancz, London.

Stravinsky, I. (1969). *The Rite of Spring: sketches 1911–1913*. Facsimile reproductions with commentary by R. Craft. Boosey and Hawkes, London.

Sudnow, D. (1978). *Ways of the hand: the organization of improvised conduct*. Routledge and Kegan Paul, London.

Sundberg, J. (1978). Synthesis of singing. *Swed. J. Musicol.* **60**, 107–12.

Sundberg, J. (1982). Perception of singing. In *The psychology of music* (ed. D. Deutsch). Academic Press, New York.

Sundberg, J. and Lindblom, B. (1976). Generative theories in language and music descriptions. *Cognition.* **4**, 99–122.

Sutherland, N. S. (1973). Object recognition. In *Handbook of perception* (eds E. C. Carterette and M. P. Friedman) Vol. 3. Academic Press, New York.

Tan, N., Aiello, R., and Bever, T. G. (1981). Harmonic structure as a determinant of melodic organization. *Memory and Cognition.* **9**, 533–9.

Taylor, J. (ed.) (1932). *Selected writings of John Hughlings Jackson*. Hodder and Stoughton, London.

Triesman, A. M. (1964). Selective attention in man. *Br. Med. Bull.* **20**, 12–16.

Tucker, W. H., Bates, R. H. T., Frykberg, S. D., Howarth, R. J., Kennedy, W. K., Lamb, M. R., and Vaughan, R. G. (1977). An interactive aid for musicians. *Int. J. Man–Machine Stud.* **9**, 635–51.

Van Noorden, L. P. A. S. (1975). Temporal coherence in the perception n of tone sequences. Unpublished doctoral dissertation, Technische Hogeschool Eindhoven, The Netherlands.

Van Nuys, K., and Weaver, H. E. (1943). Memory span and visual pauses in reading rhythms and melodies. *Psychol. Monog.* **55**, 33–50.

Vernon, M. D. (1931). Characteristics of proof-reading. *Br. J. Psychol.* **21**, 368.

Vernon, P. E. (1970). *Creativity*. Penguin, London.

Virden, P. and Wishart, T. (1977). Some observations on the social stratification of twentieth century music. In *Whose music? A sociology of musical languages* (by J. Shepherd, P. Virden, G. Vulliamy, and T. Wishart). Latimer, London.

Ward, W. D. (1963a). Absolute pitch. Part I. *Sound.* **2.3**, 14–21.

Ward, W. D. (1963b). Absolute pitch. Part II. *Sound.* **2.4**, 33–41.

Ward, W. D. and Burns, E. M. (1982). Absolute pitch. In *The psychology of music* (ed. D. Deutsch). Academic Press, New York.

Weaver, H. E. (1943). A study of visual processes in reading differently constructed musical selections. *Psychol. Monog.* **55**, 1–30.

Werfel, F. and Stefan, P. (1942). *Verdi: the man and his letters*. L. B. Fischer, New York.

Wertheim, N. and Botez, M. I. (1961). Receptive amusia: a clinical analysis. *Brain.* **84**, 19–30.

Wertheimer, M. (1923). Untersuchung zur Lehre von der Gestalt. II. *Psychol. Forsch.* **4**, 301–50.

Whitehead, A. N. (1917). *The organization of thought*. Williams and Northgate, London.

Williams, J. P. (1970). From basic research on reading to educational practice. In *Basic studies in reading* (eds H. Levin and J. P. Williams). Basic Books, New York.

Williams, L. (1980). *The dancing chimpanzee* (2nd edn.). Allison and Busby, London.

Wing, H. D. (1962). *Wing standardized tests of musical intelligence* (1957 revision). National Foundation for Educational Research, Windsor.

Wishart, T. (1977). Musical writing, musical speaking. In *Whose music? A sociology of musical language* (by J. Shepherd, P. Virden, G. Vulliamy, and T. Wishart). Latimer, London.

Wohwill, J. F. (1981). Music and Piaget: spinning a slender thread. Paper presented at a meeting of the American Psychological Association, Los Angeles, August 1981.

Wolf, T. (1976). A cognitive model of musical sight-reading. *J. Psychol. Res.* **5**, 143–71.

Woodrow, H. (1951). The perception of time. In *Handbook of experimental psychology* (ed. S. S. Stevens). Wiley, New York.

Wyke, M. A. (1977). Musical ability: a neuropsychological interpretation. In *Music and the brain* (eds M. Critchley and R. A. Henson). Heinemann, London.

Yeston, M. (ed). (1977). *Readings in Schenker analysis*. Yale University Press, New Haven.

Zenatti, A. (1969). Le developpement genetique de la perception musicale. *Monog. Francais Psychol*. No. 17.

Author index

Subject index